BIRDS OF
THE GREATER SUNDAS,
THE PHILIPPINES,
AND WALLACEA

BIRDS OF
THE GREATER SUNDAS,
THE PHILIPPINES,
AND WALLACEA

Text and Illustrations by Norman Arlott

Princeton University Press
Princeton and Oxford

DEDICATION
It is my pleasure to dedicate this book to Isla, Ella and Jacob.

Published in the United States, Canada, and the Philippine Islands
by Princeton University Press, 41 William Street, Princeton, New Jersey, 08540

press.princeton.edu

Text © 2018 Norman Arlott
Illustrations © 2018 Norman Arlott

First published by William Collins, an imprint of HarperCollins Publishers, in 2018

23 22 21 20 19 18
10 9 8 7 6 5 4 3 2 1

ISBN 978-0-691-18062-5
Library of Congress Control Number 2017961433

Edited and designed by D & N Publishing, Baydon, Wiltshire
Cartography by Martin Brown

Printed and bound in China by RRD Asia Print Solutions

CONTENTS

Maleo

Great Hornbill

♀

♂

Wallace's Standardwing

ACKNOWLEDGEMENTS

Bird books take a relatively short time to paint and write, but the knowledge that enables them to be completed is gained over many, many years. I well remember that my passion started as a very young boy bird collecting birds' eggs (now, quite rightly, frowned upon) with my father. That passion has since been enhanced by being fortunate enough to be in the field with, and inspired by, some well-known and not so well-known 'birders'. I must mention the following, who have encouraged me and allowed me to pick their brains over the years: the late John G. Williams, the late Eric Hosking, the late Crispin Fisher, Robert Gillmor, the late Basil Parsons, Brian Leflay and Moss Taylor.

This book could not have gone ahead without the help of the staff at the British Museum at Tring, especially Mark Adams and Robert Prys-Jones. David Price-Goodfellow deserves special praise for his skill, and patience, in putting together the various component parts of this book. And thanks also go to Susi Bailey for her copy-editing skills. Without publishers there would not be a book, so it gives me great pleasure to thank everyone at HarperCollins, particularly Myles Archibald and Julia Koppitz.

Last, but definitely not least, I must thank friends and family who have had to put up with my various mood changes while trying to sort out some of the more difficult aspects of putting this book together; my wife Marie probably endured more than most.

INTRODUCTION

The format of this book follows that of my Palearctic, West Indies, North America and Greenland, India and South-East Asia volumes.

Although my brief was, predominantly, to produce an 'illustrated checklist' (space would not allow me to produce a 'full' field guide), it is hoped that within these pages I have given a helpful nudge towards what to look for when searching for new birds as well as providing a reminder of birds seen.

Most of the text in this book is based on the type of notes I make before embarking on a field trip to a new area. Hopefully the text will, along with the illustrations, help to identify most birds encountered in the Greater Sundas, the Philippines and Wallacea. Obviously, the use of more in-depth tomes will be required for some of the trickier species (see Further Reading).

I can only hope that with this work I have been able to add to the pleasure of anticipation or memory, and perhaps even added some extra piece of knowledge about the birds of this vast region.

AREA AND SPECIES COVERED

This book covers the Greater Sundas, the Philippines and Wallacea (see map on pp. 12–13). Although Sumatra, Java, Bali and Borneo are known collectively as the Greater Sundas, it was decided, due mainly to their large size, to refer to each of them individually. Because of their abundance of smaller islands, the Philippines and Wallacea are referred to in a more general way, although Wallacea has been split into Sulawesi, the Lesser Sundas and the Moluccas (Maluku). This may seem 'unfair', but where deemed important, individual islands or archipelagos are mentioned from these areas. Also included are the endemic species from Christmas Island in the Indian Ocean.

I have endeavoured to include every species recorded in the region, apart from non-established introductions, and also as many of the major subspecies as possible. To keep the book to a manageable size, no juvenile plumages have been illustrated, although, when thought necessary and room permits, a short passage in 'Field notes' has been included.

PLATES

The abbreviations and symbols used on the plates are as follows:
♂ = male, ♀ = female, br = breeding, n-br = non-breeding.

NOMENCLATURE

In the main I have followed the nomenclature used by the International Ornithological Congress (IOC). I have, as in my previous volumes, tweaked the order of species to aid plate composition. In most cases this is because I prefer to have similar-looking species close to one another to help identification – after all, that is the main purpose of the book. Hopefully this will not cause too much aggravation.

I have headlined the English names I believe are used by most birders in the field, which means that in many cases I have reverted to 'old school' names rather than some of the more modern interpretations. (Most of these 'new' names, along with other well-used names, are included in parentheses.)

IDENTIFICATION

The illustrations should be all that you need to identify a specific bird, but with some of the trickier species more information is needed, hence the 'Field notes', 'Voice', 'Habitat' and 'Distribution' sections.

FIELD NOTES: Because of the need to keep text to a minimum, this section rarely mentions those aspects of a bird that should be obvious from the illustrations, e.g. wing-bars, bill shape and so on. It is used mainly to point to a bird's habits or to mention facets of identification that are hidden in a standing or perched bird.

VOICE: Probably the first sign of a bird's presence. The descriptions are shown in *italics*. Where space has allowed, I have included different interpretations of the same song. Although it is difficult to produce an accurate reproduction of bird songs or calls in the written word, this section is worth studying to get a feel for what is often the most important area of bird identification.

HABITAT: The main habitat preferences mentioned are those in which a species breeds; wintering habitats are included if appropriate.

DISTRIBUTION: Mainly general, so should be read in conjunction with the maps.

DISTRIBUTION MAPS

Distribution maps (*see* pp.373–394) are provided for many species except vagrants and those seen rarely, those with a distribution that is adequately covered in the text, species that have been recently introduced, and those that spend most of their time at sea or occur only on offshore islands. The maps should be used only as a rough guide to where a species can be found at different times of the year. Red ▓▓ areas indicate where a species may be found in the summer on its breeding grounds; blue ▓▓ shows where it is found in winter when not breeding; and purple ▓▓ areas are where a species is a year-round resident.

BIRD TOPOGRAPHY

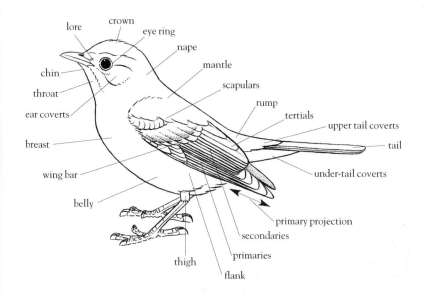

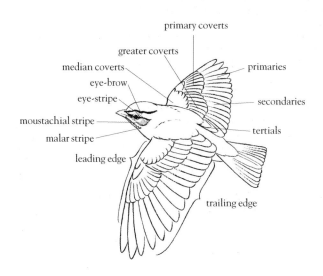

MAP OF THE REGION

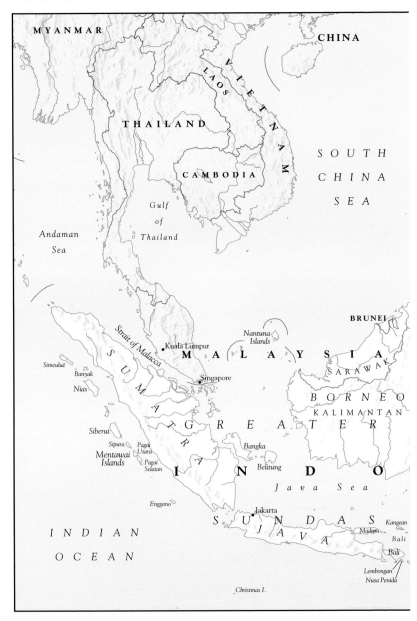

Luzon Strait

Sabtang Batan Islands

Calayan Babuyan Islands

N

miles 0 500
km 0 500

Luzon

PHILIPPINE ISLANDS

Polillo Islands

Manila

PHILIPPINES

Cantanduanes

Mindoro Romblon Samar

Calamian
Group Tablas Masbate

Panay

Cebu Leyte

Cuyo
Islands Olango

Negros Bohol

Palawan

Camiguin

Sulu Sea

Mantanani

Banggi Mindanao

Mapun Basilan Moro
Gulf

SABAH

Sulu
Archipelago

Tawi-tawi

Miangas

Balut Sarangani

Karakelong Talaud Islands

PACIFIC

OCEAN

PALAU

Celebes

Sea Tahulandang

Siau Sangihe
Islands Doi Morotai

Ruang

Maratua

Ternate

Mayu Kasiruta

Togian Islands Mandioli

Banggai Is. Bacan Is.

Taliabu Bisa

Obilatu

Sula Is.

Halmahera

Widi Waigeo

INDONESIA

Obi

Sulawesi Moluccas Ceram Sea

Makassar Strait

Boano Seram

Buru

Ambon Saparua

Wowoni Haruku

Laut

Muna Buton

Kabaena

Jampea

Kalao

Komodo

Lombok

Sumbawa Flores

Sea Flores Sea

Madu Alor

Lembata

Sumba Semau

Sawu

Rote

Miana

Tukangbesi
Islands

Kalaotoa

Wetar Atauro

EAST TIMOR Leti

Timor

NEW

GUINEA

Watubela Islands

Banda Sea

Manuk

Gunungapi Nila Kai Islands

Damar Babar Tanimbar
Islands

Moa

Arafura

Sea

LESSER SUNDAS

13

1 CASSOWARY

1 SOUTHERN CASSOWARY *Casuarius casuarius* 130–170cm FIELD NOTES Immature brown with dull bare skin areas and a much-reduced casque. Length of adult wattles and casque very variable, and bare skin colours brighter in females. Shy, usually solitary. Presence often revealed by piles of orange or purplish droppings. VOICE: Various grunts, rumblings, roars and hollow-sounding booming. HABITAT: Lowland and hill forest. DISTRIBUTION: Resident in Seram in the S Moluccas.

1

2 MALEO; SCRUBFOWL

1 MALEO *Macrocephalon maleo* 55cm FIELD NOTES: Usually encountered in pairs feeding on the ground; resorts to tree branches for roosting or when alarmed. VOICE: A nasal, vibrating braying, often answered by the female with a two-note *kuk-kuk*. HABITAT: Lowland and hill forest. Breeds communally in sandy forest areas or on sandy beaches. DISTRIBUTION: Endemic to Sulawesi.

2 MOLUCCAN SCRUBFOWL (MOLUCCAN MEGAPODE) *Eulipoa wallacei* 30cm FIELD NOTES: Shies away from breeding areas; forages on the ground, usually singly or in pairs. VOICE: A low, wavering *waaaaw*. HABITAT: Hill and montane forest. Breeds communally on sandy beaches or clearings in coastal scrub. DISTRIBUTION: Resident in the Moluccas, from Halmahera south to Buru and Seram.

3 PHILIPPINE SCRUBFOWL (PHILIPPINE MEGAPODE) *Megapodius cumingii* 32–38cm FIELD NOTES: Secretive, usually encountered feeding on the ground, singly or in small groups. Generally flies only when alarmed. VOICE: A long, mournful, drawn-out scream, said to resemble an air-raid siren. At breeding grounds issues chicken-like clucks and various *keeeee* or *kayooo* notes. HABITAT: Coastal scrub, hill and montane forest. DISTRIBUTION: Resident in Borneo, the Philippines, and Sulawesi.

4 SULA SCRUBFOWL (SULA MEGAPODE) *Megapodius bernsteinii* 35cm FIELD NOTES: Forages on the ground, singly, in pairs or in small groups. Will fly short distances if alarmed. VOICE: Duets with a mournful, hoarse two-note braying, joined by a second bird uttering a longer nasal chuckle. HABITAT: Primary forest to coastal scrub. DISTRIBUTION: Endemic to the Banggai and Sula islands.

5 TANIMBAR SCRUBFOWL (TANIMBAR MEGAPODE) *Megapodius tenimberensis* 35cm FIELD NOTES: Shy, generally encountered singly or in pairs. Usually heard rather than seen. VOICE: A loud, upslurred *kee-yu*, followed by a series of shorter, high-pitched *keyu* notes; a second bird joins in with a series of rising *kwou* notes, repeated at intervals varying from a few seconds to many minutes. HABITAT: Primary, secondary and semi-evergreen forest. DISTRIBUTION: Endemic to the Tanimbar Islands in the E Lesser Sundas.

6 DUSKY SCRUBFOWL (DUSKY MEGAPODE) *Megapodius freycinet* 35cm FIELD NOTES: Reasonably common. Pairs forage on the ground, uttering a constant clucking. Race M. f. forsteni (6b), sometimes regarded as a full species, occurs in the S Moluccas. VOICE: Duets, the first bird uttering a chuckling, rising and then falling *kejowowowowowowowowow*, the second bird joining in with two rising *keyou* notes. HABITAT: Various forests, including primary, tall secondary and swamp; also in mangroves, swamps and plantations. DISTRIBUTION: Resident in the Moluccas.

7 ORANGE-FOOTED SCRUBFOWL *Megapodius reinwardt* 35cm FIELD NOTES: Forages on the ground, usually singly or in pairs; best located by calls. When disturbed, generally runs, but will fly to hide in tree branches if alarmed. VOICE: Duets, starting with a series of melodious notes, followed by a long, descending, high-pitched, stammering *krrr-uk-uk-uk-uk-krrr*. HABITAT: Various, from lower montane forest to coastal scrub and mangrove. DISTRIBUTION: Resident in the Lesser Sundas and SE Moluccas.

3 GREBES; DUCKS

1 LITTLE GREBE *Tachybaptus ruficollis* 25cm FIELD NOTES: Usually encountered in pairs or small groups. In flight, shows whitish secondaries. The darker race *T. r. tricolor*, which occurs in Java, Sulawesi and the Lesser Sundas, is sometimes considered a full species. VOICE: A high-pitched whinnying trill and various twitterings. HABITAT: Vegetated lakes, ponds and rivers, also coastal estuaries. DISTRIBUTION: Resident in Java, the Philippines, Sulawesi and the Lesser Sundas.

2 AUSTRALIAN LITTLE GREBE (AUSTRALASIAN GREBE)
Tachybaptus novaehollandiae 23–27cm FIELD NOTES: Generally occurs in pairs or small groups. In flight, shows much white on primaries and secondaries. VOICE: A series of rapid trills. HABITAT: Freshwater lakes, ponds and swamps. DISTRIBUTION: Resident in Java and the Talaud and Sangihe islands.

3 GREAT CRESTED GREBE *Podiceps cristatus* 46–51cm FIELD NOTES: In flight, shows white secondaries and a white forewing. VOICE: A barking *rah-rah-rah* and various croaks and growls. HABITAT: Lakes, rivers and sheltered coastal waters. DISTRIBUTION: Rare vagrant.

4 BLACK-NECKED GREBE *Podiceps nigricollis* 28–34cm FIELD NOTES: Has a steep forehead. In flight, shows white secondaries. VOICE: A flute-like *poo-eeet* and a vibrant trill. HABITAT: Lakes and shallow coastal waters. DISTRIBUTION: Rare vagrant.

5 LESSER WHISTLING DUCK *Dendrocygna javanica* 38–42cm FIELD NOTES: Usually encountered in small flocks. Regularly roosts in trees. At close range, note yellow eye-ring. VOICE: In flight, utters a thin, whistled *whi-whee*. HABITAT: Mainly freshwater pools, lakes and swamps with emergent vegetation. DISTRIBUTION: Resident in Sumatra, W Java, Borneo and the W Lesser Sundas.

6 WANDERING WHISTLING DUCK *Dendrocygna arcuata* 40–45cm
FIELD NOTES: Gregarious, often in large flocks. Note white outer uppertail-coverts. VOICE: High-pitched twittering, also high-pitched whistles that are usually uttered in flight. HABITAT: Freshwater marshes, lakes and lagoons. DISTRIBUTION: Resident in Sumatra, Java, Borneo, the Philippines, Sulawesi and the Sundas.

7 SPOTTED WHISTLING DUCK *Dendrocygna guttata* 43cm FIELD NOTES: Usually found in small flocks; regularly perches in trees. VOICE: A coarse, whistled *whu-wheouw-whi*. HABITAT: Small lakes, swamps, tree-lined rivers and estuarine mangroves. DISTRIBUTION: Resident in the Philippines, Sulawesi, the S Moluccas and E Lesser Sundas.

8 SHELDUCK (COMMON SHELDUCK) *Tadorna tadorna* 58–67cm
FIELD NOTES: Unmistakable. Appears black and white in flight. VOICE: Male utters a thin, whistling *sliss-sliss-sliss*; female gives a rapid, nasal *gag-ag-ag-ag-ag-ak*. HABITAT: Inland wetlands and coastal mudflats. DISTRIBUTION: Accidental visitor to the Philippines.

9 RAJA SHELDUCK *Tadorna radjah* 48cm FIELD NOTES: Generally found in pairs or small groups; often rests on mudbanks or tree branches. In flight above, shows large white forewing; below, white with black primaries. VOICE: In flight, male utters a loud, upslurred whistle and the female a harsh rattling or grunting. HABITAT: Lakes, ponds, rivers, creeks and coastal flats. DISTRIBUTION: Resident in the Moluccas and E Lesser Sundas.

10 RUDDY SHELDUCK *Tadorna ferruginea* 61–67cm FIELD NOTES: In flight, shows extensive white forewing above and below. VOICE: Utters a honking *aakh*, also a repeated, trumpet-like *pok-pok-pok-pok*. HABITAT: Large rivers and lakes. DISTRIBUTION: Accidental visitor to the Philippines.

11 WHITE-WINGED DUCK *Asarcornis scutulata* 66–81cm FIELD NOTES: Shy and chiefly nocturnal. In flight, shows extensive white forewing. Female as male but duller. VOICE: Generally silent; in flight, may utter a wailing honk, ending with a nasal whistle. HABITAT: Swamp forest and nearby swampy areas. DISTRIBUTION: Resident in Sumatra.

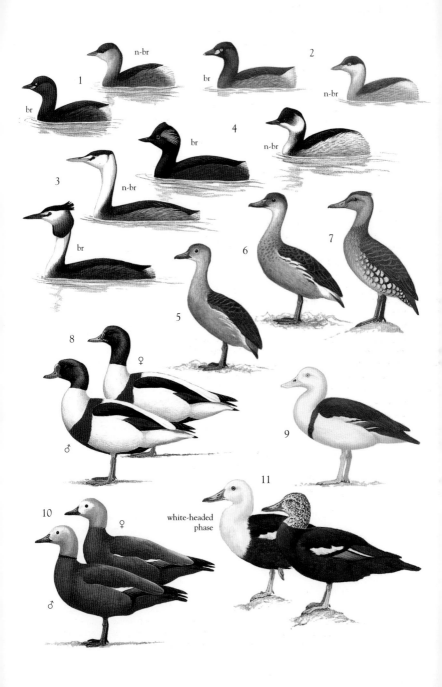

4 DUCKS

1 COTTON PYGMY GOOSE *Nettapus coromandelianus* 30–37cm FIELD NOTES: Usually seen in pairs or small parties. In flight, males show much white on base of primaries and secondaries; female wing mainly dark. Flies low with shallow, fluttering wing-beats. VOICE: Male utters a sharp, cackled *car-car-carawak*; female gives a weak quack. HABITAT: Freshwater lakes and pools with emergent vegetation. DISTRIBUTION: Mainly winter visitor to the Philippines, Borneo, Java, Sumatra and Sulawesi.

2 GREEN PYGMY GOOSE *Nettapus pulchellus* 32–36cm FIELD NOTES: Usually seen in pairs or small groups, easily overlooked while swimming among floating vegetation. In flight, shows extensive white secondaries. VOICE: In flight, utters a shrill, whistled *tii-whit* or *whit*. HABITAT: Freshwater lakes, swamps and rivers, especially with floating or submerged vegetation. DISTRIBUTION: Vagrant or non-breeding visitor to Sulawesi, the S Moluccas and Lesser Sundas.

3 GADWALL *Anas strepera* 46–55cm FIELD NOTES: Usually found in small groups. In flight, both sexes show a distinct white secondary patch on upperwing. VOICE: Male gives a sharp *ahrk* and a low whistle; female utters a mechanical quack. HABITAT: Freshwater lakes and marshes, coastal lagoons and estuaries. DISTRIBUTION: Rare vagrant.

4 WIGEON (EURASIAN WIGEON) *Anas penelope* 45–50cm FIELD NOTES: Regularly grazes away from water. In flight, male shows large white patch on upperwing, underwing grey. VOICE: Male utters a clear, whistled *wheeooo*, female a growling *krr*. HABITAT: Wet grassland, marshes, lakes, rivers and coastal waters. DISTRIBUTION: Winter visitor to the Philippines; vagrant in Borneo and Sulawesi.

5 MALLARD *Anas platyrhynchos* 50–65cm FIELD NOTES: Non-breeding male like female but bill dull yellow. VOICE: Male utters a rasped *kreep*, female a *quack-quack-quack*. HABITAT: Lakes, ponds, rivers and estuaries. DISTRIBUTION: Winter vagrant recorded in Borneo.

6 SPOT-BILLED DUCK (INDIAN or WESTERN SPOT-BILLED DUCK) *Anas poecilorhyncha* 58–63cm FIELD NOTES: In flight, upperwing shows distinctive white tertials. VOICE: Calls very similar to those of Mallard. HABITAT: Well-vegetated lakes, pools and marshes. DISTRIBUTION: Vagrant recorded in the Philippines.

7 PHILIPPINE DUCK *Anas luzonica* 48–58cm FIELD NOTES: Generally found in pairs or small parties; sometimes seen in larger flocks of 100–200. VOICE: Similar to Mallard but more harsh. HABITAT: Lakes, rivers, marshes and tidal creeks. DISTRIBUTION: Resident in the Philippines.

8 PACIFIC BLACK DUCK *Anas superciliosa* 47–60cm FIELD NOTES: Usually encountered in pairs or small groups. In flight, shows extensive white underwing coverts. VOICE: Similar to Mallard, but hoarser. HABITAT: Various wetlands, including lakes, ponds, marshes and estuaries. DISTRIBUTION: Resident in Sumatra, Java, Sulawesi and the Lesser Sundas; vagrant in Borneo.

9 SHOVELER (NORTHERN or EUROPEAN SHOVELER) *Anas clypeata* 44–52cm FIELD NOTES: Usually occurs in pairs or small groups. Due to large bill, tends to look 'front heavy' in flight. Male upperwing shows a pale blue forewing and a green speculum separated by a white wing-bar, female wing duller. VOICE: Generally silent. HABITAT: Open freshwater areas, less often on coastal lagoons and estuaries. DISTRIBUTION: Winter visitor to Philippines and Borneo.

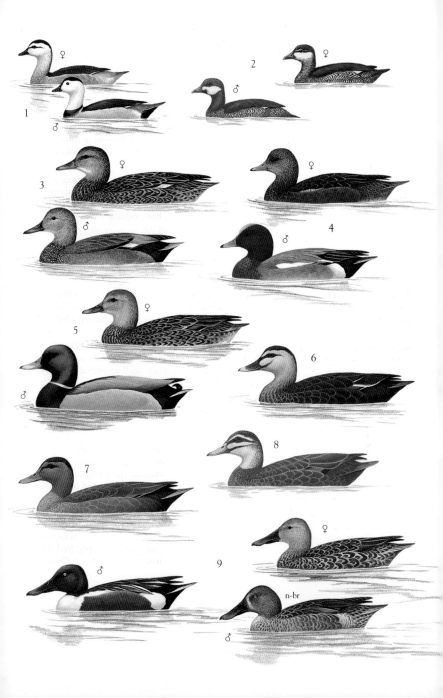

5 DUCKS

1 SUNDA TEAL *Anas gibberifrons* 42cm FIELD NOTES: Generally seen in pairs or small flocks. Male shows a 'bulge' on forehead. In flight, upperwing shows a white mid-wing panel. VOICE: Male utters a clear *pip*, female gives a wild, laughing cackle. HABITAT: Small lakes, swamps, forest streams, rich fields, mudflats and mangroves. DISTRIBUTION: Resident in Java, Sumatra, Bali, SE Borneo, Sulawesi, Sula and the Lesser Sundas.

2 GREY TEAL *Anas gracilis* 42cm FIELD NOTES: Usually occurs in pairs or small flocks. Very similar to Sunda Teal, but less brown; does not have a forehead 'bulge'. VOICE: Male gives a muted whistle, female utters a rapid series of harsh, laughing quacks. HABITAT: Lakes, swamps, rivers, lagoons and shallow coastal waters. DISTRIBUTION: Uncommon visitor to the S Moluccas and E Lesser Sundas.

3 PINTAIL (NORTHERN PINTAIL) *Anas acuta* 51–56cm (male with tail 61–66cm) FIELD NOTES: Gregarious, may consort with Garganey. Long neck and tail make for an elongated look in flight. VOICE: Generally silent but male may give a mellow *proop-proop*; female utters a series of weak quacks. HABITAT: Lakes, marshes, coastal lagoons and estuaries. DISTRIBUTION: Winter visitor to Sumatra, Java, Borneo and the Philippines.

4 TEAL (EURASIAN or COMMON TEAL) *Anas crecca* 34–38cm FIELD NOTES: Usually seen in pairs or small groups. Flight rapid with much twisting and turning. VOICE: Male utters a soft, high-pitched *preep-preep*; females generally silent, although may give a nasal quack if alarmed. HABITAT: Lakes, pools, marshes and estuaries. DISTRIBUTION: Winter vagrant, recorded from Borneo.

5 GARGANEY *Anas querquedula* 37–41cm FIELD NOTES: Gregarious, often forms large flocks and mixes freely with other duck species. Normally keeps close to cover, foraging among emergent vegetation. VOICE: Generally silent but male may utter a rattling *knerek* and the female a high, nasal quack. HABITAT: Freshwater lakes, marshes and coastal lagoons. DISTRIBUTION: Winter visitor to Sumatra, Java, Borneo, the Philippines and Wallacea.

6 POCHARD (COMMON or EUROPEAN POCHARD) *Aythya ferina* 42–49cm FIELD NOTES: Usually gregarious. In flight, shows pale grey wings. VOICE: Generally silent. HABITAT: Large open lakes, less often rivers and coastal waters. DISTRIBUTION: Rare winter visitor to the Philippines.

7 BAER'S POCHARD (BAER'S or SIBERIAN WHITE-EYE) *Aythya baeri* 41–46cm FIELD NOTES: Usually in pairs or small parties. In flight, upperwing of both sexes shows a prominent white bar across primaries and secondaries. VOICE: Generally silent. HABITAT: Lakes, ponds, marshes and rivers. DISTRIBUTION: Vagrant, recorded from the Philippines.

8 HARDHEAD *Aythya australis* 42–59cm FIELD NOTES: Usually occurs in small or large flocks. Upperwing of both sexes shows a white bar across primaries and secondaries. VOICE: Generally silent. HABITAT: Swamps and vegetated lakes; in winter, prefers large open lakes, rivers and coastal lagoons. DISTRIBUTION: Old breeding record from Java, otherwise a rare vagrant, recorded from Sulawesi and the Lesser Sundas.

9 TUFTED DUCK *Aythya fuligula* 40–47cm FIELD NOTES: Generally gregarious. In flight, upperwing of both sexes shows a prominent white bar across primaries and secondaries. VOICE: Usually silent, but may give a low growl when flushed. HABITAT: Lakes, rivers and sheltered coastal waters. DISTRIBUTION: Winter visitor to Borneo and the Philippines; rare vagrant in Sumatra and Sulawesi.

10 SCAUP (GREATER SCAUP) *Aythya marila* 40–51cm FIELD NOTES: Usually gregarious. In flight, upperwing of both sexes shows a white wing-bar across primaries and secondaries, and male forewing is pale grey. VOICE: Generally silent. HABITAT: Coastal waters, less often inland lakes. DISTRIBUTION: Rare vagrant, recorded from the Philippines.

white-undertail
variety

white-faced
variety

6 PARTRIDGES

1 GREY-BREASTED PARTRIDGE *Arborophila orientalis* 28cm FIELD NOTES: Little known; presumably forages among leaf litter in small parties. VOICE: A series of single whistles followed by a double chirping whistle, increasing in volume. HABITAT: Undergrowth in primary montane forest. DISTRIBUTION: Endemic to W and C Java.

2 SUMATRAN PARTRIDGE *Arborophila sumatrana* 28cm FIELD NOTES: Little known; actions presumably similar to previous species. VOICE: Very similar to previous species. HABITAT: Dense undergrowth in broadleaved foothill and mountain forest. DISTRIBUTION: Endemic to C and S Sumatra.

3 ROLL'S PARTRIDGE *Arborophila rolli* 28cm FIELD NOTES: Was, until recently, regarded as a subspecies of the previous species; actions are presumed to be similar. VOICE: Similar to Grey-breasted Partridge. HABITAT: Dense forest undergrowth. DISTRIBUTION: Endemic to N Sumatra.

4 JAVAN PARTRIDGE (CHESTNUT-BELLIED PARTRIDGE)
Arborophila javanica 28cm FIELD NOTES: Little recorded; presumably forages among leaf litter as other partridges. VOICE: A far-carrying series of double calls, increasing in volume and tempo. HABITAT: Hill and montane forest. DISTRIBUTION: Endemic to Java.

5 BORNEAN PARTRIDGE (RED-BREASTED PARTRIDGE)
Arborophila hyperythra 27cm FIELD NOTES: Forages in groups in thickets, on forest tracks and on river flats. Dark-chinned race *A. h. erythrophrys* (5b) occurs in the montane areas of NE Borneo. VOICE: A repeated, ringing *chii*, which increases in volume and tempo, answered by a low double note. HABITAT: Thickets, including bamboo in understorey of secondary and primary hill and montane forest. DISTRIBUTION: Endemic to Borneo.

6 RED-BILLED PARTRIDGE *Arborophila rubrirostris* 29cm FIELD NOTES: Occurs in small groups, foraging in mossy gullies and dense undergrowth. VOICE: A loud, whistled *keow*, rising in pitch and volume. HABITAT: Lower and upper montane forest. DISTRIBUTION: Endemic to N and W Sumatra.

7 CHESTNUT-NECKLACED PARTRIDGE *Arborophila charltonii* 26–32cm FIELD NOTES: Forages in small groups in secondary scrub and forest edges. VOICE: A whistled *pi pi pi*, answered with a whistled *pi-u pi-u*; also utters a short, liquid warble. HABITAT: Lowland forest and scrub. DISTRIBUTION: Resident in N Sumatra and N Borneo.

8 FERRUGINOUS PARTRIDGE *Caloperdix oculeus* 23–27cm FIELD NOTES: Forages on the forest floor, singly, in pairs or sometimes in larger parties. VOICE: A rising *pi-pi-pi-pipipipipipipi*, repeated 8–9 times, followed by a clanging *dit-duit dit-duit*; female replies with many rapid, rising, whistled notes. HABITAT: Secondary scrub, evergreen and semi-evergreen forest. DISTRIBUTION: Resident in Sumatra and Borneo.

9 CRIMSON-HEADED PARTRIDGE *Haematortyx sanguiniceps* 25cm FIELD NOTES: Forages on forest floor, often encountered on forest trails. VOICE: A harsh, high-pitched *KRO-krang*, repeated several times; also utters a harsh clucking. HABITAT: Lower montane forest, heath forest and poor forest on sandy soils in valley bottoms. DISTRIBUTION: Resident in Borneo.

10 CRESTED PARTRIDGE *Rollulus rouloul* 25cm FIELD NOTES: Generally encountered in pairs foraging among leaf litter on the forest floor. VOICE: A long series of mournful *si-ul* whistles, second note higher pitched, usually given in early morning or late evening. HABITAT: Usually lowland and hill forest, also recorded in adjacent palm groves. DISTRIBUTION: Resident in Sumatra and Borneo.

head variations

erythrophrys

5b

5

grey eye-brow
form

7 FRANCOLINS; PARTRIDGES; JUNGLEFOWL; PHEASANTS

1 CHINESE FRANCOLIN *Francolinus pintadeanus* 31–34cm FIELD NOTES: Forages on the ground. Wary, although often calls from an exposed perch. VOICE: A harsh, metallic *kak-kak-kuich ka-ka* or *wi-ta-tak-takaa*, normally repeated after lengthy pauses. HABITAT: Grassland with mixed trees and shrubs. DISTRIBUTION: Introduced in the Philippines, probably now extinct.

2 DAURIAN PARTRIDGE (MONGOLIAN or BEARDED PARTRIDGE)
Perdix dauurica 28–30cm FIELD NOTES: Usually occurs in small parties, foraging on the ground. VOICE: Various creaking calls. HABITAT: Grassland with mixed trees and shrubs. DISTRIBUTION: Introduced in the Philippines, probably now extinct.

3 BLACK PARTRIDGE *Melanoperdix niger* 24–27cm FIELD NOTES: Shy, generally encountered in pairs foraging on the forest floor, little else recorded. VOICE: A low, creaking contact call; may also utter a clear two-note whistle. HABITAT: Lowland primary and peat-swamp forest. DISTRIBUTION: Resident in Sumatra and Borneo.

4 LONG-BILLED PARTRIDGE *Rhizothera longirostris* 30–35cm FIELD NOTES: Forages on the ground, flying to rest in tree branches when alarmed, otherwise very little recorded. VOICE: A duetted, bell-like *ti-oooah-whee*, repeated over long periods. HABITAT: Lowland primary forest. DISTRIBUTION: Resident in Sumatra and Borneo.

5 HOSE'S PARTRIDGE (DULIT PARTRIDGE) *Rhizothera dulitensis* 30–35cm FIELD NOTES: Very little recorded, actions presumably similar to Long-billed Partridge. VOICE: Not recorded. HABITAT: Montane forest. DISTRIBUTION: Endemic to NE Borneo.

6 RED JUNGLEFOWL *Gallus gallus* Male 65–78cm, female 41–46cm FIELD NOTES: Generally shy; occurs singly, in pairs or occasionally in family groups. VOICE: *Cock-a-doodle-do*, similar to a farmyard cockerel, although with a more shrill and strangulated finish. HABITAT: Forest, forest edges and dense tall scrub. DISTRIBUTION: Resident in Sumatra and Java; introduced in the Philippines, Borneo, Sulawesi and the Lesser Sundas.

7 GREEN JUNGLEFOWL *Gallus varius* Male 65–75cm, female 42–46cm FIELD NOTES: Generally seen singly or in small groups, in early morning and late evening, recorded feeding in open areas such as grain fields or tracks. VOICE: Male gives a three-note *cha-aw-awk* or *chow-a-aaaar* and a slow, cackling *wok-wok-wok*; female utters a rapid *kok-kok-kok…* HABITAT: Woodland, woodland edges, plantations and grassland. DISTRIBUTION: Resident in Java, Bali and the W Lesser Sundas.

8 SALVADORI'S PHEASANT *Lophura inornata* 46–55cm FIELD NOTES: Rare, very little recorded, probably occurs in pairs. VOICE: Male utters a cluck in the breeding season. HABITAT: Montane forest with dense undergrowth. DISTRIBUTION: Endemic to SW Sumatra.

9 HOOGERWERF'S PHEASANT (ACEH PHEASANT) *Lophura hoogerwerfi* 40–50cm FIELD NOTES: Actions presumably much like Salvadori's Pheasant, with which it is often regarded as conspecific. VOICE: Not known, probably much like Salvadori's. HABITAT: Montane forest. DISTRIBUTION: Endemic to N Sumatra.

8 PHEASANTS; PEAFOWL

1 CRESTED FIREBACK *Lophura ignita* Male 65–70cm, female 56–57cm
FIELD NOTES: Wary, presence often given away by contact calls or wing-whirring sounds
of male. Recorded in small groups, usually a single male and several females. Dark race
L. i. rufa (1b) occurs in Sumatra (except SE); white-tailed race *L. i. macartneyi* (1c) is
found in SE Sumatra. VOICE: Male utters a subdued *woonk-k woonk-k*, often accompanied
by wing-whirring. When alarmed, gives a sharp *chuken chuken*. HABITAT: Lowland forest.
DISTRIBUTION: Resident in Sumatra and Borneo.

2 CRESTLESS FIREBACK *Lophura erythrophthalma* Male 47–50cm, female
42–44cm FIELD NOTES: Wary, forages on the forest floor in small groups, presumably
one male and several females. *L. e. pyronota* (2b) occurs in Borneo. VOICE: A vibrating,
throaty *purr* and a repeated, croaking *tak-takuru* or *tooktaroo*. When alarmed, utters a
loud *kak*. Wing-whirring takes place during display. HABITAT: Primary lowland forest.
DISTRIBUTION: Resident in Sumatra and Borneo.

3 BULWER'S PHEASANT *Lophura bulweri* Male 77–80cm, female 55cm
FIELD NOTES: Thought to occur in pairs or small family groups. In a spectacular display,
male greatly extends wattles and raises and spreads tail. VOICE: In breeding season, utters a
shrill, piercing cry. Other calls recorded are a metallic *kook kook* and a distinctive *bek-kia*.
HABITAT: Primary hill and submontane forest. DISTRIBUTION: Endemic to Borneo.

**4 BRONZE-TAILED PEACOCK-PHEASANT (SUMATRAN PEACOCK-
PHEASANT)** *Polyplectron chalcurum* Male 56cm, female 40cm FIELD NOTES: Very shy
and wary, presumably forages on the forest floor in pairs. VOICE: Male gives a harsh, loud,
far-carrying *karau-karau-karau*. HABITAT: Montane forest. DISTRIBUTION: Endemic to
W Sumatra.

5 BORNEAN PEACOCK-PHEASANT *Polyplectron schleiermacheri* Male 50cm,
female 36cm FIELD NOTES: Little recorded, forages quietly on the forest floor; spreads wings
during display. VOICE: A melancholic *hor-hor* or *wu-wurh*. Contact call is a loud *cack cack*.
HABITAT: Primary lowland rainforest. DISTRIBUTION: Endemic to Borneo.

6 PALAWAN PEACOCK-PHEASANT *Polyplectron napoleonis* Male 50cm, female
40cm FIELD NOTES: Secretive. Males recorded foraging singly and females in small groups,
best located by calls or clean display 'scrapes'. VOICE: A harsh, screeched *auukk*, *kratt* and
ka-reeeetch, also a two-note, see-sawing *krotchh-kritchh*, likened to hitting a metal pipe
with a piece of wood. HABITAT: Forested slopes. DISTRIBUTION: Endemic to Palawan in the
Philippines.

7 GREAT ARGUS *Argusianus argus* Male 160–200cm, female 72–76cm
FIELD NOTES: Wary, wanders into undergrowth at the least disturbance. Forages in the
mornings and evenings, spends much of the rest of the day resting in trees. Best located by
calls or display 'scrapes'. VOICE: A distinctive, repeated *kwoow-wow* and a musical *wow* that
is repeated over and over, becoming increasingly higher in pitch, giving the impression
of mounting excitement, before stopping abruptly. HABITAT: Hill and lowland forest.
DISTRIBUTION: Resident in Sumatra and Borneo.

8 GREEN PEAFOWL *Pavo muticus* Male 180–300cm, female 100–110cm
FIELD NOTES: Unmistakable. Timid and secretive. Best located when calling from roost sites.
Tends to forage near watercourses. VOICE: A repeated, trumpeting *ki-wao* or *yee-ow*. When
alarmed, gives a repeated *tak tak ker-r-r oo oo ker-r-r-oo*. Female utters a loud *AOW-aa
AOW-aa*. HABITAT: Forest margins and savannah woodland. DISTRIBUTION: Resident in Java.

pyronota

2b ♂

1 ♀

♀

♂

2

1b *rufa*

♂

♂

2 ♀

1c

macartneyi

♂

♂

3

4 ♂

♀

8 ♂

♀

5 ♂

♀

6 ♂

♀

7

♀

♂

♀

9 QUAILS; BUTTONQUAILS

1 JAPANESE QUAIL (ASIAN MIGRATORY QUAIL) *Coturnix japonica* 17–19cm
FIELD NOTES: Shy and furtive. In non-breeding plumage, the rufous face is often obscured by pale feathering. VOICE: A chattering *chrr-chuerrk-churr* and a rippled *tree-tree* when flushed. HABITAT: Rolling grassland, agricultural land, montane foothills and forest clearings. DISTRIBUTION: Winter vagrant, recorded in the Philippines.

2 BROWN QUAIL *Coturnix ypsilophora* 19cm FIELD NOTES: Generally seen in small coveys of 3–11 birds, typically elusive but occasionally recorded feeding along roadsides in the early morning or late afternoon. C. y. *pallidor* (main illustration) occurs on Sumba and Sawu in the Lesser Sundas; chestnut race C. y. *raaltenii* (2b) is found from the C to W Lesser Sundas. VOICE: Race C. y. *raaltenii* gives an *er-errrrrrhh*, the drawn-out part having an upward inflection. Flushed birds of race C. y. *pallidior* utter a loud *trrriup trrriup*. HABITAT: Rank grassland, damp areas, light scrub and overgrown gardens. DISTRIBUTION: Resident in the Lesser Sundas.

3 KING QUAIL (BLUE-BREASTED QUAIL) *Excalfactoria chinensis* 12–15cm
FIELD NOTES: Shy and furtive, most often observed when running or dust-bathing. Generally seen in pairs or small parties, running mouse-like through rank grass, pausing to feed before running on again. VOICE: A piping *ti-yu ti-yu ti-yu ti-yu ti-yu or ti-ti-yu*. When flushed, utters a weak *tir-tir-tir* or a sequence of sharp *cheeps*. HABITAT: Shrubby and swampy grassland, cultivated land and scrubby rank vegetation. DISTRIBUTION: Resident in Sumatra, Java, Borneo, the Philippines and Wallacea.

4 SMALL BUTTONQUAIL (COMMON or LITTLE BUTTONQUAIL)
Turnix sylvaticus 15–16cm FIELD NOTES: Secretive; generally adopts a crouched foraging posture but can be quite upright when crossing open ground. VOICE: A low, droning *hoooo hoooo hoooo*, also various rattling, low-pitched calls. HABITAT: Grassland, scrub and grassy areas at the edge of cultivation. DISTRIBUTION: Resident in Java, Bali and the Philippines.

5 RED-BACKED BUTTONQUAIL *Turnix maculosus* 12–16cm FIELD NOTES: Actions and habits similar to Small Buttonquail. VOICE: A deep, far-carrying, subdued *oom oom oom...* HABITAT: Dense grassland, grassy scrub and cultivation. DISTRIBUTION: Resident throughout, with a patchy distribution in Wallacea.

6 SPOTTED BUTTONQUAIL *Turnix ocellatus* 17–18cm FIELD NOTES: Shy and secretive. Forages on the ground and often seen on dirt tracks in forests; if disturbed, tends to disappear into cover, but also recorded feeding unconcerned near observers. VOICE: Female said to utter a low booming, otherwise little known. HABITAT: Very varied, including scrub, dry forest ravines, forest edges and gardens. DISTRIBUTION: Endemic to the Philippines.

7 BARRED BUTTONQUAIL *Turnix suscitator* 15–17cm FIELD NOTES: Encountered singly or in pairs; regularly forages along dirt roads or highways. When flushed, rises steeply and flies a short distance before dropping into cover. VOICE: A deep *groo groo groo*, followed by a purring *krrrr*, this continuing for several seconds, often given at night; also a far-carrying *hoon-hoon-hoon-hoon*. HABITAT: Grassland, scrub, forest edges, coastal secondary growth and cultivated areas. DISTRIBUTION: Resident in Sumatra, Java, Bali, the Philippines, Sulawesi and the W Lesser Sundas.

8 WORCESTER'S BUTTONQUAIL *Turnix worcesteri* 12–14cm FIELD NOTES: Little known, actions presumed to be similar to other buttonquails. VOICE: Unrecorded. HABITAT: Probably grassland at high elevations. DISTRIBUTION: Endemic to the Philippines.

9 SUMBA BUTTONQUAIL *Turnix everetti* 14cm FIELD NOTES: Forages in pairs. Very little else recorded, but actions probably much as other buttonquails. VOICE: Unrecorded. HABITAT: Scrubby grassland and fields. DISTRIBUTION: Endemic to Sumba Island in the Lesser Sundas.

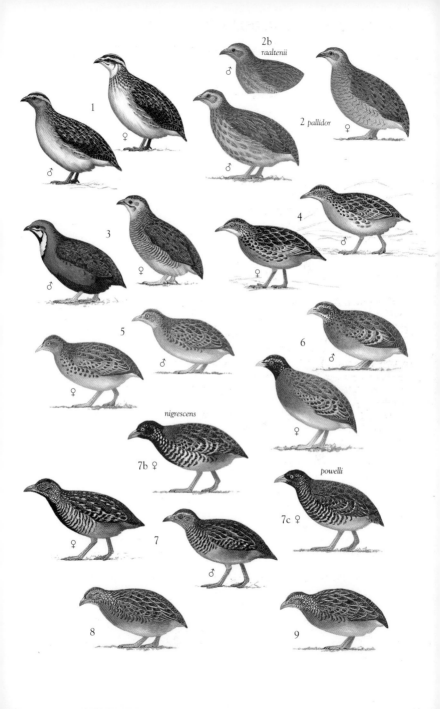

2b
raaltenii
♂

2 *pallidor*
♀

♂

1

♀

♂

3

♀

4

♀

♂

5

♂

6

♂

♀

♀

nigrescens

7b ♀

powelli

7c ♀

♀

7

♂

8

9

10 HONEYGUIDE; PICULETS; WOODPECKERS

1 MALAYSIAN HONEYGUIDE *Indicator archipelagicus* 16–18cm FIELD NOTES: Often sits motionless, usually seen in the vicinity of a beehive. Females lack the yellow shoulder patch. VOICE: A mewing, followed by an ascending rattle. HABITAT: Lowland primary forest. DISTRIBUTION: Rare resident in Sumatra and Borneo.

2 SPECKLED PICULET *Picumnus innominatus malayorum* 10cm FIELD NOTES: Agile forager, also makes aerial sallies after insects. Presence revealed by persistent tapping while searching for food. VOICE: A high-pitched *ti-ti-ti-ti-ti* and a squeaky *sik-sik-sik*. Drums with a persistent *brr-r-r brr-r-r…* HABITAT: Mixed hill primary and secondary lowland forest. DISTRIBUTION: Resident in N Borneo and Sumatra.

3 RUFOUS PICULET *Sasia abnormis* 8–10cm FIELD NOTES: Active forager, singly or in small parties. VOICE: A high-pitched *kik-ik-ik-ik-ik-ik*; also a sharp *tic* or *tsit*. HABITAT: Primary and secondary lowland and hill forest; in Borneo, favours thick, tangled vegetation in disturbed forest. DISTRIBUTION: Resident in Sumatra, Java and Borneo.

4 SULAWESI PYGMY WOODPECKER *Yungipicus temminckii* 13cm FIELD NOTES: Occurs singly or in pairs; forages from the mid-storey to the canopy. VOICE: A slightly descending, nasal trill. HABITAT: Primary and tall secondary forest, forest edges and wooded cultivation. DISTRIBUTION: Endemic to Sulawesi.

5 PHILIPPINE PYGMY WOODPECKER *Yungipicus maculatus* 14cm FIELD NOTES: Occurs singly or in pairs; regularly joins mixed-species feeding flocks. VOICE: A loud, stuttering, slightly descending trill. HABITAT: Primary and secondary forest, cloud forest, forest edges and mahogany plantations. DISTRIBUTION: Endemic to the Philippines.

6 SULU PYGMY WOODPECKER *Yungipicus ramsayi* 14cm FIELD NOTES: Actions presumably similar to Philippine Pygmy Woodpecker, with which it was often considered conspecific. VOICE: A loud, staccato *kikikikikikikiki*. HABITAT: Forests and mangroves. DISTRIBUTION: Endemic to the Sulu Islands.

7 SUNDA PYGMY WOODPECKER *Yungipicus moluccensis* 14–15cm FIELD NOTES: Forages in upper tree levels; sometimes a member of mixed-species feeding flocks. VOICE: A high-pitched trill or a whirring *trrrrr-i-i*. HABITAT: Various woodland types, including mangrove, primary and secondary forest, coastal forest and coastal gardens. DISTRIBUTION: Resident in Sumatra, Java, Borneo and W Lesser Sundas.

8 GREY-CAPPED PYGMY WOODPECKER *Yungipicus canicapillus* 14–16cm FIELD NOTES: Agile, often hanging upside down in the tops of trees and bushes. VOICE: A rattling *tit-erh-r-r-r-h* that often starts with a *kik* or *pit*; also utters a squeaky *kweek-kweek-kweeek*. HABITAT: Montane and lowland forest. DISTRIBUTION: Resident in Sumatra and Borneo.

9 FRECKLE-BREASTED WOODPECKER *Dendrocopos analis* 18–19cm FIELD NOTES: Usually encountered singly, in pairs or in small parties foraging on trunks and branches. VOICE: A ringing *tuk-tuk* and a trilled *tirri-tierrier-tierrierie*. HABITAT: Open forest, secondary forest, plantations and gardens. DISTRIBUTION: Resident in Sumatra, Java and Bali.

10 BUFF-NECKED WOODPECKER *Meiglyptes tukki* 21cm FIELD NOTES: Generally seen singly in the lower and middle storey, also a regular member of mixed-species feeding parties. Often forages low down on stumps and fallen logs. VOICE: A high, trilled *kirr-r-r* and a high-pitched *ti-ti-ti-ti-ti*. HABITAT: Primary and secondary lowland forest. DISTRIBUTION: Resident in Sumatra and Borneo.

11 BUFF-RUMPED WOODPECKER *Meiglyptes tristis* 17–18cm FIELD NOTES: Active forager, generally encountered in pairs or as a member of a mixed-species feeding party. *M. t. grammithorax* (11b) occurs in Sumatra and Borneo. VOICE: A soft, rattled *drrrrr…*, also a *pit* or *pit-pit*. HABITAT: Lowland and hill forest, also open coastal forest. DISTRIBUTION: Resident in Sumatra, Java and Borneo.

12 GREY-AND-BUFF WOODPECKER *Hemicircus concretus* 13–14cm FIELD NOTES: Forages in canopy, moving rapidly between branches and leaf clusters; best located by calls. *H. c. sordidus* (12b) occurs in Sumatra and Borneo. VOICE: A high-pitched, drawn-out *kiyow* or *kee-yew*, and a vibrating *chitter*. HABITAT: Primary and secondary lowland and hill forest, also plantations and occasionally gardens. DISTRIBUTION: Resident in Sumatra, Java and Borneo.

11b
grammithorax

12b
sordidus

11 WOODPECKERS

1 RUFOUS WOODPECKER *Micropternus brachyurus* 25cm FIELD NOTES: Usually encountered in pairs or small family groups, digging at tree-ant or termite nests; forages from the ground to the canopy. VOICE: A high-pitched, nasal *kenk kenk kenk* or *kweep-kweep-kweep*. Drumming is said to sound like a stalling motorbike. HABITAT: Primary and secondary forest, forest edges, plantations and gardens. DISTRIBUTION: Resident in Sumatra, Java and Borneo.

2 WHITE-BELLIED WOODPECKER *Dryocopus javensis* 40–48cm FIELD NOTES: Usually encountered singly, in pairs or in small groups. Noisy. Forages at all levels. VOICE: A laughing *kek-kek-kek-kek-kek...* or *kiau-kiau-kiau-kiau...*; also utters a sharp *kiyow, kyah* or *keer*. Drumming is loud and accelerating. HABITAT: Primary and occasionally secondary lowland and hill forest, also recorded in mangrove. DISTRIBUTION: Resident in Sumatra, Java (rare), Bali (rare), Borneo and the Philippines.

3 BANDED WOODPECKER *Chrysophlegma miniaceum* 25–27cm
FIELD NOTES: Unobtrusive, usually seen singly or in pairs foraging on large trunks at all levels. VOICE: A screaming *kwee* or *kwee kwee kwee*, also a mournful, descending *peew*. HABITAT: From coastal forest to montane forest. DISTRIBUTION: Resident in Sumatra, Java (rare) and Borneo.

4 CHECKER-THROATED WOODPECKER *Chrysophlegma mentale* 26–30cm
FIELD NOTES: Usually seen singly or in pairs foraging from lower to higher levels of the understorey. Sometimes joins mixed-species feeding parties. VOICE: A long series of *wi* notes; calls include *kyick* and a *kiyee... kiyee... kiyee*. HABITAT: Primary forest in lowlands, hills and mountains. DISTRIBUTION: Resident in Sumatra, W Java and Borneo.

5 GREATER YELLOWNAPE *Chrysophlegma flavinucha* 33–34cm FIELD NOTES: Often seen in small, loose groups foraging on trunks and branches; also rummages on the ground searching for ants, termites and grubs. VOICE: Calls include a long, accelerating *kwee-kwee-kwee-kwee-kwee-kwee-kwee-kwee-kwi-kwi-kwi-kwi-wi-wi-wi-wik*, a loud, plaintive *pee-u... pee-u*, and a metallic *chenk*. When disturbed, utters a laughing *kwek-kwek-kwek-kwek...* HABITAT: Mixed lower montane forest, pine forest and secondary growth. DISTRIBUTION: Resident in Sumatra.

6 CRIMSON-WINGED WOODPECKER *Picus puniceus* 24–28cm
FIELD NOTES: Generally occurs singly or in loose pairs; often forms part of mixed-species feeding flocks. VOICE: A long series of descending *kui* notes; calls include a distinctive *kee kyu*. HABITAT: Primary, secondary and logged forest, coastal scrub and gardens. DISTRIBUTION: Resident in Sumatra, Java and Borneo.

7 LESSER YELLOWNAPE *Picus chlorolophus* 25–28cm FIELD NOTES: Usually found in pairs, regularly seen as part of mixed-species feeding flocks. Often ventures to the ground in search of ants. VOICE: A loud, mournful *peee-ui, pee-a* or *pee-oow*, also a descending *kwee-kwee-kwee-kwee-kwee-kwee...* HABITAT: Lower montane forest. DISTRIBUTION: Resident in Sumatra.

8 LACED WOODPECKER *Picus vittatus* 30–33cm FIELD NOTES: Generally seen in pairs. Forages low in trees, on fallen trees and on the ground. In flight, shows a yellowish rump. VOICE: A fast, low-pitched *pew-pew-pew...*, also a *keep* or *kee-ip*. HABITAT: Open coastal forest, mangroves and plantations. DISTRIBUTION: Resident in E Sumatra, Java and Bali.

9 GREY-HEADED WOODPECKER *Picus canus dedemi* 26cm FIELD NOTES: Regularly forages on the ground in search of ants and grubs. In flight, shows a bright red rump. VOICE: A clear, whistled, descending *pew pew pew pew pew...* HABITAT: Upper montane forest. DISTRIBUTION: Rare resident in Sumatra.

12 WOODPECKERS

1 OLIVE-BACKED WOODPECKER *Dinopium rafflesii* 28cm FIELD NOTES: Forages from low to middle levels, usually singly or in pairs. VOICE: A slow *chakchakchakchakchak…*, also a similar but faster and longer call, and a single *chak*. HABITAT: Primary and secondary forest in lowlands, hills and mountains; also recorded in mangroves. DISTRIBUTION: Resident in Sumatra and Borneo.

2 COMMON FLAMEBACK *Dinopium javanense* 28–30cm FIELD NOTES: Pairs are found at all forest levels, although lower parts are preferred. VOICE: A long, trilled *ka-di-di-di-di-di-di…*, a *kow* or *kow kow*, and a *kowp-owp-owp-owp* uttered in flight. HABITAT: Open secondary forest, plantations, mangroves and gardens. DISTRIBUTION: Resident in Sumatra, Java, Bali and Borneo.

3 SPOT-THROATED FLAMEBACK *Dinopium everetti* 28–30cm FIELD NOTES: Actions presumably much as Common Flameback, with which it was considered conspecific until recently. VOICE: Probably similar to Common Flameback. HABITAT: Open woodland. DISTRIBUTION: Endemic to the Philippines (Palawan and nearby islands).

4 GREATER FLAMEBACK *Chrysocolaptes guttacristatus* 33cm FIELD NOTES: Tends to prefer large trees, working up from the lower trunk in jerky spurts and spirals. Often seen as part of mixed-species feeding flocks. VOICE: A single *kik* and a monotone *di-di-di-di-di* or similar. HABITAT: Coastal forest, open forest and forest edges. DISTRIBUTION: Resident in W and C Sumatra, Java and Borneo.

5 BUFF-SPOTTED FLAMEBACK *Chrysocolaptes lucidus* 28–34cm FIELD NOTES: Recently split from Greater Flameback; actions and habits are presumed to be similar. *C. l. rufopunctatus* (5b) occurs in the E and C Philippines; *C. l. montanus* (5c) is found on Mindanao. VOICE: Presumed to be similar to Greater Flameback. HABITAT: Primary and secondary forest and forest clearings. DISTRIBUTION: Endemic to the Philippines (Mindanao and Basilan).

6 LUZON FLAMEBACK *Chrysocolaptes haematribon* 28–34cm FIELD NOTES: Recently split from Greater Flameback; actions and habits are presumed to be similar. VOICE: Presumed to be similar to Greater Flameback. HABITAT: Primary and secondary forest, also plantations with tall trees. DISTRIBUTION: Endemic to the N Philippines.

7 YELLOW-FACED FLAMEBACK *Chrysocolaptes xanthocephalus* 28–30cm FIELD NOTES: Recently split from Greater Flameback; actions and habits are presumed to be similar. VOICE: Presumed to be similar to Greater Flameback. HABITAT: Lowland forest and plantations. DISTRIBUTION: Endemic to the C Philippines.

8 RED-HEADED FLAMEBACK *Chrysocolaptes erythrocephalus* 28–34cm FIELD NOTES: Recently split from Greater Flameback; actions and habits are presumed to be similar. VOICE: Presumed to be similar to Greater Flameback. HABITAT: Primary and secondary forest, plantations and clearings. DISTRIBUTION: Endemic to the W Philippines.

9 JAVAN FLAMEBACK *Chrysocolaptes strictus* 28–32cm FIELD NOTES: Recently split from Greater Flameback; actions and habits are presumed to be similar. VOICE: Presumed to be similar to Greater Flameback. HABITAT: Primary and secondary forest, coastal woodland and plantations. DISTRIBUTION: Resident in Java and Bali.

5b ♂
rufopunctatus

5c *montanus*

13 WOODPECKERS

1 MAROON WOODPECKER *Blythipicus rubiginosus* 23cm FIELD NOTES: Generally forages low down, at the base of trunks, on fallen logs or on the ground. Often forms part of mixed-species feeding flocks. VOICE: A wavering, high-pitched *kik-kik-kik-kik-kik-kik-kik...* that slows towards the end; also a descending *chai-chai-chai-chai* or *keek-eek-eek-eek-eek-eek*, and a *pit, pyick, kyak* and *kik-ik*. HABITAT: Primary and secondary forest, also plantations. DISTRIBUTION: Resident in Sumatra and Borneo.

2 ORANGE-BACKED WOODPECKER *Reinwardtipicus validus* 30cm FIELD NOTES: Usually encountered in pairs or small parties foraging on rotten logs, dead tree stumps, main trunks and branches. Presence often given away by loud pecking and hammering. VOICE: A rapid, trilled *ki-i-i-i-i-ik*; also noted are a squeaky *kit kit kit kit-it*, a *kee-wheet*, a *wheet wheet wheet wheet wheow*, and a chattering *cha-cha-cha*. HABITAT: Forest, from the coast to mountains. DISTRIBUTION: Resident in Sumatra, Java and Borneo.

3 SOOTY WOODPECKER *Mulleripicus funebris* 34–35cm FIELD NOTES: Usually encountered singly or in pairs foraging in the upper storeys of tall trees. M. f. fuliginosus (3b) occurs in the S Philippines. VOICE: A trilled *chil-lel-lel-lel-lel-lel...*, often repeated. HABITAT: Various forest types, including secondary, mountain oak and pine, and forest edges near plantations. DISTRIBUTION: Endemic to the Philippines.

4 ASHY WOODPECKER *Mulleripicus fulvus* 39–40cm FIELD NOTES: Generally met with in pairs, groups or singly. Forages on trunks and stout branches; also noted feeding on the ground or on rotting stumps. M. f. wallacei (4b) is found in S Sulawesi. VOICE: Various calls recorded, including a rapid, weak, even-pitched *kikikikiki...*, a laughing *hew-hew-hew-hew-hew-hew* and a soft *twee twee twee*. HABITAT: Primary and secondary forest, occasionally cultivated areas with trees, coconut groves and mangroves. DISTRIBUTION: Endemic to Sulawesi.

5 GREAT SLATY WOODPECKER *Mulleripicus pulverulentus* 45–51cm FIELD NOTES: Usually encountered in pairs or small noisy groups, flying from one tree or forest patch to another in a loose follow-my-leader fashion. Forages mainly in tall trees, searching for ants and grubs on trunks and large branches. VOICE: A whinnying *woi-kwoi-kwoi-kwoi*, often given in flight; also utters a soft *whu-ick* and a single loud *dwot*, said to sound somewhere between the bleating of a goat and the barking of a dog. HABITAT: Lowland primary forest, secondary growth, clearing edges and occasionally plantations. DISTRIBUTION: Resident in Sumatra, Java, Borneo and the Philippines.

♂

♀

1

♀

2

♂

♀

3

3b *fuliginosus* ♂

4b *wallacei* ♂

♀

5 ♂

♂

4

♀

14 BARBETS

1 FIRE-TUFTED BARBET *Psilopogon pyrolophus* 29cm FIELD NOTES: Forages in pairs or small groups in the canopy of tall trees, acrobatic when attempting to reach fruit. VOICE: A cicada-like *dddzza-ddzza* that increases to a *zz-zz-zz-zz*; also utters a whistled note and a squeak. HABITAT: Primary and secondary forest, forest edges and forest patches. DISTRIBUTION: Resident in Sumatra.

2 LINEATED BARBET *Psilopogon lineatus* 25–30cm FIELD NOTES: Variable; dark and light forms are depicted. Usually seen singly or in small groups; larger groups occur at trees laden with fruit. Juvenile less streaked. VOICE: A monotonous *kotur kotur kotur…*, also a trill followed by a long series of *poo-tak* notes. HABITAT: Open forest, secondary forest and forest edges. DISTRIBUTION: Resident in Java and Bali.

3 BROWN-THROATED BARBET *Psilopogon corvinus* 26cm FIELD NOTES: Generally favours the forest canopy, where it forages singly or as part of mixed-species feeding parties. VOICE: A ringing *hoo-too-too-too too*, *boo toot-boo too-bootootoot* or *too-ta-ta-toot*, sometimes preceded by a fast trill; also utters a rapid rattling when alarmed. HABITAT: Moist montane forest. DISTRIBUTION: Endemic to W Java.

4 GOLD-WHISKERED BARBET *Psilopogon chrysopogon* 30cm FIELD NOTES: Usually encountered in the forest canopy; favours fruiting trees. VOICE: A loud, rapid *too-tuk too-tuk too-tuk…* or *tehoop-tehoop-tehoop…*; also utters a repeated, low-pitched trill. HABITAT: Hill forest. DISTRIBUTION: Resident in Sumatra and Borneo.

5 RED-CROWNED BARBET *Psilopogon rafflesii* 25–27cm FIELD NOTES: Forages in the forest canopy, feeding on fruit and insects. VOICE: A loud *took* or *took-took* followed by a rapid, repeated series of *tuk* notes, the song sometimes ending in a fast trill. HABITAT: Lowland forest. DISTRIBUTION: Resident in Sumatra and Borneo.

6 RED-THROATED BARBET *Psilopogon mystacophanos* 23cm FIELD NOTES: Forages mainly in the forest canopy, although will descend to rummage in dense cover in the understorey. VOICE: A slow, uneven series of deep notes, *chok… chok-chok… chok… chok-chok… chok…*, also *pooh pooh lentogok lentogok*. Calls are slower and more hesitant than in other barbets, and there is also a repeated high-pitched trill, which gradually gets shorter. HABITAT: Lowland forest. DISTRIBUTION: Resident in Sumatra and Borneo.

7 BLACK-BANDED BARBET *Psilopogon javensis* 26cm FIELD NOTES: Often met with in more open or lightly wooded areas of forest. VOICE: Variable, including a repeated, ringing *tooloong-tumpook*, an accelerating *too-took too-took too-took…*, and singular *tyaap* or *tap* notes. HABITAT: Lowland and hill forest. DISTRIBUTION: Resident in Java and Bali.

8 BLACK-BROWED BARBET *Psilopogon oorti* 21–24cm FIELD NOTES: Active forager in the canopy and subcanopy. VOICE: A loud, throaty *too-took-trrrrrk*, repeated about once a second, occasionally with a soft *ta* at the beginning or end. HABITAT: Montane and submontane forest. DISTRIBUTION: Resident in Sumatra.

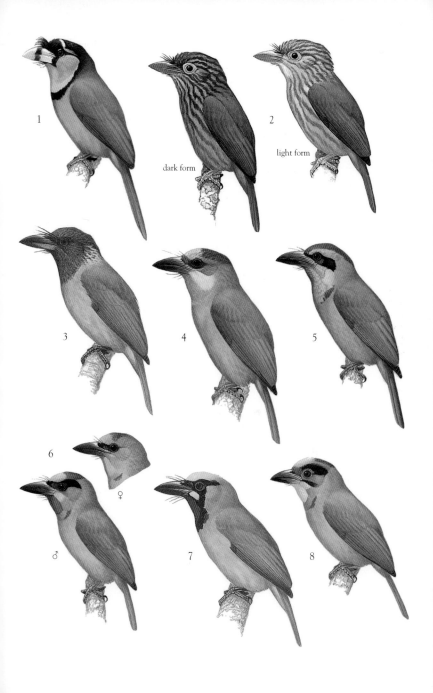

1

2

dark form

light form

3

4

5

6

♀

♂

7

8

15 BARBETS

1 MOUNTAIN BARBET *Psilopogon monticola* 20cm FIELD NOTES: Forages at all levels, often forming part of mixed-species feeding parties. VOICE: A fast *tuk tuk tuk tuk* with the odd *tu-ruk* about every 20 or so notes. HABITAT: Lower montane and hill forest, forest edges, orchards and gardens. DISTRIBUTION: Endemic to Borneo.

2 YELLOW-CROWNED BARBET *Psilopogon henricii* 21–23cm FIELD NOTES: Spends much time foraging in the tree canopy, feeding on figs and other fruits. VOICE: A short, trilled *trrok* followed by a loud *tok-tok-tok-tok*, repeated for about 10–20 seconds. HABITAT: Lowland and submontane forest. DISTRIBUTION: Resident in Sumatra and Borneo.

3 FLAME-FRONTED BARBET *Psilopogon armillaris* 20cm FIELD NOTES: Common, often encountered as part of mixed-species feeding parties in fruiting trees. VOICE: A monotonous, repeated *trrk trrk trrk trrrk* or a series of short trilling notes, *t-t-t-trrrt*, repeated endlessly. HABITAT: Primary lowland and hill forest, also fruiting trees in plantations and gardens. DISTRIBUTION: Endemic to Java and Bali.

4 GOLDEN-NAPED BARBET *Psilopogon pulcherrimus* 20cm FIELD NOTES: Forages in the mid-storey and canopy. VOICE: Variable, including a repeated, hollow *took-took-tarrrook*, also a rolling *trrr-trrr-trrrrrr* and a short series of *twaak twaak twaak…* notes. HABITAT: Mountain forest. DISTRIBUTION: Endemic to Borneo.

5 YELLOW-EARED BARBET *Psilopogon australis* 16–17cm FIELD NOTES: Generally seen in pairs or small parties, with larger groups in fruiting trees. Once considered conspecific with Blue-eared Barbet. VOICE: A fast, endlessly repeated rattle, also a repeated shrill trill. HABITAT: Primary forest, secondary forest and plantations. DISTRIBUTION: Resident in Java and Bali.

6 BLUE-EARED BARBET *Psilopogon duvaucelii* 17cm FIELD NOTES: Occurs in pairs or small groups, with larger groups in fruiting trees. VOICE: An endlessly repeated *tk-trrt tk-trrt*, *koo-turr koo-trr* or *too-rook too-rook*; also a whistled *teeow-teeow…* HABITAT: Primary and secondary forest and cultivated areas. DISTRIBUTION: Resident in Sumatra and Borneo.

7 BORNEAN BARBET *Psilopogon eximius* 15cm FIELD NOTES: Generally forages in the canopy in fruiting trees. VOICE: A rapid series of *tiuk* notes, also a fast trill. HABITAT: Mountain forest. DISTRIBUTION: Endemic to Borneo.

8 COPPERSMITH BARBET *Psilopogon haemacephalus* 17cm FIELD NOTES: Generally seen in pairs or small parties, with larger parties occurring in fruiting trees. In the Philippines, recorded calling from an exposed perch at the top of a dead tree. *P. h. cebuensis* (8b) occurs in the C Philippines; *P. i. roseus* (8c) is found in Java and Bali. VOICE: A monotonous, metallic *tuk tuk tuk tuk tuk tuk tuk…* HABITAT: Open lowland forest and forest edges. DISTRIBUTION: Resident in Sumatra, Java, Bali and the Philippines.

9 BROWN BARBET *Caloramphus fuliginosus* 17cm FIELD NOTES: Often encountered in groups, foraging on tree trunks and branches; calls constantly. *C. f. tertius* (9b) occurs in N Borneo. VOICE: A high-pitched, whistled squeak. HABITAT: Primary and secondary forest. DISTRIBUTION: Endemic to the whole of Borneo.

10 SOOTY BARBET *Caloramphus hayii* 17–20cm FIELD NOTES: Regularly found in small groups feeding from the understorey to the canopy, especially in fruiting trees; often forages acrobatically, like a tit. Recently split from Brown Barbet. VOICE: A sibilant series of *pseeee* calls, also utters a thin *pseeoo*. HABITAT: Lowland and swamp forest. DISTRIBUTION: Resident in Sumatra.

16 HORNBILLS

1 ORIENTAL PIED HORNBILL *Anthracoceros albirostris* 55–60cm
FIELD NOTES: Mainly arboreal but will descend to the ground to pick up food, usually in small groups although bigger flocks may occur post-breeding. In flight, shows prominent white tips to flight feathers and either white-tipped or plain white outer tail feathers. Apparently, race on Borneo has white outer tail feathers, but it is recorded that this tail pattern is not constant. VOICE: Various loud squeals and raucous cackles. HABITAT: Lowland primary and secondary forest, forest edges and clearings. DISTRIBUTION: Resident in Sumatra, Java, Bali and Borneo.

2 BLACK HORNBILL *Anthracoceros malayanus* 76cm FIELD NOTES: Usually seen in pairs or flocks foraging from the lower strata to the upper canopy. Recorded following gibbons to collect disturbed insects. VOICE: Harsh, grating growls and retching noises. HABITAT: Primary lowland, peat swamp and tall mangrove forest. DISTRIBUTION: Resident in Sumatra and Borneo.

3 PALAWAN HORNBILL *Anthracoceros marchei* 55cm FIELD NOTES: Usually seen in small noisy groups foraging from the ground to the canopy. VOICE: A trumpeting *kuk, kuk-kak* or *kuk-kuk-ka*. HABITAT: Primary and secondary evergreen forest, mangrove swamps and sometimes in cultivation. DISTRIBUTION: Endemic to Palawan in the Philippines.

4 SULU HORNBILL *Anthracoceros montani* 50cm FIELD NOTES: Rare. Travels in pairs or small noisy groups, foraging mainly in the forest canopy. VOICE: A raucous *ghaakh*, uttered singly or in a long series of up to 20 notes, ending with a stuttering trill and two distinct, separate notes. HABITAT: Lowland and hill forest. DISTRIBUTION: Endemic to Jolo, Sanga Sanga and Tawi-tawi in the Philippines.

5 RHINOCEROS HORNBILL *Buceros rhinoceros* 91–122cm FIELD NOTES: Arboreal. Usually encountered in pairs or small flocks. In flight, shows all-black wings and a white tail with a black subterminal band. Juveniles lack the casque. The sharp, recurved casque race *B. r. borneoensis* (5b) occurs in Borneo. VOICE: Male utters deep *hok* notes and female gives a *hak*, often duetted as *hok-hak hok-hak…* Both give a loud, throaty *ger-ronk* in flight. HABITAT: Primary lowland and hill forest. DISTRIBUTION: Resident in Sumatra, Java and Borneo.

6 GREAT HORNBILL *Buceros bicornis* 95–105cm FIELD NOTES: Generally seen in pairs or small groups; may gather in larger flocks at fruiting trees or communal roosts. Mainly arboreal, although may descend to the ground to pick up fallen fruit. In flight, shows white tips to flight feathers, a buff-white wing-bar and a white tail with a black subterminal band. Juveniles lack the casque. VOICE: A loud, reverberating *tok… tok… tok…*, also various hoarse grunts, barks and roars. In flight, utters a loud *ger-onk*. HABITAT: From lowland to submontane forest. DISTRIBUTION: Resident in Sumatra.

1

♀

2

dark form

♀

♂

♂

3

♀

♂

4

♀

♂

5

♀

♂

6

♀

♂

5b ♂
borneoensis

17 HORNBILLS

1 RUFOUS HORNBILL *Buceros hydrocorax* 60–65cm FIELD NOTES: Forages mainly in the canopy, occasionally descending to low bushes or the ground. Often seen flying across valleys or along mountain slopes in small groups. *B. h. semigaleatus* (1b) occurs in the C Philippines; *B. h. mindanensis* (1c) is found in the S Philippines. VOICE: A loud, deep *kaaww* or *aaww*. HABITAT: Primary and tall secondary forest, from sea-level to mountains. DISTRIBUTION: Endemic to the Philippines.

2 HELMETED HORNBILL *Rhinoplax vigil* 110–120cm FIELD NOTES: Usually occurs singly or in pairs, foraging in the canopy of tall trees in search of fruit, small animals, snakes and birds. VOICE: A series of loud, hollow *took* notes, quickening to *tee-poop* notes before ending in a manic laugh. In flight, utters a loud, clanking *ka-hank*. HABITAT: Tall lowland and hill forest. DISTRIBUTION: Resident in Sumatra and Borneo.

3 BUSHY-CRESTED HORNBILL *Anorrhinus galeritus* 65–70cm FIELD NOTES: Usually found in flocks of 5–15 birds, foraging in or just below the canopy. VOICE: A loud, excited *klia-klia-klia kliu-kliu* that rises and falls, often uttered by all group members and building to a screaming crescendo. HABITAT: Forest, from lowlands to hills. DISTRIBUTION: Resident in Sumatra and Borneo.

4 LUZON HORNBILL *Penelopides manillae* 45cm FIELD NOTES: Occurs in small groups of up to fifteen birds. This and the following four species were all originally described as races of the Philippine Tarictic Hornbill. VOICE: A repeated nasal *tuc* or *ta-ruc*, often extended to *ta-ruc-tuc-tuc-tuc-tuc*. HABITAT: Primary evergreen lowland forest, riverine forest and even single fruiting trees in grassland. DISTRIBUTION: Endemic to the N Philippines.

5 MINDANAO HORNBILL *Penelopides affinis* 45cm FIELD NOTES: Forages in the middle and lower forest levels, usually in small groups. *P. a. basilanicus* (5b) occurs on Basilan Island (SW Philippines). VOICE: Similar to previous species. HABITAT: Primary evergreen forest, including clearings and edges, also secondary forest. DISTRIBUTION: Endemic to the S Philippines.

6 SAMAR HORNBILL *Penelopides samarensis* 45cm FIELD NOTES: Usually encountered in pairs or small flocks. Female similar to female Mindanao Hornbill. This species is often considered a race of Mindanao Hornbill. VOICE: Similar to Luzon Hornbill. HABITAT: Moist lowland forest. DISTRIBUTION: Endemic to the EC Philippines.

7 VISAYAN HORNBILL *Penelopides panini* 45cm FIELD NOTES: Forages below the canopy and along forest edges. VOICE: A repeated, subdued, nasal *ta-ric* or *ta-ric-tic*. HABITAT: Primary evergreen forest, secondary forest and isolated fruiting trees. DISTRIBUTION: Endemic to NC Philippines.

8 MINDORO HORNBILL *Penelopides mindorensis* 45cm FIELD NOTES: Usually occurs in pairs or flocks of up to 20 birds. VOICE: Similar to Visayan Hornbill. HABITAT: Primary evergreen forest, secondary forest, forest edges and isolated fruiting trees. DISTRIBUTION: Endemic to the S Philippines.

9 WHITE-CROWNED HORNBILL *Berenicornis comatus* 75–85cm FIELD NOTES: Small parties forage in the dense tangled growth of lower storeys or on the ground; spends much time digging in bark debris searching for food. VOICE: A deep *hoo hu-hu-hu-hu-hu-hu* or *kuk kuk kuk kuk kuk*, often fading away. HABITAT: Dense vegetation, near rivers in lowland and hill forest. DISTRIBUTION: Resident in Sumatra and Borneo.

1b ♂
semigaleatus

1

♀

1c ♂

mindanensis

♀

2

♂

5b

basilanicus

5

♀

3

♀

4

♂

♀

6

♂

♂

♀

8

♀

9

♀

7

♂

♂

♂

♀

18 HORNBILLS

1 SULAWESI HORNBILL *Rhabdotorrhinus exarhatus* 45cm FIELD NOTES: Usually encountered in noisy, active pairs or small groups, foraging in the mid-canopy. VOICE: A rapid series of harsh braying and honking notes. HABITAT: Primary lowland and hill forest, tall secondary forest, swamp forest and forest edges. DISTRIBUTION: Endemic to Sulawesi.

2 WRINKLED HORNBILL *Rhabdotorrhinus corrugatus* 75cm FIELD NOTES: Usually seen in pairs or small flocks, foraging in the canopy. VOICE: A sharp, barking *kak kak-kak*, also an echoing *wakowwakowkow* or *rowwrow*. HABITAT: Lowland and swamp forest. DISTRIBUTION: Resident in Sumatra and Borneo.

3 RUFOUS-HEADED HORNBILL (WALDEN'S HORNBILL)
Rhabdotorrhinus waldeni 60–65cm FIELD NOTES: Generally occurs in small groups, foraging in the canopy; often seen flying over forest or crossing valleys. VOICE: A loud, stuttering, nasal *au-au-au-auk*. HABITAT: Forest, from coast to hills, also in large trees in clearings. DISTRIBUTION: Endemic to the C Philippines.

4 WRITHED HORNBILL *Rhabdotorrhinus leucocephalus* 60–65cm
FIELD NOTES: Usually seen in noisy, conspicuous small groups foraging in the canopy of tall trees. VOICE: A loud, nasal *auk*, uttered singly or as a series of notes. HABITAT: Primary lowland forest. DISTRIBUTION: Endemic to the Philippines.

5 KNOBBED HORNBILL *Rhyticeros cassidix* 70–80cm FIELD NOTES: Seen singly, in pairs or in flocks; some non-breeding flocks can be large, with up to 50 or so birds. Forages in the forest canopy, often mixing with other fruit-eating species. VOICE: A deep, upslurred, honking *wha wha wha wha* or similar. HABITAT: Primary lowland, hill, montane, swamp and tall secondary forest, also forest stands within cultivated areas. DISTRIBUTION: Endemic to Sulawesi.

6 WREATHED HORNBILL *Rhyticeros undulatus* 75–85cm FIELD NOTES: Generally occurs in pairs or small parties, forming larger groups where food is plentiful or at communal roosts. Forages mainly in the canopy, although will descend to the ground to pick up fallen fruit or capture animal prey. VOICE: A very loud, breathless *kuk-KWEHK*. HABITAT: Lowland, hill and peat-swamp forest. DISTRIBUTION: Resident in Sumatra, Java and Borneo.

7 SUMBA HORNBILL *Rhyticeros everetti* 55cm FIELD NOTES: Encountered singly, in pairs or in small groups, with much larger numbers at roosting sites. Forages mainly in the canopy in fruiting trees. VOICE: A short *erm-err* and a *kokokokokokoko*. HABITAT: Patches of primary forest, secondary forest and open parkland with fruiting trees. DISTRIBUTION: Endemic to the W Lesser Sundas (Sumba).

8 PLAIN-POUCHED HORNBILL *Rhyticeros subruficollis* 65–70cm
FIELD NOTES: Generally found in pairs and occasionally in small groups. Forages mainly in the treetops, although will descend to the ground to collect fallen fruit or capture small animals. VOICE: A loud *keh-keh-kehk*. HABITAT: Broadleaved evergreen and mixed deciduous forest. DISTRIBUTION: Possibly resident on Sumatra.

9 PAPUAN HORNBILL (BLYTH'S HORNBILL) *Rhyticeros plicatus* 65–85cm
FIELD NOTES: Found singly, in pairs or in small groups, foraging in the canopy of fruiting trees. VOICE: Various deep grunting and honking notes, uttered singly or in a sequence. HABITAT: Primary lowland, hill and swamp forest. DISTRIBUTION: Resident in the Moluccas.

19 TROGONS

1 JAVAN TROGON *Apalharpactes reinwardtii* 34cm FIELD NOTES: Sits quietly on a shady perch before flying off to capture insect prey; also feeds on fruit. Often forms part of mixed-species feeding flocks. VOICE: A penetrating, hoarse *chierr chierr* or loud *turrr*. HABITAT: Montane rainforest. DISTRIBUTION: Endemic to W Java.

2 SUMATRAN TROGON *Apalharpactes mackloti* 30cm FIELD NOTES: Actions and habits similar to Javan Trogon, with which it was once thought to be conspecific. VOICE: A high, whistled *wiwi wheeer-lu*, repeated every few seconds; other calls similar to Javan Trogon. HABITAT: Montane rainforest, chiefly on the lower slopes. DISTRIBUTION: Endemic to Sumatra.

3 RED-NAPED TROGON *Harpactes kasumba* 31–35cm FIELD NOTES: Sits motionless for long periods, a typical trogon behaviour; favours the middle to upper storey. Often joins mixed-species feeding flocks. VOICE: A subdued, harsh *kau kau kau kau kau*; female utters a whirring rattle. HABITAT: Primary lowland and hill forest. DISTRIBUTION: Resident in Sumatra and Borneo.

4 DIARD'S TROGON *Harpactes diardii* 32–35cm FIELD NOTES: Very unobtrusive, usually found in the middle storey; sits still for long periods. VOICE: A descending *kau kau kau kau kau kau…* HABITAT: Lowland, hill, peat-swamp and heath forest. DISTRIBUTION: Resident in Sumatra and Borneo.

5 PHILIPPINE TROGON *Harpactes ardens* 30cm FIELD NOTES: Perches in a shady location. Makes sallies to capture insects or pluck fruit from nearby trees. VOICE: A soft *nuu nu nu nu nu nu nu nuu*, accelerating at first and then gradually descending and slowing. HABITAT: Understorey or primary and secondary forest. DISTRIBUTION: Endemic to the Philippines.

6 WHITEHEAD'S TROGON *Harpactes whiteheadi* 29–31cm FIELD NOTES: Perches in the higher branches of the understorey. VOICE: A harsh, even-pitched series of notes, recorded variously as *wark wark wark wark* or *poop poop poop poop poop*; also a soft, rolling *rrrr*, sometimes followed by a loud *kekekeke* that drops in pitch. HABITAT: Dark, wet patches of mountain forest. DISTRIBUTION: Endemic to N Borneo.

7 CINNAMON-RUMPED TROGON *Harpactes orrhophaeus* 25cm FIELD NOTES: Very shy; frequents the lower to middle storey. Recorded as a member of mixed-species feeding flocks. VOICE: A weak, descending *ta-aup ta-aup ta-aup*, also an explosive *purr*. HABITAT: Primary hill and submontane forest. DISTRIBUTION: Resident in Sumatra and Borneo.

8 SCARLET-RUMPED TROGON *Harpactes duvaucelii* 23–26cm FIELD NOTES: Frequents the lower to middle storey and occasionally forest borders. Often a member of mixed-species feeding flocks. VOICE: A rapid, accelerating, descending *yau-yau-yau-yau-yau…* When alarmed, gives a quiet, whirring *kir-r-r-r*. HABITAT: Primary and logged forest. DISTRIBUTION: Resident in Sumatra and Borneo.

9 ORANGE-BREASTED TROGON *Harpactes oreskios* 25–26cm FIELD NOTES: Frequents the middle to upper storey. Recorded following mixed-species feeding flocks. *H. o. dulitensis* (9b) occurs in Borneo. VOICE: A subdued, rapid *tu tu tau-tau-tau*. HABITAT: Lowland, hill and submontane forest. DISTRIBUTION: Resident in Sumatra, Java and Borneo.

10 RED-HEADED TROGON *Harpactes erythrocephalus* 31–35cm FIELD NOTES: Unobtrusive, sits motionless for long periods in the middle to upper storey. VOICE: A mellow, descending *tyaup tyaup tyaup tyaup tyaup*; when alarmed, utters a chattering *tewirr* croak. HABITAT: Hill forest. DISTRIBUTION: Resident in Sumatra.

20 ROLLERS; BEE-EATERS; HOOPOE

1 PURPLE-WINGED ROLLER *Coracias temminckii* 30–34cm FIELD NOTES: Generally seen singly or in pairs; regularly perches in the open on a bare branch, telegraph wire or bush top. VOICE: Various harsh *krawk* notes, alternating with, or followed by, an upslurred, grating *tjorraa*. HABITAT: Forest edges, swamp forest, secondary woodland, open scrub woodland, lightly wooded cultivation and savannah. DISTRIBUTION: Endemic to Sulawesi.

2 DOLLARBIRD (ORIENTAL DOLLARBIRD, RED-BILLED or BROAD-BILLED ROLLER) *Eurystomus orientalis* 25–28cm FIELD NOTES: Often perches on the topmost branches of tall dead trees, from where acrobatic sallies are made in pursuit of flying insects. In flight, shows a large, pale blue patch on base of primaries. VOICE: A fast *krak-kak-kak-kak-kak* and a hoarse *chak*. HABITAT: Lowland forest, forest edges, clearings and lightly wooded cultivation. DISTRIBUTION: Resident and winter visitor throughout the region.

3 PURPLE ROLLER (AZURE DOLLARBIRD or AZURE ROLLER)
Eurystomus azureus 27–35cm FIELD NOTES: Uncommon, usually encountered in twos or threes sitting at the top of a tall tree; feeding actions similar to Dollarbird VOICE: Harsh, grating calls given in a steady series. HABITAT: Primary hill forest, forest edges and, occasionally, adjacent coconut groves and gardens. DISTRIBUTION: Endemic to the N Moluccas.

4 PURPLE-BEARDED BEE-EATER *Meropogon forsteni* 25–26cm FIELD NOTES: Usually found singly, in pairs or in small parties. Perches on exposed branches in the open, at the mid-storey and upper canopy, making aerial sallies after flying insects. VOICE: A quiet, high-pitched *szit*, *peet* or *sip-sip*. HABITAT: Edges of clearings and breaks in primary or tall secondary forest. DISTRIBUTION: Endemic to Sulawesi.

5 RED-BEARDED BEE-EATER *Nyctyornis amictus* 27–31cm FIELD NOTES: Often frequents the lower canopy. Sits quietly, partly hidden, before making short flying sorties to catch winged insects. VOICE: A loud, hoarse *chachachacha… quo-qua-qua-qua* or a descending *kak kak-ka-ka-ka-ka*; also recorded is a deep *kwow* or *kwok*. HABITAT: Primary and old secondary forest. DISTRIBUTION: Resident in Sumatra and Borneo.

6 BLUE-THROATED BEE-EATER *Merops viridis* 22–24cm FIELD NOTES: Colonial breeder, often in coastal sandy areas. Hawks insects from the top of trees or power lines. *M. v. americanus* (6b) occurs on the Philippines. VOICE: A short, trilled *brk brk*. In flight, utters a loud *prrrp prrrp prrrp* or *kerik-kerik-kerik*. HABITAT: Open country and clearings adjacent to forest, often near the coast. DISTRIBUTION: Resident in Sumatra, Java, Borneo and the Philippines.

7 RAINBOW BEE-EATER *Merops ornatus* 19–21cm FIELD NOTES: Generally in pairs or small groups. Immatures lack the black gorget and elongated tail feathers. VOICE: A rolling *prrrp prrrp*, *preee* or *drrrt*; when alarmed, utters a *dip-dip* or *clip-lip-lip-lip*. HABITAT: Grassy areas, forest clearings, scrub, forest edges and trees alongside rivers. DISTRIBUTION: Winter or non-breeding visitor to Wallacea; vagrant in Bali and Borneo.

8 BLUE-TAILED BEE-EATER *Merops philippinus* 23–26cm FIELD NOTES: Gregarious; hawks insects from exposed perches, such as branches and overhead wires. VOICE: A rolling *diririp* or similar, also a trilled *kwink-kwink kwink-kwink kwink*. HABITAT: Open country, coastal scrub, river margins and mangroves. DISTRIBUTION: Resident in the Philippines, Sulawesi and the Lesser Sundas; non-breeding visitor to Sumatra, Java, Bali and Borneo.

9 CHESTNUT-HEADED BEE-EATER *Merops leschenaulti* 18–20cm
FIELD NOTES: Actions similar to Blue-tailed Bee-eater. Often seen in small nomadic parties. VOICE: A *pruik* or *churit*; also recorded is a ringing *kree-kree-weet-weet-weet*. HABITAT: Open and wooded areas. DISTRIBUTION: Resident in Sumatra, Java and Bali.

10 HOOPOE (EURASIAN or COMMON HOOPOE) *Upupa epops* 26–32cm
FIELD NOTES: Unmistakable, even in flight, where it gives the impression of a giant butterfly. Crest is often fanned when alighting or alarmed. VOICE: A low *hoop-hoop-hoop* or *poop-poop-poop*. HABITAT: Open country with scattered trees, cultivation, parks and gardens. DISTRIBUTION: Vagrant, recorded from Sumatra, Borneo and the Philippines.

21 KINGFISHERS

1 LILAC-CHEEKED KINGFISHER (LILAC KINGFISHER) *Cittura cyanotis*
28cm FIELD NOTES: Usually seen singly perched at low level. Singing birds generally
sit higher in the canopy. Black-forehead race *C. c. sanghirensis* (1b) occurs on Sangihe
and Siau islands. VOICE: Three or four descending, high, piping notes, repeated at
2–3-second intervals; also gives a falcon-like *ku-ku-ku-ku* and repeated *kebekek*. Birds from
Sangihe utter a puppy-like *yap-yap*, a quavering wail and a series of upslurred whistles.
HABITAT: Primary and tall secondary lowland and hill forest, also tree-crop plantations.
DISTRIBUTION: Endemic to Sulawesi.

2 KINGFISHER (COMMON or RIVER KINGFISHER) *Alcedo atthis* 16–17cm
FIELD NOTES: First sight is often just a blue flash flying low along a river, the bird giving a
high-pitched call. Uses a prominent low perch, overhanging water, to dive for fish. Blue-
faced race *A. a. hispidoides* (2b) occurs in Sulawesi and the Moluccas. VOICE: A penetrating,
high-pitched *tseee* or *tseee ti-tee ti-tee ti-tee*. HABITAT: Rivers, streams and ponds in open
wooded areas; occasionally mangroves or estuaries. DISTRIBUTION: Resident and winter
visitor in Wallacea; winter visitor to Sumatra, Java, Bali, Borneo and the Philippines.

3 BLUE-EARED KINGFISHER *Alcedo meninting* 17cm FIELD NOTES: Tends to fish
from a low, shady perch overhanging water. VOICE: A high-pitched, shrill *seet*, also thin,
shrill contact calls. HABITAT: Streams, small rivers and pools in dense forest, also creeks and
channels in mangroves. DISTRIBUTION: Resident in Sumatra, Java, Borneo, the Philippines,
Sulawesi and the W Lesser Sundas.

4 BLUE-BANDED KINGFISHER *Alcedo euryzona* 17cm FIELD NOTES: Hunts from a
low perch near forest streams; active, always moving from perch to perch. *A. e. peninsulae*
(4b) occurs in Sumatra and Borneo; male very similar to nominate. VOICE: A high-pitched
cheep, usually given in flight. HABITAT: Streams and small rivers in lowland, hill and
submontane forest. DISTRIBUTION: Resident in Sumatra, Java and Borneo.

5 CERULEAN KINGFISHER *Alcedo coerulescens* 13cm FIELD NOTES: Usually seen
singly or in pairs; fishes from a low perch at water's edge. Female slightly greener. VOICE: A
high-pitched, penetrating *tieh tieh*. HABITAT: Water in low-lying country, including streams,
canals, fish ponds, swamps, mangroves and tidal estuaries. DISTRIBUTION: Resident in S
Sumatra, Java, Bali and W Lesser Sundas.

6 AZURE KINGFISHER *Ceyx azureus* 16–17cm FIELD NOTES: Generally encountered
singly; perches on low branches over water, diving to catch fish. VOICE: A repeated, shrill
tzeep or *peeee*. HABITAT: Wooded banks of streams and estuaries. DISTRIBUTION: Resident in
the N Moluccas and E Lesser Sundas.

7 INDIGO-BANDED KINGFISHER *Ceyx cyanopectus* 14cm FIELD NOTES: Perches on
branches or rocks, diving to catch fish. *C. c. nigrirostris* (7b) occurs in the WC Philippines.
VOICE: A thin, high-pitched single note. HABITAT: Thickly forested streams and rivers, also
palm swamps and mangroves. DISTRIBUTION: Endemic to the Philippines.

8 SOUTHERN SILVERY KINGFISHER *Ceyx agentatus* 15cm FIELD NOTES: Perches
on low stream-side branches or rocks, diving to catch fish. VOICE: A high-pitched *wheeet*.
HABITAT: Forested streams, rivers and pools. DISTRIBUTION: Endemic to the S Philippines.

9 NORTHERN SILVERY KINGFISHER *Ceyx flumenicola* 14cm FIELD NOTES: Recently
split from the previous species; actions presumed to be similar. VOICE: No known difference
from previous species. HABITAT: Forested streams, rivers and pools. DISTRIBUTION: Endemic
to the SC Philippines.

10 LITTLE KINGFISHER *Ceyx pusillus* 11cm FIELD NOTES: Catches fish from a low
perch. VOICE: A high-pitched, repeated *tsee* or *tzweeip*. HABITAT: Mainly mangroves, also
forest streams and swamp forest. DISTRIBUTION: Resident in the N Moluccas and Kai Islands
in the S Moluccas.

1 ♂

1b sanghirensis

♂

♀

2b hispidoides

2

4b ♀ peninsulae

4

♀

3

♂

5

6

7b ♂ nigrirostris

7

♀

♂

8

9

10

22 KINGFISHERS

1 MOLUCCAN DWARF KINGFISHER *Ceyx lepidus* 14cm FIELD NOTES: Usually solitary; uses a low perch as a vantage point to look for insects etc. This and the following three species are often thought to be conspecific. VOICE: A shrill, wheezy *tzeeip*. HABITAT: Primary and secondary forest. DISTRIBUTION: Endemic to the Moluccas except Buru.

2 SULA DWARF KINGFISHER *Ceyx wallacii* 14cm FIELD NOTES: Habits presumed similar to previous species. VOICE: Unknown. HABITAT: Forested areas. DISTRIBUTION: Endemic to the Sula Islands.

3 BURU DWARF KINGFISHER *Ceyx cajeli* 14cm FIELD NOTES: Habits presumed similar to Moluccan Dwarf Kingfisher. VOICE: Unknown. HABITAT: Forested areas. DISTRIBUTION: Endemic to the S Moluccas (Buru Island).

4 DIMORPHIC DWARF KINGFISHER *Ceyx margarethae* 14cm FIELD NOTES: Variable; dark and light morphs occur, light morph depicted. Habits presumed similar to the Moluccan Dwarf Kingfisher. VOICE: A *pe-teeeet pe-teeeet*. HABITAT: Primary and secondary forest. DISTRIBUTION: Endemic to the C and S Philippines.

5 ORIENTAL DWARF KINGFISHER *Ceyx erithaca* 14cm FIELD NOTES: Perches low down on vegetation or rocks. VOICE: A high-pitched *tsriet-tsriet* or a soft *tjie-tjie-tjlie*. HABITAT: Shady streams or pools in forests and occasionally mangroves. DISTRIBUTION: Nominate form is found in Sumatra, Java and Bali; rufous form '*rufidorsa*' (5b) occurs in Sumatra, Java, Borneo, the W Philippines and the W Lesser Sundas.

6 PHILIPPINE DWARF KINGFISHER *Ceyx melanurus* 12–13cm FIELD NOTES: Solitary; perches low down. *C. m. mindanensis* (6b) occurs in the S Philippines. VOICE: A high-pitched *zeeeep*. HABITAT: Dense primary lowland and secondary forest. DISTRIBUTION: Endemic to the Philippines.

7 SULAWESI DWARF KINGFISHER *Ceyx fallax* 12cm FIELD NOTES: Uses a low perch from which to catch insect or amphibian prey. VOICE: A high-pitched *seeee*. HABITAT: Well-shaded lowland forest. DISTRIBUTION: Endemic to Sulawesi.

8 STORK-BILLED KINGFISHER *Pelargopsis capensis* 35cm FIELD NOTES: Sits well concealed on a waterside branch. *P. c. gigantea* (8b) occurs in the S Philippines; Lesser Sundas race has a browner head and ear-coverts. VOICE: Calls include a *ke-ke-ke-ke*, a *kak kak kak* and a pleasant *peer… peer… peer*. HABITAT: Shady waters in wooded areas and mangroves. DISTRIBUTION: Resident in Sumatra, Java, Borneo, the Philippines and W Lesser Sundas.

9 BLACK-BILLED KINGFISHER (GREAT-BILLED KINGFISHER) *Pelargopsis melanorhyncha* 35–37cm FIELD NOTES: Perches on a partly concealed branch, singly or in pairs. *P. m. dichrorhyncha* (9b) occurs in the Banggai archipelago. VOICE: A loud *kak*, *kak-ka* or *ke-kak*. HABITAT: Coastal woodland and scrub. DISTRIBUTION: Endemic to Sulawesi and the Sula Islands.

10 RUDDY KINGFISHER *Halcyon coromanda* 25cm FIELD NOTES: Found singly or in pairs. Some races show a varying amount of lilac flush to upperparts. VOICE: A high, descending *titititititititi…* HABITAT: Coastal woodland and forested streams DISTRIBUTION: Resident in Sumatra, Java, Borneo, the Philippines, Sulawesi and the Sula Islands.

11 WHITE-BREASTED KINGFISHER *Halcyon smyrnensis* 27–28cm FIELD NOTES: In flight, shows a pale blue patch at base of primaries. *H. s. gularis* (11b) occurs in the Philippines. VOICE: A trilling *kililili* or *kee kee kee*. HABITAT: Open areas, secondary growth and coastal wetlands. DISTRIBUTION: Resident in Sumatra, Java and the Philippines; vagrant in Borneo.

12 BLACK-CAPPED KINGFISHER *Halcyon pileata* 28cm FIELD NOTES: In flight, shows white patches at base of primaries. Occasionally perches on exposed branches or wires. VOICE: A ringing, cackling *kikikikikiki*. HABITAT: Coastal and inland wetlands. DISTRIBUTION: Winter visitor to Sumatra, Java, Borneo, the Philippines and N Sulawesi.

13 JAVAN KINGFISHER *Halcyon cyanoventris* 27cm FIELD NOTES: Perches on treetops, exposed side branches, wires or posts. In flight, shows white patches at base of primaries. VOICE: A loud scream, a loud *tjie-rie-rie-rie-rie*, and a repeated *tjeu* or *tschrii*. HABITAT: Various, including coastal mangroves, scrub, and wooded and cultivated country. DISTRIBUTION: Resident in Java and Bali.

8b
gigantea

9b
dichrorhyncha

6
mindanensis

11b
gularis

23 KINGFISHERS

1 RUFOUS-LORED KINGFISHER (WINCHELL'S KINGFISHER) *Todiramphus winchelli* 25cm FIELD NOTES: More often heard than seen; usually perches in the canopy, although will descend to the ground to pick up prey. *T. w. mindanensis* (1b) occurs in the S Philippines; *T. w. nigrorum* (1c) is found in the C Philippines. VOICE: A loud, harsh, ascending *chup-chup-chep-chep-chep-chep*, repeated every few seconds; also a faster *chup-chup-chup-chu-chu-chu-chu…*, rising at first, then descending and slowing. HABITAT: Undisturbed or little-disturbed forest. DISTRIBUTION: Endemic to the S Philippines.

2 BLUE-AND-WHITE KINGFISHER *Todiramphus diops* 19–21cm FIELD NOTES: Perches in the open on branches or wires; generally found singly or in pairs, occasionally in small groups. VOICE: A warbling *tu-tu-tu-k-k* and a high, descending, three-note nasal whistle, repeated endlessly. HABITAT: Secondary woodland, forest edges, mangrove edges, cultivated groves and wooded gardens. DISTRIBUTION: Endemic to the N Moluccas.

3 LAZULI KINGFISHER *Todiramphus lazuli* 22cm FIELD NOTES: Perches among shaded branches, dead branches and sometimes overhead wires. VOICE: A rapid, loud, high *ke-ke-ke-ke-ke-ke*. HABITAT: Partly cleared forest, forest edges, swampy woodland and occasionally mangroves. DISTRIBUTION: Endemic to the S Moluccas.

4 FOREST KINGFISHER *Todiramphus macleayii* 20cm FIELD NOTES: Perches conspicuously on bare branches or overhead wires, plunging to the ground to capture prey. VOICE: A harsh, strident *scissor-weeya scissor-weeya*, a chattering *kreek-kreek*, and various loud whistles and screeches. HABITAT: Open woodland, forest edges, cultivated areas and savannah. DISTRIBUTION: Non-breeding visitor to SE Wallacea.

5 SOMBRE KINGFISHER *Todiramphus funebris* 30cm FIELD NOTES: Arboreal, perching inconspicuously in lower crown or mid-storey levels. Dives to the ground to capture prey. VOICE: A slow *ki… ki… ki…* HABITAT: Open cultivated lowlands, coconut plantations and gardens. DISTRIBUTION: Endemic to the N Moluccas.

6 COLLARED KINGFISHER (MANGROVE or WHITE-COLLARED KINGFISHER) *Todiramphus chloris* 23–25cm FIELD NOTES: Conspicuous, bold and noisy, especially early in the day. VOICE: A harsh *krerk-krerk-krerk-krerk* that often ends with *jew-jaw* notes; also utters a shrieking *kick kyew kick kyew…* HABITAT: Open wooded country, coastal woodland, cultivation, parks and gardens. DISTRIBUTION: Resident in Sumatra, Java, Bali, Borneo, the Philippines, Sulawesi and the Lesser Sundas.

7 TALAUD KINGFISHER *Todiramphus enigma* 21cm FIELD NOTES: Often seen perched in close proximity to a river. VOICE: A repeated *kekee-kekee-kekee-kekee-kekee*. HABITAT: Forest and forest edges. DISTRIBUTION: Endemic to N Sulawesi.

8 BEACH KINGFISHER *Todiramphus saurophagus* 26–30cm FIELD NOTES: Usually seen perched on a bare branch, rock, post or even driftwood, at the fringes of the seashore. Occasionally hovers before diving to catch fish or crabs. VOICE: A loud, deep *kill kill*, *kee-kee-kee* or *kiokiokiokio*. HABITAT: Mangrove and coastal woodland. DISTRIBUTION: Resident in the Moluccas.

9 SACRED KINGFISHER *Todiramphus sanctus* 18–23cm FIELD NOTES: Usually encountered in pairs, sitting on an exposed perch. Most prey is taken from the ground, although will dive for fish. VOICE: A rapid, high-pitched *kik-kik-kik-kik*; also utters a rasping *schssk schssk*. HABITAT: Mangroves, open country and cultivation. DISTRIBUTION: Non-breeding visitor throughout Wallacea, Sumatra, Java and Borneo.

10 CINNAMON-BANDED KINGFISHER *Todiramphus australasia* 21cm FIELD NOTES: Usually perches in the mid- to upper storey in pairs or singly. *T. a. dammerianus* (10b) occurs in the E Lesser Sundas. VOICE: A rapid, descending trill, also a series of weak, wheezy *ch-w'hee* notes and single yapping notes. HABITAT: Primary and tall secondary forest, forest edges, monsoon woodland and open forest, also shady trees in cultivation or villages. DISTRIBUTION: Endemic to the Lesser Sundas.

1 ♂ 1b ♀
mindanensis
♀
1c ♂
nigrorum
2
♀
3 ♂
♀
♂
4 ♀
♂
5
♀
6
7
♂
8
9
10
10b
dammerianus

24 KINGFISHERS

1 BANDED KINGFISHER *Lacedo pulchella* 21–25cm FIELD NOTES: Often sits motionless for long periods. Hunts insects from a forest perch and sometimes hawks in the tree canopy. *L. p. melanops* (1b) occurs in Borneo. VOICE: A long, whistled *wheeeoo* followed by up to fifteen short *chi-wiu* whistles that gradually fade away; also utters a sharp *wiak* or *wiak wiak*. HABITAT: Hill and submontane forest. DISTRIBUTION: Resident in Sumatra, Java and Borneo.

2 WHITE-RUMPED KINGFISHER (GLITTERING KINGFISHER)
Caridonax fulgidus 30cm FIELD NOTES: Generally sits unobtrusively on a low forest branch, diving to the forest floor to capture prey. Usually seen singly, in pairs or occasionally in small groups. VOICE: A series of rapid, harsh notes, *kuff-kuff-kuff*, also a long series of puppy-like yaps. HABITAT: Primary and tall secondary moist forest, monsoon forest, lightly wooded cultivation and scrub with tall trees. DISTRIBUTION: Endemic to the Lesser Sundas.

3 RUFOUS-COLLARED KINGFISHER *Actenoides concretus* 24–25cm
FIELD NOTES: Perches in the lower storey, keeping still, apart from a slowly wagging tail and alert head movements. VOICE: A rising, whistled *kwee-i*, repeated every second for about ten seconds. HABITAT: Lowland and hill forest. DISTRIBUTION: Resident in Sumatra and Borneo.

4 SPOTTED KINGFISHER *Actenoides lindsayi* 25cm FIELD NOTES: Perches quietly in shady areas of the understorey, generally singly or in pairs. VOICE: A loud, ringing, whistled *ptuuooo* precedes the main call, which is a stuttering, rising *tu-tu-tu-tu-tu* followed by a descending *tuuu tuu-a tuu-a tuu-a*; when alarmed, gives a rasping chatter. HABITAT: Lowland and hilly forest. DISTRIBUTION: Endemic to the Philippines.

5 BLUE-CAPPED KINGFISHER (HOMBRON'S KINGFISHER)
Actenoides hombroni 28cm FIELD NOTES: Perches in dark areas in the forest understorey, singly or in pairs. VOICE: Calls include a loud, repeated *ki-aw* or *te-u* and a woodpecker-like *kaaa-a-a-a*; the main call is similar to that of a Spotted Kingfisher. HABITAT: Mid-montane and lower mossy forest. DISTRIBUTION: Endemic to the S Philippines.

6 GREEN-BACKED KINGFISHER *Actenoides monachus* 31cm FIELD NOTES: A quiet, solitary bird, typically perching in the lower mid-storey, often close to a tree trunk; drops to the forest floor to pick up prey from the leaf litter. *A. m. capucinus* (6b) occurs in E, SE and S Sulawesi. VOICE: A haunting series of long, mournful, ascending and descending whistled notes; also a shorter *huuuuwEEEEu*. Calls are usually given in the early morning or in overcast weather. HABITAT: Primary and secondary forest. DISTRIBUTION: Endemic to Sulawesi.

7 SCALY-BREASTED KINGFISHER (REGENT KINGFISHER)
Actenoides princeps 24cm FIELD NOTES: Usually solitary. Perches in shadowy areas of forest, from low levels to the understorey. *A. p. erythrorhamphus* (7b) occurs in NW and C Sulawesi; *A. p. regalis* (7c) is found in NE Sulawesi. VOICE: A series of soft, mournful whistles, the first notes rolling and the latter ones rising in pitch and then falling. HABITAT: Primary and tall secondary hill and montane forest. DISTRIBUTION: Endemic to Sulawesi.

8 COMMON PARADISE KINGFISHER *Tanysiptera galatea* 33–43cm
FIELD NOTES: Very variable. Two races depicted: *T. g. emiliae* (main illustration) occurs on Rau Island; *T. g. margarethae* (8b) occurs on Bacan Island. Perches, semi-concealed in dark forest understorey, darting to the ground or nearby foliage to take prey. VOICE: A series of separate, mournful whistles that accelerate into a short trill; also utters shrill squawks and a rasping chatter. HABITAT: Primary and tall secondary forest, remnant forest patches and coastal scrub. DISTRIBUTION: Resident in the Moluccas (except Kai Islands).

25 CUCKOOS

1 CHANNEL-BILLED CUCKOO *Scythrops novaehollandiae* 58–65cm
FIELD NOTES: Usually seen singly or in flocks of up to ten birds; frequents the canopy and occasionally seen in lower foliage. Noisy early and late. VOICE: A loud, drawn-out, rising scream, often repeated; also utters a shorter, down-slurred scream. HABITAT: Forest edges, monsoon forest, lightly wooded areas and mangroves. DISTRIBUTION: Local resident in Wallacea; non-breeding visitor to the Moluccas.

2 CHESTNUT-WINGED CUCKOO (RED-WINGED CUCKOO)
Clamator coromandus 41–47cm FIELD NOTES: Generally stays hidden in the canopy foliage, although regularly forages in low vegetation in search of prey. VOICE: A metallic, whistled *thu-thu thu-thu thu-thu…*, also a harsh *chee-ke-kek* or *crititititit*. HABITAT: Forest clearings, scrub forest, mangroves, cultivation and gardens. DISTRIBUTION: Winter visitor to Sumatra, Java, Borneo, the Philippines and Sulawesi.

3 PHILIPPINE DRONGO-CUCKOO *Surniculus velutinus* 24–25cm
FIELD NOTES: Secretive. Arboreal. Sluggish while searching in tree foliage. Often thought conspecific with Square-tailed Drongo-cuckoo. VOICE: An ascending *wu wu wu waa waa wee* or *wi wi wi wi…* HABITAT: Lowland forest and forest edges. DISTRIBUTION: Endemic to the Philippines.

4 SQUARE-TAILED DRONGO-CUCKOO *Surniculus lugubris* 24–25cm
FIELD NOTES: Actions similar to previous species. VOICE: Loud, clear, mellow whistles, rising up the scale. HABITAT: Primary forest, forest edges and secondary scrub. DISTRIBUTION: Resident in Sumatra, Java, Bali, Borneo and the W Philippines.

5 FORK-TAILED DRONGO-CUCKOO *Surniculus dicruroides* 24–25cm
FIELD NOTES: Sluggish, arboreal forager in the tree canopy; calls from a bare treetop branch. VOICE: A rising *pip-pip-pip-pip-pip-pip*; also gives a shrill, accelerating *phew phew phewphewphewphew* that falls away. HABITAT: Broadleaved evergreen and deciduous forest, secondary growth, plantations and occasionally mangroves. DISTRIBUTION: Vagrant, recorded in Borneo.

6 MOLUCCAN DRONGO-CUCKOO *Surniculus musschenbroeki* 24cm
FIELD NOTES: Presence usually given away by calls; generally encountered singly or in pairs foraging in upper tree levels. Often considered conspecific with Square-tailed Drongo-cuckoo. VOICE: A rising, whistled *ki ki ki ki ki ki ki ki*, repeated and sometimes becoming hoarse and frantic. HABITAT: Primary and tall secondary forest and forest edges. DISTRIBUTION: Resident in Sulawesi and the N Moluccas.

26 CUCKOOS

1 MOUSTACHED HAWK-CUCKOO *Hierococcyx vagans* 28–30cm FIELD NOTES: Forages in the canopy. Best located by call. VOICE: A loud, monotonous *peu-peu*, also an ascending sequence of mellow notes that accelerates to fever pitch and then ends abruptly. HABITAT: Lowland and hill forest, and forest edges. DISTRIBUTION: Resident in Sumatra and Borneo; vagrant in Java.

2 LARGE HAWK-CUCKOO *Hierococcyx sparverioides* 38–40cm FIELD NOTES: Secretive, foraging inconspicuously in foliage; best located by call. VOICE: A screaming *pi-pee-ha… pi-pee-ha* that leads to a frenetic climax. HABITAT: Various, from thickets to montane forest. DISTRIBUTION: Non-breeding visitor to Java, Borneo, the Philippines and Sulawesi.

3 DARK HAWK-CUCKOO *Hierococcyx bocki* 31cm FIELD NOTES: Formerly thought to be a race of the previous species; actions and habits are presumed to be similar. VOICE: A two-note, whistled *pee-ha pee-ha* or *pi-phu pi-phu*. HABITAT: Hill and montane forest. DISTRIBUTION: Resident in Sumatra and Borneo.

4 MALAYSIAN HAWK-CUCKOO *Hierococcyx fugax* 28–30cm FIELD NOTES: Arboreal; skulks, usually low down, moving higher when calling. VOICE: A shrill, insistent *gee-whizz… gee-whizz…*, often followed by rapid *ti-tu-tu* notes that accelerate to a shrill crescendo and end with a slower *tu-tu-tu*. HABITAT: Forest, secondary growth, thickets and plantations. DISTRIBUTION: Resident in Sumatra and Borneo.

5 RUFOUS HAWK-CUCKOO *Hierococcyx hyperythrus* 28–30cm FIELD NOTES: Skulking, usually foraging low down in bushes or understorey. VOICE: A shrieking *joo-ichi joo-ichi*. HABITAT: Woodland and scrub. DISTRIBUTION: Non-breeding visitor to Borneo, the Philippines, Sulawesi and the S Moluccas.

6 HODGSON'S HAWK-CUCKOO *Hierococcyx nisicolor* 28–30cm FIELD NOTES: Arboreal, skulking and foraging in the understorey. VOICE: Similar to Malaysian Hawk-cuckoo but with a rapid *trrrrr-tititititirrrtrrr* at the end. HABITAT: Montane forest. DISTRIBUTION: Non-breeding visitor to Sumatra, Java and Borneo.

7 PHILIPPINE HAWK-CUCKOO *Hierococcyx pectoralis* 29cm FIELD NOTES: Shy, generally seen singly or in pairs; forages at all levels. VOICE: A *wheet wheet wheet wheet tu*, repeated nine or ten times, getting louder and faster, and ending in a frantic finish. HABITAT: Lowland to montane forest and secondary growth. DISTRIBUTION: Endemic to the Philippines.

8 PALLID CUCKOO *Cacomantis pallidus* 31–32cm FIELD NOTES: Often perches in the open; generally solitary, although recorded in small groups in Australia. VOICE: An eight-note ascending and accelerating whistle; female gives a hoarse whistle. HABITAT: Open woodland, clearings and open areas with trees. DISTRIBUTION: Non-breeding visitor to the N Moluccas and Lesser Sundas.

9 BANDED BAY CUCKOO *Cacomantis sonneratii* 24cm FIELD NOTES: More frequently heard than seen, although often calls from an exposed perch. VOICE: A shrill *pi-pi-pew-pew* or *smoke-yer-pepper*. HABITAT: Open forest, secondary growth, scrub and cultivated areas. DISTRIBUTION: Resident in Sumatra, Java and Borneo.

27 CUCKOOS

1 PLAINTIVE CUCKOO *Cacomantis merulinus* 23cm FIELD NOTES: Mainly arboreal; a restless forager among foliage at the top of trees, sometimes making sallies after flying insects or dropping to the ground to pick up prey. VOICE: A repeated *tay… ta… teee…*, also a descending, accelerating, trilled *pwee pwee pwee pee-pee-pee-pee*. HABITAT: Open woodland, secondary forest and cultivated areas. DISTRIBUTION: Resident in Sumatra, Java, Borneo, the Philippines and Sulawesi.

2 BRUSH CUCKOO *Cacomantis variolosus* 23cm FIELD NOTES: Secretive, more often heard than seen. *C. v. infaustus* (2b) is found in the N and E Moluccas. VOICE: A repeated series of 4–10 clear whistles, *weep weep weep weep weep…* HABITAT: Forest, from coastal areas to mountains. DISTRIBUTION: Resident in Sula Island, E Lesser Sundas and the Moluccas.

3 RUSTY-BREASTED CUCKOO *Cacomantis sepulcralis* 21–25cm FIELD NOTES: Forages among foliage of trees and bushes. Sometimes considered conspecific with Brush Cuckoo. VOICE: A melancholy, descending *whi whi whi whi whi…*, also an accelerating series of *whi-wibu* notes. HABITAT: Forest, forest edges, secondary growth and plantations. DISTRIBUTION: Resident in Sumatra, Java, Bali, Borneo, Sulawesi, Sula Islands, S Moluccas and the Lesser Sundas.

4 MOLUCCAN CUCKOO *Cacomantis aeruginosus* 24cm FIELD NOTES: Usually solitary, its presence often given away by its calls. VOICE: A long series of rapidly repeated piping whistles that slows slightly towards the end; also short, high-pitched, whistled notes, repeated monotonously. HABITAT: Montane forest. DISTRIBUTION: Endemic to the N Moluccas.

5 SULAWESI CUCKOO *Cuculus crassirostris* 38cm FIELD NOTES: Shy, perching in a leafy area of the mid-storey, often close to the trunk; usually seen singly or in pairs, its presence revealed by its calls. VOICE: A far-carrying, mellow *ho-hoo* or *hoo-oo-oo*; also a cooing *ko ko ku ku*, the last note barely audible. HABITAT: Primary and tall secondary hill forest, and forest edges. DISTRIBUTION: Endemic to Sulawesi.

6 INDIAN CUCKOO *Cuculus micropterus* 33cm FIELD NOTES: Usually forages in the tree canopy. Has wide-spaced barring on underparts and a dark subterminal band on tail. Some birds can look much browner on back. VOICE: A loud, persistent whistle, often transcribed as *one-more-bottle*; female makes a bubbling call. HABITAT: Lowland and hill forest. DISTRIBUTION: Resident and non-breeding visitor to Sumatra, Java and Borneo; non-breeding visitor to the Philippines; vagrant in the N Moluccas.

7 ORIENTAL CUCKOO *Cuculus optatus* 30–33cm FIELD NOTES: Forages in the canopy. Lacks a dark subterminal tail bar. VOICE: A low *hoop hoop hoop*, also a harsh *gaak-gaak ga-ak-ak-ak*; female has a bubbling call. HABITAT: Lowland forest and forest edges. DISTRIBUTION: Non-breeding visitor to Borneo.

8 HIMALAYAN CUCKOO *Cuculus saturatus* 30–32cm FIELD NOTES: Secretive, foraging in the forest canopy. Underparts tinged buff. VOICE: A *hoop hoop-hoop* or *tun-tadun*. HABITAT: Lowland to submontane forest. DISTRIBUTION: Winter visitor to Sumatra, Java, Borneo, the Philippines and Wallacea.

9 SUNDA LESSER CUCKOO *Cuculus lepidus* 26–29cm FIELD NOTES: Secretive, best located by voice. Forages mainly in the forest canopy. Once regarded as conspecific with the similar-looking, but larger, Himalayan Cuckoo. VOICE: A loud *kuk hoo hoo hoo*, also a mellow *pu-pu*; female has a bubbling call. HABITAT: Primary hill and mountain forest. DISTRIBUTION: Resident in Sumatra, Java, Borneo and the Lesser Sundas.

28 CUCKOOS

1 LITTLE BRONZE CUCKOO *Chrysococcyx minutillus* 15–16cm
FIELD NOTES: Unobtrusive, tends to forage in dense foliage. 'Dark-backed Bronze Cuckoo'
C. m. rufomerus (1b) occurs in the Lesser Sundas; 'Pied Bronze Cuckoo' *C. m. crassirostris*
(1c) is found in the Moluccas. VOICE: A descending *rhew rhew rhew rhew* or *teu teu teu teu
teu…*, sometimes including a rising, screeching *wireg-reeg-reeg*; also utters a high-pitched,
drawn-out trill. HABITAT: Coastal scrub, mangroves, secondary growth, forest edges, parks
and gardens. DISTRIBUTION: Resident in Sumatra, Java, Borneo, the Philippines, Sulawesi,
the Moluccas and the Lesser Sundas.

2 HORSFIELD'S BRONZE CUCKOO *Chrysococcyx basalis* 16cm   FIELD NOTES: Forages
at all levels, from the ground up. Sometimes occurs in small parties. VOICE: A descending,
high-pitched, whistled *peeer* or *tseeeuw*, incessantly repeated. HABITAT: Coastal scrub,
and coastal and subcoastal woodland. DISTRIBUTION: Non-breeding visitor to Java, Bali,
Sulawesi and the Lesser Sundas; vagrant in Sumatra and Borneo.

3 ASIAN EMERALD CUCKOO (ORIENTAL EMERALD CUCKOO)
Chrysococcyx maculatus 18cm   FIELD NOTES: Favours the branches and foliage of the
tree canopy; active forager, often making aerial sallies to capture flying insects. VOICE: A
loud, descending *kee-kee-kee*; also a *chweek* given in flight. HABITAT: Lowland forest and
secondary growth. DISTRIBUTION: Winter visitor to Sumatra.

4 SHINING BRONZE CUCKOO *Chrysococcyx lucidus* 17cm   FIELD NOTES: Usually
solitary. Inconspicuous forager from low scrub to treetops. VOICE: Generally silent; may utter
an upward-inflected *fleei*, which is rapidly repeated and often ends with a descending *pee-
eerr*. HABITAT: Woodland, woodland edges, scrubby secondary growth and village gardens.
DISTRIBUTION: Non-breeding visitor to the Lesser Sundas.

5 VIOLET CUCKOO *Chrysococcyx xanthorhynchus* 17cm   FIELD NOTES: Secretive,
creeping among foliage in search of prey; often perches at the top of a tall tree when calling.
VOICE: A loud, sharp, repeated *tee-wit*, often uttered in flight; also a descending, trilled
seer-se-seer seeseeseesee. HABITAT: Lowland and hill forest, forest edges, secondary forest,
mangroves and plantations. DISTRIBUTION: Resident in Sumatra, Java, Borneo and the
Philippines.

6 BLACK-EARED CUCKOO *Chrysococcyx osculans* 20cm   FIELD NOTES: Forages low
down in shrubby vegetation; usually solitary. VOICE: A quiet, drawn-out, descending,
plaintive *piiieeer*; also a cheerful *peeowee* or *cheeowee*. HABITAT: Open woodland and open
scrubland. DISTRIBUTION: Winter visitor to the Moluccas and E Lesser Sundas.

29 MALKOHAS

1 GREEN-BILLED MALKOHA *Phaenicophaeus tristis* 38cm FIELD NOTES: Skulking. Forages in dense thickets; best located when flying, weakly, from one thicket to another. VOICE: A mellow, nasal *oh-oh-oh-oh* and a frog-like *ko ko ko ko*; utters a peculiar chuckle when flushed. HABITAT: Hill to submontane forest. DISTRIBUTION: Resident in Sumatra.

2 BLACK-BELLIED MALKOHA *Phaenicophaeus diardi* 38cm FIELD NOTES: Forages in dense undergrowth and creepers. Often occurs in small parties. VOICE: A gruff *gwuap*, a hurried *gwagaup* and a loud *pauk*. HABITAT: Lowland and hill forest, swamp forest and secondary growth. DISTRIBUTION: Resident in Sumatra and Borneo.

3 CHESTNUT-BELLIED MALKOHA *Phaenicophaeus sumatranus* 40–41cm FIELD NOTES: Secretive, creeping through trees and thickets. VOICE: A low *tok tok…*, also a thin, high-pitched mewing. HABITAT: Primary lowland and secondary forest, forest edges and scrub. DISTRIBUTION: Resident in Sumatra and Borneo.

4 CHESTNUT-BREASTED MALKOHA *Phaenicophaeus curvirostris* 42–49cm FIELD NOTES: Often sits motionless in the canopy; moves around waving its tail like a squirrel. Often a member of mixed-species feeding groups. VOICE: A low, clucking *kuk kuk kuk* and a faster *kok-kok-kok…*; when agitated, utters a cat-like *miaou*. HABITAT: Primary and secondary forest, from lowland to hills, also plantations. DISTRIBUTION: Resident in Sumatra, Java, Bali, Borneo and the W Philippines.

5 RAFFLE'S MALKOHA *Rhinortha chlorophaea* 32–35cm FIELD NOTES: Moves steadily among mid-storey foliage and creepers. Often gathers in small parties. VOICE: A series of descending, mewing notes; a hoarse, strained *heeah* and harsh croaking sounds. HABITAT: Primary and secondary lowland forest, forest edges, heath forest and gardens. DISTRIBUTION: Resident in Sumatra and Borneo.

6 RED-BILLED MALKOHA *Zanclostomus javanicus* 42cm FIELD NOTES: Actions much as other malkohas. VOICE: A frog-like *uc uc uc uc uc…*, which occasionally ends in a quick *uc-uc-uc*; also a whistled *who-oo*, repeated every ten seconds. HABITAT: Lowland, hill and submontane forest. DISTRIBUTION: Resident in Sumatra, Java and Borneo.

7 YELLOW-BILLED MALKOHA *Rhamphococcyx calyorhynchus* 51–53cm FIELD NOTES: Usually encountered singly, in pairs or in small parties; forages in thick vegetation, creeping around squirrel-like. VOICE: A nasal rattle that accelerates and then fades away; also a drawn-out nasal whining, said to sound like a branch creaking in a breeze. HABITAT: Primary and tall secondary lowland, hill and occasionally submontane forest, forest edges, open woodland, wooded cultivation and scrub. DISTRIBUTION: Endemic to Sulawesi.

8 SCALE-FEATHERED MALKOHA *Dasylophus cumingi* 40–41cm FIELD NOTES: Usually seen singly or in small groups, foraging in dense foliage in the understorey or sometimes in the canopy. VOICE: An explosive, high-pitched *quizzzzz-kid* or *whizzzzz-kid*. HABITAT: Forest, forest edges and secondary growth. DISTRIBUTION: Endemic to the N Philippines.

9 RED-CRESTED MALKOHA (ROUGH-CRESTED MALKOHA) *Dasylophus superciliosus* 41–42cm FIELD NOTES: Travels slowly through dense forest understorey, with the odd short flight, singly or in small groups. VOICE: A repeated, guttural, metallic *cheuk*. HABITAT: Lowland forest, secondary growth and forest edges. DISTRIBUTION: Endemic to the N Philippines.

30 COUCALS

1 BLACK-HOODED COUCAL *Centropus steerii* 46cm FIELD NOTES: Secretive, more often heard than seen; skulks in dense foliage and vines in the understorey and canopy. VOICE: A loud *hoooot hoot-hoot-hoot-hoot-hoot…*, which descends and becomes softer. HABITAT: Lowland primary forest. DISTRIBUTION: Endemic to the NC Philippines (Mindoro).

2 PHILIPPINE COUCAL *Centropus viridis* 41–43cm FIELD NOTES: Skulks through dense vegetation, although often sits atop bushes and tall grass. The all-black race C. v. mindorensis (2b) occurs on Mindoro. The rare white morph occurs on Luzon. VOICE: Various calls, including a rapid *coo-coo-coo-coo…* or *boop-boop-boop-boop…*, and a distinctive *chi-gook, chi-gook-gook* or *chi-go-go gook*. HABITAT: Grassland, cultivation, secondary growth and thickets. DISTRIBUTION: Endemic to the Philippines.

3 JAVAN COUCAL (SUNDA COUCAL) *Centropus nigrorufus* 46cm FIELD NOTES: Typical coucal skulking habits. VOICE: Not described, but said to be similar to Greater Coucal. HABITAT: Coastal marshes, thickets, swamps, mangroves and tall grasses near mangroves. DISTRIBUTION: Endemic to Java.

4 GREATER COUCAL *Centropus sinensis* 48cm FIELD NOTES: Skulks in vegetation; when searching for prey, often walks with tail held horizontally. Juvenile has underparts narrowly barred white, rufous upperparts barred dark brown, black tail narrowly barred white and head brownish black. VOICE: A deep *hoop-hoop-hoop-hoop-hoop-hoop*, descending and then rising. HABITAT: Secondary forest, forest edges, reedy riverbanks, mangroves and cultivated areas. DISTRIBUTION: Resident in Sumatra and Borneo.

5 LESSER COUCAL *Centropus bengalensis* 31–33cm FIELD NOTES: Typical coucal skulking habits. VOICE: A deep *whoop whoop whoop whoop kurook kurook kurook…*, which increases in tempo and descends in pitch. HABITAT: Swamps, grassland, scrub and forest edges. DISTRIBUTION: Resident throughout, except the SE Moluccas.

6 BLACK-FACED COUCAL *Centropus melanops* 42–48cm FIELD NOTES: Skulks in dense foliage in the middle and upper canopy, usually singly or in pairs. VOICE: A loud *wooooop wooooop wooooop*, also a descending *boop boop boop boop*. HABITAT: Lowland forest and forest edges. DISTRIBUTION: Endemic to the S and SE Philippines.

7 BAY COUCAL *Centropus celebensis* 44–50cm FIELD NOTES: Usually found in pairs or small groups, skulking in dense vegetation from the undergrowth to the lower canopy. VOICE: An accelerating, deep *hoo hoo hoo hoo hoo hoo hoo hoo hoo*, which starts high and then falls, slows and then rises with the last two or three notes; also gives a long series of upslurred *woop* notes. HABITAT: Primary and tall secondary lowland and hill forest, forest edges and dense undergrowth. DISTRIBUTION: Endemic to Sulawesi.

8 RUFOUS COUCAL *Centropus unirufus* 38–42cm FIELD NOTES: Generally encountered in small, noisy groups of up to twelve bird or so. Forages in the understorey in dense undergrowth, particularly favouring bamboo thickets. VOICE: A snapping *squip whip* or *squip whip whip whip*, often given by groups moving through trees. HABITAT: Lowland and hill forest with thick undergrowth and bamboo. DISTRIBUTION: Endemic to the N Philippines.

white morph

2b *mindorensis*

1

2

3

4

5

n-br

br

6

7

8

31 COUCALS; GROUND-CUCKOOS; KOELS

1 GOLIATH COUCAL *Centropus goliath* 62–70cm FIELD NOTES: Usually found in pairs or small groups, clambering around from the undergrowth to the mid-storey and occasionally higher. VOICE: A persistent series of deep *ooom* notes; when alarmed, utters a harsh, guttural *kcau* or *kcau-kuc*. HABITAT: Primary forest, forest edges and dense forest undergrowth. DISTRIBUTION: Endemic to the N Moluccas.

2 PHEASANT COUCAL *Centropus phasianinus* 53–80cm FIELD NOTES: Generally seen in pairs or singly. Forages by clambering around in vegetation, or walking or running to capture prey. VOICE: A long, descending and then rising series of loud, hollow notes; also a series of loud, harsh, hissing notes. HABITAT: Swampy grassland, secondary monsoon forest and fringing grassland. DISTRIBUTION: Resident in the E Lesser Sundas (Timor).

3 KAI COUCAL *Centropus spilopterus* 53–62cm FIELD NOTES: Often considered a race of *C. phasianus*. Usually found singly or in pairs. Frequently conspicuous in secondary cultivation and in trees with few leaves. VOICE: A far-carrying series of short, ascending and descending *bop* notes. HABITAT: Lightly wooded cultivation, forest edges, remnant forest patches and scrub. DISTRIBUTION: Endemic to the S Moluccas (Kai Islands).

4 SHORT-TOED COUCAL *Centropus rectunguis* 37cm FIELD NOTES: Shy and skulking, solitary. Spends time on the ground foraging for prey. VOICE: A series of four or five resonant, booming notes, *buup buup buup buup*, which descend towards the end, repeated every few seconds. HABITAT: Lowland primary forest, riverine scrub and coastal scrub. DISTRIBUTION: Resident in Sumatra and Borneo.

5 BORNEAN GROUND-CUCKOO *Carpococcyx radiceus* 60cm FIELD NOTES: Forages on the ground, often following swarms of army ants, or pigs or bears to capture disturbed grubs and worms. VOICE: A far-carrying *whoo-hooh whoo-hooh whoo-hooh*. HABITAT: Alluvial and swamp forest, also undisturbed lowland riverine forest. DISTRIBUTION: Endemic to Borneo.

6 SUMATRAN GROUND-CUCKOO *Carpococcyx viridis* 55cm FIELD NOTES: Little recorded, known to be a shy ground forager and very rare. VOICE: A coughing *heh heh heh* and a loud *tock-tor*. HABITAT: Forest in hilly areas. DISTRIBUTION: Endemic to Sumatra.

7 ASIAN KOEL *Eudynamys scolopaceus* 40–43cm FIELD NOTES: Unobtrusive, usually keeping to dense foliage; first sign is often of a bird flying from tree to tree. VOICE: A shrill *ko-el ko-el ko-el* that increases in scale and pitch before ending abruptly; also a descending, bubbling *wreep-wreep-wreep-wreep-wreepwreepwreep*. HABITAT: Open woodland, forest edges, scrub, cultivation, parks and gardens. DISTRIBUTION: Resident in Sumatra, Java, the Philippines, N Moluccas and W Lesser Sundas; winter visitor to Borneo.

8 BLACK-BILLED KOEL *Eudynamys melanorhynchus* 36–44cm FIELD NOTES: Occurs singly, in pairs and in small groups; usually shy, often heard rather than seen. Frequents the mid-storey and canopy. VOICE: Various calls, including a melancholy series of *kuOw* notes, which starts low and then gets louder and higher in pitch; also a loud bubbling, which rises and then quickly falls away, and a constant-pitched *whu-wu-wu-ki-ki-ki-ki-ki-ki*. HABITAT: Primary and tall secondary lowland, hill and submontane forest, riverine forest, forest edges and lightly wooded areas. DISTRIBUTION: Endemic to Sulawesi and the Sula Islands.

9 PACIFIC KOEL *Eudynamys orientalis* 39–47cm FIELD NOTES: Actions and habits similar to Asian Koel. *E. o. cyanocephalus* (9b) is a winter visitor to the Lesser Sundas and S Moluccas. VOICE: A loud, dreary *kooeei* or *ko-el*, a rapid bubbling call and a high-pitched, nasal *keel*. HABITAT: Coastal forest, secondary forest, forest edges, cultivation with trees and forest gardens. DISTRIBUTION: Resident in the Lesser Sundas; winter visitor to the S Moluccas and Lesser Sundas.

dark form ♀

rufous form

9b cyanocephalus

32 COCKATOOS

1 PALM COCKATOO *Prosciger aterrimus* 55–60cm FIELD NOTES: Usually seen singly or in pairs; forages in trees and occasionally on the ground to pick up fallen fruit. VOICE: Calls include peculiar whistles and a hoarse, nasal screech. HABITAT: Lowland and hill forest and forest edges. DISTRIBUTION: Introduced in the S Moluccas (Kai Islands) but no recent sightings.

2 YELLOW-CRESTED COCKATOO *Cacatua sulpurea* 33cm FIELD NOTES: Occurs singly, in pairs or in small groups, with larger groups at roosts. Forages mainly in the lower canopy, or on the ground when raiding crops. *C. s. citrinocristata* (2b) occurs on Sumba Island in the Lesser Sundas. VOICE: A raucous screeching and a variety of whistles and squeaks. HABITAT: Primary and tall secondary lowland and hill forest, forest edges, monsoon forest, tall scrubby woodland, wooded scrub and cultivation. DISTRIBUTION: Resident in Sulawesi and the Lesser Sundas.

3 SULPHUR-CRESTED COCKATOO *Cacatua galerita* 45–55cm
FIELD NOTES: Conspicuous; occurs singly, in pairs or in small, noisy groups. Forages in trees, also on the ground when raiding crops. VOICE: A loud, raucous screech. HABITAT: Monsoon forest, open woodland, forest edges and lightly wooded cultivation. DISTRIBUTION: Introduced to the S Moluccas.

4 SALMON-CRESTED COCKATOO *Cacatua moluccensis* 46–52cm
FIELD NOTES: Usually encountered singly, in pairs or in small groups. Inconspicuous, except when flying to and from roosts. Forages quietly in the upper mid-storey and canopy. VOICE: Harsh screeches and a nasal, staccato chatter. HABITAT: Primary and tall secondary lowland and hill forest. DISTRIBUTION: Endemic to the S Moluccas.

5 WHITE COCKATOO *Cacatua alba* 46cm FIELD NOTES: Noisy and conspicuous; occurs singly, in pairs, in small groups or in large groups in late afternoon. Frequents the canopy. VOICE: A short, nasal, high-pitched screech. HABITAT: Primary and tall secondary lowland and hill forest, forest edges and forest remnants. DISTRIBUTION: Endemic to the N Moluccas.

6 PHILIPPINE COCKATOO (RED-VENTED COCKATOO)
Cacatua haematuropygia 30cm FIELD NOTES: Generally seen singly, in pairs or in flocks of up to 30 or so. Non-breeding groups nomadic; often raids crops. The only all-white land bird in the Philippines. VOICE: Various raucous calls, which can be very loud when groups are calling together. HABITAT: Lowland, riverine and mangrove forest, forest edges and adjacent open ground. DISTRIBUTION: Endemic to the Philippines.

7 TANIMBAR CORELLA *Cacatua goffiniana* 31–32cm FIELD NOTES: Often seen in large flocks. Regularly perches on bare branches at the top of tall trees. When crest is raised, pink feather bases are exposed. VOICE: Various loud, harsh screeches. HABITAT: Primary and tall secondary lowland forest, forest edges, clearings; also crop fields adjacent to forest. DISTRIBUTION: Endemic to the E Lesser Sundas.

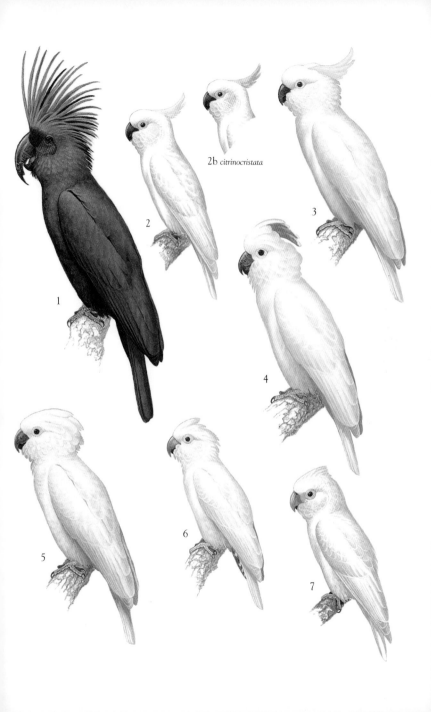

2b *citrinocristata*

33 PARROTS

1 RED-AND-BLUE LORY *Eos histrio* 31cm FIELD NOTES: Usually found in pairs or small flocks, with much larger flocks at communal roosts. *E. h. challengeri* (1b) occurs on Miangas Island. VOICE: Short, harsh, chattering screeches. HABITAT: Primary lowland and hill forest; also coconut plantations. DISTRIBUTION: Endemic to the islands north of Sulawesi.

2 VIOLET-NECKED LORY *Eos squamata* 23–27cm FIELD NOTES: Found in pairs or small flocks, and larger flocks when feeding in flowering or fruiting trees. *E. s. obiensis* (2b) occurs on Obi and Bisa islands. VOICE: Loud, shrill, harsh, rapidly repeated screeches. HABITAT: Primary and tall secondary lowland and hill forest, forest edges, scrubby secondary growth, mangroves and coconut plantations. DISTRIBUTION: Resident in the N Moluccas.

3 RED LORY *Eos bornea* 30cm FIELD NOTES: Generally seen in pairs or small parties, occasionally found in much larger groups. Feeds in flowering or fruiting trees. Noisy. VOICE: Screeches and more musical, bell-like notes. HABITAT: Primary and tall secondary lowland and hill forest, mangroves, coconut plantations and around human habitation. DISTRIBUTION: Endemic to the S Moluccas.

4 BLUE-STREAKED LORY *Eos reticulata* 31cm FIELD NOTES: Frequents flowering trees, usually in pairs or small flocks. VOICE: A drawn-out, nasal screech or screeches; also utters starling-like chatters and whistles. HABITAT: Primary and secondary lowland forest, open forest, mangroves, wooded cultivation and coconut plantations. DISTRIBUTION: Endemic to the E Lesser Sundas.

5 BLUE-EARED LORY *Eos semilarvata* 24cm FIELD NOTES: Found singly, in pairs and in small groups; visits flowering trees and shrubs to feed. VOICE: A loud screech. HABITAT: Primary montane forest and upper montane heath. DISTRIBUTION: Endemic to the S Moluccas (Seram).

6 CHATTERING LORY *Lorius garrulus* 30cm FIELD NOTES: Usually seen in pairs, occasionally in larger groups when feeding in flowering trees. *L. g. flavopalliatus* (6b) occurs on Bacan, Obi, Obilatu, Kasiruta and Mandioli islands. VOICE: A loud, nasal, disyllabic bugle; in flight, gives a loud, harsh, quavering bray. HABITAT: Primary and tall secondary lowland and hill forest, forest edges; occasionally visits coconut groves. DISTRIBUTION: Endemic to the N Moluccas.

7 PURPLE-NAPED LORY *Lorius domicella* 28cm FIELD NOTES: Generally seen singly or in pairs, foraging acrobatically to extract various seeds. VOICE: Recorded only as having a melodious call. HABITAT: Submontane forest. DISTRIBUTION: Endemic to the S Moluccas.

8 RED-CHEEKED PARROT *Geoffroyus geoffroyi* 21–30cm FIELD NOTES: Frequents the canopy, in small groups, in pairs or singly. Often sits prominently on an exposed branch. *G. g. cyanicollis* (8b) occurs in the N Moluccas; *G. g. keyensis* (8c) is found in the S Moluccas (Kai Islands). VOICE: Short, repeated *kee* notes. HABITAT: Primary and tall secondary forest, monsoon forest and woodland, forest edges, coastal woodland, mangroves, scrub and parkland. DISTRIBUTION: Resident in the Moluccas and Lesser Sundas.

9 BLUE-RUMPED PARROT *Psittinus cyanurus* 18–19cm FIELD NOTES: Pairs or small parties are usually seen foraging in the upper branches, or flying above the forest canopy. *P. c. abbotti* (9b) occurs on islands off NW Sumatra (Simeulue and Siumat). VOICE: A sharp *chi-chi-chi* and *chew-ee*, also a high-pitched *peep*. HABITAT: Lowland forest, swamp forest, mangroves and cultivated areas. DISTRIBUTION: Resident in Sumatra and Borneo.

1b
challengeri

2b
obiensis

1

2

riciniata

3

4

5

6

6b
flavopalliatus

7

8b
cyanicollis

♂

♀

8

♂

8

♂

8c *keyensis*

9b
abbotti

♂

♀

♂

9

♀

34 PARROTS

1 GUAIABERO *Bolbopsittacus lunulatus* 16–17cm FIELD NOTES: Occurs singly or in pairs, with larger parties often occurring in fruiting trees. VOICE: A high-pitched *zeet* or *zeet zeet*. HABITAT: Forest and forest edges, secondary growth, clearings with scattered trees, mangroves and orchards. DISTRIBUTION: Endemic to the Philippines.

2 ORNATE LORIKEET *Trichoglossus ornatus* 23–25cm FIELD NOTES: Usually in pairs and small flocks, often in larger flocks at flowering trees. VOICE: Short, squeaky, screeching notes interspersed with rolling screeches. HABITAT: Forest edges, tall secondary forest, coastal woodland, swamp forest, mangroves, wooded cultivation and coconut plantations. DISTRIBUTION: Endemic to Sulawesi.

3 OLIVE-HEADED LORIKEET *Trichoglossus euteles* 25cm FIELD NOTES: Occurs in small flocks, with larger flocks at flowering trees. VOICE: A rapid, buzzy trill, a drawn-out wheezy call, and a series of harsh squeaks, twitters and whistles. HABITAT: Primary montane forest, forest edges, secondary growth and savannah woodland. DISTRIBUTION: Endemic to the C Lesser Sundas.

4 CITRINE LORIKEET (YELLOW-AND-GREEN LORIKEET) *Trichoglossus flavoviridis* 21cm FIELD NOTES: Usually in pairs or small flocks; larger flocks at flowering trees. *T. f. meyeri* (4b) from Sulawesi. VOICE: Calls include a high-pitched screech, squeaky chatters, and dry *ksk* notes interspersed with thin whistles. HABITAT: Primary hill and montane forest and forest edges. DISTRIBUTION: Endemic to Sulawesi and the Sula Islands.

5 COCONUT LORIKEET *Trichoglossus haematodus* 25–30cm FIELD NOTES: Usually in pairs, groups or large flocks, especially at flowering trees. This and the following four species are often considered to be races of the Rainbow Lorikeet *T. moluccanus*. VOICE: A repeated harsh screech in flight, and a strident *peaow peaow peaow* when perched. HABITAT: Most types of lowland and lower montane wooded country, coconut and other plantations, and suburban areas. DISTRIBUTION: Resident in the S Moluccas.

6 SUNSET LORIKEET *Trichoglossus forsteni* 25–30cm FIELD NOTES: See Coconut Lorikeet. *T. f. djampeanus* (6b) occurs on Jampea Island. VOICE: As Coconut Lorikeet. HABITAT: Most types of lower and montane woodland. DISTRIBUTION: Resident in Bali, W Lesser Sundas (Lombok and Sumbawa), and islands in the Flores Sea (Jampea and Kalaotoa).

7 LEAF LORIKEET (FLORES LORIKEET) *Trichoglossus weberi* 25cm FIELD NOTES: See Coconut Lorikeet. VOICE: Similar to Coconut Lorikeet. HABITAT: Rainforest and *Casuarina* trees. DISTRIBUTION: Endemic to the Lesser Sundas (Flores).

8 RED-COLLARED LORIKEET *Trichoglossus rubritorquis* 26cm FIELD NOTES: See Coconut Lorikeet. VOICE: As Coconut Lorikeet. HABITAT: Presumed to be similar to Coconut Lorikeet. DISTRIBUTION: Resident in the E Lesser Sundas.

9 MARIGOLD LORIKEET *Trichoglossus capistratus* 26cm FIELD NOTES: See Coconut Lorikeet. VOICE: As Coconut Lorikeet. HABITAT: Primary and secondary forest, dry woodland and plantations. DISTRIBUTION: Endemic to the C Lesser Sundas.

10 MINDANAO LORIKEET *Trichoglossus johnstoniae* 18cm FIELD NOTES: Usually occurs in pairs or noisy flocks; regularly seen in flight as flocks fly between trees. VOICE: Calls include a sharp *chick, chick-it* or *twick-it*. HABITAT: Montane forest and forest edges. DISTRIBUTION: Endemic to the S Philippines.

11 IRIS LORIKEET *Psitteuteles iris* 20cm FIELD NOTES: Usually occurs in small parties, occasionally in large flocks. Frequents flowering trees. VOICE: Various shrill screeches and whistles. HABITAT: Primary and tall secondary monsoon, lowland, hill and submontane forest. DISTRIBUTION: Endemic to the E Lesser Sundas.

12 BLUE-FRONTED LORIKEET *Charmosyna toxopei* 16cm FIELD NOTES: Usually found in small flocks. VOICE: A shrill *ti… ti… ti… ti… ti-ti-ti*. HABITAT: Primary and secondary forest. DISTRIBUTION: Endemic to the S Moluccas (Buru).

13 RED-FLANKED LORIKEET *Charmosyna placentis* 16–19cm FIELD NOTES: Frequents upper canopy levels, feeding in flowering trees, usually in pairs or small flocks. VOICE: A dry *tst* and sharp *skeesk* notes. HABITAT: Lowland forest, forest edges, coastal trees and plantations. DISTRIBUTION: Resident in the Moluccas.

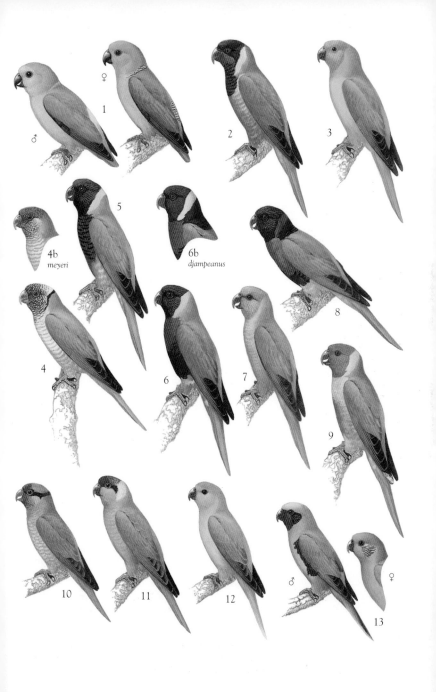

4b
meyeri

6b
djampeanus

35 PARROTS

1 MONTANE RACQUET-TAIL *Prioniturus montanus* 30cm FIELD NOTES: Occurs singly, in pairs or in small flocks; noisy when flying through or over forest. Immatures lack the spatules. VOICE: Calls include a hacking *kak-kak-kak-kak ak ak ak…*, loud, harsh notes and a note like a swinging rusty gate. HABITAT: Mid-montane forest. DISTRIBUTION: Endemic to the N Philippines.

2 MINDANAO RACQUET-TAIL *Prioniturus waterstradti* 27cm FIELD NOTES: Once considered a race of Montane Racquet-tail; actions presumed to be similar. Immatures lack the spatules. VOICE: Presumably similar to the previous species. HABITAT: Dense montane forest, ridgetop forest and stunted mossy forest. DISTRIBUTION: Endemic to the S Philippines.

3 BLUE-HEADED RACQUET-TAIL *Prioniturus platenae* 27cm FIELD NOTES: Occurs singly, in pairs or in small groups, foraging in the canopy. Noisy, especially in flight. Immatures lack the spatules. VOICE: Similar to Montane Racquet-tail. HABITAT: Lowland forest, scrub and mangroves. DISTRIBUTION: Endemic to the W Philippines.

4 GREEN RACQUET-TAIL *Prioniturus luconensis* 29cm FIELD NOTES: Forages in the canopy and understorey, usually in pairs or small parties; very active in the late afternoon. Immatures lack the spatules. VOICE: Calls include a harsh *aaaak*, a horse-like whinnying, a ringing *liiinng* and a *yuur-witt*, the last syllable rising sharply. HABITAT: Lowland forest, forest edges and nearby cultivated areas. DISTRIBUTION: Endemic to the N Philippines.

5 BLUE-CROWNED RACQUET-TAIL *Prioniturus discurus* 27cm FIELD NOTES: Occurs in small, noisy groups or pairs. Immatures lack the spatules. VOICE: Various squeals, squeaks and harsh notes. HABITAT: Primary and secondary forest, mangroves, orchards and banana plantations. DISTRIBUTION: Endemic to the Philippines.

6 MINDORO RACQUET-TAIL *Prioniturus mindorensis* 27cm FIELD NOTES: Recently split from the previous species; habits presumed to be similar. Immatures lack the spatules. VOICE: Presumably similar to the previous species. HABITAT: Humid forest, mainly in the lowlands. DISTRIBUTION: Endemic to Mindoro in the S Philippines.

7 BURU RACQUET-TAIL *Prioniturus mada* 32cm FIELD NOTES: Forages in the crowns of forest trees, usually in small flocks. Immatures lack the spatules. VOICE: A repeated pleasant whistling, a musical *si-quie*, a rapidly repeated *kwii kwii kwii* and a low-pitched *squr-squr*. HABITAT: Primary lowland, hill and montane forest. DISTRIBUTION: Endemic to the S Moluccas.

8 GOLDEN-MANTLED RACQUET-TAIL *Prioniturus platurus* 28cm FIELD NOTES: Regularly seen flying over the forest canopy in small or large, noisy flocks; otherwise quite secretive and hard to see. Immatures lack the spatules. *P. p. sinerubris* (8b) occurs in the Sula Islands (Taliabu). VOICE: Calls include a harsh, nasal *kaaa*, a *krrrik* or *krrrri*, and a repeated nasal *quelie*. HABITAT: Primary and tall secondary lowland and montane forest, mangroves and lightly wooded cultivation. DISTRIBUTION: Endemic to Sulawesi and the Sula Islands.

9 YELLOW-BREASTED RACQUET-TAIL *Prioniturus flavicans* 37cm FIELD NOTES: Usually seen singly, in pairs or in small groups; generally quiet and inconspicuous as it forages in the thick foliage of the crowns of tall trees. Regularly joins mixed-species feeding flocks. Immatures lack the spatules. VOICE: Calls include a drawn-out screech with an alternating pitch, a series of three repeated nasal, barking screeches, and a higher-pitched nasal bugling or yodelling. HABITAT: Primary lowland and hill forest, and nearby lightly wooded cultivation. DISTRIBUTION: Endemic to Sulawesi.

10 BLUE-WINGED RACQUET-TAIL *Prioniturus verticalis* 30cm FIELD NOTES: Noisy in flight; foraging actions similar to other racquet-tails. Immatures lack the spatules. VOICE: Calls include a harsh, rasping *aaaaak* and a squeaky *lee-aaack*. HABITAT: Primary lowland forest, forest edges and mangroves. DISTRIBUTION: Endemic to the Philippines (Sulu Archipelago).

36 PARROTS

1 GREAT-BILLED PARROT *Tanygnathus megalorynchos* 33–43cm FIELD NOTES: Seen singly, in pairs or in small parties; larger flocks at roosts. Nomadic, occasionally flying between small islands. Feeds in the canopy of fruiting trees; sometimes perches on exposed branches or in dead trees. *T. m. subaffinis* (1b) is found in the E Lesser Sundas. VOICE: A harsh, reedy *ke-rarr ke-rarr*; a series of repeated quavering, nasal notes; and a harsh repeated note given in flight. HABITAT: Primary and secondary lowland and hill forest, forest edges, mangroves, coastal woodland, wooded cultivation, plantations and gardens. DISTRIBUTION: Resident over much of Wallacea; possibly resident in the S Philippines (Balut and Sarangani).

2 BLUE-NAPED PARROT *Tanygnathus lucionensis* 31cm FIELD NOTES: Occurs singly, in pairs or in small parties; feeds on fruit and seeds in upper tree levels. *T. l. talautensis* (2b) is found on the Talaud Islands (N of Sulawesi). VOICE: A piercing shriek and a harsh *awwwk-awwwk*. HABITAT: Forest, forest edges, remnant patches of forest within cultivation, wooded cultivation and coconut groves. DISTRIBUTION: Resident in Borneo, the Philippines, and the Sangihe and Talaud islands (N of Sulawesi).

3 BLACK-LORED PARROT *Tanygnathus gramineus* 40cm FIELD NOTES: Usually seen singly, more often heard than seen, little else recorded. Female has pink-grey bill. VOICE: Similar to the Great-billed Parrot, but more drawn out and higher pitched. HABITAT: Montane forest. DISTRIBUTION: Endemic to the S Moluccas (Buru).

4 BLUE-BACKED PARROT *Tanygnathus sumatranus* 32cm FIELD NOTES: Forages in the canopy, singly, in pairs or in small groups; often flies low, only a few metres above the ground. *T. s. everetti* (4b) occurs in the S and C Philippines. VOICE: A harsh, squawking *nyak nyak…*, a *nyak* followed by a high-pitched screech, a quavering or yodelling screech, and a loud, piercing *kei*. HABITAT: Forest and forest edges, swamp forest, tall secondary woodland, remnant forest patches and coconut plantations. DISTRIBUTION: Resident in the Philippines, Sulawesi, and the Sangihe, Talaud and Sula islands.

5 ECLECTUS PARROT *Eclectus roratus* 35–42cm FIELD NOTES: Noisy and conspicuous; usually seen singly, in pairs and occasionally in small parties foraging in the canopy. Often perches on partially exposed branches. *E. r. reideli* (5b) occurs in the E Lesser Sundas (Tanimbar Islands); *E. r. vosmaeri* (5c) is found in the N Moluccas. VOICE: A series of loud, hoarse, rapidly repeated screeches, generally given in flight; also a ringing, metallic squeal, uttered when perched. HABITAT: Primary and tall secondary lowland and hill forest, mangroves and plantations. DISTRIBUTION: Resident in the Moluccas and E Lesser Sundas.

6 MOLUCCAN KING PARROT *Alisterus amboinensis* 35cm FIELD NOTES: More often seen in flight; forages from mid-storey to canopy. *A. a. hypophonius* (6b) from N Moluccas (Halmahera). VOICE: A series of high-pitched, ringing, upslurred whistles; in flight, utters a dry *chack chack*. HABITAT: Primary and secondary lowland and hill forest; occasionally gardens. DISTRIBUTION: Resident in Sulawesi (Banggai Islands), the Sula Islands and the Moluccas.

7 OLIVE-SHOULDERED PARROT *Aprosmictus jonquillaceus* 35cm FIELD NOTES: Occurs singly, in pairs and occasionally in small groups, more often seen flying across forest openings; forages mainly from the mid-storey to the canopy. VOICE: Short, harsh, grating squawks. HABITAT: Primary and tall secondary monsoon forest, savannah woodland, cultivation and scrubby secondary growth. DISTRIBUTION: Resident in Sulawesi (Banggai Islands), the Sula Islands and the Moluccas.

8 ROSE-BREASTED PARAKEET (RED-BREASTED PARAKEET) *Psittacula alexandri* 33–38cm FIELD NOTES: Usually seen in small parties, with larger groups where food is plentiful. VOICE: A short, nasal *kaihk*, often repeated. HABITAT: Open forest, groves and cultivation. DISTRIBUTION: Resident in Sumatra (Simeulue, Banyak and Nias islands), Java, Bali and Borneo.

9 LONG-TAILED PARAKEET *Psittacula longicauda* 40–48cm FIELD NOTES: Usually found in small flocks, with larger gatherings at rich food sources. VOICE: A high-pitched *pee-yo pee-yo pee-yo* and a nasal, quavering *graak graak graak*. HABITAT: Open lowland and coastal forest, forested swamps, secondary forest and plantations. DISTRIBUTION: Resident in Sumatra and Borneo.

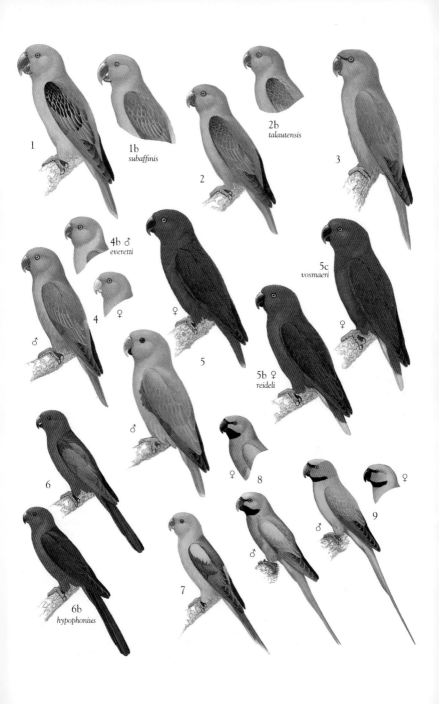

1   1b *subaffinis*

2   2b *talautensis*

3

4b ♂ *everetti*

4   ♂   ♀

5   ♀   5c *vosmaeri*

5   ♂   5b ♀ *reideli*

6

6b *hypophonius*

7   8 ♀   ♂   9 ♀   ♂

37 PARROTS

1 YELLOW-CAPPED PYGMY PARROT *Micropsitta keiensis* 9cm FIELD NOTES: Occurs in pairs or small parties. Forages on trunks and large branches. VOICE: A series of short, weak, high-pitched notes. HABITAT: All types of woodland areas. DISTRIBUTION: Resident in the S Moluccas (Kai Islands).

2 RED-BREASTED PYGMY PARROT *Micropsitta bruijnii* 8–9cm FIELD NOTES: Frequents upper tree levels; acrobatic forager, seen singly, in pairs or in small parties. VOICE: A thin, high-pitched *tsee-tsee*. HABITAT: Primary and disturbed hill and montane forest; occasionally lowland forest. DISTRIBUTION: Resident in the S Moluccas (Buru and Seram).

3 BLUE-CROWNED HANGING PARROT *Loriculus galgulus* 12–14cm FIELD NOTES: Usually encountered in pairs or small parties. VOICE: A shrill *tsi, tsrri* or *tsi-tsi-tsi*. HABITAT: Lowland forest; occasionally montane forest and plantations. DISTRIBUTION: Resident in Sumatra, Borneo and possibly W Java.

4 PHILIPPINE HANGING PARROT *Loriculus philippensis* 14cm FIELD NOTES: Occurs singly, in pairs, and in larger groups at feeding sites; favours flowering and fruiting trees. *L. p. apicalis* (4b) is found in the S Philippines; *L. p. chrysonotus* (4c) occurs on Cebu; *L. p. bonapartei* (4c) occurs in the Sulu Archipelago; *L. p. regulus* (4e) is found in the C Philippines. VOICE: A sharp twittering. HABITAT: All types of forest, forest patches and gardens. DISTRIBUTION: Endemic to the Philippines.

5 SULA HANGING PARROT *Loriculus sclateri* 14cm FIELD NOTES: Sometimes considered conspecific with the Moluccan Hanging Parrot; actions presumed to be similar. VOICE: Presumably similar to Moluccan Hanging Parrot. HABITAT: Primary and secondary forest, and partially cleared adjacent areas. DISTRIBUTION: Endemic to the Sula Islands.

6 SANGIHE HANGING PARROT *Loriculus catamene* 12cm FIELD NOTES: Usually found in pairs or small flocks; favours flowering coconut palms. VOICE: A dry, staccato, high, disyllabic whistle and an upslurred *sh-ui*. HABITAT: Remnant forest patches, coconut and mixed tree-crop plantations. DISTRIBUTION: Endemic to Sangihe Islands (N of Sulawesi).

7 CAMIGUIN HANGING PARROT *Loriculus camiguinensis* 14cm FIELD NOTES: Forages in the canopy. Feeds on the seeds of wild bananas, fruits, berries and blossoms. Considered by some authorities to be a race of the Philippine Hanging Parrot. VOICE: A high-pitched *tziit-tziit-tziit*. HABITAT: Upland forest. DISTRIBUTION: Endemic to the S Philippines (Camiguin Island).

8 SULAWESI HANGING PARROT (GREAT HANGING PARROT) *Loriculus stigmatus* 15cm FIELD NOTES: Usually occurs singly, in pairs or in small parties; larger numbers are found when feeding in flowering or fruiting trees. VOICE: A high-pitched *tsu-tsee* or *tsu-tsee-tsee*. HABITAT: Primary and tall secondary lowland and hill forest, forest edges, lightly wooded cultivation, mangroves, scrub and coconut plantations. DISTRIBUTION: Endemic to Sulawesi.

9 MOLUCCAN HANGING PARROT *Loriculus amabilis* 11cm FIELD NOTES: Forages in the crowns of tall flowering and fruiting trees; singly, in pairs or in small parties. VOICE: A rapid, weak, high-pitched, buzzing call. HABITAT: Primary and secondary lowland forest, coastal woodland and mangroves. DISTRIBUTION: Endemic to the N Moluccas.

10 YELLOW-THROATED HANGING PARROT *Loriculus pusillus* 12cm FIELD NOTES: Feeds on flowers, buds and small fruits. VOICE: A shrill, ringing *sree-ee*, given in flight. HABITAT: Rainforest, from sea-level to mountains, and open areas with *Casuarina* trees. DISTRIBUTION: Endemic to Java and Bali.

11 WALLACE'S HANGING PARROT *Loriculus flosculus* 11–12cm FIELD NOTES: Favours fruiting fig trees or other soft fruit and flowering trees. Usually in pairs or small groups. VOICE: A hoarse *chi-chi-chi-chi-chi*, given during display; in flight, utters a screeching *strrt strrt*. HABITAT: Primary hill forest. DISTRIBUTION: Endemic to the W Lesser Sundas (Flores).

12 PYGMY HANGING PARROT *Loriculus exilis* 10–11cm FIELD NOTES: Forages in the crowns of tall trees, feeding on flowers and fruits. VOICE: A short, dry, thin, weak *pssst*. HABITAT: Primary lowland and hill forest; occasionally visits mangroves and trees in open country. DISTRIBUTION: Endemic to Sulawesi.

4b
apicalis

4c
chrysonotus

4d

4e
regulus

bonapartei

38 SWIFTLETS

1 WATERFALL SWIFTLET (GIANT SWIFTLET) *Hydrochous gigas* 16cm
FIELD NOTES: Gregarious, often in the company of other swifts. Usually seen over hilly or mountainous terrain. VOICE: Sharp *wicker* notes. HABITAT: Mountain forest with nearby waterfalls. DISTRIBUTION: Resident in Sumatra and Borneo.

2 GLOSSY SWIFTLET (WHITE-BELLIED SWIFTLET) *Collocalia esculenta*
10cm FIELD NOTES: Gregarious. Has a banking and gliding flight, interspersed with fluttering, bat-like wing-beats. *C. e. marginata* (2b) is found in the W and N Philippines; *C. e. spilura* (2c) occurs on the N Moluccas. Work is being carried out to split the Glossy Swiftlet into numerous new full species. VOICE: A sharp twitter. HABITAT: Open and forested areas. DISTRIBUTION: Resident and widespread over the region, except Java, Bali and the W Lesser Sundas (Lombok).

3 CAVE SWIFTLET (LINCHI SWIFTLET) *Collocalia linchi* 10cm FIELD NOTES: Flies low, often in loose flocks. VOICE: A high-pitched *cheer-cheer*. HABITAT: Over forest and open country, from sea-level to mountains. DISTRIBUTION: Resident in Borneo, Sumatra, Java, Bali, and the W Lesser Sundas (Lombok).

4 BORNEAN SWIFTLET *Collocalia dodgei* 9–10cm FIELD NOTES: Often considered a race of the Cave Swiftlet; actions presumably similar. VOICE: Presumed to be similar to Cave Swiftlet. HABITAT: Mountainous areas. DISTRIBUTION: Endemic to N Borneo.

5 PYGMY SWIFTLET *Collocalia troglodytes* 9cm FIELD NOTES: Forages in small groups above forests, clearings and inland water. VOICE: A short, throaty *chirp*. HABITAT: Lowland forests and inland waters. DISTRIBUTION: Endemic to the Philippines.

6 PHILIPPINE SWIFTLET *Aerodramus mearnsi* 10–11cm FIELD NOTES: Forages above forests and in clearings. VOICE: A rhythmic series of *wi-ch-chew* notes. HABITAT: Submontane forests with nearby caves. DISTRIBUTION: Endemic to the Philippines.

7 HALMAHERA SWIFTLET *Aerodramus infuscatus* 10cm FIELD NOTES: Usually forages in flocks of 10–30 birds, often in the company of other swiftlets. VOICE: A long, rhythmic series of *wee-chi-chi* notes. HABITAT: Ranges over forests, disturbed areas and open areas. DISTRIBUTION: Endemic to the N Moluccas.

8 SULAWESI SWIFTLET *Aerodramus sororum* 10cm FIELD NOTES: Actions presumed to be similar to the previous species, with which it is considered by some authorities to be conspecific. VOICE: Presumably similar to the previous species. HABITAT: Presumably similar to the previous species. DISTRIBUTION: Endemic to Sulawesi.

9 SERAM SWIFTLET *Aerodramus ceramensis* 10cm FIELD NOTES: Considered by some authorities to be a race of the Halmahera Swiftlet; actions presumed to be similar. VOICE: Presumably similar to Halmahera Swiftlet. HABITAT: Presumably similar to Halmahera Swiftlet. DISTRIBUTION: Endemic to the S Moluccas.

10 VOLCANO SWIFTLET *Aerodramus vulcanorum* 14cm FIELD NOTES: Occurs in fast-flying flocks around open peaks and ridges of the highest mountains. VOICE: A piercing *teeree-teeree-teeree*. HABITAT: Mountains and volcanic rims. DISTRIBUTION: Endemic to W Java.

1

2

2b
marginata

2c
spilura

3

4

5

6

7

8

9

10

39 SWIFTLETS; SWIFTS

1 WHITEHEAD'S SWIFTLET *Aerodramus whiteheadi* 14cm FIELD NOTES: Little recorded; note broad head. VOICE: Unrecorded. HABITAT: Forested mountain areas. DISTRIBUTION: Endemic to the Philippines.

2 MOSSY-NEST SWIFTLET *Aerodramus salangana* 12cm FIELD NOTES: Forages over, and sometimes inside, forests. VOICE: Shrill twitterings, chirrups and burbling notes. HABITAT: Primary forest with nearby caves. DISTRIBUTION: Resident in Sumatra, Java and Borneo; vagrant in the Philippines.

3 UNIFORM SWIFTLET *Aerodramus vanikorensis* 13cm FIELD NOTES: Gregarious, usually in small to large flocks, often alongside other swiftlet species. VOICE: A *zoo-zu-chee-chee* and a squeaky trill. HABITAT: Various, including forest, grassland, ponds and mangroves, all with nearby caves. DISTRIBUTION: Resident in Sulawesi, the Moluccas and the E Lesser Sundas.

4 AMELINE SWIFTLET *Aerodramus amelis* 13cm FIELD NOTES: Considered by some authorities to be a race of the Uniform Swiftlet; actions presumed to be similar. VOICE: Presumably similar to Uniform Swiftlet. HABITAT: Similar to Uniform Swiftlet. DISTRIBUTION: Endemic to the Philippines.

5 BLACK-NEST SWIFTLET *Aerodramus maximus* 13cm FIELD NOTES: Gregarious, often in the company of other swifts. Most active during the crepuscular period. VOICE: Shrill chirrups and burbling calls. HABITAT: Lowlands to highlands in a range of habitats, including dense forest near breeding sites. DISTRIBUTION: Resident in Sumatra, Java and Borneo.

6 EDIBLE-NEST SWIFTLET *Aerodramus fuciphagus* 12cm FIELD NOTES: Gregarious, often in the company of other swifts and swallows. VOICE: A loud, metallic *zwing.* HABITAT: Open areas, offshore islets, forest and mangroves. DISTRIBUTION: Resident in Sumatra, Java, Borneo, the Lesser Sundas and islands in the Flores Sea.

7 GERMAIN'S SWIFTLET *Aerodramus germani* 11–12cm FIELD NOTES: Gregarious, often flying alongside other swifts and swallows. VOICE: Various *chip* notes, otherwise similar to the previous species. HABITAT: Open areas, islets, coasts and over forest. DISTRIBUTION: Resident in Borneo and the Philippines.

8 ASIAN PALM SWIFT *Cypsiurus balasiensis* 13cm FIELD NOTES: Slim. Often seen in small, fast-flying groups; flies with fluttering wing-beats interspersed with short glides. VOICE: A trilling *te-he-he-he-he* or *tititee.* HABITAT: Open country, cultivation and urban areas, usually with nearby palms. DISTRIBUTION: Resident in Sumatra, Java, Bali, Borneo, the Philippines and Sulawesi.

9 FORK-TAILED SWIFT (PACIFIC SWIFT) *Apus pacificus* 17–18cm FIELD NOTES: Forages over forest and hilltops, coasts and urban areas. Pale fringes below, especially on belly and undertail-coverts. VOICE: A high-pitched *skree-ee-ee.* HABITAT: Forested regions, and open and urban areas. DISTRIBUTION: Winter visitor or passage migrant to the region; possibly resident in the N Philippines.

10 HOUSE SWIFT *Apus nipalensis* 15cm FIELD NOTES: Has a fluttering, bat-like flight, combined with short glides. Often nests in groups under building eaves, bridges or cliff faces. VOICE: A shrill, whickering scream. HABITAT: Urban, open, mountain and occasionally forested areas, often near water. DISTRIBUTION: Resident in Sumatra, Borneo, the Philippines and Sulawesi.

40 SWIFTS; TREESWIFTS

1 PHILIPPINE SPINETAIL (PHILIPPINE SPINE-TAILED SWIFT, PHILIPPINE NEEDLETAIL) *Mearnsia picina* 14cm FIELD NOTES: Usually seen alone or in small groups, foraging above forests or nearby cleared areas. Sometimes seen with other swift species flying low, through passes or along logging tracks. VOICE: Unrecorded. HABITAT: Forest areas. DISTRIBUTION: Endemic to the Philippines.

2 SILVER-RUMPED SPINETAIL *Raphidura leucopygialis* 11cm FIELD NOTES: Flight is fluttery and erratic. Usually seen singly or in small groups. VOICE: A high-pitched *tirrr-tirrr* and a rapid chattering. HABITAT: Primary and secondary growth and plantations; often close to water, including estuarine areas. DISTRIBUTION: Resident in Sumatra, Java and Borneo.

3 WHITE-THROATED NEEDLETAIL (NEEDLE-TAILED SWIFT) *Hirundapus caudacutus* 21–22cm FIELD NOTES: Flight is fast and powerful. Often migrates with other swift species. White horseshoe shape from undertail to flanks. VOICE: A weak, high-pitched twittering. HABITAT: Forested and open areas. DISTRIBUTION: Passage migrant in Java and Borneo.

4 SILVER-BACKED NEEDLETAIL *Hirundapus cochinchinensis* 20–22cm FIELD NOTES: Usually encountered over forests, in small groups. Fast and powerful flight. White horseshoe shape from undertail to flanks. VOICE: A soft, rippling *trp-trp-trp-trp-trp*. HABITAT: Forested regions from lowlands to mountains, especially near water. DISTRIBUTION: Winter visitor to Sumatra and Java.

5 BROWN-BACKED NEEDLETAIL *Hirundapus giganteus* 23–25cm FIELD NOTES: Typical powerful flight, wings making a whooshing sound when overhead. White horseshoe shape from undertail to flanks. Usually seen hawking insects over forest, grassland or marshes. Drinks at pools or rivers by scooping up water in flight. VOICE: A slow, rippling trill, a squeaky *cirrwiet cirrwiet* and a thin *chiek*. HABITAT: Forested and open areas. DISTRIBUTION: Resident in Sumatra, Java, Bali, Borneo and the W Philippines.

6 PURPLE NEEDLETAIL *Hirundapus celebensis* 25cm FIELD NOTES: Very fast flight, wings producing a jet-like 'swoosh' if heard at close range. White horseshoe shape from undertail to flanks. VOICE: Unrecorded. HABITAT: Forest in lowlands and hills, open country and urban areas. DISTRIBUTION: Resident in the Philippines and N Sulawesi.

7 GREY-RUMPED TREESWIFT *Hemiprocne longipennis* 21–25cm FIELD NOTES: Makes aerial sorties, from a favourite bare branch in the tree canopy. Usually seen singly, in pairs or in small groups. VOICE: A harsh, piercing *ki ki-ki-kew*, a staccato *chi-chi-chi-chew* and a *too-it*. HABITAT: Well-exposed bare branches in forests and open woodland areas. DISTRIBUTION: Resident in Sumatra, Java, Bali, Borneo, the Philippines (Sulu Archipelago), W Lesser Sundas (Lombok), Sulawesi and the Sula Islands.

8 MOUSTACHED TREESWIFT *Hemiprocne mystacea* 28–31cm FIELD NOTES: Usually found in pairs or loose groups, at dusk may form larger flocks. Perches on open branches to make aerial sallies after flying insects, generally more active at twilight. VOICE: Calls include a short, hard *skip* and a buzzing *krerr*; in flight, utters a high-pitched, down-slurred *kiiee*. HABITAT: Open areas with trees, forest edges, riverine areas, mangroves and coastal woodland. DISTRIBUTION: Resident in the Moluccas, except the Kai Islands.

9 WHISKERED TREESWIFT *Hemiprocne comata* 15–17cm FIELD NOTES: Spends much time perched on exposed branches, making short flights to capture insects. In flight from below, shows a dark underwing with a white trailing edge. VOICE: Variously recorded as a high-pitched *she-she-she-she-shoo-shee*, a squeaky *peoop* or *peeoop peoop-poo* and a *cheer-ter cheer-ter*; also utters a plaintive *chew*. HABITAT: Forest edges and clearings. DISTRIBUTION: Resident in Sumatra, Borneo and the Philippines, except Palawan.

41 OWLS

1 MINAHASSA MASKED OWL *Tyto inexspectata* 30cm FIELD NOTES: Generally seen singly or in pairs, very rarely observed. VOICE: Recorded as being similar to Sulawesi Masked Owl, but weaker and less deep. HABITAT: Primary and lightly disturbed hill and lower montane forest. DISTRIBUTION: Endemic to Sulawesi.

2 TALIABU MASKED OWL *Tyto nigrobrunnea* 32cm FIELD NOTES: Often considered a race of the Minahassa Masked Owl; actions presumed to be similar. VOICE: Only records are of a hissing. HABITAT: Rainforest and selectively logged lowland forest. DISTRIBUTION: Endemic to Taliabu in the Sula Islands.

3 SULAWESI MASKED OWL *Tyto rosenbergii* 43–46cm FIELD NOTES: Rarely seen during daylight hours. Generally hunts in clearings, cultivation and forest edges. VOICE: A hoarse, dry, almost hissing screech. HABITAT: Lightly wooded cultivation, tall dead trees in open country, grassland, forest edges, plantations and suburban areas. DISTRIBUTION: Endemic to Sulawesi.

4 LESSER MASKED OWL (MOLUCCAN MASKED OWL) *Tyto sororcula* 29–31cm FIELD NOTES: Little recorded. *T. s. cayelii* (4b) occurs on Buru; *T. s. almae* (4c) is found on Seram. Some authorities believe this species to be a race of the Australian Masked Owl *T. novaehollandiae*. VOICE: Unrecorded. HABITAT: Rainforest, and primary and mature monsoon forest. DISTRIBUTION: Resident in the S Moluccas and E Lesser Sundas.

5 BARN OWL *Tyto alba* 33–35cm FIELD NOTES: Usually nocturnal but can be seen hunting during daylight hours; hunts close to the ground with an undulating flight and much hovering before dropping onto prey. Some authorities split the species into two, the Eastern Barn Owl and Western Barn Owl, but it seems more work needs to be undertaken before all agree. VOICE: A shrill, hoarse *shrrreeeeee*; also various chuckling, snoring and hissing sounds. HABITAT: Cultivation, open country, forest remnants with nearby grassland or marshland, mangroves, and suburban and urban areas. DISTRIBUTION: Resident in Sumatra, Java, Bali, Borneo (introduced), the Lesser Sundas and islands in the Flores Sea.

6 EASTERN GRASS OWL *Tyto longimembris* 32–38cm FIELD NOTES: Crepuscular and nocturnal. When quartering an area searching for prey, flight is low with frequent gliding and hovering. VOICE: Similar to Barn Owl. HABITAT: Grassland. DISTRIBUTION: Resident in Borneo, the Philippines, Sulawesi and the W Lesser Sundas.

7 ORIENTAL BAY OWL *Phodilus badius* 29cm FIELD NOTES: Nocturnal. Often seen perching in saplings near the forest floor, presumably to hunt for rats; also hunts under the canopy with a fast, twisting flight as it negotiates vertical tree trunks. VOICE: A series of eerie whistles with an upward inflection, which rise and then fade away. HABITAT: Mainly primary lowland and hill forest, occasionally montane forest. DISTRIBUTION: Resident in Sumatra, Java, Bali, Borneo and possibly the Philippines.

8 SHORT-EARED OWL *Asio flammeus* 37cm FIELD NOTES: Generally active during daylight hours. Quarters hunting area in a low flight, often hovering before dropping onto prey. VOICE: Generally silent, but may utter various barking sounds. HABITAT: Open country with scattered bushes, scrubby hillsides, and coastal grassland and marshes. DISTRIBUTION: Winter visitor or winter vagrant to Borneo and the Philippines.

42 SCOPS OWLS

1 GIANT SCOPS OWL *Otus gurneyi* 30cm FIELD NOTES: Usually forages high in the understorey. Roosts during the day in the fork of tree trunks. VOICE: A loud *wokkk* or *waookk*, or a rasping *owwwkkk*. HABITAT: Forest and forest edges, from lowlands to mountains; also recorded in small clumps of trees in grassland. DISTRIBUTION: Endemic to the S Philippines.

2 RINJANI SCOPS OWL *Otus jolandae* 22cm FIELD NOTES: Presumed to be similar to other scops owls, resting in cover by day; calls from early evening and throughout the night. VOICE: A single, clear whistle. HABITAT: Forest, from lowland to foothills; also recorded in forest patches in more open country. DISTRIBUTION: Endemic to Lombok in the W Lesser Sundas.

3 WHITE-FRONTED SCOPS OWL *Otus sagittatus* 25–28cm FIELD NOTES: Nocturnal. Little recorded information. VOICE: A hollow, whistled *hooo*. HABITAT: Lowland forest. DISTRIBUTION: Possibly resident in Sumatra.

4 REDDISH SCOPS OWL *Otus rufescens* 20cm FIELD NOTES: Hunts low down in the understorey, otherwise little recorded information. VOICE: A hollow *hoooo* that fades at the finish. HABITAT: Lowland forest. DISTRIBUTION: Resident in Sumatra, Java and Borneo.

5 MOUNTAIN SCOPS OWL *Otus spilocephalus* 17–21cm FIELD NOTES: Nocturnal. Hunts beneath the tree canopy, reported as keeping low to the ground. Roosts by day in a tree hollow. *O. s. luciae* (main illustration) is found in Borneo; *O. s. vandewateri* (5b) occurs in Sumatra. VOICE: A soft, far-carrying *plew plew* or *hoo hoo*. HABITAT: Moist montane forest. DISTRIBUTION: Resident in Sumatra and Borneo.

6 SIMEULUE SCOPS OWL *Otus umbra* 18cm FIELD NOTES: Poorly studied, with little recorded information. VOICE: Two steady notes followed by a higher, rising, inflected note, *pook-pook-pupook*; female gives a long whine. HABITAT: Remnant forest patches, forest edges and clove plantations. DISTRIBUTION: Endemic to Simeulue Island off NW Sumatra.

7 JAVAN SCOPS OWL *Otus angelinae* 20cm FIELD NOTES: Secretive; little recorded information. VOICE: Calls include a soft *wook-wook*, a hissing *tch-tschschsch* and a *poo-poo* alarm call. HABITAT: Montane forest. DISTRIBUTION: Endemic to W Java.

8 MANTANANI SCOPS OWL *Otus mantananensis* 18cm FIELD NOTES: Hunts at woodland edges and in clearings. VOICE: A goose-like honk followed by three gruff, lower-pitched, gruff notes. HABITAT: Lowland and foothill forest, woodland and plantations. DISTRIBUTION: Resident on Mantanani Island off NW Borneo and on islets south of Palawan.

9 SANGIHE SCOPS OWL *Otus collari* 19–20cm FIELD NOTES: Little recorded information. VOICE: A high-pitched, downslurred, fluty whistle, *kleeeeer*. HABITAT: Forest, mixed plantations, secondary growth and agricultural areas with trees and bushes. DISTRIBUTION: Endemic to the Sangihe Islands, north of Sulawesi.

10 ENGGANO SCOPS OWL *Otus enganensis* 20cm FIELD NOTES: Little recorded information. VOICE: A harsh croak, reported as similar to Moluccan Scops Owl (Plate 43). HABITAT: Little recorded, presumed to be wooded areas and forest edges. DISTRIBUTION: Endemic to Enggano Island off SW Sumatra.

5
luciae

5b
vandewateri

brown morph

rufous morph

43 SCOPS OWLS

1 LUZON SCOPS OWL *Otus longicornis* 18cm FIELD NOTES: Can be quite approachable; usually perches in the understorey. VOICE: A loud, far-carrying *whoo-hooo whoo-hooo*. HABITAT: Submontane and montane mossy forest, mixed pine forest and rainforest. DISTRIBUTION: Endemic to Luzon in the N Philippines.

2 MINDORO SCOPS OWL *Otus mindorensis* 17cm FIELD NOTES: Quite common in suitable habitats. Roosts by day in tree hollows or dense foliage. VOICE: A soft, delicate *po-wo* or *wo-wo*. HABITAT: Montane forest. DISTRIBUTION: Endemic to Mindoro in the N Philippines.

3 MINDANAO SCOPS OWL *Otus mirus* 19–20cm FIELD NOTES: Little recorded information, apparently rare. VOICE: A far-carrying, whistled *paww piaww*. HABITAT: Mid-montane and montane forest. DISTRIBUTION: Endemic to the S Philippines.

4 RYUKU SCOPS OWL (ELEGANT SCOPS OWL) *Otus elegans* 20cm FIELD NOTES: Nocturnal. Hunts along forest edges. VOICE: Various, reported as a repeated, hoarse, cough-like *uhu*, *kuru* or *u-kuruk*, or a soft *poo-pup* or *pooo poo-pup*. HABITAT: Dense evergreen forest. DISTRIBUTION: Resident in the N Philippines (Batan, Sabtang and Calayan islands).

5 ORIENTAL SCOPS OWL *Otus sunia* 18cm FIELD NOTES: Nocturnal. Hunts from a perch or in flight, usually along forest edges. VOICE: A toad-like *wuk-tuk-tah*, *wut-chu-chraaii* or similar. HABITAT: Broadleaved evergreen forest, mixed deciduous forest, forest edges, clearings and sometimes gardens. DISTRIBUTION: Vagrant or winter visitor to Sumatra.

6 SULAWESI SCOPS OWL *Otus manadensis* 21cm FIELD NOTES: Usually seen singly or in pairs, generally hiding in dense foliage. VOICE: A clear, plaintive whistle with a rising inflection. HABITAT: Primary and tall secondary lowland and hill forest, forest edges, lightly wooded cultivation, scrub and remnant forest patches. DISTRIBUTION: Endemic to Sulawesi.

7 SULA SCOPS OWL *Otus sulaensis* 20cm FIELD NOTES: Little recorded information; thought to hunt for insects and other invertebrates and small vertebrates. VOICE: A series of rapid, resonant notes or a long, churring song. HABITAT: Primary and disturbed secondary forest. DISTRIBUTION: Endemic to the Sula Islands.

8 SIAU SCOPS OWL *Otus siaoensis* 19cm FIELD NOTES: Little recorded information. Known from only a single species collected in 1866. VOICE: Unrecorded. HABITAT: Forest. DISTRIBUTION: Endemic to Siau Island, north of Sulawesi.

9 MOLUCCAN SCOPS OWL *Otus magicus* 21cm FIELD NOTES: Usually encountered singly or in pairs perched high in trees; feeds on invertebrates and small vertebrates. *O. m. albiventris* (9b) occurs in the Lesser Sundas. VOICE: A harsh, raven-like croak. HABITAT: Primary forest, coastal swamp forest and secondary forest. DISTRIBUTION: Resident in the Moluccas and W and C Lesser Sundas.

10 FLORES SCOPS OWL *Otus alfredi* 19–21cm FIELD NOTES: Little recorded information. Known from very few specimens. VOICE: Unrecorded. HABITAT: Presumed to occur in montane forest. DISTRIBUTION: Endemic to Flores Island in the Lesser Sundas.

brown
morph

rufous
morph

9b
albiventris

44 SCOPS OWLS; OWLETS

1 RAJAH SCOPS OWL *Otus brookii* 23cm FIELD NOTES: Little recorded information. Probably rare. Feeds mainly on insects. VOICE: A monotonous, explosive *whaooo*. HABITAT: Montane rainforest. DISTRIBUTION: Resident in Sumatra and Borneo.

2 SUNDA SCOPS OWL *Otus lempiji* 20cm FIELD NOTES: Hunts from a perch, dropping onto insects and occasionally small birds. VOICE: A soft, upward-inflected *wooup*. HABITAT: Secondary forest, forest edges, plantations, open areas with scattered trees, parks and well-wooded gardens. DISTRIBUTION: Resident in Sumatra, Java, Bali and Borneo.

3 MENTAWAI SCOPS OWL *Otus mentawi* 20cm FIELD NOTES: Occasionally perches on exposed branches. VOICE: A series of *po-po* notes followed by descending, single *po* notes. HABITAT: Lowland forest and secondary growth. DISTRIBUTION: Endemic to islands off W Sumatra.

4 PALAWAN SCOPS OWL *Otus fuliginosus* 20cm FIELD NOTES: Keeps to the dense understorey, quite low to the ground. VOICE: A deep, harsh, growling *krarr-kruarr, wach grarhrhrh* or *wach waaarwwwhhh*. HABITAT: Forest, secondary growth and trees in mixed cultivation in lowland. DISTRIBUTION: Endemic to Palawan in the Philippines.

5 PHILIPPINE SCOPS OWL *Otus megalotis* 23–28cm FIELD NOTES: Usually seen singly or in pairs in the forest understorey. VOICE: A harsh *oiik oiik oiik oiik*. HABITAT: Forest and forest edges. DISTRIBUTION: Endemic to the N Philippines.

6 EVERETT'S SCOPS OWL *Otus everetti* 22–23cm FIELD NOTES: Occurs singly or in pairs; presumed to feed on invertebrates. VOICE: A loud, repeated *wkuach*. HABITAT: Humid lowland forest, forest edges and secondary growth. DISTRIBUTION: Endemic to the S Philippines.

7 NEGROS SCOPS OWL *Otus nigrorum* 20cm FIELD NOTES: Little recorded information; presumably similar to the two previous species. VOICE: A series of rapid *quick-quick* notes. HABITAT: Dense lowland and montane tropical forest. DISTRIBUTION: Endemic to the C Philippines.

8 WALLACE'S SCOPS OWL *Otus silvicola* 23–25cm FIELD NOTES: Generally seen singly or in pairs; perches high, often in a concealed position. VOICE: A gruff *rrow* and a steady series of *whumph* notes. HABITAT: Primary and tall secondary hill and montane forest, forest edges and degraded forest, cultivation and around human habitation. DISTRIBUTION: Endemic to the W Lesser Sundas (Sumbawa and Flores).

9 COLLARED OWLET *Glaucidium brodiei* 16–17cm FIELD NOTES: Crepuscular and diurnal. Bold, fierce hunter, seen taking birds as large as itself. Has eye-like markings on back of head. VOICE: A mellow, bell-like *hoo hoo-hoo hooo* or *toot-tootoot-toot*. HABITAT: Broadleaved evergreen hill forest. DISTRIBUTION: Resident in Sumatra and Borneo.

10 JAVAN OWLET *Glaucidium castanopterum* 24cm FIELD NOTES: Mainly nocturnal, but sometimes active by day. Pounces on prey from a perch, including insects, mice, small birds and occasionally small reptiles. VOICE: A rapid trill, descending in pitch and increasing in volume. HABITAT: Primary and secondary forest, and trees in suburban areas. DISTRIBUTION: Endemic to Java.

rufous morph

rufous morph

rufous morph

45 OWLS; HAWK OWLS

1 BARRED EAGLE OWL *Bubo sumatranus* 40–46cm FIELD NOTES: Nocturnal and crepuscular. Hunts from a perch, from where it drops onto small mammals and insects. Hops when on the ground. VOICE: A loud *whooa-who whooa-who*, also a quacking *gagagagogogo*. HABITAT: Lowland and hill forest. DISTRIBUTION: Resident in Sumatra, Java, Bali and Borneo.

2 PHILIPPINE EAGLE OWL *Bubo philippensis* 50–51cm FIELD NOTES: Little recorded information. Reported roosting in trees by day; presumed to prey on small mammals or birds. *B. p. mindanensis* (2b) occurs in the S Philippines. VOICE: A deep, resonating *hoo-hoo-hoo…* HABITAT: Forest and forest edges, often near water. DISTRIBUTION: Endemic to the Philippines.

3 BUFFY FISH OWL *Ketupa ketupu* 38–44cm FIELD NOTES: Captures fish in its talons by swooping from a perch or walking and wading into shallow water. VOICE: A loud, monotonous *kootookookootook…*, a ringing *pof pof pof*, a musical *to-whee to-whee*, and various hisses, mews and shrieks. HABITAT: Along rivers in primary forest, coastal forest and rice fields in hills. DISTRIBUTION: Resident in Sumatra, Java and Borneo.

4 SPOTTED WOOD OWL *Strix seloputo* 45–47cm FIELD NOTES: Hunts from a perch, preying mainly on small rodents, small birds and insects. *S. s. wiepkeni* (4b) is found in the W Philippines. VOICE: A deep *who*, which usually starts with a rolling *huhuhuwhuwhu*; also a resonant, rising *hoop-hoong* and a deep growling. HABITAT: Lowland forest, mangroves and clusters of trees near human habitation. DISTRIBUTION: Resident in Sumatra, Java and the W Philippines.

5 BROWN WOOD OWL *Strix leptogrammica* 47–53cm FIELD NOTES: Nocturnal. Shy, resting during the day in dense foliage. *S. l. niasensis* (5b) occurs on Nias Island off W Sumatra. VOICE: A low, hollow *tok tu-hoo tok-tu-hoo*; also eerie shrieks and chuckles. HABITAT: All types of forest, from coasts to mountains. DISTRIBUTION: Resident in Sumatra, Java and Borneo.

6 BARKING OWL *Ninox connivens* 40–45cm FIELD NOTES: Usually seen singly or in pairs. Roosts during the day, in foliage in the mid-storey and canopy. Hunts and calls from an open perch. VOICE: A pair of dog-like barking notes, *wuff-wuff*, given by the male; female utters a higher-pitched *wok-wok*. HABITAT: Woodland, scrub and forest edges, often near watercourses and swamps. DISTRIBUTION: Resident in the N Moluccas.

7 SUMBA BOOBOOK *Ninox rudolfi* 35–40cm FIELD NOTES: Seen singly or in pairs, sometimes in small dispersed groups. Occasionally seen during daylight hours. VOICE: A series of monotonous, cough-like notes, uttered continuously. HABITAT: Primary and tall secondary forest, forest edges and remnant forest patches. DISTRIBUTION: Endemic to Sumba in the W Lesser Sundas.

1

2

2b
mindanensis

3

4

4b
wiepkeni

5

5b
niasensis

6

7

46 HAWK OWLS

1 TOGIAN HAWK OWL (TOGIAN BOOBOOK) *Ninox burhani* 25cm
FIELD NOTES: Usually seen in pairs, but singles and threes both recorded. Nocturnal; roosts in thick foliage. VOICE: A gruff, low-pitched *kok-ko-ro-ok*, usually repeated and occasionally preceded by a single croaking note. HABITAT: Disturbed and degraded lowland forest.
DISTRIBUTION: Endemic to the Togian Islands off Sulawesi.

2 SOUTHERN BOOBOOK *Ninox boobook* 27cm FIELD NOTES: Occurs singly or in pairs. Roosts by day in thick foliage. *N. b. fusca* (main illustration) occurs on Timor; *N. b. ocellata* (2b) is found on Sawu Island in the Lesser Sundas. VOICE: A simple *bru-bruk*. HABITAT: Primary and tall secondary lowland forest, monsoon hill forest and monsoon woodland.
DISTRIBUTION: Resident in the E Lesser Sundas and the Kai Islands in the S Moluccas.

3 BROWN HAWK OWL *Ninox scutulata* 32–33cm FIELD NOTES: Crepuscular and nocturnal. Recorded hunting flying insects in the manner of a nightjar, sometimes in groups. Tends to frequent the same perch over a prolonged period. VOICE: A haunting *whu-up*, *pung-ok*, *oo-uk* or *coo-oo*. HABITAT: Open forest, forest edges, woodland and wooded cultivation. DISTRIBUTION: Resident in, and winter visitor to, Sumatra, W Java, Borneo and the Philippines; winter visitor to Wallacea.

4 CHOCOLATE BOOBOOK *Ninox randi* 27–33cm FIELD NOTES: Formerly considered a subspecies of the Brown Hawk Owl; actions and habits presumed to be similar. VOICE: A series of low-pitched *whoop* notes. HABITAT: Primary lowland rainforest, secondary forest and mangroves. DISTRIBUTION: Endemic to the Philippines except Palawan.

5 LUZON HAWK OWL (PHILIPPINE HAWK OWL) *Ninox philippensis* 20cm
FIELD NOTES: Roosts during daylight in the darker parts of the forest. Preys on insects and rodents. VOICE: A series of *cuk* notes, interspersed with softer *boo* or *boo-boo* notes, starting quietly, then accelerating and getting louder. HABITAT: Primary and secondary rainforest, and remnant forest patches. DISTRIBUTION: Endemic to the N and C Philippines.

6 SULU HAWK OWL *Ninox reyi* 19–20cm FIELD NOTES: Formerly regarded as a subspecies of the Luzon Hawk Owl; actions presumed to be similar. VOICE: A hollow, wooden knocking in short phrases, starting with low *clucks*, getting louder and higher in pitch, then slowing and dropping in pitch, before becoming louder and higher pitched again. HABITAT: Subtropical or tropical moist lowland forest, also montane forest.
DISTRIBUTION: Endemic to the Sulu Archipelago in the Philippines.

7 MINDANAO HAWK OWL *Ninox spilocephala* 18cm FIELD NOTES: Recently split from the Luzon Hawk Owl; actions presumed to be similar. Main prey probably insects. VOICE: A long series of low-pitched, mellow, dove-like double notes. HABITAT: Primary lowland rainforest and secondary forest. DISTRIBUTION: Endemic to the S Philippines.

8 MINDORO HAWK OWL *Ninox mindorensis* 20cm FIELD NOTES: Recently split from the Luzon Hawk Owl; presumably nocturnal and roosts in dense cover. VOICE: A series of high-pitched whistles, which often start with high, tittering toots. HABITAT: Primary and secondary forest, remnant forest patches and open woodland. DISTRIBUTION: Endemic to Mindoro in the N Philippines.

9 ROMBLON HAWK OWL *Ninox spilonotus* 26cm FIELD NOTES: Formerly considered a subspecies of the Luzon Hawk Owl; actions presumed to be similar. VOICE: A series of short, hoarse whistles that fall in pitch, starting slowly and then changing into three- or four-note versions. HABITAT: Remnants of primary and tall secondary forest. DISTRIBUTION: Endemic to Sibuyan and Tablas islands in the C Philippines.

10 CEBU HAWK OWL *Ninox rumseyi* 25cm FIELD NOTES: Recently split from the Luzon Hawk Owl; habits presumed to be similar. Preys on rats and small birds. VOICE: Gruff, staccato *chucks* and plaintive, down-slurred notes with occasional tree-frog-like *bwick* notes; also recorded are clear, bell-like *duit* notes and hoarse screeches. HABITAT: Forests.
DISTRIBUTION: Endemic to Cebu in the C Philippines.

1

2

fusca

2b *ocellata*

3

4

5

6

7

8

9

10

47 HAWK OWLS

1 CAMIGUIN HAWK OWL *Ninox leventisi* 25cm FIELD NOTES: Formerly considered a subspecies of the Luzon Hawk Owl (Plate 46); actions presumed to be similar. VOICE: Duets with short, low-pitched strophes, repeated and with many rapid, irregular, barking notes per strophe. HABITAT: Forest and forest edges. DISTRIBUTION: Endemic to Camiguin Island in the S Philippines.

2 OCHRE-BELLIED HAWK OWL *Ninox ochracea* 29cm FIELD NOTES: Usually seen singly or in pairs; recorded hunting from horizontal branches in the mid-storey or lower canopy, usually overlooking open areas or forest roads. VOICE: A loud series of hoarse *kau* notes that slows near the end, and including *wuu kau* notes as it develops. HABITAT: Primary and tall secondary lowland, hill and lower montane forest; also recorded in riverine forest. DISTRIBUTION: Endemic to Sulawesi.

3 CINNABAR BOOBOOK *Ninox ios* 22cm FIELD NOTES: Nocturnal. Reported to use an exposed branch to make short sallies to capture flying insects. VOICE: A hard *wruck-wruck*. HABITAT: Mid-elevation forest. DISTRIBUTION: Endemic to Sulawesi.

4 HANTU HAWK OWL (SERAM BOOBOOK) *Ninox squamipila* 27–39cm FIELD NOTES: Perches in the mid-storey and lower canopy, often on exposed branches or stumps. Roosts during daylight in dense foliage. *N. s. hantu* (4b) occurs on Buru Island in the S Moluccas. VOICE: A far-carrying, mellow *wooo wooo wu wu wu wu*. HABITAT: Primary and tall secondary forest, selectively logged forest and forest edges in lowlands and hills. DISTRIBUTION: Endemic to Seram and Buru in the S Moluccas.

5 HALMAHERA BOOBOOK *Ninox hypogramma* 27–39cm FIELD NOTES: Formerly considered to be a race of the Hantu Hawk Owl; actions presumed to be similar. VOICE: Gruff two-note phrases, evenly pitched and far-carrying. HABITAT: Tropical lowland rainforest and tall secondary forest. DISTRIBUTION: Endemic to Halmahera and Bacan in the N Moluccas.

6 TANIMBAR BOOBOOK *Ninox forbesi* 30cm FIELD NOTES: Formerly considered a race of the Hantu Hawk Owl; habits presumed to be similar. VOICE: A *ku-kuk ku-kuk ku-kuk*. HABITAT: Primary and tall secondary lowland and hill forest. DISTRIBUTION: Endemic to the Tanimbar Islands in the E Lesser Sundas.

7 CHRISTMAS ISLAND HAWK OWL (CHRISTMAS BOOBOOK) *Ninox natalis* 26–29cm FIELD NOTES: During daylight, hides in dense thickets or thick foliage in the mid-canopy of trees. Preys on insects, small birds and rats. VOICE: A simple *bru-bruk*, repeated many times; also a low, barking *ow-ow-ow*. HABITAT: Tropical rainforest, monsoon forest and scrub. DISTRIBUTION: Endemic to Christmas Island.

8 SPECKLED HAWK OWL (SPECKLED BOOBOOK) *Ninox punctulata* 27cm FIELD NOTES: Usually encountered singly or in pairs. Has been reported foraging along small streams in forests. VOICE: A long series of *toi toi toi toi* or *wher wher wher wher* notes, rising and accelerating before ending with a lower-pitched *toi*; also reported is a *toi-toi-toi-seeeet*. HABITAT: Primary lowland and hill forest, forest edges and tall secondary forest; occasionally found in cultivation near human habitation. DISTRIBUTION: Endemic to Sulawesi.

9 LITTLE SUMBA HAWK OWL *Ninox sumbaensis* 23cm FIELD NOTES: Little recorded information; presumed to be similar to other hawk owls. VOICE: A subdued, flute-like *duu* or *puu*. HABITAT: Remnant patches of primary forest, and disturbed primary and secondary forest. DISTRIBUTION: Endemic to Sumba Island in the W Lesser Sundas.

48 FROGMOUTHS

1 LARGE FROGMOUTH *Batrachostomus auritus* 40–43cm FIELD NOTES: Nocturnal. During daylight, stays motionless in the tree canopy. Makes sallies from a perch to take insects. VOICE: A tremulous *prrrrooh prrrrooh prrrrooh…* HABITAT: Lowland forest. DISTRIBUTION: Resident in Sumatra and Borneo.

2 DULIT FROGMOUTH *Batrachostomus harterti* 34–37cm FIELD NOTES: Little recorded information; presumed to be nocturnal, with actions similar to the previous species. VOICE: A repeated, loud, trumpeting *whooooooaaah.* HABITAT: Submontane forest. DISTRIBUTION: Endemic to Borneo.

3 PHILIPPINE FROGMOUTH *Batrachostomus septimus* 23cm FIELD NOTES: Nocturnal; more often heard than seen. Typical frogmouth habits; perches upright, resembling a broken branch, and feeds by making aerial sallies to capture flying insects or by gleaning insects or other invertebrates from leaves. VOICE: A harsh, growling *kaaoo, kaaww, paaww* or *pa-paaww.* HABITAT: Forest and forest edges. DISTRIBUTION: Endemic to the Philippines.

4 GOULD'S FROGMOUTH *Batrachostomus stellatus* 21–25cm FIELD NOTES: Nocturnal. Sits motionless during daylight hours; little other recorded information. VOICE: Male utters an eerie, weak *woah-weeo,* occasionally just a *weeo;* female utters a growling, rapid, high-pitched yapping. HABITAT: Primary lowland and hill forest. DISTRIBUTION: Resident in Sumatra and Borneo.

5 SHORT-TAILED FROGMOUTH *Batrachostomus poliolophus* 20–22cm FIELD NOTES: Little recorded; actions presumed to be similar to Philippine Frogmouth. VOICE: Unrecorded. HABITAT: Submontane primary forest and mixed pine forest. DISTRIBUTION: Endemic to Sumatra.

6 BORNEAN FROGMOUTH *Batrachostomus mixtus* 20–22cm FIELD NOTES: Formerly considered to be a race of the Short-tailed Frogmouth; actions presumed to be similar to Philippine Frogmouth. VOICE: A pure, whistled *pwau* or *weeow,* repeated every 2–3 seconds. HABITAT: Submontane and montane forest. DISTRIBUTION: Endemic to Borneo.

7 BLYTH'S FROGMOUTH *Batrachostomus affinis* 19–24cm FIELD NOTES: During the day, sits very upright with beak pointing skywards, often close to the ground. Feeding actions probably much like other smaller frogmouths. VOICE: Male gives a plaintive whistle, female utters a maniacal laugh. HABITAT: Dense lowland rainforest. DISTRIBUTION: Resident in Sumatra and Borneo.

brown morph

chestnut morph

dark morph

chestnut
morph

49 FROGMOUTHS; NIGHTJARS

1 JAVAN FROGMOUTH *Batrachostomus javensis* 19–25cm FIELD NOTES: Typical frogmouth. Sits upright with beak pointing skyward while resting in the daytime, usually not far from the ground. Presumably makes sallies to capture invertebrate prey. VOICE: Hoarse *gwaa* notes, descending in pitch; also various barks, trills and whistles. HABITAT: Moist lowland and hill forest. DISTRIBUTION: Endemic to Java.

2 PALAWAN FROGMOUTH *Batrachostomus chaseni* 21–22cm FIELD NOTES: Nocturnal. Little recorded; actions presumed to be much as other smaller frogmouths. VOICE: A plaintive, whistled *pheuuuuuuuuuuuu*, also a harsh, mournful, growling *kawwrreerr*. HABITAT: Forest and secondary growth, including dense tangles of vines and bamboo. DISTRIBUTION: Endemic to the W Philippines.

3 SUNDA FROGMOUTH *Batrachostomus cornutus* 23–28cm FIELD NOTES: Plumage very variable. Reported resting during the day on low branches, sometimes with bill wide open (due to heat?). VOICE: A descending series of *gwaa* notes. HABITAT: Secondary forest and forest edges. DISTRIBUTION: Resident in Sumatra, Java and Borneo.

4 MOLUCCAN OWLET-NIGHTJAR *Aegotheles crinifrons* 29cm FIELD NOTES: Encountered singly, in pairs and occasionally in small groups. Feeds on small flying insects, which are captured during short sallies from perches in the mid-storey. VOICE: A weak, upslurred scream, followed by three more unhurried screams on the same pitch; when alarmed, issues various manic screams, cackles and cat-like yowling. HABITAT: Primary and tall secondary lowland and hill forest, forest edges and selectively logged forest; occasionally in lightly wooded cultivation and coconut plantations. DISTRIBUTION: Endemic to the N Moluccas.

5 SATANIC NIGHTJAR (HEINRICH'S NIGHTJAR) *Eurostopodus diabolicus* 26cm FIELD NOTES: Feeds aerially, presumably mainly in twilight and at night, around small openings or breaks in forests. VOICE: A bubbling trill and a *plip-plop*. HABITAT: Primary and selectively logged montane forest. DISTRIBUTION: Endemic to Sulawesi.

6 SPOTTED NIGHTJAR *Eurostopodus argus* 30cm FIELD NOTES: Found singly, in pairs or in small groups. Roosts by day on the ground. In flight, shows a white patch on four outermost primaries. VOICE: A rapid series of ascending *whaw* notes, followed by a bubbling gobble. HABITAT: Savannah, grassland and rainforest edges. DISTRIBUTION: Winter visitor to the E Lesser Sundas.

7 MALAYSIAN EARED NIGHTJAR *Lyncornis temminckii* 25–28cm FIELD NOTES: Forages in flight over open areas, forest clearings, forest edges, cultivation and water. VOICE: A repeated *tut-wee-ow*. HABITAT: Lowland primary and secondary forest, and secondary growth; in Borneo, favours dipterocarp forest, alluvial forest, scrubland, grassland, grassy swampland and coastal vegetation. DISTRIBUTION: Resident in Sumatra and Borneo.

8 GREAT EARED NIGHTJAR *Lyncornis macrotis* 40cm FIELD NOTES: Forages in twilight over forest and forest clearings, flying with leisurely wing-beats, much like a small harrier. VOICE: A wailing *pee-wheeoo wheeoo wheeoo*, given in flight and when perched. HABITAT: Forest and forest edges. DISTRIBUTION: Resident on Simeulue Island off NW Sumatra, the Philippines, Sulawesi and the Sula Islands.

1   ♂   ♀

grey morph

♂

2

brown morph

♂

4

dark morph

rufous morph

3

♀

5

6

7

8

50 NIGHTJARS

1 GREY NIGHTJAR *Caprimulgus jotaka* 28–32cm FIELD NOTES: Crepuscular and nocturnal. Captures insects in aerial pursuits with a buoyant, agile flight. In flight, male shows white patch on outer primaries and on tail corners; female patches buff. VOICE: A rapid *tuk tuk tuk tuk…* HABITAT: Open areas in lowlands. DISTRIBUTION: Winter visitor to Sumatra, Java, Bali, Borneo, the Philippines and the N Moluccas.

2 LARGE-TAILED NIGHTJAR *Caprimulgus macrurus* 33cm FIELD NOTES: Crepuscular and nocturnal. Captures insects by making aerial sorties from perches or the ground, also hawks after flying insects. In flight, male shows white patch on outer primaries and on tail corners; female patches buff. VOICE: A resonant *tok tok tok…* HABITAT: Open forest edges, forest clearings, secondary growth and cultivation. DISTRIBUTION: Resident in Sumatra, Java, Bali, Borneo, the Philippines, Lesser Sundas and Moluccas.

3 MEES'S NIGHTJAR *Caprimulgus meesi* 25–29cm FIELD NOTES: Crepuscular and nocturnal. Makes feeding sorties from an exposed branch and possibly the ground. Calls from both exposed branches and the ground. Formerly thought conspecific with Large-tailed Nightjar. In flight, male shows white patch on outer primaries and tail corners; female patches buff. VOICE: A high-pitched *piok-piok* or *weelp-weelp.* HABITAT: Dense scrubland with scattered small trees and forest edges. DISTRIBUTION: Resident in Flores in the Lesser Sundas.

4 PHILIPPINE NIGHTJAR *Caprimulgus manillensis* 23–25cm FIELD NOTES: Forages at twilight and nocturnally, launching sallies after flying insects from the ground or an exposed perch. In flight, shows white patch on outer primaries and tail corners. VOICE: A harsh, pounding *chuck chur*, repeated, sometimes for several minutes. HABITAT: Primary and secondary forest, pine forest, secondary growth, scrub and bamboo. DISTRIBUTION: Resident in the Philippines, except Palawan.

5 SULAWESI NIGHTJAR *Caprimulgus celebensis* 26cm FIELD NOTES: Crepuscular and nocturnal. Hawks insects over small patches of grassland, alone or in pairs. Reported singing from *Pandanus* palms and other trees at the edges of coastal scrub. In flight, shows white patch on outer primaries and tail corners. VOICE: A rapid, accelerating series of *chuck* notes, the last note softer and fading away. HABITAT: Dry coastal scrub and mangrove edges; in Sula, also occurs along logging roads in lowland forest. DISTRIBUTION: Endemic to Sulawesi and the Sula Islands.

6 SAVANNA NIGHTJAR *Caprimulgus affinis* 23cm FIELD NOTES: Crepuscular and nocturnal. In flight, male shows white patch on primaries and white tail sides. VOICE: A repeated *chweep.* HABITAT: Dry open coastal woodland, open woodland, cultivation, dry riverbeds and near human habitation. DISTRIBUTION: Resident in Sumatra, Java, Borneo, the Philippines, Sulawesi and the Lesser Sundas.

7 BONAPARTE'S NIGHTJAR *Caprimulgus concretus* 20cm FIELD NOTES: Crepuscular and nocturnal. Makes aerial sorties after flying insects from a perch; often forages along rivers. VOICE: A low, mournful, double-noted *waouuuu.* HABITAT: Primary lowland forest, often near rivers. DISTRIBUTION: Resident in Sumatra and Borneo.

8 SALVADORI'S NIGHTJAR *Caprimulgus pulchellus* 24cm FIELD NOTES: Crepuscular and nocturnal. Forages over forest clearings and near cliffs; flight is slow, with flapping wing-beats and frequent glides. Also makes short sallies from a perch to capture insects. In flight, male shows white patch on outer primaries and tail corners; female patches buff. VOICE: Five *tock* notes, given in an irregular pattern. HABITAT: Montane and submontane forest, often on cliffs or cliff faces; occasionally in small marshy areas. DISTRIBUTION: Resident in Sumatra and Java.

51 PIGEONS; DOVES

1 ROCK DOVE (FERAL PIGEON) *Columba livia* 31–34cm FIELD NOTES: The common 'pest' of many towns and villages. Plumage very variable. VOICE: A moaning *gootr-goo gootr-goo*. HABITAT: Towns and cities. DISTRIBUTION: Resident in Borneo and Wallacea.

2 SILVERY PIGEON *Columba argentina* 34–38cm FIELD NOTES: Rare. Often associates with Pied Imperial Pigeon (Plate 62); note black tip on undertail feathers on Silvery Pigeon is level across all feathers, while on very similar Pied Imperial Pigeon black tip extends up the central feathers. VOICE: Unrecorded. HABITAT: Mangroves, woodland and coconut groves. DISTRIBUTION: Resident on islands off Sumatra and SW Borneo.

3 METALLIC PIGEON *Columba vitiensis* 37–41cm FIELD NOTES: Feeds in the canopy and on the ground. In flight, usually in small flocks. *C. v. halmaheira* (main illustration) is found in the Moluccas and Banggai and Sula islands. *C. v. metallica* (3b) occurs in the Lesser Sundas; *C. v. griseogularis* (3c) is found in the Philippines and on islands off E Borneo. VOICE: A deep *wuuuu woooo*. HABITAT: Various forests, from lowlands to mountains. DISTRIBUTION: Resident in the Philippines, Banggai and Sula islands, Moluccas, Lesser Sundas and islands off E Borneo.

4 RED TURTLE DOVE (RED COLLARED DOVE) *Streptopelia tranquebarica* 31–33cm FIELD NOTES: Feeds mainly on the ground. In flight, tail shows white sides and greyish-white corners. VOICE: A deep *cru-u-u-u-u* or *groo-gurr-goo*. HABITAT: Open country, groves, secondary woodland, scrub and gardens. DISTRIBUTION: Resident in the Philippines and Sulawesi.

5 SUNDA COLLARED DOVE (ISLAND COLLARED DOVE) *Streptopelia bitorquata* 31cm FIELD NOTES: Usually seen alone or in pairs; feeds on the ground, rests in trees or on wires. Formerly thought conspecific with Philippine Collared Dove. VOICE: A repeated, throaty, purring *crrrruw*. HABITAT: Mangroves, open wooded areas, lightly wooded cultivation and forest edges. DISTRIBUTION: Resident in Java, Bali and the Lesser Sundas.

6 PHILIPPINE COLLARED DOVE *Streptopelia dusumieri* 30–33cm FIELD NOTES: Feeds on the ground, rests in trees. Usually seen alone or in pairs. Regarded by some authorities as a race of the previous species. VOICE: A sad *tuk-mm-mm* or hoarse *cook-oo-COO-oo*. HABITAT: Open areas with scattered trees and scrub. DISTRIBUTION: Resident in the Philippines; vagrant recorded in Borneo.

7 SPOTTED DOVE (NECKLACE DOVE) *Spilopelia chinensis* 30cm FIELD NOTES: Forages mainly on the ground; perches in trees, on overhead wires or on buildings. In flight, shows white corners to dark tail. VOICE: A melodious *coo croo-oo croo-oo* or *coocoo croor-croor*. HABITAT: Cultivated areas, open forest and around human habitation. DISTRIBUTION: Resident throughout the region.

8 WHITE-EARED BROWN DOVE *Phapitreron leucotis* 23cm FIELD NOTES: Occurs singly or in pairs; forages mainly in trees but will feed on the ground. Best located by its call. *P. l. nigrorum* (8b) occurs in the C Philippines. VOICE: A *hoot-ho hoot-ho hoot hoot hoot hoot-hoot-hoot* that accelerates and descends down the scale. HABITAT: Dense woodland, open woodland and edges of cultivated fields. DISTRIBUTION: Endemic to the Philippines.

9 AMETHYST BROWN DOVE *Phapitreron amethystinus* 26–27cm FIELD NOTES: Found singly or in pairs foraging in the mid-storey or canopy. *P. a. maculipectus* (9b) occurs on Negros in the C Philippines. VOICE: A soft, deep, hollow *hoot hoot-hoot hoot hoot hoot*. HABITAT: Primary and secondary forest, from lowlands to mountains. DISTRIBUTION: Endemic to the Philippines.

10 TAWITAWI BROWN DOVE *Phapitreron cinereiceps* 26–27cm FIELD NOTES: Frequents the mid-storey or canopy, alone or in pairs. VOICE: A deep, resonating *hoot hoot toot toot-toot-toot-toot-toot*, which accelerates and then tails off. HABITAT: Lowland forest. DISTRIBUTION: Endemic to the Philippines on Tawi-tawi Island in the Sulu Archipelago.

11 MINDANAO BROWN DOVE *Phapitreron brunneiceps* 26–27cm FIELD NOTES: Frequents the mid-storey or canopy. Formerly considered conspecific with Tawitawi Brown Dove. VOICE: A short, fast *hoot toot-toot-toot-toot*. HABITAT: Forest, from mid-altitude to mountains. DISTRIBUTION: Endemic to the S Philippines.

114

52 CUCKOO-DOVES

1 BARRED CUCKOO-DOVE *Macropygia unchall* 37–41cm FIELD NOTES: Usually seen in pairs or small flocks. Acrobatically clambers around tree branches foraging for small fruits; on the ground, carries tail slightly raised. VOICE: A booming *croo-oom*. HABITAT: Submontane forest, occasionally in gardens and coconut plantations. DISTRIBUTION: Resident in Sumatra, Java, Bali and the W Lesser Sundas.

2 AMBOYNA CUCKOO-DOVE (SLENDER-BILLED CUCKOO-DOVE) *Macropygia amboinensis* 35–37cm FIELD NOTES: Usually seen in pairs or small groups. Feeds on small fruits, seeds and nuts, taken from shrubs up to the canopy; occasionally feeds or takes grit on the ground. VOICE: A *whoop-whoop*. HABITAT: Rainforest, rainforest regrowth, woodland and scrubland. DISTRIBUTION: Resident in the S Moluccas.

3 SULTAN'S CUCKOO-DOVE *Macropygia doreya* 33–37cm FIELD NOTES: Occurs singly, in pairs or in flocks. Often perches on exposed branches and dead trees. Formerly considered a race of the previous species. M. d. albicapilla (3b) occurs in Sulawesi and satellite islands. VOICE: Nominate race not recorded; M. d. albicapilla utters a rising *kuoow* and a series of upslurred notes, *uwoop uwoop uwoop uwoop…* HABITAT: Primary and tall secondary forest, forest edges, swamp forest and lightly wooded cultivation; occasionally in lightly wooded scrub. DISTRIBUTION: Resident in Sulawesi and the N Moluccas.

4 RUDDY CUCKOO-DOVE *Macropygia emiliana* 30–37cm FIELD NOTES: Forages from the mid-storey to the canopy, usually singly or in pairs. VOICE: A series of down-slurred, mournful *whu* notes. HABITAT: Primary lowland and hill forest, tall secondary forest and open forest areas. DISTRIBUTION: Resident in Java, Bali and the W Lesser Sundas.

5 ENGGANO CUCKOO-DOVE *Macropygia cinnamomea* 30–32cm FIELD NOTES: Formerly considered a race of Ruddy Cuckoo-dove; habits presumed to be similar. VOICE: A loud *poh wa wao*. HABITAT: Primary lowland and secondary forest, and open forest areas. DISTRIBUTION: Endemic to Enggano Island off S Sumatra.

6 BARUSAN CUCKOO-DOVE *Macropygia modiglianii* 30–37cm FIELD NOTES: Formerly considered a race of Ruddy Cuckoo-dove; habits presumed to be similar. VOICE: Unreported. HABITAT: Primary and tall secondary forest, and open forest areas. DISTRIBUTION: Resident on the islands off W Sumatra, except Enggano.

7 TIMOR CUCKOO-DOVE (BARRED-NECKED CUCKOO DOVE) *Macropygia magna* 44cm FIELD NOTES: Generally inconspicuous unless calling. Usually seen singly, in pairs or in small flocks; forages in the mid-storey and lower canopy. VOICE: A series of three well-spaced notes: a long upslurred note followed by two shorter notes. HABITAT: Primary and tall secondary monsoon forest, forest edges and secondary scrub. DISTRIBUTION: Endemic to the E Lesser Sundas.

53 CUCKOO-DOVES

1 TANIMBAR CUCKOO-DOVE *Macropygia timorlaoensis* 38–43cm
FIELD NOTES: Occurs singly, in pairs or in small groups, feeding in the mid-storey and lower canopy. Formerly considered a race of Timor Cuckoo-dove (Plate 52). VOICE: A slightly hoarse, mellow *koowuck-whuuuu*, repeated, sometimes monotonously. HABITAT: Monsoon forest, secondary growth and forest edges. DISTRIBUTION: Endemic to the Tanimbar Islands in the E Lesser Sundas.

2 FLORES SEA CUCKOO-DOVE *Macropygia macassariensis* 38–43cm
FIELD NOTES: Formerly considered a race of Timor Cuckoo-dove (Plate 52); habits presumably similar to the previous species. VOICE: Unreported. HABITAT: Monsoon forest, secondary growth and forest edges. DISTRIBUTION: Resident in SW Sulawesi, islands south of Sulawesi and the E Lesser Sundas.

3 PHILIPPINE CUCKOO-DOVE *Macropygia tenuirostris* 36–41cm FIELD NOTES: Usually encountered in pairs or small flocks. Acrobatic forager in trees when searching for fruits, seeds and nuts. VOICE: A distinctive *boo boo boo-wow*, often repeated for several minutes. HABITAT: Forest, secondary growth and forest clearings. DISTRIBUTION: Resident in the Philippines and Borneo.

4 LITTLE CUCKOO-DOVE *Macropygia ruficeps* 30cm FIELD NOTES: Usually occurs in pairs or small flocks. Feeds on the ground and in trees, generally in the mid-storey or lower canopy. M. r. nana (4b) is found in Borneo. VOICE: A soft, monotonous *wup-wup-wup-wup-wup…*, also a rapidly repeated *croo-wuck croo-wuck croo-wuck*. HABITAT: Submontane forest. DISTRIBUTION: Resident in Sumatra, Java, Bali, the Lesser Sundas and Borneo.

5 GREAT CUCKOO-DOVE *Reinwardtoena reinwardti* 48–53cm FIELD NOTES: Usually found singly, but may be seen in pairs or small flocks. Feeds in trees and sometimes on the ground. VOICE: A loud, clear *wh wuk-wu wuk-wu wuk-wu wuk-wu wuck-wu wuck-wu*. HABITAT: Primary and secondary forest, forest edges and, occasionally, nearby gardens. DISTRIBUTION: Resident in the Moluccas.

6 WHITE-FACED CUCKOO-DOVE *Turacoena manadensis* 36–40cm
FIELD NOTES: Found singly or in pairs. Frequents the mid-storey and canopy, often feeds in the open on fruiting trees and shrubs. VOICE: A throaty *tik ko-koo* or *wok woo woo*. HABITAT: Wooded gorges and patches of dense woodland in relatively open country. DISTRIBUTION: Endemic to Sulawesi.

7 SULA CUCKOO-DOVE *Turacoena sulaensis* 36cm FIELD NOTES: Formerly considered a race of White-faced Cuckoo-dove; actions and habits presumed to be similar. VOICE: Untranscribed, although sonograph material suggests differences from White-faced Cuckoo-dove. HABITAT: Wooded gorges and patches of woodland in relatively open country. DISTRIBUTION: Endemic to the Sula and Banggai islands.

8 BLACK CUCKOO-DOVE *Turacoena modesta* 38–39cm FIELD NOTES: Forages at the top of small trees and shrubs, usually alone or in pairs. VOICE: A series of upslurred *ho-wuk* notes that starts slowly and accelerates towards the end. HABITAT: Primary and tall secondary monsoon forest, woodland and tall secondary growth. DISTRIBUTION: Endemic to the E Lesser Sundas.

54 DOVES

1 PACIFIC EMERALD DOVE *Chalcophaps longirostris timorensis* 23–28cm
FIELD NOTES: Occurs singly, in pairs or in small groups. Feeds on the ground on fallen fruit, roosts in trees. In flight, shows two pale bars on lower back. VOICE: A low, moaning *coo coo coo coo coo coo*, starting quietly and then rising; also utters a nasal *hoo-hoo-hoo*.
HABITAT: Forest, forest edges, secondary growth, scrub and thickets. DISTRIBUTION: Resident to the E Lesser Sundas, and S and SE Moluccas.

2 EMERALD DOVE (COMMON EMERALD DOVE) *Chalcophaps indica* 23–27cm
FIELD NOTES: Feeds on the ground, often on forest tracks. Seen singly, in pairs or in small groups, especially under fruiting trees. In flight, shows two pale bars on lower back. VOICE: A soft, drawn-out *tuk-hoop*, *hoo-hoo* or *tk-hoon*. HABITAT: Broadleaved, semi-evergreen and mixed deciduous forest. DISTRIBUTION: Resident throughout the region, except the E Lesser Sundas and SE Moluccas.

3 STEPHAN'S EMERALD DOVE *Chalcophaps stephani* 24–25cm FIELD NOTES: Feeds on the ground on fallen fruit and seeds; singly, in pairs or, at rich feeding sites, in small groups. In flight, shows two pale bars on lower back. VOICE: A soft *tuu* followed by a series of short notes, *du-du-duu-duu-duu-duu*… HABITAT: Primary lowland and hill forest; occasionally in secondary coastal woodland. DISTRIBUTION: Resident in Sulawesi, the Sula Islands and the Kai Islands in the S Moluccas.

4 ZEBRA DOVE *Geopelia striata* 21–22cm FIELD NOTES: Feeds mainly on the ground, usually in pairs or small groups. VOICE: A high-pitched, soft trilling that leads to a series of rapid *coo* notes. HABITAT: Open country with scrub, cultivation, parks and gardens. DISTRIBUTION: Resident in Sumatra, Java, Bali, Borneo, the Philippines, Sulawesi, the W Lesser Sundas and S Moluccas.

5 BARRED DOVE *Geopelia maugeus* 21–24cm FIELD NOTES: Found singly, in pairs or in small groups. Feeds on the ground. VOICE: Calls include a down-slurred, purring *prrrrr*, a falsetto and a monotonous *ooo-loo*. HABITAT: Lightly wooded open country, open scrubby monsoon woodland, edges of mangroves, grassland with scattered trees and cultivation. DISTRIBUTION: Endemic to the SE Moluccas and Lesser Sundas.

6 LUZON BLEEDING-HEART *Gallicolumba luzonica* 25–26cm FIELD NOTES: Forages on the forest floor and along forest trails and roads. VOICE: A soft *aa-ooooot* that rises at the end. HABITAT: Forest and secondary growth, from lowlands to mid-mountain. DISTRIBUTION: Endemic to the N Philippines.

7 MINDORO BLEEDING-HEART *Gallicolumba platenae* 25–26cm FIELD NOTES: Forages on the ground. Little reported. VOICE: Unrecorded, suspected to be similar to Negros Bleeding-heart. HABITAT: Lowland forest with dry floors and thick undergrowth. DISTRIBUTION: Endemic to Mindoro in the Philippines.

8 MINDANAO BLEEDING-HEART *Gallicolumba crinigera* 26–27cm
FIELD NOTES: Forages on the forest floor. *G. p. laytensis* (8b) occurs in the C Philippines.
VOICE: A soft *co-co-oooot*, also an *a-ooooo*. HABITAT: Primary and secondary forest. DISTRIBUTION: Endemic to the S Philippines.

9 NEGROS BLEEDING-HEART *Gallicolumba keayi* 25–26cm FIELD NOTES: Little recorded, presumed similar to others of the genus. VOICE: 20–25 bubbling notes.
HABITAT: Primary and secondary forest. DISTRIBUTION: Endemic to the WC Philippines.

10 SULU BLEEDING-HEART *Gallicolumba menagei* 28cm FIELD NOTES: Feeds on the forest floor. VOICE: Unrecorded. HABITAT: Primary and secondary forest. DISTRIBUTION: Endemic to Tawi-tawi Island in the Sulu Archipelago.

11 SULAWESI GROUND DOVE *Gallicolumba tristigmala* 32–33cm FIELD NOTES: Forages on the ground, singly or in pairs. Shy, tends to run when disturbed. *G. t. auripectus* (11b) occurs in SC and SE Sulawesi. VOICE: Similar to Hoopoe (Plate 20), but softer. HABITAT: Primary lowland, hill and mountain forest. DISTRIBUTION: Endemic to Sulawesi.

12 WETAR GROUND DOVE *Alopecoenas hoedtii* 25cm FIELD NOTES: Apparently solitary, little else reported. VOICE: Unrecorded. HABITAT: Lowland and hill monsoon forest and woodland. DISTRIBUTION: Endemic to the E Lesser Sundas.

55 GREEN PIGEONS

1 CINNAMON-HEADED GREEN PIGEON *Treron fulvicollis* 25–27cm
FIELD NOTES: Reported as feeding mainly in small fruiting trees. *T. f. baramensis* (1b)
occurs in Borneo. VOICE: A variable whistled phrase, consisting of 14 or so *coo* notes.
HABITAT: Coastal forest, mangroves, swamp forest and open scrub. DISTRIBUTION: Resident
in Sumatra and Borneo.

2 LITTLE GREEN PIGEON *Treron olax* 21–27cm FIELD NOTES: Arboreal, feeding from
the mid-storey to the canopy, usually in groups of up to eight birds. VOICE: A high-pitched
wiiiiii-iiu-iiu-iiu-iiu-iiui-iiuwu, repeated after short intervals. HABITAT: Coastal, primary,
secondary and submontane forest. DISTRIBUTION: Resident in Sumatra, Java and Borneo.

3 PINK-NECKED GREEN PIGEON *Treron vernans* 26–32cm FIELD NOTES: Feeds
from the mid-storey to the canopy, usually in small flocks, with larger flocks at rich feeding
sites. VOICE: Foraging groups utter a hoarse, rasping *krrak krrak…* HABITAT: Forest and forest
edges, plantations, bamboo and mangroves. DISTRIBUTION: Resident in Sumatra, Java, Bali,
Borneo, the Philippines, Sulawesi, the W Lesser Sundas and N Moluccas.

4 ORANGE-BREASTED GREEN PIGEON *Treron bicinctus* 29cm FIELD NOTES: Feeds
on fruits and berries in small flocks, with larger flocks at rich fruiting trees. VOICE: A
modulated, mellow whistle followed by gurgling notes, also a croaking note and chuckling
call. HABITAT: Small fruit-bearing trees and bushes. DISTRIBUTION: Resident in Java and
Bali.

5 BURU GREEN PIGEON *Treron aromaticus* 28cm FIELD NOTES: Occurs singly,
in pairs or in small groups. Formerly considered a race of the Sri Lanka Green Pigeon
T. pompadora. VOICE: Undescribed. HABITAT: Forest, forest edges and tall secondary growth.
DISTRIBUTION: Endemic to Buru in the S Moluccas.

6 PHILIPPINE GREEN PIGEON *Treron axillaris* 28cm FIELD NOTES: Occurs singly,
in pairs or in small groups. Originally considered a race of the Sri Lanka Green Pigeon
T. pompadora. VOICE: A mournful *coo* and a series of mellow whistles. HABITAT: Primary and
secondary evergreen forest and forest patches. DISTRIBUTION: Endemic to the Philippines.

7 THICK-BILLED GREEN PIGEON *Treron curvirostra* 24–31cm FIELD NOTES: Arboreal.
Feeds on fruits and berries, usually in small flocks, with larger flocks at rich food
sites. VOICE: Low-pitched, throaty whistles; also gives a hoarse *goo-goo* while feeding.
HABITAT: Various forests, including broadleaved evergreen, semi-evergreen and mixed
deciduous; also mangroves and secondary growth. DISTRIBUTION: Resident in Sumatra, Java,
Borneo and the Philippines.

8 GREY-CHEEKED GREEN PIGEON *Treron griseicauda* 25cm FIELD NOTES: Usually
occurs in small or large flocks; generally feeds in the crown of tall trees, although
regularly perches on exposed branches. VOICE: A jumble of melodious gurgles, coos and
whistles; also utters a sad, howling *kuwu kuwu*. HABITAT: Lowland forest, remnant forest
patches, forest edges, lightly wooded cultivation, scrub with scattered trees and gardens.
DISTRIBUTION: Resident in Java, Bali, Sulawesi and the Sula Islands.

56 GREEN PIGEONS

1 FLORES GREEN PIGEON *Treron floris* 29cm FIELD NOTES: Wary and generally inconspicuous. Usually encountered in small flocks, with larger flocks in fruiting trees. VOICE: Generally silent, although low grunts have been reported. HABITAT: Primary and tall secondary forest patches, coastal forest, woodland, lightly wooded cultivation and scrub. DISTRIBUTION: Endemic to the W Lesser Sundas.

2 SUMBA GREEN PIGEON *Treron teysmannii* 29cm FIELD NOTES: Found singly, in pairs or in small flocks. Generally quiet and inconspicuous. Forages mainly in the crown of fruiting trees. VOICE: Includes an *awop-awop-a-where-rup*, a mellow, coughing *korrr* and a *awhereu* advertising call. HABITAT: Remaining areas of primary, selectively logged and tall secondary forest; also visits fruiting trees in parkland savannah. DISTRIBUTION: Endemic to Sumba in the W Lesser Sundas.

3 TIMOR GREEN PIGEON *Treron psittaceus* 32cm FIELD NOTES: Usually encountered in small flocks, also singly or in pairs; wary and inconspicuous. Forages in fruiting trees. VOICE: A series of descending seesawing notes, also a complex jumble of moderately high-pitched bubbling and gargling notes. HABITAT: Primary and tall secondary lowland monsoon forest. DISTRIBUTION: Endemic to the E Lesser Sundas.

4 LARGE GREEN PIGEON *Treron capellei* 35–36cm FIELD NOTES: Forages in small groups of up to a dozen birds, in fruiting trees. VOICE: A variable, deep, nasal, creaking *oo-oo-aah oo-oo-aah aa-aa-aah* and a *oooOOah oo-aah…* HABITAT: Primary lowland forest and forest patches. DISTRIBUTION: Resident in Sumatra, Java and Borneo.

5 SUMATRAN GREEN PIGEON *Treron oxyurus* 34cm FIELD NOTES: Usually occurs in nomadic flocks, but never far from forests. VOICE: A ringing *oo-oowao-oowau* or similar. HABITAT: Thick hill and mountain forest. DISTRIBUTION: Endemic to Sumatra and W Java.

6 WEDGE-TAILED GREEN PIGEON (SINGING GREEN PIGEON)
Treron sphenurus 30–33cm FIELD NOTES: Acrobatic forager in fruiting trees; occurs singly, in pairs or in small flocks. VOICE: A series of musical whistling or fluting notes, also a curious grunting. HABITAT: Oak–laurel and montane heath forest. DISTRIBUTION: Resident in Sumatra and Java.

7 WHISTLING GREEN PIGEON *Treron formosae* 35cm FIELD NOTES: Forages in the tree canopy on small fruits. VOICE: A *po-po-peh*. HABITAT: Forest and forest patches. DISTRIBUTION: Resident on islands in the N Philippines.

8 NICOBAR PIGEON (HACKLED, WHITE-TAILED or VULTURINE PIGEON) *Caloenas nicobarica* 40cm FIELD NOTES: Usually forages at dawn or dusk, mainly on the ground, on fallen fruit. Female has browner upperparts, a smaller cere and shorter hackles. VOICE: Usually silent, although recorded as uttering a short, soft cooing and pig-like grunts, the latter generally given during disputes. HABITAT: Wooded islands, coastal woodland, bushes and mangroves. DISTRIBUTION: Resident throughout the region, especially on small forested islands.

57 FRUIT DOVES

1 BLACK-BACKED FRUIT DOVE (BANDED FRUIT DOVE) *Ptilinopus cinctus*
30–32cm FIELD NOTES: Usually seen singly, in pairs and occasionally in small groups. Mainly frequents the mid-storey and lower canopy. *P. c. ottonis* (1b) is found Damar, Nila and Babar in the E Lesser Sundas; *P. c. albocinctus* (1c) occurs on Lombok, Sumbawa and Flores in the W Lesser Sundas. VOICE: A series of evenly pitched, muted *whoo* notes; *P. c. albocinctus* gives a series of disyllabic *wh-oo* notes. HABITAT: Primary and tall secondary lowland, hill and montane forest, *Casuarina* groves and coastal woodland. DISTRIBUTION: Resident in Bali and the Lesser Sundas.

2 PINK-HEADED FRUIT DOVE *Ptilinopus porphyreus* 29cm FIELD NOTES: Usually encountered singly or in pairs. Shy and inconspicuous. VOICE: A soft *hoo*. HABITAT: Oak–laurel forest and montane heath forest. DISTRIBUTION: Endemic to Sumatra, Java and Bali.

3 RED-NAPED FRUIT DOVE *Ptilinopus dohertyi* 33cm FIELD NOTES: Generally quiet and inconspicuous, although sometimes perches in the open at the top of tall trees, especially along limestone ridges. Frequents the mid-storey up to the canopy; often forages, slowly and methodically in the outer foliage, singly or in pairs. VOICE: A soft, deep *woo-oo*. HABITAT: Remaining patches of primary and tall secondary forest, including forests on the near-vertical walls of limestone gorges. DISTRIBUTION: Endemic to Sumba in the W Lesser Sundas.

4 FLAME-BREASTED FRUIT DOVE *Ptilinopus marchei* 34–38cm
FIELD NOTES: Generally frequents the forest canopy. Very shy; usually flies off, with much noisy wing-flapping, before being located. VOICE: A deep *hooot* or *hooot hooot*. HABITAT: Montane mossy forest. DISTRIBUTION: Endemic to the N Philippines.

5 YELLOW-BREASTED FRUIT DOVE *Ptilinopus occipitalis* 29–30cm
FIELD NOTES: Frequents the mid- and upper canopy, singly or in small flocks; larger flocks may occur in fruiting trees. VOICE: A deep, resonating *hhooott* or *hoorrrr hoorrrr*. HABITAT: Lowland and mid-elevation primary forest. DISTRIBUTION: Endemic to the Philippines.

6 RED-EARED FRUIT DOVE *Ptilinopus fischeri* 34cm FIELD NOTES: Generally seen singly or in pairs, occasionally in small groups. Quiet and inconspicuous. Feeds on small fruits in the mid-storey and lower canopy. *P. f. centralis* (6b) is found C and SE Sulawesi; *P. f. meridionalis* (6c) occurs in S Sulawesi. VOICE: A soft, rising, frog-like *oowup*. HABITAT: Primary hill and montane forest. DISTRIBUTION: Endemic to Sulawesi.

7 CREAM-BELLIED FRUIT DOVE *Ptilinopus merrilli* 32cm FIELD NOTES: Shy. Forages in the canopy and sometimes the understorey. *P. m. faustinoi* (7b) occurs in N Luzon. VOICE: A soft, stuttering *crruuoop*, descending at the start and rising at the end, repeated in a pulsating sequence; also utters a soft, purring *rrrrrr*, repeated for several minutes. HABITAT: Primary and selectively logged forest. DISTRIBUTION: Endemic to the N Philippines.

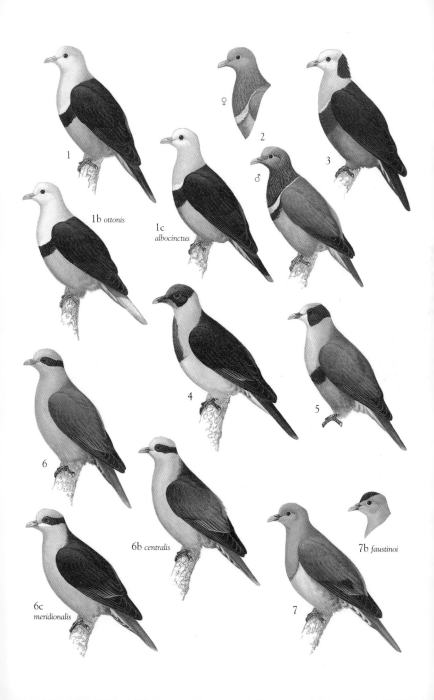

1b *ottonis*

1c *albocinctus*

2 ♀

3

♂

4

5

6

6b *centralis*

6c *meridionalis*

7

7b *faustinoi*

58 FRUIT DOVES

1 JAMBU FRUIT DOVE (CRIMSON-HEADED FRUIT DOVE) *Ptilinopus jambu*
22–28cm FIELD NOTES: Generally forages in trees, although recorded feeding on the ground on fallen fruits. VOICE: A soft, repeated *hooo*, although generally silent. HABITAT: Mangroves, coastal woodland and open wooded areas. DISTRIBUTION: Resident in Sumatra, W Java and Borneo.

2 BLACK-CHINNED FRUIT DOVE (BLACK-THROATED FRUIT DOVE) *Ptilinopus leclancheri* 26–28cm FIELD NOTES: Feeds in fruiting trees. Immature similar to female but lacks the pectoral band. VOICE: A well-spaced *whoo - whoo - whoo...*, also a deep, hollow *rooooooo* and a long *whohooo*. HABITAT: Patches of lowland and secondary growth. DISTRIBUTION: Resident in the Philippines.

3 BANGGAI FRUIT DOVE (MAROON-CHINNED FRUIT DOVE)
Ptilinopus subgularis 33–36cm FIELD NOTES: Usually seen singly, in pairs or in small flocks. Formerly considered conspecific with the next two species. VOICE: A series of 20 *whoop* notes. HABITAT: Primary forest, also some secondary and disturbed forest. DISTRIBUTION: Endemic to the Banggai Islands off E Sulawesi.

4 OBERHOLSER'S FRUIT DOVE *Ptilinopus epius* 33–36cm FIELD NOTES: Forages in trees, feeding on fruits. Formerly considered a race of the previous species. VOICE: A series of 7–8 *whoop* notes. HABITAT: Dense primary and secondary forest in lowlands and hills. DISTRIBUTION: Endemic to Sulawesi.

5 SULA FRUIT DOVE *Ptilinopus mangoliensis* 33–36cm FIELD NOTES: Generally forages in the canopy of large fruiting trees. Formerly considered a race of Banggai Fruit Dove. VOICE: A series of 11 *whoop* notes. HABITAT: Dense primary and secondary forest. DISTRIBUTION: Endemic to Sula Islands.

6 SCARLET-BREASTED FRUIT DOVE *Ptilinopus bernsteinii* 28cm
FIELD NOTES: Generally seen singly or in pairs, foraging in the mid-storey and lower canopy. VOICE: A mournful, slow, hoarse *oo-oooh*; also gives a growling call. HABITAT: Primary lowland, hill and montane forest, forest edges, lightly wooded cultivation and, occasionally, bamboo groves. DISTRIBUTION: Endemic to the N Moluccas.

7 WALLACE'S FRUIT DOVE *Ptilinopus walacii* 26cm FIELD NOTES: Usually occurs in groups of 3–50 or more. Shy and inconspicuous. VOICE: Generally silent, but may utter a low *hoo hoo hoo hoo*. HABITAT: Primary and tall secondary lowland forest, forest edges, open secondary woodland, scrub and mangroves. DISTRIBUTION: Tanimbar Islands and surrounding areas.

8 SUPERB FRUIT DOVE *Ptilinopus superbus* 23–24cm FIELD NOTES: Inconspicuous, usually seen singly or in pairs in the mid-storey and canopy, often with other fruit-eating pigeons. *P. s. temminckii* (8b) occurs in Sulawesi. VOICE: A repeated, slow series of upslurred *whup* notes that accelerates slightly and begins with a single drawn-out, even-pitched note. *P. s. temminckii* produces a slow *coo* and a series of 6–11 *hoo* notes, starting slowly, rising and occasionally accelerating as it fades away. HABITAT: Primary and tall secondary lowland, hill and lower montane forest, also remnant forest patches in secondary scrub and cultivation. DISTRIBUTION: Resident in Sulawesi and the Moluccas.

59 FRUIT DOVES

1 BLUE-CAPPED FRUIT DOVE *Ptilinopus monacha* 18cm FIELD NOTES: Occurs singly, in pairs and sometimes in small groups. Generally quiet. VOICE: A slow, monotonous *who-oo*, also a single upslurred note and a short series of accelerating upslurred notes. HABITAT: Scrubby coastal woodland, tall secondary growth and forest edges, mangroves and coconut plantations with a mixed understorey of tall scrub. DISTRIBUTION: Endemic to the N Moluccas.

2 ROSE-CROWNED FRUIT DOVE *Ptilinopus regina* 21–23cm
FIELD NOTES: Inconspicuous, best located by its call. Found singly, in pairs or in small groups of up to fifteen birds. *P. r. xanthogaster* (2b) occurs in the SE Moluccas. VOICE: A long series of upslurred *wuu* notes; also a loud, accelerating series of 10–20 or more *hoo* notes, starting slowly and ending with notes descending and running together. HABITAT: Forest, monsoon woodland and scrub, coastal and riparian woodland and mangroves. DISTRIBUTION: Resident in the SE Moluccas and Lesser Sundas.

3 WHITE-BIBBED FRUIT DOVE *Ptilinopus rivoli* 23–24cm FIELD NOTES: Usually encountered singly, in pairs and occasionally in small groups. Often associates with other fruit doves in the mid-storey and canopy of fruiting trees. VOICE: A series of ascending, then descending, *hoo* notes. HABITAT: Primary and tall secondary coastal, lowland, hill and montane forest. DISTRIBUTION: Resident in the Moluccas.

4 CLARET-BREASTED FRUIT DOVE *Ptilinopus viridis* 20–21cm
FIELD NOTES: Frequents the canopy. Often perches conspicuously on high, exposed branches, especially in the early morning and late afternoon. Usually occurs singly or in pairs. VOICE: A mournful *a-huh-hoo wo wo wo wo wo wo wo wo wo wo wo wo* that tails off towards the end. HABITAT: Primary and tall secondary coastal, lowland and hill forest, forest edges, lightly wooded cultivation and small coastal islets. DISTRIBUTION: Resident in the S Moluccas.

5 GREY-HEADED FRUIT DOVE *Ptilinopus hyogastrus* 23–24cm FIELD NOTES: Occurs singly, in pairs and sometimes in groups of 20 or more birds, especially in fruiting trees. Regularly perches on exposed treetop branches or overhead wires, particularly in the early morning and late afternoon. VOICE: A soft, slightly mournful, repeated *who-huu*. HABITAT: Forest edges, secondary growth, grassland with scattered trees, lightly wooded cultivation and mangroves; occasionally occurs near human habitation. DISTRIBUTION: Endemic to the N Moluccas.

6 CARUNCULATED FRUIT DOVE *Ptilinopus granulifrons* 20–24cm
FIELD NOTES: Usually forages in twos or threes in the canopy of fruiting trees, often along with other fruit-eating species. VOICE: Unrecorded. HABITAT: Primary and secondary lowland and hill forest, forest edges, selectively logged forest, lightly wooded cultivation and coastal scrub. DISTRIBUTION: Endemic to Obi in the N Moluccas.

7 BLACK-NAPED FRUIT DOVE *Ptilinopus melanospilus* 21–27cm FIELD NOTES: Found singly, in pairs or in small flocks; large flocks of 20–100 birds are on record, usually occurring at fruiting trees or roosts. Often mixes with other fruit-eating birds. VOICE: A *hoo hoo*, repeated every few seconds, often for several minutes. HABITAT: Primary, selectively logged and tall secondary forest, forest edges, open woodland, lightly wooded cultivation, scrub and urban areas. DISTRIBUTION: Resident in Java, Bali, the Lesser Sundas, S and W Philippines, Sulawesi, the Sula Islands and Doi in the N Moluccas, also on many smaller islands off Sumatra and Borneo.

8 NEGROS FRUIT DOVE *Ptilinopus arcanus* 16–17cm FIELD NOTES: Known from only a single female specimen. Habits presumed to be as other fruit doves. May be extinct. VOICE: Unrecorded. HABITAT: Forest at 1,200m. DISTRIBUTION: Endemic to Negros in the Philippines.

60 PIGEONS

1 PINK-BELLIED IMPERIAL PIGEON *Ducula poliocephala* 42cm FIELD NOTES: Usually seen singly, in pairs or in small groups foraging in the canopy. Shares roosts with other imperial pigeons. VOICE: A deep, booming *booouuum booouuum*. HABITAT: Primary forest, undisturbed secondary growth and forest edges. DISTRIBUTION: Endemic to the Philippines.

2 WHITE-BELLIED IMPERIAL PIGEON *Ducula forsteni* 43–52cm FIELD NOTES: Occurs singly, in pairs and occasionally in large flocks, especially in fruiting trees. Generally vocal and conspicuous, regularly perching on exposed branches above the canopy. Forages in the lower canopy or mid-storey. VOICE: A very deep, far-carrying *uu-uum*. HABITAT: Primary hill and montane forest. DISTRIBUTION: Endemic to Sulawesi and the Sula Islands.

3 MINDORO IMPERIAL PIGEON *Ducula mindorensis* 47cm FIELD NOTES: Generally seen singly or in pairs, occasionally in small flocks; forages in the understorey and canopy. VOICE: A deep, resonating, two-syllable note. HABITAT: Montane forest and occasionally lowland forest. DISTRIBUTION: Endemic to Mindoro in the Philippines.

4 GREY-HEADED IMPERIAL PIGEON *Ducula radiata* 36–39cm FIELD NOTES: Shy. Occurs singly or in flocks of up to 20 birds. Occasionally mixes with other pigeons in fruiting trees. Forages in the mid-storey and lower canopy. VOICE: A subdued *huh*. HABITAT: Primary hill and montane forest, forest edges and occasionally lowland forest. DISTRIBUTION: Endemic to Sulawesi.

5 SPOTTED IMPERIAL PIGEON (GREY-NECKED IMPERIAL PIGEON) *Ducula carola* 33–36cm FIELD NOTES: Generally seen in small or large flocks, sometimes associating with flocks of Green Imperial Pigeons in lowlands. *D. c. mindanensis* (5b) is found in Mindanao. VOICE: A deep, descending *hu hu hu hu hu-hu-hu-huhu*, the last notes quieter and accelerating. HABITAT: Lowland to mossy montane forest and forest edges. DISTRIBUTION: Endemic to the Philippines.

6 GREEN IMPERIAL PIGEON *Ducula aenea* 40–47cm FIELD NOTES: Usually seen in pairs or small flocks. In the early morning, regularly perches on dead branches at the top of trees, before dispersing to feed. Forages in the canopy. *D. a. oenothorax* (6b) occurs on Enggano Island off SW Sumatra; *D. a. paulina* (6c) is found on Sulawesi, and the Togian, Banggai and Sula islands. VOICE: A deep, hollow *currr-whoo*. HABITAT: Primary, secondary evergreen and monsoon forest, also mangroves. DISTRIBUTION: Resident in Sumatra, Java, Bali, Borneo, the Philippines, Sulawesi, the Sula Islands and the W Lesser Sundas.

7 SPECTACLED IMPERIAL PIGEON *Ducula perspicillata* 41cm FIELD NOTES: Occurs singly, in pairs and in small flocks. Generally quite vocal and conspicuous, especially in the early morning and late afternoon, when birds tend to perch in the open. VOICE: A hurried series of 6–8 moderately low-pitched, short *hoo* notes. HABITAT: Primary, coastal, lowland and hill forest, forest edges, tall secondary forest, lightly wooded cultivation and mangroves. DISTRIBUTION: Resident from Buru northwards in the Moluccas.

8 SERAM IMPERIAL PIGEON *Ducula neglecta* 43cm FIELD NOTES: Formerly considered a race of the previous species; habits and actions presumed to be similar. VOICE: A deep, rolling *wooo*. HABITAT: Primary and selectively logged evergreen forest. DISTRIBUTION: Endemic to Seram and nearby Boano, Ambon and Saparua islands in the S Moluccas.

61 PIGEONS

1 BLUE-TAILED IMPERIAL PIGEON (ELEGANT or YELLOW-EYED IMPERIAL PIGEON) *Ducula concinna* 45cm FIELD NOTES: Usually encountered in flocks of up to 40 birds, although sometimes alone or in pairs. Forages in the upper mid-storey and canopy. Nomadic, recorded flying between islands in search of food. VOICE: A gruff, growled *urrauw*, interspersed with loud, drawn-out, upslurred growls. HABITAT: Primary and secondary forest, forest edges and lightly wooded cultivation. DISTRIBUTION: Resident on small islands in the Moluccas.

2 SPICE IMPERIAL PIGEON *Ducula myristicivora* 41–43cm FIELD NOTES: Perches on high, exposed branches in the early morning and late afternoon, usually alone, in pairs and occasionally in small flocks. VOICE: A harsh, far-carrying, short, upward-inflected, disyllabic growl; also a short, harsh *koor*. HABITAT: Primary and tall secondary lowland forest and mangroves. DISTRIBUTION: Possibly resident on Widi Island in the N Moluccas.

3 CHRISTMAS IMPERIAL PIGEON *Ducula whartoni* 42–45cm FIELD NOTES: Forages mainly in the canopy, sometimes in larger flocks at fruiting trees. VOICE: A series of slurred, cooing notes, *rroow... rroow... rroow*; also reported is a deep, booming call. HABITAT: Inland primary and secondary rainforest, also littoral forest when trees are in fruit. DISTRIBUTION: Endemic to Christmas Island.

4 PINK-HEADED IMPERIAL PIGEON *Ducula rosacea* 44cm FIELD NOTES: Occurs singly, in pairs or in flocks of up to 20 birds. Frequents the canopy, often in the company of other imperial pigeons. VOICE: A deep, muted, drawn-out *hoo-ooo*, also reported as *hoo hoo hoo-oo hoo-oo hoo-oo*. HABITAT: Primary, selectively logged, tall secondary coastal, lowland and hill forest, forest edges, scrubby woodland, lightly wooded cultivation and small offshore islets. DISTRIBUTION: Resident on islands in the Java Sea and Flores Sea, the Lesser Sundas and locally in the Moluccas.

5 GREY IMPERIAL PIGEON *Ducula pickeringii* 40cm FIELD NOTES: Usually seen singly or in pairs. May travel between islands in search of food. *D. p. langhornei* (5b) occurs in the C Sulu Archipelago. VOICE: A deep, gruff *o-oow* or *oot aaooooh*. HABITAT: Primary and tall secondary coastal forest, lowland forest, degraded monsoon forest and lightly wooded cultivation. DISTRIBUTION: Resident on small islands north of Sulawesi, the Sulu Archipelago and islands off NE Borneo.

6 CINNAMON-BELLIED IMPERIAL PIGEON *Ducula basilica* 41–42cm FIELD NOTES: Presence revealed by loud calls. Singles, pairs or small flocks are usually found in the mid-storey and lower canopy; also reported perching on tall emergent trees overlooking the surrounding forest. *D. b. obiensis* (6b) occurs on Obi Island in the N Moluccas. VOICE: An unhurried, deep, throaty growl preceded by a brief, hoarse *oo* or *whoo*. HABITAT: Primary lowland and hill forest, disturbed forest and lightly wooded cultivation. DISTRIBUTION: Endemic to the N Moluccas.

7 MOUNTAIN IMPERIAL PIGEON *Ducula badia* 43–51cm FIELD NOTES: Usually seen in pairs or small parties. VOICE: A clicking or clucking sound followed by a deep, resonant, booming double or triple note, *whroom whroom* or *whroom whroom whroom*. HABITAT: Montane forest, but visits fruiting trees in lowlands and mangroves. DISTRIBUTION: Resident in Sumatra, W Java and Borneo.

8 DARK-BACKED IMPERIAL PIGEON *Ducula lacernulata* 35–45cm FIELD NOTES: Usually encountered in the forest canopy in small groups; occasionally found singly or in pairs. *D. l. willami* (8b) occurs in E Java and Bali; *D. l. sasakensis* (8c) is found in the W Lesser Sundas. VOICE: A muted series of short *whu* notes. HABITAT: Hill and montane forest, wooded cultivation, and *Casuarina* forest in Flores. DISTRIBUTION: Resident in Java, Bali and the W Lesser Sundas.

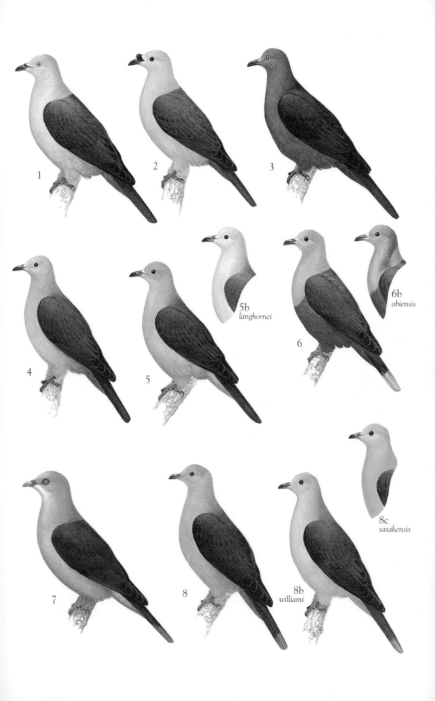

1

2

3

4

5

5b
langhornei

6

6b
obiensis

7

8

8b
williami

8c
sasakensis

62 PIGEONS

1 TIMOR IMPERIAL PIGEON *Ducula cineracea* 39–45cm FIELD NOTES: Forages in the dense foliage of the canopy, alone, in pairs or in small groups. VOICE: A short series of rapid, deep, muted, resonant *hu* notes, resulting in a quavering sound; also reported is a deep *hoo hoo* call. HABITAT: Montane forest, preferring areas of monsoon woodland. DISTRIBUTION: Endemic to Timor and Wetar in the E Lesser Sundas.

2 PIED IMPERIAL PIGEON *Ducula bicolor* 35–42cm FIELD NOTES: Usually found in flocks or small parties. Typically roosts on small islands and islets, visiting coastal areas of larger islands to feed. VOICE: Variable, calls including a deep purring, a chuckling *hu-hu-hu*, a *cru-croo*, a deep *wuum wuum* and a *whoo whoo whoo hoo hoo*. HABITAT: Coastal forest, mangroves and plantations. DISTRIBUTION: Resident on islands off Sumatra, Java, Bali, islands off Borneo, the S and W Philippines, islands off Sulawesi, the Moluccas, and Komodo and the Tanimbar Islands in the E Lesser Sundas.

3 SILVER-TIPPED IMPERIAL PIGEON *Ducula luctuosa* 37–38cm FIELD NOTES: Gregarious; usually gathers in small flocks, although very large flocks recorded, especially prior to dusk. VOICE: Calls include a growling *coo-cooo*, a low *wh-hoo*, a single loud, upslurred *whooo* and a smooth *woooo*. HABITAT: Forest edges, open wooded areas, lightly wooded cultivation and mangroves. DISTRIBUTION: Endemic to Sulawesi and the Sula Islands.

4 SOMBRE PIGEON *Cryptophaps poecilorrhoa* 46cm FIELD NOTES: Usually found singly, occasionally in pairs. Favours the subcanopy in undisturbed forest. VOICE: Unrecorded. HABITAT: Primary hill and montane forest. DISTRIBUTION: Endemic to Sulawesi.

5 PAPUAN MOUNTAIN PIGEON *Gymnophaps albertisii* 33–36cm FIELD NOTES: Forages in the canopy, singly, in pairs or in flocks; little information reported. VOICE: A quiet, low-pitched, upslurred *woooooooo m*; also soft, querulous whistles. HABITAT: Montane forest. DISTRIBUTION: Resident on Bacan Island in the N Moluccas.

6 BURU MOUNTAIN PIGEON *Gymnophaps mada* 33–39cm FIELD NOTES: Little recorded information. Occurs singly, in pairs or in small flocks. VOICE: Unrecorded. HABITAT: Hill and montane forest, occasionally visiting lowland and disturbed forest to feed. DISTRIBUTION: Endemic to Buru in the S Moluccas.

7 SERAM MOUNTAIN PIGEON *Gymnophaps stalkeri* 33–39cm FIELD NOTES: Formerly considered a race of the previous species; habits and actions presumed to be similar. VOICE: Unrecorded. HABITAT: Hill and montane forest. DISTRIBUTION: Endemic to Seram in the S Moluccas.

8 WESTERN CROWNED PIGEON *Goura cristata* 66–75cm FIELD NOTES: Unmistakable. Forages on the ground, singly or in small groups; roosts in trees. VOICE: A very low, deep *oom*. HABITAT: Lowland forest. DISTRIBUTION: Resident in Seram, probably introduced.

63 CRAKES; RAILS

1 RED-NECKED CRAKE *Rallina tricolor* 23–30cm FIELD NOTES: Forages on the forest floor, along shallow streams or in shallow pools, singly and occasionally in pairs or small groups. VOICE: A repeated, descending *nark-nak-nak* or *kare-kare-kare*, also a monotonous *tock tock tock…* Contact calls include a low *um um um* and a repeated soft *plop*. HABITAT: Primary and tall secondary lowland rainforest, monsoon forest and swamp forest. DISTRIBUTION: Resident in the S Moluccas and E Lesser Sundas.

2 RED-LEGGED CRAKE *Rallina fasciata* 23–25cm FIELD NOTES: Occurs singly or in pairs. Skulks; probably nocturnal. VOICE: A loud *gogogogok*, a nasal *pek pek pek*, a *girrr* and a slow, descending trill. HABITAT: Reedy swamps and marshes, watercourses, and wet areas in forest or secondary growth; also open hillsides and grassland in the Philippines. DISTRIBUTION: Resident and winter visitor to Sumatra, Java, Bali, Borneo, the Philippines, Moluccas and Lesser Sundas.

3 SLATY-LEGGED CRAKE *Rallina eurizonoides* 27cm FIELD NOTES: Shy, active mainly at dawn or dusk; if flushed, may fly to perch in tree branches. VOICE: A persistent *kek-kek-kek-kek…* or *ow-ow-ow-ow…* HABITAT: Forest with dense understorey, forest streams, dense scrub and long grass. DISTRIBUTION: Resident in Sulawesi, the Sula Islands and the Philippines; winter visitor to Sumatra and W Java.

4 CALAYAN RAIL *Gallirallus calayanensis* 30cm FIELD NOTES: Forages on the ground, singly or in small groups; tends to run away if disturbed. VOICE: A series of hoarse, staccato *ngeck* notes. HABITAT: Primary and secondary forest on coralline limestone. DISTRIBUTION: Endemic to Calayan Island in the N Philippines.

5 BUFF-BANDED RAIL *Gallirallus philippensis* 30cm FIELD NOTES: Usually seen alone, occasionally in small, loose groups; forages along water edges, tracks or roadsides. VOICE: A braying *coo-aw-000-aw-000-aw-000-aw*, a creaking *swit-swit* and a squeaking *krek-krek-krek*. HABITAT: Drier parts of marshes, grassland, canefields, rank grassland and open hills. DISTRIBUTION: Resident in Borneo, the Philippines and widely in Wallacea.

6 BARRED RAIL *Gallirallus torquatus* 33–35cm FIELD NOTES: Very shy. Usually found singly, in pairs or occasionally in small groups. Regularly forages along little-used tracks. G. t. sulcirostris (6b) occurs on the Banggai and Sula islands. VOICE: Loud, discordant, harsh croaking and screaming, often lasting several seconds. HABITAT: Rank grassland at the borders of primary and tall secondary lowland and hill forest, mangroves, mixed scrub and cultivation. DISTRIBUTION: Resident in the Philippines, Sulawesi and the nearby Banggai and Sula islands.

7 SLATY-BREASTED RAIL *Gallirallus stiatus* 29cm FIELD NOTES: Skulking; normally forages in dense vegetation, although often reported feeding in the open, especially at dawn or dusk. VOICE: A sharp *terrik*, which may be strung together as a 'song'; also a noisy *ka-ka-ka*. HABITAT: Swamps, reed-beds, rice fields, mangroves, and rank grass and scrub bordering creeks and streams. DISTRIBUTION: Resident in Sumatra, Java, Bali, Borneo, the Philippines and Sulawesi; vagrant in the Lesser Sundas.

8 INDIAN WATER RAIL (BROWN-CHEEKED RAIL) *Rallus indicus* 23–28cm FIELD NOTES: Secretive, but will forage in the open when not disturbed. VOICE: A long, clear, piping *kyu*, also a repeated metallic, slurred *shrink shrink*. HABITAT: Marshes. DISTRIBUTION: Vagrant in Borneo.

9 BROWN-BANDED RAIL *Lewinia mirifica* 21–22cm FIELD NOTES: Little recorded information; habits presumed to be similar to Lewin's Rail. VOICE: Unrecorded. HABITAT: Submontane and pine forest mixed with grasses and shrubs. DISTRIBUTION: Endemic to Luzon in the Philippines.

10 LEWIN'S RAIL *Lewinia pectoralis* 23–27cm FIELD NOTES: Secretive and wary, mainly active at dusk and dawn, and on overcast days. Very difficult to flush, uses runways in dense vegetation to escape when disturbed. VOICE: A loud, repeated *grr-eek grr-eek*, also a loud, metallic *jik-jik-jik-jik…* HABITAT: Rank regrowth, dense grass and scrub, usually near water. DISTRIBUTION: Resident in Flores in the Lesser Sundas.

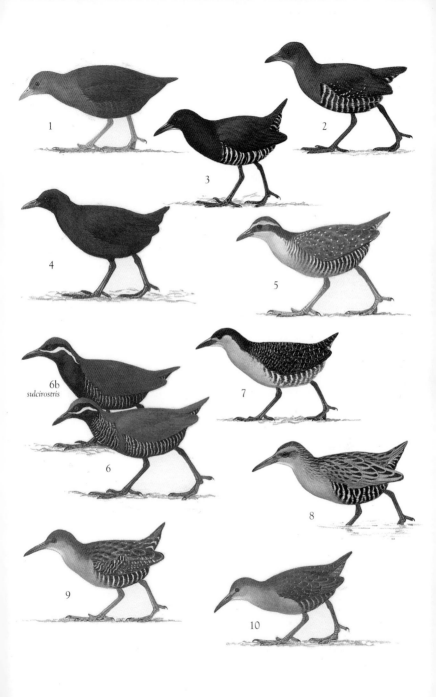

6b
sulcirostris

64 RAILS

1 SNORING RAIL *Aramidopsis plateni* 29cm FIELD NOTES: Forages in dense cover, singly, in pairs or in small family groups; reported to search for crabs in mountain forest streams. VOICE: A quiet snore, consisting of a brief wheeze followed by a drawn-out *ee-orrrr*; also utters a brief, deeply sighing *hmmmm*. HABITAT: Primary and tall secondary lowland, hill and montane forest, also dense wet secondary growth bordering forest. DISTRIBUTION: Endemic to Sulawesi.

2 BLUE-FACED RAIL *Gymnocrex rosenbergii* 30cm FIELD NOTES: Elusive. Occurs alone and occasionally in pairs. Favours moist areas within forest. VOICE: Utters a quiet clucking. HABITAT: Primary and tall secondary lowland and hill forest, remnant patches of dense secondary forest and bushy abandoned rice fields. DISTRIBUTION: Endemic to Sulawesi.

3 BARE-EYED RAIL *Gymnocrex plumbeiventris* 30–33cm FIELD NOTES: Usually solitary and secretive. Runs to and fro around the forest floor in search of food, continually uttering grunting noises. VOICE: A continuous, grunting *uw uw uw uw…*; also utters a loud, gulping *wow-wow-wow-wow*. HABITAT: Primary and tall secondary lowland forest. DISTRIBUTION: Resident in the N Moluccas.

4 TALAUD RAIL *Gymnocrex talaudensis* 33–35cm FIELD NOTES: Little recorded information, said to be extremely shy. VOICE: A series of fifteen or more of rapid, high-pitched *peet-peet-peet* notes. HABITAT: Patches of wet grass and rank vegetation at the edge of lowland forest. DISTRIBUTION: Endemic to the Talaud Islands, northeast of Sulawesi.

5 ISABELLINE BUSH-HEN *Amaurornis isabellina* 35–40cm FIELD NOTES: Generally shy, although regularly forages, quite openly, along the edges of and within recently cleared areas in dense vegetation. VOICE: A jumble of sharp, slightly pulsating screeches and chattering notes, usually given by several birds together. HABITAT: Dense, rank grassland, overgrown cultivation, low scrub mixed with grass and tall grass bordering forest. DISTRIBUTION: Endemic to Sulawesi.

6 PLAIN BUSH-HEN *Amaurornis olivacea* 30cm FIELD NOTES: Generally seen alone, although may occur in groups in suitable habitats. More often heard than seen. VOICE: A raspy, growling *kaawww keerrr*. HABITAT: Dry grassland, scrub, forest plantations and logged areas. DISTRIBUTION: Endemic to the Philippines.

7 PALE-VENTED BUSH-HEN (RUFOUS-TAILED BUSH-HEN)
Amaurornis moluccana 30cm FIELD NOTES: Shy and secretive. Usually keeps to dense cover; wades or swims in streams, generally keeping within shaded areas. Formerly considered conspecific with the previous species. VOICE: A series of shrieks or cat-like wails, decreasing in volume. HABITAT: Dense rank grass and scrub bordering streams, swamps, marshy areas and forest. DISTRIBUTION: Resident on the Sangihe and Talaud islands (north of Sulawesi); also the Kai Islands in the S Moluccas and the Tanimbar Islands in the E Lesser Sundas.

8 TALAUD BUSH-HEN *Amaurornis magnirostris* 30–31cm FIELD NOTES: Shy but inquisitive, although runs at the slightest disturbance. VOICE: A series of frog-like notes or low-pitched barks. HABITAT: Forest with adjacent scrub, rank vegetation, swampy patches and overgrown cultivation. DISTRIBUTION: Endemic to Karakelong Island in the Talaud Archipelago, north of Sulawesi.

9 WHITE-BREASTED CRAKE (WHITE-BREASTED WATERHEN)
Amaurornis phoenicurus 28–33cm FIELD NOTES: Unmistakable. Often seen in the open, and climbing in bushes and trees. *A. p. leucomelanus* (9b) occurs on Sulawesi, Moluccas and the Lesser Sundas. VOICE: Various loud grunts and chuckles. HABITAT: Various wet areas. DISTRIBUTION: Resident throughout the region, except the N Moluccas.

10 DRUMMER RAIL (INVISIBLE RAIL) *Habroptila wallacii* 35cm FIELD NOTES: Usually solitary. Occasionally seen crossing open areas. VOICE: Reported to utter a low drum-beating sound, *wak wak wak*, which is given at the same time as a *tuk tuk tuk* sound made with the wings. HABITAT: Forest, dense swampy thickets (especially Sago *Metroxylon sagu* swamp), marsh edges, secondary growth and forest edges. DISTRIBUTION: Endemic to Halmahera in the N Moluccas.

9b
leucomelanus

65 CRAKES; WATERCOCK; SWAMPHEN; MOORHENS; COOT; FINFOOT

1 BAILLON'S CRAKE *Porzana pusilla* 17–19cm FIELD NOTES: Forages at dawn or dusk, close to or in dense cover. VOICE: A dry frog-like rattle. HABITAT: Marshes, paddyfields, and around lakes and ponds. DISTRIBUTION: Possibly resident in Sumatra, Borneo, Sulawesi, Seram in the Moluccas and Flores in the Lesser Sundas; winter visitor to the Philippines and Java.

2 RUDDY-BREASTED CRAKE *Porzana fusca* 21–23cm FIELD NOTES: Secretive, although often seen at the edge of reed-beds. VOICE: A harsh *tewk* that often speeds up and is followed by a descending trill. HABITAT: Marshes, paddyfields, along streams, dry bush and forest paths. DISTRIBUTION: Resident in Sumatra, Java and Bali, possibly Borneo, the Philippines, Sulawesi and the W Lesser Sundas.

3 BAND-BELLIED CRAKE *Porzana paykullii* 20–22cm FIELD NOTES: Secretive. Rarely seen, often heard. VOICE: Brief trills, like the sound of a wooden rattle. HABITAT: Open inland swamps, wet grassland, damp woodland and paddyfields. DISTRIBUTION: Winter visitor to Sumatra, Java and Borneo; vagrant in Sulawesi.

4 SPOTLESS CRAKE *Porzana tabuensis* 15–18cm FIELD NOTES: Secretive. Forages in deep cover; sightings are usually of a bird darting from one patch of cover to another. Clambers in vegetation and along branches. VOICE: A loud, sewing-machine-like *purr*, and a loud *pit* that is often interspersed with a harsh, nasal *harr*. HABITAT: Wet grasslands, marshes. DISTRIBUTION: Resident in the N Philippines and on Timor in the S Moluccas.

5 WHITE-BROWED CRAKE *Porzana cinerea* 19–22cm FIELD NOTES: Forages at dawn and dusk, taking cover at the slightest disturbance. More often heard. VOICE: A loud, nasal, chattering *chika*, repeated 10–12 times; also a repeated nasal *hee* note. HABITAT: Wet grassland, marshes, paddyfields and rank vegetation bordering streams. DISTRIBUTION: Resident throughout the region.

6 WATERCOCK *Gallicrex cinerea* 42–43cm FIELD NOTES: Mainly crepuscular, skulking; readily swims. VOICE: A long series of *kok* notes, followed by a series of hollow *utumb* notes and ending with a short series of *kluk* notes. HABITAT: Swamps, marshes, paddyfields and mangroves. DISTRIBUTION: Resident in the Philippines; resident and winter visitor in Sumatra and Borneo; winter visitor to Sulawesi and the W Lesser Sundas.

7 PURPLE SWAMPHEN *Porphyrio porphyrio* 45–50cm FIELD NOTES: Readily forages in the open, generally close to cover. Walks on floating vegetation and clambers among reeds and bushes. *P. p. indicus* (main illustration) is found in Sumatra, Java, Borneo, Sulawesi and the S Philippines; *P. p. pulverulentus* (7b) occurs in the Philippines. Both forms depicted are often treated as full species. VOICE: A series of plaintive, nasal rattles, ending in a crescendo; also a low *chuk-chuk* and a trumpeting *toot*. HABITAT: Dense reed-beds and fringing vegetation by lakes, ponds and rivers. DISTRIBUTION: Resident throughout the region.

8 MOORHEN (COMMON MOORHEN) *Gallinula chloropus* 32–35cm FIELD NOTES: Usually keeps to the edge of cover, although regularly seen walking in the open. Readily swims. VOICE: A bubbling *krrrk* or *kurr-ik*; when alarmed, utters a *kik-kik-kik*. HABITAT: Marshes, lakes and watercourses with surrounding emergent vegetation. DISTRIBUTION: Resident and migrant in the region, except the Moluccas.

9 DUSKY MOORHEN *Gallinula tenebrosa* 30cm FIELD NOTES: Forages in the open and swims amid aquatic vegetation. VOICE: Various shrieks, screeches and yelps, also a nasal *kerk*. HABITAT: Lakes, ponds and swamps with aquatic vegetation. DISTRIBUTION: Resident in Wallacea and possibly SE Borneo.

10 COOT (EURASIAN or COMMON COOT) *Fulica atra* 36–38cm FIELD NOTES: Usually seen swimming, although regularly grazes on waterside banks. VOICE: Various metallic notes. HABITAT: Open water with fringing vegetation. DISTRIBUTION: Rare winter visitor or vagrant to Borneo, Java, Bali, the Philippines, the W Lesser Sundas and S Moluccas.

11 MASKED FINFOOT *Heliopais personatus* 43–55cm FIELD NOTES: Secretive, usually swimming below overhanging vegetation. VOICE: A high-pitched, bubbling, grunting *quack*. HABITAT: Shady jungle rivers and dense mangrove swamps. DISTRIBUTION: Winter visitor or vagrant in Sumatra; vagrant in Java and Borneo.

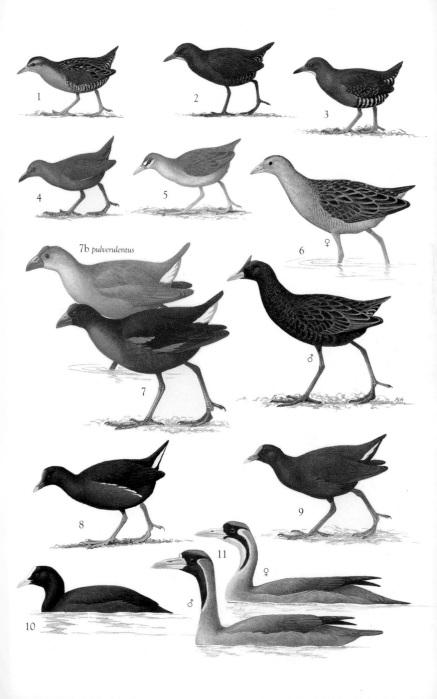

7b *pulverulentus*

66 PLOVERS

1 LAPWING (NORTHERN LAPWING, GREEN PLOVER, PEEWIT)
Vanellus vanellus 28–31cm FIELD NOTES: Generally occurs in pairs or flocks. In flight from above, looks black with white lower rump and white-tipped primaries. VOICE: A plaintive *pee-wit* or *wee-ip*. HABITAT: Grassland, margins of lakes and rivers, and on estuaries. DISTRIBUTION: Vagrant in NW Borneo.

2 JAVANESE LAPWING (JAVAN or JAVANESE WATTLED LAPWING)
Vanellus macropterus 28cm FIELD NOTES: Little recorded information. Not reported since 1940; possibly extinct. VOICE: Unrecorded. HABITAT: Open areas near freshwater ponds, agricultural land and river deltas. DISTRIBUTION: Endemic to Java.

3 MASKED LAPWING *Vanellus miles* 33–37cm FIELD NOTES: Noisy and conspicuous, usually encountered in small flocks. In flight, shows white uppertail-coverts and base of tail. VOICE: A grating, staccato *keer-ki-ki-ki-ki* or *krik-krik-krik*, a sharp *kek* and a slurred, descending *kreerk-kreerk*. HABITAT: Grassland near water, also lake and swamp margins. DISTRIBUTION: Irregular visitor to the S Moluccas, E Lesser Sundas and Christmas Island.

4 RED-WATTLED LAPWING (RED-WATTLED PLOVER) *Vanellus indicus* 32–35cm
FIELD NOTES: Occurs in pairs or small parties. In flight from above, wing appears dark with a white bar on secondary-coverts; rump, uppertail-coverts and base of tail white; tail mainly black with a white tip. VOICE: A shrill *did-he-do-it* or *kree-dee-der*; when alarmed, gives a sharp *trint trint trint*. HABITAT: Open areas, agricultural land, and river, lake and marsh margins. DISTRIBUTION: Winter visitor or vagrant to Sumatra.

5 GREY-HEADED LAPWING *Vanellus cinereus* 34–37cm FIELD NOTES: Normally occurs in small flocks. Non-breeding birds have a whitish throat. In flight from above, shows much white on secondaries, secondary-coverts and rump; tail black with white sides. VOICE: A plaintive *chee-it*; when disturbed, utters a rasping *cha-ha-eet* or a sharp *pink*. HABITAT: Marshland, swampy grassland, paddyfields and river margins. DISTRIBUTION: Vagrant in Borneo, the Philippines and Sulawesi.

6 PACIFIC GOLDEN PLOVER (ASIAN or EASTERN GOLDEN
PLOVER) *Pluvialis fulva* 23–26cm FIELD NOTES: Occurs singly, in pairs or in small flocks. VOICE: A rapid *chu-wit* and a drawn-out *klu-ee*. HABITAT: Coastal lagoons, mudflats, lake and river margins, grassland and fields. DISTRIBUTION: Winter visitor throughout the region.

7 GREY PLOVER (BLACK-BELLIED PLOVER) *Pluvialis squatarola* 27–30cm
FIELD NOTES: Occurs singly, in pairs or in small parties. In flight from above, shows white rump and wing-bar. In non-breeding plumage, underwing white with prominent black axillary patches. VOICE: A mournful *tlee-oo-ee*. HABITAT: Mainly coastal mudflats and beaches. DISTRIBUTION: Winter visitor throughout the region.

67 PLOVERS

1 RINGED PLOVER (COMMON RINGED PLOVER) *Charadrius hiaticula* 18–20cm
FIELD NOTES: Usually seen singly or in pairs. In flight, upperwing shows bold white wing-bar.
VOICE: A mellow, rising *too-lee*; when alarmed, gives a soft *too-weep*. HABITAT: Shores of
coasts, lakes and rivers. DISTRIBUTION: Winter vagrant in Borneo and the W Philippines.

2 LONG-BILLED PLOVER *Charadrius placidus* 19–21cm FIELD NOTES: Usually seen
singly or in loose groups. In flight, upperwing shows inconspicuous white wing-bar. VOICE: A
clear *pewee*, also a pleasant *tudulu*. HABITAT: Lakes and river margins, marshes, coastal pools
and paddyfields. DISTRIBUTION: Vagrant in Borneo and Bali.

3 LITTLE RINGED PLOVER *Charadrius dubius* 14–17cm FIELD NOTES: Usually seen
singly or in small groups. Yellow eye-ring. In flight, upperwing shows inconspicuous white
wing-bar. VOICE: A descending *pee-oo*; when alarmed, utters a *pip-pip-pip*. HABITAT: Margins
of lakes and rivers, marshes, mudflats and estuaries. DISTRIBUTION: Resident in the
Philippines; winter visitor throughout the region.

4 KENTISH PLOVER *Charadrius alexandrinus* 15–17cm FIELD NOTES: Often mixes
with other small plovers, when its quicker movements may stand out. In flight, upperwing
shows white wing-bar. VOICE: A soft, clear *pit* or *pit-pit-pit*; when alarmed, gives a hard
prrr, too-eet or *pweep*. HABITAT: Sandy shores of coasts, lagoons, saltpans and lakes.
DISTRIBUTION: Winter visitor to Sumatra, Java, Bali, Borneo and the N Philippines.

5 WHITE-FACED PLOVER *Charadrius dealbatus* 16–17cm FIELD NOTES: Considered
by some authorities to be a race of the previous species; actions presumed to be
similar. VOICE: Generally silent, otherwise no known difference from previous species.
HABITAT: Sandy areas, mudflats, saltpans and reclaimed land. DISTRIBUTION: Winter visitor
to Sumatra, the Philippines and Sulawesi; vagrant in Borneo.

6 RED-CAPPED PLOVER *Charadrius ruficapillus* 14–16cm FIELD NOTES: Occurs
singly, in pairs or in small groups. Active and tame. Formerly considered a race of Kentish
Plover. VOICE: A rapid, hard trill; other calls similar to Kentish Plover. HABITAT: Coastal
and subcoastal sandy and shell beaches, brackish and saltwater mudflats and sandflats.
DISTRIBUTION: Casual winter visitor to the Lesser Sundas and possibly E Java.

7 MALAYSIAN PLOVER *Charadrius peronii* 14–16cm FIELD NOTES: Usually
encountered in pairs or small flocks. In flight, upperwing shows prominent white wing-bar,
especially at base of primaries. VOICE: A soft *whit* or *twik*. HABITAT: Undisturbed sandy, coral
and shell beaches, also adjacent mudflats. DISTRIBUTION: Resident in Sumatra, Bali, Borneo,
the Philippines, Sulawesi and Lesser Sundas.

8 JAVAN PLOVER *Charadrius javanicus* 15cm FIELD NOTES: Formerly considered a race
of Kentish Plover; actions and habits presumed to be similar. VOICE: A soft, rising *kweek
kweek*. HABITAT: Coastal lowlands. DISTRIBUTION: Resident in Java, Bali and Sumbawa in
the W Lesser Sundas.

9 LESSER SAND PLOVER *Charadrius mongolus* 19–21cm FIELD NOTES: Gregarious,
often in large flocks, also mixing with other plovers. In flight, upperwing shows a white
wing-bar. *C. m. atrifrons* (9b) occurs in Sumatra. VOICE: A short *drrit*, and a sharp *chitik* or
chiktik. HABITAT: Mainly coastal mudflats and sandflats. DISTRIBUTION: Winter visitor or
migrant throughout the region.

10 ORIENTAL PLOVER *Charadrius veredus* 22–25cm FIELD NOTES: Occurs singly or in
small parties; has a strong, powerful flight, often with erratic turns. VOICE: Trilling calls and
a short piping *klink*; in flight, utters a sharp, whistled *chip-chip-chip*. HABITAT: Dry grassland,
dry areas near wetlands, and coastal mudflats and sandflats. DISTRIBUTION: Winter visitor or
migrant throughout the region.

11 GREATER SAND PLOVER *Charadrius leschenaultii* 22–25cm
FIELD NOTES: Gregarious. In flight, upperwing shows a prominent white wing-bar. VOICE: A
soft *trrri*, also a melodious *pipruirr*. HABITAT: Mainly coastal wetlands. DISTRIBUTION: Winter
visitor or migrant throughout the region.

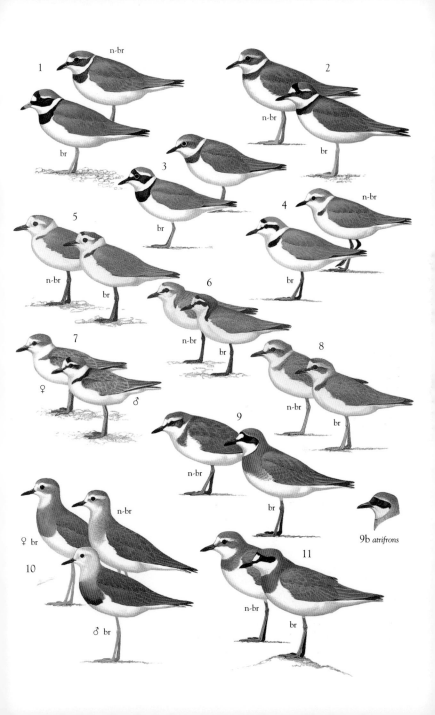

68 WOODCOCKS; SNIPE

1 WOODCOCK (EURASIAN WOODCOCK) *Scolopax rusticola* 33–35cm
FIELD NOTES: Usually encountered when flushed, after which it makes a zigzagging flight through trees before dropping out of sight. VOICE: Generally silent, but may utter a *schaap* or *schaap schaap*. HABITAT: Woodland and plantations with wet areas for feeding. DISTRIBUTION: Vagrant in Borneo and possibly the Philippines.

2 JAVAN WOODCOCK (DUSKY WOODCOCK) *Scolopax saturata* 30cm
FIELD NOTES: Nocturnal. Makes a roding display-flight at dawn or dusk, usually over forest clearings. VOICE: A nasal *queet* and a rapid, squealing *quo-quo-quo-quo*, both given during display-flight and the latter also given while perched. HABITAT: Damp montane forest, with moderate to dense undergrowth. DISTRIBUTION: Resident in Sumatra and Java.

3 SULAWESI WOODCOCK *Scolopax celebensis* 30–35cm FIELD NOTES: Skulks away from danger, reported making short flights over treetops at dusk; little other recorded information. VOICE: Unrecorded. HABITAT: Dense montane woodland, especially where there is some open ground below the canopy; also in bamboo thickets. DISTRIBUTION: Endemic to Sulawesi.

4 MOLUCCAN WOODCOCK (OBI WOODCOCK) *Scolopax rochussenii* 32–40cm
FIELD NOTES: Elusive; best seen during dusk roding display-flight, when with shallow wing-beats it makes circling or linear flights over treetops, watercourses or swampy areas. VOICE: Gives an explosive trill during display-flight. HABITAT: Lowland, montane and slightly disturbed forest, near rivers or streams. DISTRIBUTION: Endemic to Obi and Bacan islands in the N Moluccas.

5 BUKIDNON WOODCOCK *Scolopax bukidnonensis* 33cm FIELD NOTES: Usually solitary and nocturnal. Makes a wide oval display-flight over forest clearings, at dawn or dusk. VOICE: During display-flight, utters a metallic, staccato, clicking *pip-pip-pip-pip-pip*, with a growling *gro-a gro-a* between the calls. HABITAT: Mid-altitude and montane forest, especially mossy forest. DISTRIBUTION: Endemic to the Philippines.

6 SWINHOE'S SNIPE (CHINESE SNIPE) *Gallinago megala* 27–29cm FIELD NOTES: At rest, primaries extend beyond tertials. In flight, toes project slightly beyond tail and underwing is uniformly barred. VOICE: Sometimes utters a gruff *scaap* when flushed. HABITAT: Marshes, flooded grassland and paddyfields; sometimes drier areas such as rice stubble. DISTRIBUTION: Winter visitor to Java, Bali, Borneo, the Philippines and throughout Wallacea.

7 PIN-TAILED SNIPE (PINTAIL SNIPE) *Gallinago stenura* 25–27cm FIELD NOTES: At rest, tertials overlap primaries and tail appears short. In flight, toes project well beyond tail and underwing is uniformly barred. Flushed flight is short and not as towering as Snipe. Supercilium wider at base of bill than Snipe. VOICE: When flushed, may utter a low-pitched, weak *scaap*, *squik* or *etch*. HABITAT: Marshes, paddyfields and wet grassland, and sometimes drier areas. DISTRIBUTION: Winter visitor to Sumatra, Java, Bali, Borneo, the Philippines, Sulawesi and the W Lesser Sundas.

8 SNIPE (COMMON SNIPE) *Gallinago gallinago* 25–27cm FIELD NOTES: Usually feeds close to cover. When flushed, flies off in a rapid, erratic, zigzagging, towering manner. In flight, secondaries show a white trailing edge and pale banding on underwing-coverts. VOICE: Utters a harsh *scaap* when flushed. HABITAT: Various wet areas, including marshes, swampy ground, and lake and river edges. DISTRIBUTION: Winter visitor to Borneo and the Philippines.

9 JACK SNIPE *Lymnocryptes minimus* 17–19cm FIELD NOTES: Secretive, tending to wait until nearly trodden on before being flushed; flies away with less erratic movements than Snipe. VOICE: May utter a weak *gah* when disturbed. HABITAT: Marshes, flooded land, and wet grassy areas surrounding lakes, ponds and rivers. DISTRIBUTION: Winter visitor or vagrant to the Philippines and possibly Borneo.

69 DOWITCHERS; GODWITS; CURLEWS

1 LONG-BILLED DOWITCHER *Limnodromus scolopaceus* 27–30cm
FIELD NOTES: Usually gregarious, occurring in small groups. In flight, shows a white oval on lower back, white trailing edge to flight feathers, and distinct black and white barring on tail. VOICE: A sharp *kik* or *kik-kik-kik-kik*; when alarmed, gives a *kreeek*. HABITAT: Various wetlands, both inland and coastal. DISTRIBUTION: Vagrant in Bali and Borneo.

2 ASIAN DOWITCHER (ASIATIC or SNIPE-BILLED DOWITCHER) *Limnodromus semipalmatus* 33–36cm FIELD NOTES: Often associates with godwits. In flight, shows a whitish lower back, barred and streaked dark grey; tail white, barred dark grey. VOICE: A yelping *chep-chep* or *chowp*, also a soft, human-like *kiawow*. HABITAT: Coastal wetlands. DISTRIBUTION: Winter visitor to Sumatra, Java and Borneo; migrant to the Philippines; vagrant in Sulawesi and the Lesser Sundas.

3 BLACK-TAILED GODWIT *Limosa limosa* 40–44cm FIELD NOTES: Gregarious, often associating with Bar-tailed Godwits and other waders. In flight, shows bold white wing-bar on upperwing, white rump and black tail. VOICE: A *kek*, *tuk* or *kip*, usually repeated. HABITAT: Mudflats, coastal pools, marshes and lake shores. DISTRIBUTION: Winter visitor or migrant throughout the region.

4 BAR-TAILED GODWIT *Limosa lapponica* 37–41cm FIELD NOTES: Gregarious, often seen with Black-tailed Godwits and other waders. In flight, shows white from rump to mid-back; tail barred black and white. VOICE: A barking *kak-kak*, and *kirric* or similar. HABITAT: Estuaries, muddy or sandy shores, and coastal pools. DISTRIBUTION: Winter visitor throughout the region.

5 LITTLE CURLEW (LITTLE WHIMBREL) *Numenius minutus* 29–32cm
FIELD NOTES: Usually encountered in groups. Lacks white rump. In flight, underwing-coverts buff with black bars. VOICE: In flight, utters a whistled *te-te-te* or a rougher *tchew-tchew-tchew*; when alarmed, utters a short *kweek-ek*. HABITAT: Short grassland, bare cultivation and freshwater margins. DISTRIBUTION: Migrant to Java, Borneo, the Philippines and Wallacea.

6 WHIMBREL *Numenius phaeopus* 40–46cm FIELD NOTES: Usually found in small parties. Nominate form shows a white rump in flight; *N. p. variegatus* (not depicted) has a white rump variably barred dark brownish grey, sometimes showing little contrast with rest of mantle. Both races occur throughout, the latter more common. VOICE: A tittering, flat-toned *tetti-tetti-tetti-tet*, *bibibibibibi* or similar. HABITAT: Coastal wetlands and nearby grassland, marshes, mangroves and along large rivers. DISTRIBUTION: Winter visitor throughout the region.

7 CURLEW (EURASIAN, WESTERN or COMMON CURLEW) *Numenius arquata* 50–60cm FIELD NOTES: Usually occurs in small parties. In flight, shows a white rump and lower back. Female slightly larger and longer-billed. VOICE: A far-carrying *cour-lee* and a low *whaup*; gives a stammering *tututu* or *tyuyuyuyu* when disturbed. HABITAT: Mudflats, sandflats, lake margins, and flooded and dry grassland. DISTRIBUTION: Winter visitor or migrant to Sumatra, Java, Bali, Borneo, the Philippines, Lesser Sundas and Moluccas.

8 BRISTLE-THIGHED CURLEW *Numenius tahitiensis* 40–44cm FIELD NOTES: Usually occurs singly, in pairs or in small groups. In flight, shows a bright cinnamon rump. VOICE: A rippling *whe-whe-whe-whe*, a ringing *whee-wheeoo* and a whistled *chi-u-it*. HABITAT: Coastal areas and dry areas well away from the shore. DISTRIBUTION: Accidental vagrant in the Philippines.

9 EASTERN CURLEW (FAR EASTERN or AUSTRALIAN CURLEW) *Numenius madagascariensis* 60–66cm FIELD NOTES: Shy; may mix with flocks of Curlews. Note no white rump in flight. Female larger and longer-billed. VOICE: A far-carrying *cour-lee*, flatter in tone than Curlew; when disturbed, utters a strident *ker-ker-ee-ker-ee*. HABITAT: Coastal mudflats, beaches and estuaries. DISTRIBUTION: Winter visitor or migrant throughout the region.

70 SANDPIPERS

1 GREY-TAILED TATTLER (POLYNESIAN, SIBERIAN or GREY-RUMPED TATTLER, GREY-RUMPED SANDPIPER) *Tringa brevipes* 24–27cm
FIELD NOTES: Generally occurs singly or in loose parties. Walks with a bobbing rear end. In flight, slate-grey underwing contrasts with white belly. VOICE: In flight, utters an upslurred *tu-whip*; when alarmed, gives a *klee, klee-klee* or *weet-weet*. HABITAT: Tidal mudflats, beaches, rocky shores, reefs and occasionally inland lakes. DISTRIBUTION: Winter visitor to Java, Bali, Borneo, the Philippines and Wallacea. Rare visitor to Sumatra.

2 SPOTTED REDSHANK (DUSKY REDSHANK) *Tringa erythropus* 29–32cm
FIELD NOTES: Moulting birds have a non-breeding-type plumage blotched with black. In flight, shows a white oval in centre of back. Often wades up to belly when foraging. VOICE: In flight, utters a distinctive *chu-it*; when alarmed, gives a short *chip*. HABITAT: Upper reaches of estuaries, coastal lagoons, lakes and marshes. DISTRIBUTION: Migrant to Borneo and the Philippines.

3 GREENSHANK (COMMON or GREATER GREENSHANK) *Tringa nebularia* 30–35cm FIELD NOTES: Usually seen singly, but sometimes in larger groups at roost. In flight, shows a white rump and back; feet project slightly beyond tail. VOICE: A ringing *chew-chew-chew*; when alarmed, gives a *kiu-kiu-kiu*. HABITAT: Wide variety of coastal and inland wetlands. DISTRIBUTION: Local winter visitor throughout the region.

4 REDSHANK (COMMON REDSHANK) *Tringa totanus* 27–29cm FIELD NOTES: Wary; takes noisily to flight at the slightest disturbance, usually the first in a group of waders to take to the air. In flight, shows a white oval in centre of back, and striking white secondaries and inner primaries. VOICE: A piping *teu-hu teu-hu-hu* or similar; when alarmed, utters a loud *tli-tli-tli-tli*. HABITAT: Wide variety of coastal and inland waters. DISTRIBUTION: Winter visitor throughout the region.

5 SPOTTED GREENSHANK (NORDMANN'S GREENSHANK) *Tringa guttifer* 30–35cm FIELD NOTES: Wary. Often wades up to belly. In flight, shows a white rump and back; tail pale grey; legs do not protrude beyond tail. VOICE: A piercing *keyew* and a harsh *gwark*. HABITAT: Mainly coastal wetlands. DISTRIBUTION: Scarce migrant to Sumatra, Borneo and the Philippines.

6 LESSER YELLOWLEGS *Tringa flavipes* 23–25cm FIELD NOTES: Active forager, often running through water looking for prey. In flight, shows a square white rump; toes project well beyond tail. VOICE: A flat, harsh *tew-tew* or *tew*. HABITAT: Wide variety of coastal and inland wetlands. DISTRIBUTION: Vagrant in Sumatra.

7 GREEN SANDPIPER *Tringa ochropus* 21–24cm FIELD NOTES: Usually seen singly. Wary, flushing quite readily. In flight, shows a white rump and black and white barring on tail. VOICE: A musical *tlueet-wit-wit*; when alarmed, utters a sharp *wit-wit-wit*. HABITAT: Edges of lakes, pools, rivers and streams. DISTRIBUTION: Winter visitor to Sumatra, Borneo and the Philippines; vagrant in Java and Sulawesi.

8 MARSH SANDPIPER *Tringa stagnatilis* 22–25cm FIELD NOTES: Usually seen singly or in scattered parties. In flight, looks like a small Greenshank, but feet project well beyond tail. VOICE: A plaintive *keeuw* or *kyu-kyu-kyu*; when flushed, utters a loud *yip*. HABITAT: Marshes, ponds, lakes and coastal waters. DISTRIBUTION: Winter visitor to Sumatra, Java, Bali, Borneo, the Philippines and Wallacea.

9 WOOD SANDPIPER *Tringa glareola* 19–21cm FIELD NOTES: Often found in scattered groups. In flight, shows a white rump and a white tail with narrow black bars. VOICE: A high-pitched *chiff-iff-iff*; when alarmed, utters a *chip* or *chip-chip-chip*. HABITAT: Lakes, pools and marshes, less often on coastal wetlands. DISTRIBUTION: Winter visitor throughout the region.

71 SANDPIPERS; STINTS

1 GREAT KNOT (GREATER or EASTERN KNOT, GREAT SANDPIPER)
Calidris tenuirostris 26–28cm FIELD NOTES: Usually occurs in flocks, often in the company of other waders. In flight, upperwing shows a narrow white wing-bar; lower rump white, sparsely marked with dark specks, appearing white; tail dark grey. VOICE: A low *nyut-nyut*, also a harsh *chuker-chuker-chuker* and a soft *prrt*. HABITAT: Mainly sandy or muddy coastal shores. DISTRIBUTION: Scarce migrant or winter visitor throughout the region.

2 KNOT (RED or LESSER KNOT) *Calidris canutus* 23–25cm FIELD NOTES: Usually in small parties. In flight, upperwing shows a narrow white wing-bar; lower rump white, finely barred blackish, appearing grey. VOICE: A soft, nasal *knut*, *wutt* or *whet*; utters a *kikkiik* when alarmed. HABITAT: Sandy or muddy coastal shores. DISTRIBUTION: Migrant to Sumatra, Java, Borneo, the Philippines and Wallacea.

3 SANDERLING *Calidris alba* 20–21cm FIELD NOTES: Usually in small parties feeding along the water's edge. Typically makes rapid runs, interspersed with quick dips to pick up food. In non-breeding plumage, upperwing shows a dark leading edge and a broad white wing-bar. VOICE: In flight, utters a *twick* or *kip*, often repeated and forming a quick trill. HABITAT: Sandy or muddy coastal shores. DISTRIBUTION: Migrant and winter visitor throughout the region.

4 LITTLE STINT *Calidris minuta* 12–14cm FIELD NOTES: Has a quick 'running around' foraging action, similar to the much more common Red-necked Stint. In juvenile plumage, shows distinct pale 'braces' on mantle. VOICE: A short *stit-tit*. HABITAT: Freshwater and saltwater wetlands. DISTRIBUTION: Vagrant in Borneo and the Philippines.

5 RED-NECKED STINT (RUFOUS-NECKED STINT) *Calidris ruficollis* 13–16cm FIELD NOTES: Forages with a continual pecking, 'running around' action. Non-breeding and juvenile very similar to Little Stint, although rear end appears more attenuated and bill is slightly blunter and shorter. VOICE: A coarse *chit*, *kreep*, *creek* or *chritt*. HABITAT: Saltwater and freshwater wetlands. DISTRIBUTION: Winter visitor throughout the region.

6 TEMMINCK'S STINT *Calidris temminckii* 13–15cm FIELD NOTES: Has a slow, deliberate foraging action, often among waterside vegetation. When alarmed, flees with a towering, jinking flight. At rest, white-sided tail projects beyond wing-tips. Legs greenish yellow. VOICE: A rapid *tirirririr* or trilled *trirr*. HABITAT: Marshes, lake and pond edges, paddyfields, saltpans and estuaries. DISTRIBUTION: Winter visitor to Borneo; vagrant in the Philippines.

7 LONG-TOED STINT *Calidris subminuta* 13–16cm FIELD NOTES: Regularly forages among waterside vegetation. When alarmed, often stands upright with neck extended; if flushed, flees with a towering flight on weak, fluttery wing-beats. Juvenile has pronounced white 'braces' on mantle. VOICE: A soft *prrt*, *chrrup* or *chulip*, and a sharp *tik-tik-tik*. HABITAT: Marshes, edges of lakes and pools, and on estuaries. DISTRIBUTION: Winter visitor to the region.

8 SHARP-TAILED SANDPIPER *Calidris acuminata* 17–21cm FIELD NOTES: Usually occurs in small groups, often mixed with other waders. VOICE: A soft *wheep*, *pleep* or *trrt*, also a twittering *prrt-wheep wheep*. HABITAT: Freshwater and coastal wetlands. DISTRIBUTION: Passage migrant throughout the region.

9 DUNLIN (RED-BACKED SANDPIPER) *Calidris alpina* 16–17cm FIELD NOTES: Walks quickly, interspersed with short runs, probing and pecking vigorously. In flight, shows a white wing-bar and white sides to rump and uppertail-coverts. VOICE: A rasping *kreeeep* and a low *beep*. HABITAT: Coastal mudflats, seashore, marshes, lakeside and riversides. DISTRIBUTION: Vagrant in the Philippines, and possibly Java, Borneo and Wallacea.

10 CURLEW SANDPIPER *Calidris ferruginea* 18–23cm FIELD NOTES: Regularly wades, often up to belly in shallows. In flight, upperwing shows a white wing-bar and a white lower rump and uppertail-coverts. VOICE: A rippling *chirrup*. HABITAT: Coastal mudflats, lagoons, saltmarshes and estuaries; less common on inland wetlands. DISTRIBUTION: Winter visitor and migrant to the whole region.

72 SANDPIPERS; RUFF; TURNSTONE; PHALAROPES

1 BROAD-BILLED SANDPIPER *Calidris falcinellus* 16–18cm FIELD NOTES: Often forages among stint flocks. In non-breeding plumage, upperwing shows dark lesser wing-coverts and leading edge, and a white wing-bar. VOICE: A buzzing *chrrreet* or *treet*. HABITAT: Coastal creeks, lagoons and mudflats. DISTRIBUTION: Migrant or winter visitor to the region.

2 RUFF *Calidris pugnax* 26–32cm FIELD NOTES: Moulting birds have a non-breeding-type plumage splattered with dark blotches on the breast. Flamboyant breeding plumage rarely seen in wintering areas. Females are known as Reeves. VOICE: Normally silent; migrating flocks may utter a shrill *hoo-ee*. HABITAT: Lake, pool and river margins, marshes, wet grassland and coastal mudflats. DISTRIBUTION: Winter visitor or migrant to the region, nowhere common.

3 TEREK SANDPIPER *Xenus cinereus* 22–25cm FIELD NOTES: Usually seen singly or in small, scattered groups. Often feeds in an active, dashing manner. In flight, upperwing shows a wide white trailing edge. VOICE: In flight, utters a rippling *du-du-du-du-du* or a mellow *chu-du-du*. HABITAT: Mainly coastal wetlands. DISTRIBUTION: Passage migrant and winter visitor to the region.

4 COMMON SANDPIPER *Actitis hypoleucos* 19–21cm FIELD NOTES: Bobs rear end while walking. Flies, often low, with stiff, flicking wing-beats. Upperwing shows a white bar. VOICE: In flight, gives a piping *tswee-wee-we*; when alarmed, utters a *sweet-eet*. HABITAT: Various freshwater and saltwater wetlands. DISTRIBUTION: Winter visitor to the region.

5 TURNSTONE (RUDDY TURNSTONE) *Arenaria interpres* 21–26cm FIELD NOTES: Typically forages by flicking over small stones, shells or seaweed in search of small invertebrates. In flight, shows striking black and white patterning. VOICE: A rapid, staccato *trik-tuk-tuk-tuk*, *tuk-e-tuk* or *chit-uk*; when alarmed, gives a sharp *chick-ik*, *kuu* or *teu*. HABITAT: Stony, rocky and sandy shores, also mudflats. DISTRIBUTION: Widespread winter visitor or migrant to the region.

6 RED-NECKED PHALAROPE (NORTHERN PHALAROPE) *Phalaropus lobatus* 18–19cm FIELD NOTES: Forages mainly while swimming, usually at sea in small flocks. Thin bill. In flight, upperwing shows a white wing-bar. VOICE: In flight, gives a short *twick*, *clip* or *kip*. HABITAT: At sea, on coastal waters, and sometimes on inland rivers or paddyfields. DISTRIBUTION: Passage migrant to the seas of the region, occasionally inland.

7 GREY PHALAROPE (RED PHALAROPE) *Phalaropus fulicarius* 21–22cm FIELD NOTES: Forages mainly by swimming. Short, thick bill. In flight, shows a white wing-bar. VOICE: In flight, utters a sharp *pic*. HABITAT: Generally pelagic, but sometimes (usually when storm-blown) occurs inland. DISTRIBUTION: Vagrant recorded off Borneo and Luzon in the Philippines.

8 PAINTED SNIPE (GREATER PAINTED-SNIPE) *Rostratula benghalensis* 23–28cm FIELD NOTES: Mainly crepuscular. Secretive. Flies with dangling legs. VOICE: In display, female utters a soft *koh koh koh*, likened to blowing across the top of an empty bottle; also various hisses and growls. HABITAT: Marshes, swamps and paddyfields. DISTRIBUTION: Resident in Sumatra, Java, Borneo and the Philippines, and Lombok, Sumbawa and Flores in the W Lesser Sundas.

9 AUSTRALIAN PRATINCOLE *Stiltia isabella* 24cm FIELD NOTES: Usually occurs singly or in small groups. Forages on the ground or by hawking insects in the air. In flight, shows exceptionally long wings, white rump and short squarish tail. Underwing-coverts black. VOICE: A shrill, sweet *hoo-wee-too* or *hoo-wee*. HABITAT: Open grassland. DISTRIBUTION: Regular winter visitor to Wallacea; scarce visitor to Sumatra, Java, Bali and Borneo.

10 ORIENTAL PRATINCOLE *Glareola maldivarum* 23–26cm FIELD NOTES: Generally gregarious. In flight, shows a white rump and forked tail. Underwing-coverts chestnut. VOICE: A sharp *kyik*, *chik-chik* or *chet*, also a rising *trooeet* and a *ter-ack*. HABITAT: Bare flats, dry paddyfields, marshes, lake and river margins, and coastal pools. DISTRIBUTION: Resident and migrant to Borneo and the Philippines; migrant throughout rest of region.

73 THICK-KNEE; OYSTERCATCHERS; STILTS; AVOCET; JACANAS

1 BEACH THICK-KNEE (BEACH STONE-CURLEW) *Esacus magnirostris* 53–57cm
FIELD NOTES: Mainly crepuscular or nocturnal, spending the day resting in shade. Usually seen singly, in pairs or in small groups. VOICE: A harsh, wailing *wee-loo*; utters a weak, yapping *quip*, *peep* or rising *quip-ip-ip* when alarmed. HABITAT: Coastal shores, often near mangroves. DISTRIBUTION: Resident throughout the region.

2 OYSTERCATCHER (EURASIAN OYSTERCATCHER) *Haematopus ostralegus* 40–46cm FIELD NOTES: Usually occurs in small groups. In flight, shows a broad white bar across all flight feathers of upperwing, white rump and uppertail-coverts, and mainly black tail. VOICE: A sharp *kleep* or *kle-eap*, and a quiet *weep*. HABITAT: Mudflats and rocky coasts; also feeds inland on short grassy areas. DISTRIBUTION: Vagrant in Borneo and Olango in the C Philippines.

3 PIED OYSTERCATCHER *Haematopus longirostris* 42–50cm FIELD NOTES: Occurs singly, in pairs or in small groups. Conspicuous and noisy, but wary. In flight, shows black primaries and mainly white secondaries, white rump and uppertail-coverts, and mainly black tail. VOICE: A piping *kleep*. HABITAT: Prefers remote sandy beaches and mudflats. DISTRIBUTION: Resident in the S Moluccas and E Lesser Sundas.

4 BLACK-WINGED STILT *Himantopus himantopus* 35–40cm FIELD NOTES: Usually seen in small groups. Juvenile crown and hind-neck pattern varies from white to slate grey. VOICE: A sharp *kek*, a high-pitched *kikikikik* and a yelping *kee-ack*. HABITAT: Various wetlands, including saltmarsh, saltpans, lakes and marshes. DISTRIBUTION: Migrant to N Borneo and the C Philippines.

5 PIED STILT (BLACK-NECKED STILT) *Himantopus leucocephalus* 35–40cm
FIELD NOTES: Often considered a race of Black-winged Stilt; actions and habits similar. VOICE: Similar to Black-winged Stilt, but softer and more nasal. HABITAT: Similar to Black-winged Stilt. DISTRIBUTION: Resident in Java, Bali, the Philippines and Wallacea; migrant to Sumatra and Borneo; has bred in Borneo.

6 AVOCET (PIED AVOCET) *Recurvirostra avosetta* 42–45cm FIELD NOTES: Usually gregarious. Readily swims, upending like a dabbling duck to feed. VOICE: A melodious *kluit-kluit-kluit*; when alarmed, utters a harsh *kloo-eet*. HABITAT: Mainly shallow saline or brackish lakes, lagoons, saltpans and estuaries. DISTRIBUTION: Vagrant in Borneo and Palawan in the W Philippines.

7 BRONZE-WINGED JACANA *Metopidius indicus* 28–31cm FIELD NOTES: Forages by walking on floating vegetation or wading in shallow water. Juvenile has brown upperparts and white underparts with a pinkish suffusion on neck and breast, and a chestnut crown and small white supercilium. VOICE: A harsh grunt; when alarmed, utters a wheezy, piping *seek-seek-seek*. HABITAT: Lakes and ponds with floating and emergent vegetation. DISTRIBUTION: Resident in Sumatra and Java.

8 COMB-CRESTED JACANA *Irediparra gallinacea* 23cm FIELD NOTES: Usually seen alone or in pairs. Walks with ease on floating vegetation. Juvenile resembles adult but lacks black breast-band and head wattles. VOICE: A thin, twittering call in flight, and a nasal alarm call. HABITAT: Freshwater lakes, ponds and swamps with abundant floating and emergent vegetation. DISTRIBUTION: Resident in SE Borneo and Mindanao in the S Philippines, and widely but patchily in Wallacea.

9 PHEASANT-TAILED JACANA (WATER-PHEASANT) *Hydrophasianus chirurgus* 31–58cm FIELD NOTES: Often gregarious. Forages by walking on floating vegetation, and swimming or wading in shallow water. In flight, shows striking white wings. VOICE: A far-carrying, mewing *me-e-ou* or *me-onp*; flocks utter a nasal *tewn*. HABITAT: Well-vegetated lakes, ponds and marshes; on migration, also frequents rivers and mangroves. DISTRIBUTION: Resident in the Philippines; winter visitor to Sumatra and Java; vagrant in Bali and Borneo, and possibly Wallacea.

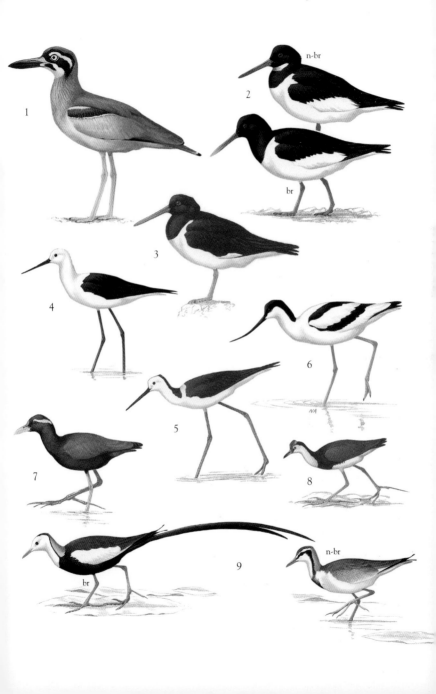

74 SKUAS; GULLS

1 ARCTIC SKUA (PARASITIC JAEGER) *Stercorarius parasiticus* 41–46cm
FIELD NOTES: Acrobatically chases and harries seabirds, attempting to make them disgorge food. In flight, shows a white flash at the base of the primaries. VOICE: Generally silent. HABITAT: Pelagic. DISTRIBUTION: Probably a regular winter visitor to the seas of the region.

2 POMARINE SKUA (POMARINE JAEGER) *Stercorarius pomarinus* 46–51cm
FIELD NOTES: The bulkiest of the 'smaller' skuas. Aggressive pursuer of seabirds in order to steal food, even going as far as killing the object of the chase. In flight, shows a white flash at base of primaries. VOICE: Generally silent. HABITAT: Coastal waters. DISTRIBUTION: Migrant to the seas of the region.

3 SOUTH POLAR SKUA (BROWN or MACCORMICK'S SKUA)
Stercorarius antarcticus 61–66cm FIELD NOTES: In flight, shows a white flash at base of primaries. Various morphs occur, grading from pale to dark. VOICE: Generally silent. HABITAT: Pelagic. DISTRIBUTION: Winter vagrant to the seas of the region.

4 LONG-TAILED SKUA (LONG-TAILED JAEGER) *Stercorarius longicaudus* 48–53cm
FIELD NOTES: In flight, shows no, or little, white at base of primaries. Less piratical than other skuas; when indulging in harassment, tends to pick on terns. VOICE: Generally silent. HABITAT: Coastal waters. DISTRIBUTION: Winter migrant or vagrant to the seas off Java, Bali, Borneo and the Lesser Sundas.

5 BLACK-TAILED GULL *Larus crassirostris* 44–47cm FIELD NOTES: Upperwing primaries black with small white tips, outer feather may have a small subterminal spot. VOICE: A plaintive mewing. HABITAT: Rocky islands, cliffs, seashores, rivers and lakes. DISTRIBUTION: Vagrant in Borneo and the Philippines.

6 SLATY-BACKED GULL *Larus schistisagus* 55–67cm FIELD NOTES: In flight, shows a broad white trailing edge to wing; often has an indistinct white band dividing the slaty upperwing from the black outer primaries, the latter with a white subterminal spot on outer feather. VOICE: A low *klook-klook-klook-klook*. HABITAT: Coastal. DISTRIBUTION: Vagrant in the Philippines.

7 VEGA GULL *Larus vegae* 57–64cm FIELD NOTES: In flight, upperwing shows black-tipped outer primaries with a white subterminal spot on two outermost feathers. VOICE: A laughing *keeah-keeah-keeah-keeah-keah-kau-kau...* HABITAT: Coasts and along rivers. DISTRIBUTION: Vagrant in the Philippines.

8 FRANKLIN'S GULL *Leucophaeus pipixcan* 32–38cm FIELD NOTES: In flight, shows grey centre to tail, grey upperwing with white trailing edge, and broad white tips to outer primaries, broken by a black subterminal band. VOICE: A soft *kruk* and a shrill *guk*. HABITAT: Coastal lagoons, sandbanks, lakes, rivers and marshes. DISTRIBUTION: Vagrant in the Philippines.

9 BROWN-HEADED GULL *Chroicocephalus brunnicephalus* 41–45cm FIELD NOTES: Outermost primaries of upperwing white with broad black tips, broken by a subterminal white spot on outermost feather. VOICE: A harsh *gek gek* or *grarhh*, a wailing *ko-yek ko-yek* and a raucous *kreeak*. HABITAT: Coastal waters, lakes and large rivers. DISTRIBUTION: Vagrant in Sumatra.

10 SAUNDERS'S GULL *Chroicocephalus saundersi* 29–32cm FIELD NOTES: Buoyant, tern-like flight. Inner primaries form a black wedge, making underwing pattern diagnostic; upperwing grey with black subterminal tips on white primaries. VOICE: A shrill *eek eek*. HABITAT: Coastal areas. DISTRIBUTION: Vagrant in the Philippines.

11 BLACK-HEADED GULL *Chroicocephalus ridibundus* 37–43cm FIELD NOTES: In flight, upperwing pale grey and outer primaries white, tipped black. VOICE: A high-pitched *karr* or *krreearr*, and a sharp *kek-kek*. HABITAT: Coasts, lakes, rivers and various inland grasslands. DISTRIBUTION: Winter visitor to Borneo, the Philippines, Sulawesi and the N Moluccas.

12 SABINE'S GULL *Xema sabini* 27–33cm FIELD NOTES: Distinctive tricoloured upperwing pattern: grey coverts, black outer primaries and coverts, and white inner primaries and secondaries. Tail forked. VOICE: A grating *krrr*. HABITAT: Mainly pelagic. DISTRIBUTION: Vagrant off the coast of Sumatra.

75 TERNS

1 CASPIAN TERN *Hydroprogne caspia* 47–54cm FIELD NOTES: Feeds mainly by hovering and then plunge-diving, also picks from water surface; sometimes harasses food from other terns and gulls. In flight, upperwing shows grey outer primaries with darker tips, underwing shows dark outer primaries; tail shallowly forked. VOICE: A loud, croaking *kraah*, *krah-krah* or *kree-ahk*. HABITAT: Coastal waters, mudflats, inland lakes, rivers and marshes. DISTRIBUTION: Vagrant in Sumatra, Borneo, Luzon in the Philippines and Timor in the Lesser Sundas.

2 GULL-BILLED TERN *Gelochelidon nilotica* 33–43cm FIELD NOTES: Feeds by hawking insects or dipping to pick up prey from water or ground. Flight gull-like. VOICE: A nasal *kay-did*, *kay-tih-did*, *gur-WICK*, *ger-erk* or *kay-vek*; also a metallic *kak-kak* and a *kvay-kvay* when alarmed. HABITAT: Coasts, saltmarshes, brackish and freshwater lakes, pools and rivers. DISTRIBUTION: Winter visitor to the region.

3 LITTLE TERN *Sternula albifrons* 22–28cm FIELD NOTES: Very active forager, feeds by plunge-diving, which is preceded by prolonged hovering. Tail deeply forked. VOICE: A rapid *kirrikikki kirrikiki*, a sharp *kik-kik* and a rasping *zr-e-e-e-p*. HABITAT: Sand bars and shingle banks on coasts, lakes and rivers. DISTRIBUTION: Resident in Sumatra, Java, Borneo, the Philippines and Sulawesi; otherwise a winter visitor to the region.

4 LESSER CRESTED TERN *Thalasseus bengalensis* 36–41cm FIELD NOTES: Feeds mainly by hovering and then plunge-diving. Inner webs of outer primaries form an indistinct silver wedge on upperwing; outer primaries on underwing show dusky tips. Rump and tail pale grey, the latter deeply forked. VOICE: A harsh *krrik-krrik* or *kerrick*. HABITAT: Coastal waters. DISTRIBUTION: Winter visitor to Sumatra, Java, Bali, Borneo and Wallacea.

5 CHINESE CRESTED TERN *Thalasseus bernsteini* 42cm FIELD NOTES: Outer webs of outer primaries on upperwing blackish; underwing white. Tail deeply forked, with longer tail streamers than in other crested terns. VOICE: Harsh, high-pitched cries. HABITAT: Coastal waters. DISTRIBUTION: Rare visitor or vagrant in Borneo, the Philippines and the N Moluccas.

6 GREATER CRESTED TERN (SWIFT TERN) *Thalasseus bergii* 43–53cm FIELD NOTES: Feeds mainly by plunge-diving, but also picks from surface of water. Underwing shows dark greyish tips to outer primaries; rump and tail same colour as upperparts; tail deeply forked. VOICE: A grating *krrik* or *kee-rit*, also a high-pitched *kree-kree*. HABITAT: Coastal waters. DISTRIBUTION: Resident and winter visitor in the region; breeds on islands off Sumatra, Sulawesi, the Lesser Sundas and the Moluccas.

7 BLACK-NAPED TERN *Sterna sumatrana* 34–35cm FIELD NOTES: Feeds mainly by plunge-diving, but also by skimming low and picking prey from water surface. Outer web of outermost primary blackish; tail deeply forked, with long outer tail feathers. VOICE: A sharp *tsii-chee-chi-chip* and a *chit-chit-chit-er*, uttered when excited or alarmed. HABITAT: Rocky islets, coastal bays and lagoons. DISTRIBUTION: Resident and winter visitor; breeds on islets off Sumatra, Java, Bali, Borneo and the Philippines, and in Wallacea.

8 ROSEATE TERN *Sterna dougallii* 33–38cm FIELD NOTES: Feeds mainly by plunge-diving, usually from a greater height than Common Tern; also picks food from surface of water. Tail deeply forked, with very long outer tail feathers. VOICE: A rasping *kraak* or *zraaach*, also a short, soft *cher-vik*. HABITAT: Offshore islets and coastal waters. DISTRIBUTION: Resident in Sumatra, Java, Borneo, the Philippines and the Moluccas.

9 COMMON TERN *Sterna hirundo* 32–39cm FIELD NOTES: Feeds mainly by plunge-diving, also picks food from surface of water. In flight from below, inner primaries appear translucent. Tail deeply forked, with long outer tail feathers. *S. h. longipennis* (9b) is the common race in the region; red-bill races possibly occur off Sumatra and Borneo. VOICE: A rapid *kye-kye-kye-kye…* and a *kirri-kirri-kirri*; when alarmed, utters a screeching *kreeearh* or *kreee-eer* and a sharp *kik*. HABITAT: Coasts and large inland waters. DISTRIBUTION: Winter visitor to the region.

1

n-br br

2

n-br br

3

n-br br

4

n-br br

5

n-br br

6

n-br br

7

br

8

n-br br

9b
longipennis

n-br br

9

76 TERNS; NODDIES

1 GREY-BACKED TERN (SPECTACLED TERN) *Onychoprion lunatus* 38cm
FIELD NOTES: Feeds mainly by plunge-diving. Underwing shows grey-brown primaries and secondaries. Tail grey, white-edged and deeply forked, with long outer tail feathers. VOICE: High-pitched screeching, less harsh than that of Sooty Tern. HABITAT: Offshore and pelagic waters. DISTRIBUTION: Uncommon visitor to the N Moluccas.

2 ALEUTIAN TERN *Onychoprion aleuticus* 32–34cm FIELD NOTES: Feeds by dipping to take food from water surface. Underwing white with a dark trailing edge to secondaries and dusky outer primaries; rump and tail white, the latter deeply forked. VOICE: A soft, wader-like *twee-ee-ee*. HABITAT: Coastal and pelagic waters. DISTRIBUTION: Vagrant in Borneo.

3 BRIDLED TERN *Onychoprion anaethetus* 34–36cm FIELD NOTES: Flight very buoyant. Feeds by plunge-diving and by dipping to pick food off water surface. Underwing mainly white, with dusky tips to primaries and secondaries; rump and tail dark grey, the latter deeply forked and with long white outer tail feathers. VOICE: A yapping *wep-wep* or *wup-wup*. HABITAT: Mainly pelagic, coming to small islets only to roost or breed. DISTRIBUTION: Resident in the region.

4 SOOTY TERN (WIDEAWAKE TERN) *Onychoprion fuscatus* 36–45cm
FIELD NOTES: Feeds mainly by dipping and picking food from water surface. Underwing white with dusky primaries and dusky tips to secondaries. Rump and tail blackish, the latter deeply forked and with long white outer tail feathers. VOICE: A distinctive *ker-wacki-wah, ker-wacki-wack* or *wide-awake*; also utters a short *kraark*. HABITAT: Mainly pelagic, rarely coming to land apart from during the breeding season. DISTRIBUTION: Resident throughout the region.

5 WHITE-WINGED TERN (WHITE-WINGED BLACK TERN)
Chlidonias leucopterus 23–27cm FIELD NOTES: Foraging flight is buoyant, with regular dips to pick up food from water surface. Underwing-coverts black, rump white, tail pale grey and very shallowly forked; in non-breeding plumage, underwing whitish with grey primaries and secondaries, and many birds with vestiges of black coverts in the form of lines or patches. VOICE: A harsh, high-pitched *kreek*, a soft *kek* and a rasping *kesch* or *chr-re re*. HABITAT: Coastal lagoons, estuaries, marshes, paddyfields, lakes, pools and large rivers. DISTRIBUTION: Winter visitor to the region.

6 WHISKERED TERN *Chlidonias hybrida* 23–29cm FIELD NOTES: Buoyant foraging flight, with regular dips to pick up food from water surface; may also plunge-dive. Rump grey, paler in non-breeding plumage; tail shallowly forked. VOICE: A rasping *cherk* and a *kek* or *kek-kek*. HABITAT: Vegetated lakes, marshes, paddyfields, coastal pools and mudflats. DISTRIBUTION: Winter visitor throughout the region.

7 WHITE TERN (FAIRY TERN) *Gygis alba* 25–30cm FIELD NOTES: Dives to capture small fish. Tail forked. Immature white, with greyish-brown mottling on mantle, nape and ear-coverts, and outer webs of outer primaries dark grey. VOICE: A guttural *heech heech*. HABITAT: Pelagic. DISTRIBUTION: Vagrant off Sumatra, the W Lesser Sundas and the N Moluccas.

8 BROWN NODDY (COMMON NODDY) *Anous stolidus* 38–45cm FIELD NOTES: Feeds mainly by hovering and dipping to pick prey from water surface. Underwing-coverts slightly paler than flight feathers. Tail wedge-shaped, but may look forked during moult of central feathers. VOICE: A crow-like *kwok-kwok*, *karruuk* or *krao*. HABITAT: Pelagic; breeds on small islands, islet, sand bars and shoals. DISTRIBUTION: Resident in seas throughout the region. Breeds on sand bars and shoals off the Philippines and on isolated islands, especially Gunungapi and Manuk in the Banda Sea.

9 BLACK NODDY (WHITE-CAPPED NODDY) *Anous minutus* 35–39cm
FIELD NOTES: Feeding actions similar to Brown Noddy. Underwing-coverts brownish black, contiguous with flight feathers. Tail wedge-shaped, but may look forked during moult of central feathers. VOICE: A distinctive *tik-tikoree*. HABITAT: Pelagic away from breeding sites. DISTRIBUTION: Breeds on the E coast of Sumatra and reefs in the Sulu Sea; wanderer to Java, Bali, Borneo and Wallacea.

77 OSPREY; BAZAS; HONEY BUZZARDS; BAT HAWK; VULTURE

1 OSPREY *Pandion haliaetus* 55–63cm FIELD NOTES: Feeds on fish; hovers, then swoops to capture prey, in talons, from just below water surface. The resident race, *P. h. cristatus* (not illustrated), is slightly smaller and often has a whiter face, although face pattern is variable and often not separable from nominate race; it is sometimes considered a full species. VOICE: When alarmed, gives a hoarse, sharp *kew-kew-kew-kew*. HABITAT: Lakes, rivers, coastal lagoons and estuaries. DISTRIBUTION: Resident in Java, Bali, Sulawesi, the Lesser Sundas and the Moluccas; winter migrant throughout the region.

2 JERDON'S BAZA *Aviceda jerdoni* 41–48cm FIELD NOTES: Shy. Crepuscular. Hunts from a perch, making short sorties to grab prey, usually insects, lizards or frogs. *A. j. celebensis* (2b) occurs on Sulawesi and the Sula Islands. VOICE: A plaintive *pee-ow*; during display, utters an excited, mewing *kip-kip-kip* or *kikiya kikiya*. HABITAT: DISTRIBUTION: Resident in Sumatra, Borneo, the Philippines, Sulawesi and the Sula Islands.

3 PACIFIC BAZA *Aviceda subcristata* 35–46cm FIELD NOTES: Usually seen singly or in pairs, sometimes in groups. Often perches conspicuously in the tops of trees. Snatches insects and lizards from foliage. *A. s. reinwardtii* (3b) occurs on Boano, Seram, Ambon and Haruku in the S Moluccas. VOICE: A breezy, high-pitched *whee-chu*, often repeated and uttered more rapidly when excited. HABITAT: Primary and tall secondary lowland and hill forest, forest edges and lightly wooded cultivation. DISTRIBUTION: Resident in the Lesser Sundas and Moluccas.

4 BLACK BAZA *Aviceda leuphotes* 30–35cm FIELD NOTES: Flight crow-like, interspersed with level-winged glides. Regularly hovers in front of, or hangs from, foliage to capture prey. VOICE: A soft, quavering squealed or whistled *tcheeoua*. HABITAT: Forested hills with glades and streams. DISTRIBUTION: Winter visitor to Sumatra and, rarely, Java.

5 CRESTED HONEY BUZZARD (ORIENTAL HONEY BUZZARD)
Pernis ptilorhynchus 52–68cm FIELD NOTES: Plumage very variable, especially underparts. Often seen soaring over forests, flying with deep, steady wing-beats interspersed with glides. *P. p. philippensis* (5b) occurs on the Philippines. VOICE: A high-pitched *wee-wey-uho* or *weehey-weehey* and a shrill, whistled *wheyeeee*. HABITAT: Forested lowlands and hills. DISTRIBUTION: Resident in the Philippines; resident in, and winter visitor to, Sumatra, Java and Borneo; winter visitor to Sulawesi.

6 BARRED HONEY BUZZARD *Pernis celebensis* 50–58cm FIELD NOTES: Usually seen singly, in pairs or occasionally in small groups; regularly soars high over forests, partly cleared ridges and valleys. VOICE: A sharp *whit-weee-oooo* or *weee-oooo*. HABITAT: Forest, forest edges and partially cleared areas. DISTRIBUTION: Endemic to Sulawesi.

7 STEERE'S HONEY BUZZARD (PHILIPPINE HONEY BUZZARD)
Pernis steerei 51–57cm FIELD NOTES: Secretive, tends to 'hide' in dense foliage, although regularly soars high over forests. Formerly regarded as a race of the previous species. VOICE: Loud screaming or ringing calls. HABITAT: Lowland to submontane forest and forest edges. DISTRIBUTION: Endemic to the Philippines.

8 BAT HAWK *Macheiramphus alcinus* 41–51cm FIELD NOTES: Crepuscular. Hunts bats as they leave or return to caves. Flight is rapid, with shallow, stiff wing-beats. Juvenile white below with variable blackish blotches. VOICE: A high, yelping *kwik-kwik-kwik-kwik*. HABITAT: Open areas near forests, near bat caves and around human habitation. DISTRIBUTION: Resident in Sumatra, Borneo and Sulawesi.

9 INDIAN WHITE-BACKED VULTURE (WHITE-BACKED VULTURE)
Gyps bengalensis 75–85cm FIELD NOTES: In flight from above, adult shows prominent white rump. Soars with wings held in a shallow 'V'. VOICE: Generally silent away from breeding sites. HABITAT: Open country. DISTRIBUTION: Vagrant; unconfirmed old record from NW Borneo. Due to the massive population crash, unlikely to be seen in the region any time soon?

78 EAGLES

1 WHITE-BELLIED SEA EAGLE *Haliaeetus leucogaster* 66–71cm FIELD NOTES: Snatches fish from water, occasionally feeds on carrion. Juvenile generally brown above and pale cinnamon below; tail white with a black subterminal band. VOICE: A loud, honking *kank kank kank kank…*, also a faster *ken-ken-ken-ken* and a *ka ka-kaaa*. HABITAT: Rocky coasts, islets and sometimes large lakes. DISTRIBUTION: Resident throughout the region.

2 LESSER FISH EAGLE *Haliaeetus humilis* 53–68cm FIELD NOTES: Swoops on fish from mid-stream rocks or overhanging branches. Regularly perches on exposed dead trees along rivers and lake margins. VOICE: A plaintive, gull-like *pheeow-pheeoow-pheeow…*, also a *hak hak hak hak* and a series of *kahAW* notes. HABITAT: Lakes and large, fast-flowing forest rivers. DISTRIBUTION: Resident in Sumatra, Borneo and Sulawesi.

3 GREY-HEADED FISH EAGLE *Haliaeetus ichthyaetus* 69–74cm FIELD NOTES: Swoops to take surface-feeding fish. Often perches on bare limbs overlooking water. Juvenile has pale head and underparts variously streaked brown; tail pale grey with darker greyish bars. VOICE: A squawking *kwok*, harsh screams, a repeated *chee-warr* and, during display, a far-carrying *tiu-weeeu*. HABITAT: Rivers and lakes in wooded country, coastal lagoons and estuaries. DISTRIBUTION: Resident in Sumatra, W Java, Borneo, the Philippines and possibly Sulawesi.

4 BONELLI'S EAGLE *Aquila fasciata* 65–72cm FIELD NOTES: Occurs in pairs; soars over wooded ridges and valleys, with wings held level. Juvenile generally more rufous, underwing-coverts pale rufous. VOICE: Generally silent; during display, utters a fluting *klu-klu-klu-kluee*. HABITAT: Primary and tall secondary foothill and montane forest, lightly wooded hills, submontane forest, cultivation, scrub and plantations. DISTRIBUTION: Resident in the Lesser Sundas.

5 GURNEY'S EAGLE *Aquila gurneyi* 74–85cm FIELD NOTES: Generally seen singly, occasionally in pairs or threes. Hunts by quartering over forest or nearby open areas, gliding on flat or slightly raised wings. In flight, juvenile shows pale cinnamon-buff head, underparts and underwing-coverts, and dark-barred greyish flight feathers with black primary tips. VOICE: A nasal, piping, downslurred note. HABITAT: Primary lowland and hill forest, coastal forest, forest edges and plantations. DISTRIBUTION: Resident in the Moluccas.

6 BOOTED EAGLE *Hieraaetus pennatus* 50–57cm FIELD NOTES: In head-on flight, shows white 'headlights' at joint of neck and wing. Glides on arched wings. Plumage variable, especially on underwing-coverts. VOICE: A shrill, chattering *ki-ki-ki…* and a buzzard-like *hiyaah*. HABITAT: Forested areas with nearby open land. DISTRIBUTION: Vagrant in Bali.

7 PYGMY EAGLE *Hieraaetus weiskei* 38–48cm FIELD NOTES: Usually occurs singly. Glides on level wings, low over canopy or forest edges; often perches in the open on treetop branches. VOICE: Generally silent; gives a whistling *sip sip see* during display flight. HABITAT: Primary rainforest, riparian and monsoon forest, and forest edges. DISTRIBUTION: Resident in the Moluccas, north from Seram.

8 RUFOUS-BELLIED EAGLE *Lophotriorchis kienerii* 53–61cm FIELD NOTES: Soars high above forest canopy, often making spectacular falcon-like stoops to take prey. Juvenile white below, including underwing-coverts. VOICE: A low-pitched *whi-whi-whi-whi yii*. HABITAT: Broadleaved evergreen forest. DISTRIBUTION: Resident in Sumatra, Java, Borneo, the Philippines and Sulawesi; possibly resident in the Lesser Sundas.

9 PHILIPPINE EAGLE *Pithecophaga jefferyi* 90–100cm FIELD NOTES: Occurs singly or in pairs. Frequently soars above forests on the lookout for small to medium animals. VOICE: A loud, plaintive, whistled *waaaauu waaaauu waaaauu* or *waa-leee-ahhh*. HABITAT: Forest, logged forest and forest edges, from lowlands to mountains. DISTRIBUTION: Endemic to the Philippines.

10 BLACK EAGLE *Ictinaetus malaiensis* 69–81cm FIELD NOTES: Often seen soaring low over forest canopy, with wings held in a shallow 'V', searching for eggs and nestlings. VOICE: A plaintive *kleeee-kee* or *hee-lee-leeuw*. HABITAT: Lowland, hill and montane forest. DISTRIBUTION: Resident in Sumatra, Java, Borneo, Sulawesi and the C Moluccas.

79 KITES; HAWK-EAGLES

1 BLACK-SHOULDERED KITE (BLACK-WINGED KITE) *Elanus caeruleus* 31–35cm
FIELD NOTES: Often hovers while searching for prey. In flight, shows a large black patch on upperwing-coverts. VOICE: A plaintive *wheep wheep*. HABITAT: Grasslands with scattered trees and cultivation. DISTRIBUTION: Resident in Sumatra, Borneo, Java, Bali, the Philippines, Sulawesi and the Lesser Sundas.

2 BLACK KITE *Milvus migrans* 55–60cm FIELD NOTES: Gregarious scavenger. Flight loose with much twisting of tail. *M. m. lineatus* (2b) (Black-eared Kite), a vagrant in Borneo and the W Philippines, is often considered a separate species. VOICE: A whinnying *pee-errrr*. HABITAT: Open areas, wetlands and urban areas. DISTRIBUTION: Resident in Sulawesi and the Lesser Sundas; winter visitor to Sumatra; vagrant in Borneo and the W Philippines.

3 BRAHMINY KITE *Haliastur indus* 45–51cm FIELD NOTES: Usually occurs singly or in pairs. Scavenger, especially around harbours and rubbish dumps. VOICE: A wheezy squeal. HABITAT: Forest edges, open country, lakes, rivers, flooded paddyfields, coastal lagoons, estuaries and fishing harbours. DISTRIBUTION: Resident throughout the region.

4 CHANGEABLE HAWK-EAGLE *Nisaetus cirrhatus* 58–77cm FIELD NOTES: Often uses a concealed forest perch from which to make short dashes after prey. Dark morph similar to Black Eagle (Plate 78), but slimmer and with longer tail. *N. c. limnaeetus* (main illustration) occurs in Sumatra, Java, Borneo, Sulawesi and the Philippines; *N. c. vanheurni* (4b) occurs on Simeulue Island off Sumatra. VOICE: A series of shrill whistles. HABITAT: Lowland forests. DISTRIBUTION: Resident in Sumatra, Java, Bali, Borneo, and the S and W Philippines.

5 FLORES HAWK-EAGLE *Nisaetus floris* 75–79cm FIELD NOTES: Formerly considered a race of the previous species; actions presumed to be similar. VOICE: Unrecorded. HABITAT: Submontane forest, lowland rainforest and nearby cultivation. DISTRIBUTION: Endemic to the Lesser Sundas.

6 BLYTH'S HAWK-EAGLE *Nisaetus alboniger* 50–58cm FIELD NOTES: Soars over canopy with wings held level; when chasing prey, adopts an agile accipiter-like flight through trees. Juvenile has unmarked cinnamon-buff underparts and head, except for black crest feathers. VOICE: Various shrill whistles. HABITAT: Upland forests. DISTRIBUTION: Resident in Sumatra and Borneo.

7 JAVAN HAWK-EAGLE *Nisaetus bartelsi* 60cm FIELD NOTES: Actions presumed to be similar to Changeable Hawk-eagle; preys on large birds, small mammals and lizards. Immature has unmarked, pale buff underparts and head, apart from dark crest feathers. VOICE: Harsh, high-pitched cries. HABITAT: Tropical hill and mountain forest, and open wooded areas. DISTRIBUTION: Endemic to Java.

8 SULAWESI HAWK-EAGLE *Nisaetus lanceolatus* 55–64cm FIELD NOTES: Usually seen singly. Perches in the tree canopy, sometimes conspicuously. Juvenile superficially similar to Flores Hawk-eagle. VOICE: A descending *kluuu-kluuu-kluuu-kluuu-kluuu-kluuu…*, preceded by an upward-inflected disyllabic note; also a rapid *kee-kee-kee-kee…* HABITAT: Primary and tall secondary lowland, hill and montane forest, forest edges and nearby open country. DISTRIBUTION: Endemic to Sulawesi and the Sula Islands.

9 PHILIPPINE HAWK-EAGLE *Nisaetus philippensis* 56–67cm FIELD NOTES: Often stays concealed in the canopy. Little recorded information; presumed to be similar to others of the genus. Juvenile similar to Flores Hawk-eagle except for long, dark crest feathers. VOICE: A screamed *wheeet whit* or *du-wheeet whit*. HABITAT: Forest and advanced secondary growth, from lowlands to mountains. DISTRIBUTION: Endemic to the N Philippines.

10 PINSKER'S HAWK-EAGLE *Nisaetus pinskeri* 54–61cm FIELD NOTES: Formerly considered a race of the previous species; actions presumed to be similar. VOICE: A *wheee-whit*, similar to previous species. HABITAT: Mature forest from lowland to low mountains. DISTRIBUTION: Endemic to the S and C Philippines.

11 WALLACE'S HAWK-EAGLE *Nisaetus nanus* 45–49cm FIELD NOTES: Hunting actions probably similar to others of the genus. Juvenile has unmarked buff head and underparts, except for black crest feathers. VOICE: A shrill, high-pitched *yik-yee* or *kliit-kleeik*. HABITAT: Primary lowland forest. DISTRIBUTION: Resident in Sumatra and Borneo.

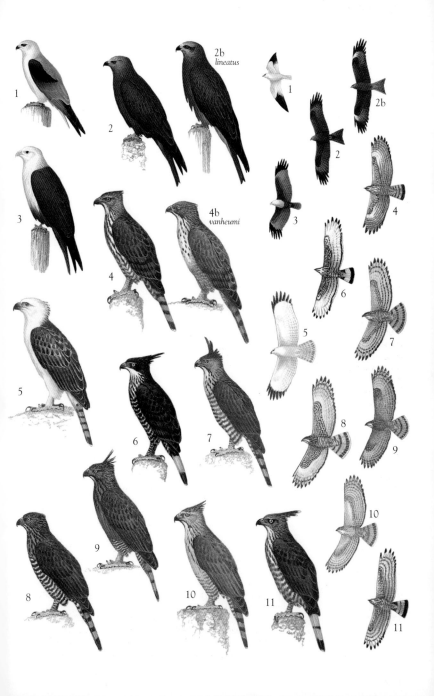

2b
lineatus

4b
vanheumi

80 SERPENT EAGLES; HARRIERS

1 CRESTED SERPENT EAGLE *Spilornis cheela* 56–74cm FIELD NOTES: Often seen soaring and calling high over forests. Variable. Races depicted are: S. c. *pallidus* from lowland Borneo (main illustration); S. c. *sipora* (1b) from Mentawai Island, off Sumatra; and S. c. *abbotti* (1c) from Simeulue Island off Sumatra. VOICE: A shrill *kwee-kwee-kwee…* HABITAT: Well-wooded areas. DISTRIBUTION: Resident in Sumatra, Java, Bali, Borneo and the W Philippines.

2 MOUNTAIN SERPENT EAGLE *Spilornis kinabaluensis* 55–58cm FIELD NOTES: Hunts along mountain ridges and dry riverbeds. Formerly considered a race of the previous species. VOICE: A long, thin scream and a drawn-out *kiillii.* HABITAT: Stunted ridgetop montane forest. DISTRIBUTION: Endemic to Borneo.

3 SULAWESI SERPENT EAGLE *Spilornis rufipectus* 46–54cm FIELD NOTES: Generally seen singly or in pairs. Noisy and conspicuous, often perching on exposed treetop branches. Regularly flies over forest canopy. VOICE: A variable, far-carrying, high-pitched whistle, which occasionally ends in a weak chatter. HABITAT: Primary lowland, hill and montane forest, tall secondary scrub woodland, forest edges, lightly wooded cultivation and adjacent grassland. DISTRIBUTION: Endemic to Sulawesi and the Sula Islands.

4 PHILIPPINE SERPENT EAGLE *Spilornis holospilus* 47–53cm FIELD NOTES: Often perches at the forest edge. Soars high over forests and forest edges, usually calling. Hunts in the canopy. VOICE: A whistled *seee-ap weep weep*, which may also be interspersed with a *aahhe-e-a reep.* HABITAT: Forest and forest edges. DISTRIBUTION: Endemic to the N and S Philippines.

5 SHORT-TOED EAGLE (SHORT-TOED SNAKE EAGLE) *Circaetus gallicus* 62–67cm FIELD NOTES: Often hovers before dropping on prey. Regularly perches on exposed branches, singly or in pairs; soars over canopy and grasslands. VOICE: Generally silent, but may utter various musical, mewing and creaking notes. HABITAT: Primary and tall secondary monsoon woodland, savanna woodland, mixed scrub and lightly wooded cultivation. DISTRIBUTION: Resident in the Lesser Sundas.

6 MARSH HARRIER (WESTERN or EURASIAN MARSH HARRIER) *Circus aeruginosus* 48–56cm FIELD NOTES: Generally flies close to the ground, quartering reed-beds or open grassland using a series of flaps followed by a glide, with wings held in a shallow 'V'. Drops feet first to capture prey. VOICE: Generally silent, but may utter a cackling *chek-ek-ek-k-ek* when alarmed. HABITAT: Reed-beds, grassland, cultivated fields and saltmarshes. DISTRIBUTION: Probable winter visitor to Sumatra and Borneo.

7 EASTERN MARSH HARRIER *Circus spilonotus* 47–55cm FIELD NOTES: Foraging actions similar to previous species, which was formerly considered conspecific. Intensity of head markings variable, often leading to a blackish face or head. VOICE: Generally silent; may utter a mewing *keeau* at roost sites. HABITAT: Marshes, grassland and paddyfields. DISTRIBUTION: Winter visitor to Sumatra, Borneo and the Philippines.

8 SPOTTED HARRIER *Circus assimilis* 50–61cm FIELD NOTES: Occurs singly or in pairs. Hunts low over open country; regularly perches on isolated posts or dead trees. VOICE: A short, shrill whistle and a rapid chatter. HABITAT: Grassland, paddyfields, scrub and cultivation. DISTRIBUTION: Resident in Sulawesi and Sumba in the Lesser Sundas; possibly also on the Sula Islands and Timor in the Lesser Sundas.

9 HEN HARRIER *Circus cyaneus* 44–52cm FIELD NOTES: Foraging actions similar to Marsh Harrier but with quicker wing-beats and shorter glides. Glides with wings held level or in a shallow 'V'. VOICE: When alarmed, male utters a *chek-ek-ek-ek* and female a twittering *chit-it-it-it-it-it-et-it-et-it-et.* HABITAT: Open grassland, marshes and coastal marshes. DISTRIBUTION: Rare winter visitor or vagrant to Borneo.

10 PIED HARRIER *Circus melanoleucos* 41–49cm FIELD NOTES: Hunting actions similar to Hen Harrier. VOICE: Generally silent; female may utter a *chak-chak-chak-chak-chak* when alarmed. HABITAT: Open grassland, marshes and paddyfields. DISTRIBUTION: Winter visitor to Borneo and the Philippines; has bred on Luzon in the Philippines.

81 SPARROWHAWKS

1 CRESTED GOSHAWK *Accipiter trivirgatus* 30–46cm FIELD NOTES: Often perches, prominently at the top of a dead tree overlooking a clearing; also hunts from a low perch in forests. Usual flight consists of stiff wing-beats followed by short glides, often high above the forest canopy. *A. t. javanicus* (1b) occurs in Java and Bali. VOICE: A loud, repeated *weeee-aaa*, also a shrill *he-he-hehehehe* or similar. HABITAT: Primary forest and forest edges. DISTRIBUTION: Resident in Sumatra, Java, Bali, Borneo and the Philippines.

2 SULAWESI GOSHAWK *Accipiter griseiceps* 28–37cm FIELD NOTES: Usually seen singly. Favours forest interiors; hunts from a perch in dense foliage, swooping to capture prey on the ground. VOICE: A high-pitched, quite faint *tseee-tseee-tseee*. HABITAT: Primary lowland, hill and montane forest, mangroves and occasionally tall secondary woodland. DISTRIBUTION: Endemic to Sulawesi.

3 SHIKRA *Accipiter badius* 30–36cm FIELD NOTES: Usually hunts from a hidden, leafy perch, taking prey from trees or on the ground. Changes perch with a low flap and glide flight. VOICE: A piping *keeu-keeu-keeu* and a shrill *kewick*. HABITAT: Open woodland, forest edges and wooded cultivation. DISTRIBUTION: Uncommon winter visitor to Sumatra.

4 VARIABLE GOSHAWK *Accipiter hiogaster* 30–45cm FIELD NOTES: Occurs singly or in pairs; frequently seen either soaring over forests or dashing along forest edges. *A. h. sylvestris* (4b) occurs in the Lesser Sundas; *A. h. pallidiceps* (4c) is found on Buru in the Moluccas; *A. h. albiventris* (4d) occurs on the Kai Islands in the S Moluccas; *A. h. griseogularis* (4e) is found in the C and N Moluccas. VOICE: A series of high-pitched, upslurred notes. HABITAT: Primary and tall secondary lowland and hill forest, forest edges, monsoon woodland, savannah scrub and plantations. DISTRIBUTION: Resident in the Moluccas and Lesser Sundas.

5 CHINESE SPARROWHAWK *Accipiter soloensis* 27–35cm FIELD NOTES: Generally hunts from a perch in tree foliage, pouncing on frogs, lizards and insects. Female larger, with slight barring below. VOICE: A rapid, accelerating piping that descends in pitch. HABITAT: Various woodlands, often near wetlands. DISTRIBUTION: Winter visitor to Sumatra, Java, Borneo, the Philippines, Sulawesi, the N Moluccas and probably the Lesser Sundas.

6 SPOT-TAILED SPARROWHAWK *Accipiter trinotatus* 26–30cm FIELD NOTES: Perches in the forest understorey, close to the trunk, singly or in pairs. Active hunter of lizards, snakes, frogs, birds and insects. VOICE: A descending series of 4–6 *ke* notes. HABITAT: Primary lowland, hill and lower montane forest, tall secondary forest and mangroves. DISTRIBUTION: Endemic to Sulawesi.

7 MOLUCCAN GOSHAWK *Accipiter henicogrammus* 37–43cm FIELD NOTES: Occurs singly, in pairs, and occasionally in family groups. Inconspicuous, often perching in shaded areas of the mid-storey, close to the trunk. VOICE: Calls include a series of upslurred, slightly accelerating screams and a longer series of ascending whistles, the last few notes more shrieking. HABITAT: Interior of primary lowland and hill forest, occasionally also forest edges. DISTRIBUTION: Endemic to the N Moluccas.

8 BROWN GOSHAWK *Accipiter faciatus* 33–55cm FIELD NOTES: Encountered singly, occasionally in pairs. Hunts from a concealed perch in the lower canopy or mid-storey. *A. f. hellmayri* (8b) occurs on Timor and nearby small islands. VOICE: A high-pitched *ki-ki-ki-ki…* HABITAT: Monsoon forest and woodland, forest edges, lightly wooded cultivation and scrub. DISTRIBUTION: Resident in the Lesser Sundas, Buru in the S Moluccas, and islands in the Flores Sea.

9 JAPANESE SPARROWHAWK *Accipiter gularis* 29–34cm FIELD NOTES: Sometimes in small flocks during migration. Often perches hidden in tree foliage. VOICE: A shrill *kek-kek-kek*, a repeated, squealing *tchew-tchew-tchew* and a loud *ki-weer*. HABITAT: Lightly wooded areas, forest edges and open country with patches of trees. DISTRIBUTION: Winter visitor to Sumatra, Java, Bali, Borneo, the Philippines, Sulawesi and the Lesser Sundas.

1b
javanicus

1

2

3

1

2

4c
pallidiceps

5

3

4

4b
sylvestris

5

6

4d
albiventris

4e
griseogularis

6

4d

7

4

8b
hellmayri

7

8

8

9

♂

♀

♂

9

♀

1 BESRA *Accipiter virgatus* 29–36cm FIELD NOTES: Perches inconspicuously before dashing out to capture prey, mainly birds. *A. v. confusus* (1b) is found in the Philippines; *A. v. vanbemmeli* (1c) occurs in Sumatra. VOICE: A rapid *tchew-tchew-tchew* and a *wu wu wit-tit-tit-tit-tit…* HABITAT: Forest, from lowlands to mountains. DISTRIBUTION: Resident in Sumatra, Java, Bali, Borneo, the Philippines and Flores in the Lesser Sundas.

2 DWARF SPARROWHAWK (SULAWESI SMALL SPARROWHAWK)
Accipiter nanus 23–28cm FIELD NOTES: Occurs singly or in pairs. Forages mainly in the forest interior, also along forest tracks and roads. Stoops to capture large insects and small birds. VOICE: A thin, high-pitched *kiliu*, sometimes followed by a sharp, rapid *ki-ki-ki-ki-ki*. HABITAT: Primary hill and montane forest. DISTRIBUTION: Endemic to Sulawesi.

3 RUFOUS-NECKED SPARROWHAWK *Accipiter erythrauchen* 26–33cm
FIELD NOTES: Perches inconspicuously in dense canopy foliage, singly or occasionally in pairs. Dashes from cover to capture small birds. VOICE: A rapid series of high-pitched staccato notes. HABITAT: Primary forest in lowlands and hills, tree plantations and logged lowland forest. DISTRIBUTION: Endemic to the Moluccas.

4 VINOUS-BREASTED SPARROWHAWK *Accipiter rhodogaster* 26–33cm
FIELD NOTES: Usually solitary, sometimes in pairs. Often perches on exposed branches in the canopy, otherwise favours the forest interior. VOICE: A rapid *hihihihihi*. HABITAT: Primary and tall secondary lowland and hill forest, lightly wooded cultivation and mangroves. DISTRIBUTION: Endemic to Sulawesi and the Sula Islands.

5 SPARROWHAWK (EURASIAN or NORTHERN SPARROWHAWK)
Accipiter nisus 28–38cm FIELD NOTES: Surprises avian prey by dashing from a hidden perch, or chasing birds with a stealthy, agile flight. Usually alone. VOICE: When alarmed, utters a rapid *kew-kew-kew-kew-kew*. HABITAT: Forests, scrub forests, open woodland and wooded cultivation. DISTRIBUTION: Vagrant in Borneo.

6 MEYER'S GOSHAWK *Accipiter meyerianus* 48–56cm FIELD NOTES: Generally seen alone, usually soaring low over forests; occasionally seen perched at the edge of a forest clearing or hunting along forest streams. VOICE: A repeated, loud, nasal, upslurred *whi-i-yu*, also a slurred *ka-ah*. HABITAT: Primary lowland and hill forest. DISTRIBUTION: Resident in the Moluccas.

7 RUFOUS-WINGED BUZZARD *Butastur liventer* 35–41cm FIELD NOTES: Solitary but not shy. Regularly hunts from a tree perch near open areas. Makes short flights to capture ground-based prey, such as small mammals, lizards, frogs, crabs and insects. Soars with wings held level. VOICE: A shrill *pit-piu*, also a high-pitched *eeoe-tsut*. HABITAT: Dry forest, secondary growth, savannah, paddyfields and urban areas. DISTRIBUTION: Resident in Java and Sulawesi.

8 GREY-FACED BUZZARD *Butastur indicus* 46cm FIELD NOTES: Often forms large flocks during migration. Hunts frogs, lizards and rodents, typically using the top of a dead tree as a lookout site. VOICE: A tremulous *chit-kwee*. HABITAT: Wooded country with nearby open areas. DISTRIBUTION: Winter visitor to Sumatra, Java, Borneo, the Philippines, Sulawesi and the N Moluccas.

9 WHITE-EYED BUZZARD *Butastur teesa* 36–43cm FIELD NOTES: Sits for long periods on a prominent perch, from where it drops onto ground-based prey, mainly small mammals, lizards, frogs, crabs and snakes. VOICE: A melancholic *pit-weer pit-weer*. HABITAT: Dry, open country with scattered trees and scrub. DISTRIBUTION: Vagrant in Sulawesi.

10 BUZZARD (COMMON BUZZARD) *Buteo buteo* 51–57cm FIELD NOTES: Regularly perches in the open on posts or trees. Soars with wings held in a shallow 'V'. Plumage very variable. VOICE: A mewing *peeeeooo*. HABITAT: Open country with scattered trees, open forest and forest edges. DISTRIBUTION: Vagrant in Java, Bali, Borneo and the Philippines.

83 FALCONETS; FALCONS

1 BLACK-THIGHED FALCONET *Microhierax fringillarius* 15–17cm FIELD NOTES: Seeks a prominent, exposed perch from where to make short sorties to catch prey. VOICE: A shrill *kee kee kee* and squealing *kweer*. HABITAT: Forest clearings, forest edges and wooded cultivation. DISTRIBUTION: Resident in Sumatra, Java, Bali and Borneo.

2 WHITE-FRONTED FALCONET *Microhierax latifrons* 14–16cm FIELD NOTES: Perches on dead branches on a tall tree, from where dashing sorties are used to pursue insects or birds. VOICE: Undescribed, presumably similar to previous species. HABITAT: Lowland primary forest and forest edges. DISTRIBUTION: Endemic to Borneo.

3 PHILIPPINE FALCONET *Microhierax erythrogenys* 15–18cm FIELD NOTES: Occurs singly, in pairs or in family groups. Favours the canopy or the upper branches of dead trees. Makes aerial forays after insects or small birds, picks lizards off trees or the ground. VOICE: A high-pitched, rapid *chik-chik-erk-erk*, also a continuous squeaky *pew pew pew pew…* HABITAT: Open forest, forest edges and clearings, from lowlands to mid-mountain. DISTRIBUTION: Endemic to the Philippines.

4 COMMON KESTREL *Falco tinnunculus* 31–37cm FIELD NOTES: Frequently hovers while searching for food, or uses a prominent post or branch from which to drop onto prey. VOICE: A shrill *kee-kee-kee-kee* and a trilling *vriii*. HABITAT: Open areas, cliffs and around human habitation. DISTRIBUTION: Winter visitor to the Philippines.

5 SPOTTED KESTREL *Falco moluccensis* 26–32cm FIELD NOTES: Perches on dead trees and hovers while searching for prey. VOICE: A shrill, repeated *kee-kee-kee-kee, kiek-kiek-kiek-kiek* or similar. HABITAT: Grassland with scattered trees, lightly wooded cultivation, forest edges and clearings, and around human habitation. DISTRIBUTION: Resident in Java, Bali and Wallacea (apart from the Kai Islands in the S Moluccas); vagrant in Borneo.

6 NANKEEN KESTREL *Falco cenchroides* 28–35cm FIELD NOTES: Usually occurs singly. Actions similar to Kestrel. VOICE: A rapid, shrill *ki-ki-ki…* and a slow *tek-tek-tek*. HABITAT: Open country and farmland with scattered trees. DISTRIBUTION: Winter visitor or vagrant to Java, Bali, the Lesser Sundas and the Moluccas; breeds on Christmas Island.

7 AMUR FALCON (EASTERN RED-FOOTED FALCON) *Falco amurensis* 28–30cm FIELD NOTES: Highly agile flight when pursuing flying insects; also hovers. VOICE: A shrill *kew-kew-kew-kew*. HABITAT: Open country and wooded areas. DISTRIBUTION: Vagrant in the Philippines.

8 MERLIN *Falco columbarius* 25–30cm FIELD NOTES: Pursuit flight is often dashing, slightly undulating, with twists and turns, usually at low level. VOICE: Generally silent. HABITAT: Open country. DISTRIBUTION: Vagrant in the Philippines.

9 HOBBY (EURASIAN or NORTHERN HOBBY) *Falco subbuteo* 30–36cm FIELD NOTES: Fast and acrobatic in pursuit of aerial prey, which include insects or small birds. Regularly perches on isolated trees. VOICE: A rapid *kew-kew-kew-kew…* HABITAT: Open and wooded areas. DISTRIBUTION: Vagrant in Java, Borneo and the Lesser Sundas.

10 ORIENTAL HOBBY *Falco severus* 27–30cm FIELD NOTES: Actions and habits similar to Hobby. VOICE: A rapid *ki-ki-ki-ki*. HABITAT: Forest edges and clearings, cultivation, lakes and swamps. DISTRIBUTION: Resident in Java, Bali, the Philippines, Sulawesi, the Sula Islands and the Moluccas; possibly resident in Sumatra; vagrant in Borneo.

11 AUSTRALIAN HOBBY *Falco longipennis* 33cm FIELD NOTES: Perches conspicuously, usually singly. Swift, agile aerial hunter of birds, insects and bats. VOICE: A weak, high-pitched *ki-ki-ki-ki-ki…* HABITAT: Lightly wooded grassland, open areas, wooded cultivation, edges of coastal and lowland monsoon forest. DISTRIBUTION: Resident in the Moluccas and Lesser Sundas.

12 PEREGRINE *Falco peregrinus* 36–48cm FIELD NOTES: Kills prey in mid-air following a fast pursuit and a high-speed stoop with closed wings. *F. p. ernesti* (main illustration) occurs in the Philippines and Indonesia; *F. p. calidus* (12b) occurs as a winter visitor to the region. VOICE: Slightly pulsating, hoarse screams and a sharp *kek-kek-kek…* HABITAT: Includes open areas, wetlands, forest edges and cliffs (coastal and inland). DISTRIBUTION: Resident and winter visitor to the region.

84 FRIGATEBIRDS; TROPICBIRDS; BOOBIES

1 GREAT FRIGATEBIRD *Fregata minor* 85–100cm FIELD NOTES: Takes fish by dipping to sea surface; also pursues other seabirds, forcing them to regurgitate food, and scavenges around boats. Often flocks with Lesser Frigatebirds. During breeding season, male inflates red skin of throat. Juvenile has pale head and white belly, separated by a black breast-band, the latter tending to fade as the bird ages. VOICE: Generally silent. HABITAT: Mainly maritime, coming to land to breed and roost; nests on flat ground or trees. DISTRIBUTION: Present year-round; breeds on Christmas Island and islands in the Banda and Flores seas.

2 LESSER FRIGATEBIRD *Fregata ariel* 71–81cm FIELD NOTES: Often occurs in large flocks, mixed with Great Frigatebirds. Feeding actions similar to Great Frigatebird. Males inflate throat-patch during breeding season. Juvenile has a pale head, a white belly and axillaries separated by a thin, darkish breast-band, the latter fading as the head darkens. VOICE: Generally silent. HABITAT: Mainly maritime, coming to land to breed or roost. DISTRIBUTION: Present year-round; breeds on Christmas Island; possibly breeds on islands in the Banda Sea.

3 CHRISTMAS FRIGATEBIRD *Fregata andrewsi* 90–100cm FIELD NOTES: Feeding behaviour similar to Great Frigatebird. Males inflate throat skin during breeding season. Juvenile similar to juvenile Lesser Frigatebird but with a wider breast-band. VOICE: Generally silent away from breeding sites. HABITAT: Mainly maritime, coming to land to breed and roost. DISTRIBUTION: Breeds on Christmas Island; non-breeding visitor to seas off Sumatra, Java, Bali and Borneo; vagrant elsewhere.

4 WHITE-TAILED TROPICBIRD *Phaethon lepturus* 70–82cm FIELD NOTES: Flight consists of fluttering wing-beats followed by long glides. Feeds by hovering and then plunge-diving on half-closed wings. *P. l. fulvus* (4b) breeds on Christmas Island and wanders to seas off Sumatra, Java and Borneo. VOICE: A squeaky *chip-chip-chip*. HABITAT: Pelagic and coastal waters; breeds in rocky crevices or sheltered ground scrapes. DISTRIBUTION: Breeds on Christmas Island, Java and Bali; wanders to seas throughout the region.

5 RED-TAILED TROPICBIRD *Phaethon rubricauda* 78–81cm FIELD NOTES: Actions similar to White-tailed Tropicbird. VOICE: A harsh, rapid *keek-keek-keek...* HABITAT: Pelagic; breeds mainly on cliffs. DISTRIBUTION: Breeds on Christmas Island, and possibly Bali and islets in the Banda Sea; waders to seas off Sumatra, Java and the Philippines.

6 ABBOTT'S BOOBY *Papasula abbotti* 71cm FIELD NOTES: Tends to have a more leisurely flight than other boobies, with slow flaps and languid glides. VOICE: Generally silent away from breeding grounds. HABITAT: Pelagic post-breeding; breeds on trees. DISTRIBUTION: Endemic breeder on Christmas Island; wanders to the seas off Sumatra and Java, and also noted in the Banda and Ceram seas.

7 RED-FOOTED BOOBY *Sula sula* 66–77cm FIELD NOTES: Feeds by angled plunge-diving. Variations in the dark morph include a white-tailed form and a white-headed, white-tailed form. VOICE: Generally silent at sea. HABITAT: Maritime away from breeding sites. DISTRIBUTION: Resident in the region; breeds on islets or reefs in the Philippines, Flores and Banda seas, and on Christmas Island; wanders off the coasts of Sumatra, Java and Borneo.

8 MASKED BOOBY *Sula dactylatra* 81–92cm FIELD NOTES: Feeds by plunge-diving, tending to dive at a steeper angle than other boobies. VOICE: Generally silent away from breeding grounds. HABITAT: Maritime away from breeding sites. DISTRIBUTION: Resident in the region; breeds on reefs or islets in the Philippines and Banda Sea.

9 BROWN BOOBY *Sula leucogaster* 64–74cm FIELD NOTES: Feeds by angled plunge-diving. Gregarious. VOICE: Generally silent away from breeding areas. HABITAT: Maritime away from breeding sites. DISTRIBUTION: Resident in the region; breeds on islets and reefs in the Philippines, and the Banda and Flores seas.

85 PELICANS; CORMORANTS

1 WHITE PELICAN (GREAT WHITE PELICAN) *Pelecanus onocrotalus* 140–175cm
FIELD NOTES: Often fishes cooperatively, birds forming a semicircle to push fish into shallows, enabling each bird to scoop up a pouchful of fish. Non-breeding adults have a paler pouch. Juvenile brownish on wings and neck. VOICE: In flight, may utter a deep croak. HABITAT: Lakes, rivers and sheltered coastal waters. DISTRIBUTION: Vagrant in Java and possibly Sumatra.

2 SPOT-BILLED PELICAN *Pelecanus philippensis* 140cm FIELD NOTES: Sociable, often feeds cooperatively like previous species. Non-breeding birds have a paler bill and facial skin. VOICE: Fishing groups may utter a deep bleating noise. HABITAT: Large lakes, lagoons, rivers and estuaries. DISTRIBUTION: Winter visitor to Sumatra and the Philippines.

3 AUSTRALIAN PELICAN *Pelecanus conspicillatus* 150cm FIELD NOTES: Gregarious, usually in small groups or large flocks. Often fishes in groups. Rests on sand bars, branches and man-made objects. Non-breeding birds have a paler pouch. VOICE: Generally silent. HABITAT: Lakes, swamps, coastal lagoons and coral reefs. DISTRIBUTION: Vagrant in Sumatra, Java and Wallacea.

4 INDIAN DARTER (ORIENTAL DARTER or SNAKEBIRD) *Anhinga melanogaster* 85–97cm FIELD NOTES: Often sits on an exposed perch with wings outstretched. Non-breeding plumage duller. Often swims with only neck and head visible. In flight, holds neck in a distinct kink. VOICE: Breeding birds utter a loud *chigi chigi chigi chigi* and various grunts and croaks. HABITAT: Lakes, marshes and large rivers. DISTRIBUTION: Resident throughout the region.

5 CORMORANT (GREAT CORMORANT) *Phalacrocorax carbo* 80–100cm
FIELD NOTES: Regularly perches prominently with wings outstretched. In flight, outstretched neck shows a slight kink. VOICE: Generally silent. HABITAT: Lakes, rivers and coastal waters. DISTRIBUTION: Vagrant in Borneo, the Philippines and the SE Moluccas.

6 LITTLE BLACK CORMORANT *Phalacrocorax sulcirostris* 61cm FIELD NOTES: Usually seen singly or in small or large flocks. Often perches conspicuously on dead trees near water. In flight, outstretched neck shows a slight kink. VOICE: Generally silent; at breeding sites utters various barks and croaks. HABITAT: Lakes, ponds and coastal waters. DISTRIBUTION: Resident in Java and Wallacea; vagrant in Borneo.

7 LITTLE PIED CORMORANT *Microcarbo melanoleucos* 55–65cm FIELD NOTES: Usually occurs singly or in parties of up to 20 birds. Perches conspicuously, usually on waterside trees. In flight, outstretched neck shows a slight kink. Black cap of juvenile extends down to eye level. VOICE: Generally silent; at breeding sites utter various cooing and clicking sounds. HABITAT: Swamps, lakes, pools, rivers, coastal lagoons, mangroves and estuaries. DISTRIBUTION: Resident in Wallacea; vagrant in Java, Bali and Borneo.

8 LITTLE CORMORANT *Microcarbo niger* 51cm FIELD NOTES: Regularly sits with wings held open. In flight, outstretched neck shows a slight kink. VOICE: Generally silent; at breeding sites utters various grunts, groans and roaring sounds, also a low-pitched *ah-ah-ah* and *kok-kok-kok*. HABITAT: Freshwater wetlands, mangroves and estuaries. DISTRIBUTION: Resident in Java, rare breeder in Borneo; vagrant in Sumatra.

86 HERONS

1 CATTLE EGRET *Bubulcus ibis* 48–53cm FIELD NOTES: Sociable, often roosting in large numbers. Regularly seen feeding on insects disturbed by grazing animals. Frequently perches in trees. VOICE: In flight, may give a harsh, croaking *ruk* or *kok*. HABITAT: Various wetlands and grasslands. DISTRIBUTION: Resident or winter visitor throughout the region, except the Kai Islands in the S Moluccas.

2 PIED HERON *Egretta picata* 50cm FIELD NOTES: Regularly occurs in small or large parties. Active, stalking forager, although recorded 'hovering' before dropping onto prey. Juvenile is brownish grey with a white head. VOICE: In flight, utters a loud *awk* or *ohrk*. HABITAT: Various wetlands, including lakes, mudflats and estuaries. DISTRIBUTION: Resident in Sulawesi; migrant to the E Lesser Sundas and S Moluccas.

3 WHITE-FACED HERON *Egretta novaehollandiae* 61–74cm FIELD NOTES: Occurs singly, in pairs or in small flocks; sometimes associates with other wading species. Active, stalking forager. VOICE: Generally silent; in flight, may utter a drawn-out, guttural croak. HABITAT: Freshwater and brackish swamps, paddyfields, lake margins and rivers. DISTRIBUTION: Resident on Christmas Island and in the Lesser Sundas; non-breeding visitor to the S Moluccas and Bali; vagrant in Borneo.

4 PACIFIC REEF HERON (EASTERN REEF EGRET) *Egretta sacra* 58–66cm FIELD NOTES: Breeding birds have a short, inconspicuous nape crest. Feeding action is lethargic, with a more rapid pursuit when potential prey is spotted. VOICE: A hoarse croak and a harsh *arrk* when alarmed. HABITAT: Rocky shores, beaches and mudflats. DISTRIBUTION: Resident throughout the region.

5 LITTLE EGRET *Egretta garzetta* 55–65cm FIELD NOTES: At onset of breeding, lores become yellow, yellow-orange or reddish. Often feeds by dashing to and fro with wings held open. Non-breeding adults and juveniles lack the head, breast and back plumes. The black-footed race *E. g. nigripes* (not depicted) breeds in Wallacea and occurs elsewhere in the region. VOICE: Utters a harsh *aaah* or *kgarrk* during disputes or when alarmed. HABITAT: Lakes, rivers, marshes, paddyfields, tidal creeks and estuaries. DISTRIBUTION: Widespread resident and non-breeding visitor to the region.

6 CHINESE EGRET (SWINHOE'S EGRET) *Egretta eulophotes* 65–68cm FIELD NOTES: In non-breeding birds bill is dark towards the tip, and they and juveniles lack head and back plumes. Regularly feeds alongside other herons, often foraging by dashing to and fro with wings held open and flapped. VOICE: Generally silent. HABITAT: Tidal mudflats, coastal bays, coastal lagoons and mangroves. DISTRIBUTION: Rare winter visitor to Sumatra, Borneo, the Philippines and Sulawesi.

7 INTERMEDIATE EGRET (YELLOW-BILLED or PLUMED EGRET) *Ardea intermedia* 65–72cm FIELD NOTES: Bill becomes black for a short time during breeding season. Non-breeding birds and juveniles lack plumes. Slow stalker when foraging. VOICE: Utters a harsh *kwark* or *kuwark* when disturbed. HABITAT: Freshwater lakes, rivers and marshes; also tidal creeks and mangrove swamps. DISTRIBUTION: Resident and non-breeding visitor to the region.

8 GREAT WHITE EGRET (GREAT EGRET) *Ardea alba* 85–102cm FIELD NOTES: Regularly walks stealthily with neck erect. For a short while prior to breeding, bill becomes blacker, lores bluish and tibia pink-red. Non-breeding and juvenile birds lack back plumes. VOICE: Generally silent, although may give a throaty croak. HABITAT: Freshwater and saltwater wetlands. DISTRIBUTION: Resident and non-breeding visitor to the region.

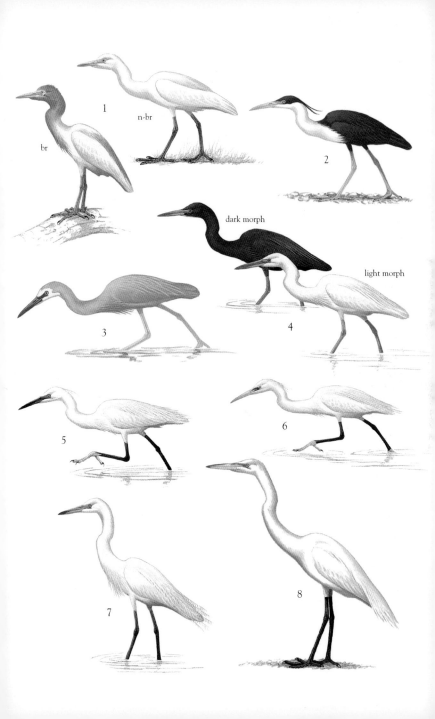

br

1

n-br

2

dark morph

light morph

3

4

5

6

7

8

87 HERONS

1 GREY HERON *Ardea cinerea* 90–98cm FIELD NOTES: Generally forages alone. Often stands motionless at water's edge or on a branch. Underwing-coverts grey, contrasting with dark flight feathers. VOICE: In flight, utters a harsh *frahnk*. HABITAT: Variety of wetlands, including lakes, marshes, rivers, tidal creeks and mangroves. DISTRIBUTION: Resident in Sumatra, Java, Bali and the W Lesser Sundas; non-breeding visitor to Borneo and the Philippines.

2 GREAT-BILLED HERON (SUMATRAN HERON) *Ardea sumatrana* 115cm FIELD NOTES: Generally shy and wary, foraging alone or in pairs. Underwing-coverts grey, contrasting little with flight feathers. VOICE: Occasional loud, harsh croaks. HABITAT: Mangroves, undisturbed beaches, reefs and large rivers near coasts. DISTRIBUTION: Widespread resident in the region.

3 PURPLE HERON *Ardea purpurea* 78–90cm FIELD NOTES: Secretive, tending to prefer the cover of aquatic vegetation. Underwing-coverts appear all dark. VOICE: In flight, utters a harsh *frahnk*, higher-pitched than that of Grey Heron. HABITAT: Marshes and lakes with dense aquatic vegetation; post-breeding, often visits more open waters. DISTRIBUTION: Resident throughout the region, except the N Moluccas.

4 BLACK-CROWNED NIGHT HERON *Nycticorax nycticorax* 58–65cm FIELD NOTES: Mainly crepuscular or nocturnal; usually forages alone, but small groups may be seen flying from daytime roosts. Juvenile has brown upperparts with buff-white spots; head, neck and breast buff, streaked brown. VOICE: In flight, utters a frog-like croak. HABITAT: Wetland areas with border vegetation and mangroves. DISTRIBUTION: Resident in Java, Borneo, Sulawesi and possibly the Philippines; non-breeding visitor to Sumatra; vagrant in the Lesser Sundas.

5 NANKEEN NIGHT HERON *Nycticorax caledonicus* 55–59cm FIELD NOTES: Nocturnal. By day, rests in the cover of leafy trees. Best sighted in the early evenings as birds leave colonial roosts to visit feeding sites. Juvenile very similar to juvenile of previous species, but neck and breast streaking more prominent. VOICE: In flight, gives a loud *kyok* or *kwok*. HABITAT: Swamps, ponds, lakes, mangroves and forest-lined creeks and rivers. DISTRIBUTION: Resident in Java, Borneo, the Philippines and Wallacea.

6 MALAYAN NIGHT HERON *Gorsachius melanolophus* 49cm FIELD NOTES: Mainly crepuscular or nocturnal. Secretive, generally foraging alone. Primaries are tipped white. VOICE: A series of deep *oo* notes. HABITAT: Marshes and streams in dense forest. DISTRIBUTION: Breeding resident in the Philippines; non-breeding migrant to rest of region.

7 JAPANESE NIGHT HERON *Gorsachius goisagi* 48–50cm FIELD NOTES: Skulking. Solitary. Mainly nocturnal. Primaries with extensive rufous tips. VOICE: A deep *bou-bou*, usually uttered at night. HABITAT: Dense undergrowth in forests, usually near water. DISTRIBUTION: Winter visitor to Borneo, the Philippines and N Sulawesi.

8 STRIATED HERON *Butorides striata* 40–48cm FIELD NOTES: Often forages alone, among vegetation on the banks of rivers or lakes; may use the same location for a number of days. Juvenile brown above with pale wing spots, underparts and neck streaked dark. VOICE: May utter a harsh *kyah* if disturbed. HABITAT: Mangroves, rivers and streams in or near forests, lakes and coastal mudflats. DISTRIBUTION: Widespread resident and winter visitor to the region.

9 CHINESE POND HERON *Ardeola bacchus* 42–45cm FIELD NOTES: Stands motionless while waiting for prey. In flight, shows white wings and tail. VOICE: Generally silent; may utter a harsh croak in flight or when alarmed. HABITAT: Marshes, paddyfields, ditches, ponds and coastal waters. DISTRIBUTION: Winter visitor to Sumatra, Borneo and the Philippines.

10 JAVAN POND HERON *Ardeola speciosa* 45cm FIELD NOTES: Crepuscular. Stands still waiting for prey. In flight, shows white wings and tail. VOICE: When flushed, may give a harsh *kaa kaa*; in flight, utters a squawk. HABITAT: Various inland and coastal wetlands. DISTRIBUTION: Resident in Java, Bali, Borneo, the Philippines and the W Lesser Sundas; non-breeding visitor to Sumatra.

88 BITTERNS; IBISES

1 YELLOW BITTERN *Ixobrychus sinensis* 30–40cm FIELD NOTES: Skulking, mainly crepuscular or nocturnal. In flight, shows buffy upperwing-coverts, black flight feathers and tail. Juvenile buff above with dark streaking, whitish below with brownish streaks on foreneck and breast. VOICE: In flight, utters a sharp *kakak kakak*. HABITAT: Vegetation surrounding marshes, lakes and flooded paddyfields. DISTRIBUTION: Resident in Sumatra, Borneo, the Philippines, Sulawesi and Flores in the Lesser Sundas; non-breeding visitor elsewhere.

2 VON SCHRENCK'S BITTERN *Ixobrychus eurhythmus* 33–39cm
FIELD NOTES: Skulking, usually solitary. In flight, upperwing-coverts buff, flight feathers greyish, tail black. Juvenile similar to adult female. VOICE: A low, repeated *gup*; in flight, utters a low squawk. HABITAT: Marshes, pools and paddyfields near forests, also well-vegetated open wetlands. DISTRIBUTION: Winter visitor to Sumatra, Java, Borneo, the Philippines and Sulawesi.

3 CINNAMON BITTERN *Ixobrychus cinnamomeus* 40–41cm FIELD NOTES: Secretive. Generally forages alone, usually crepuscular. Juvenile dark brown above with pale mottling, buff-white below with heavy, dark brown streaking. VOICE: A low *kwok-kwok-kwok…*, sometimes ending with two or three quieter notes. In flight, utters a croak. HABITAT: Various wetland areas, including flooded paddyfields, swamps and reed-beds. DISTRIBUTION: Resident in Sumatra, Java, Borneo, the Philippines, Sulawesi, the Sula Islands and the W Lesser Sundas.

4 BLACK BITTERN (YELLOW-NECKED or MANGROVE BITTERN)
Dupetor flavicollis 54–66cm FIELD NOTES: Secretive, skulking in dense cover; mainly crepuscular. Juvenile like female, but with pale fringes on upperparts. VOICE: In flight, utters a hoarse croak. HABITAT: Freshwater wetlands, swamp forest and mangroves. DISTRIBUTION: Resident and migrant to the region.

5 BITTERN (GREAT or EURASIAN BITTERN) *Botaurus stellaris* 70–80cm
FIELD NOTES: Secretive, more often seen in flight. Juvenile less distinctly marked. VOICE: In flight, utters a harsh, nasal *kau* or *krau*. HABITAT: Freshwater and brackish reed-beds. DISTRIBUTION: Vagrant in Borneo and the Philippines.

6 WHITE-SHOULDERED IBIS *Pseudibis davisoni* 75–85cm FIELD NOTES: Forages on riverbanks. Roosts and nests in tall trees. In flight, shows a white patch on inner forewing. Juvenile browner, with a dirty white collar. VOICE: Utters a hoarse, screaming *ERRRRRRRROH*, alongside a subdued *ohhaaa ohhaaa* and *errr-ah*; also other screams and honking sounds. HABITAT: Riverside forest. DISTRIBUTION: Rare resident in Borneo.

7 AUSTRALIAN WHITE IBIS *Threskiornis molucca* 65–75cm FIELD NOTES: Occurs singly, in pairs or in parties of up to 35 birds. Often perches high in isolated dead trees and on fallen riverside trees. Juvenile has bare skin flecked with white feathers, black tertials and lacks plumes. VOICE: Generally silent, but occasionally gives harsh croaks and honks. HABITAT: Swamps, moist and newly burned grassland, coastal mudflats, mangroves and margins of larger rivers. DISTRIBUTION: Resident in the E Lesser Sundas and S Moluccas.

8 BLACK-HEADED IBIS (ORIENTAL or BLACK-NECKED IBIS)
Threskiornis melanocephalus 65–75cm FIELD NOTES: Usually seen in small groups. Wades in shallow water, moving bill from side to side as it sifts water. Breeds in colonies. Juvenile has bare skin restricted to face. VOICE: Generally silent; makes strange grunts at breeding sites. HABITAT: Marshes, paddyfields, saltmarshes and coastal mudflats. DISTRIBUTION: Breeds in Java and possibly Sumatra; winter visitor to the Philippines; vagrant in Borneo and Sulawesi.

9 GLOSSY IBIS *Plegadis falcinellus* 55–65cm FIELD NOTES: Usually found in small groups. Juvenile resembles adult but lacks sheen, and neck and head are flecked with white. VOICE: A grunting *grru* or *graa*; at breeding sites utters grunting and croaking sounds. HABITAT: Various wetlands, including marshes, lakes and coastal lagoons. DISTRIBUTION: Resident in Java, the Philippines and Sulawesi; winter visitor or vagrant elsewhere.

89 SPOONBILLS; STORKS; CRANE

1 ROYAL SPOONBILL *Platalea regia* 74–81cm FIELD NOTES: Occurs singly, in pairs or in small parties. Wades and sweeps bill from side to side, sifting water for food. Non-breeding birds lack crest and yellow tinge on underparts. VOICE: Generally silent. HABITAT: Swamps, lagoons and tidal mudflats. DISTRIBUTION: Vagrant in Java, Bali, Wallacea and possibly Borneo.

2 BLACK-FACED SPOONBILL (LESSER SPOONBILL) *Platalea minor* 60–84cm FIELD NOTES: Usually found in groups. Feeding actions similar to previous species. Non-breeding birds lose the yellow tinge to crest and breast. Juvenile has black tips to primaries. VOICE: Generally silent. HABITAT: Tidal mudflats, saltmarshes, estuaries and inland lakes. DISTRIBUTION: Rare vagrant in Borneo and the Philippines.

3 MILKY STORK *Mycteria cinerea* 92–97cm FIELD NOTES: Non-breeding birds have a pinkish-yellow bill. Juvenile is dingy grey-brown, head and neck browner; facial skin and bill pale yellow. VOICE: Generally silent. During breeding, utters screaming, hissing sounds, along with bill-clapping. HABITAT: Tidal mudflats and mangroves; flooded forests in Cambodia. DISTRIBUTION: Resident in Sumatra, Java, Bali and possibly Sulawesi; vagrant in the Lesser Sundas.

4 ASIAN OPENBILL (ASIAN OPENBILL STORK) *Anastomus oscitans* 68–81cm FIELD NOTES: Usually gregarious. In non-breeding adult, blacks are more brownish, neck and head are greyish, and bill is grey. In flight, underwing shows white coverts and black flight feathers, tail black. Juvenile brownish grey with a darker mantle. VOICE: Generally silent. HABITAT: Freshwater marshes, shallow lakes, lagoons and paddyfields. DISTRIBUTION: Possible vagrant in Sumatra.

5 WOOLLY-NECKED STORK *Ciconia episcopus* 75–92cm FIELD NOTES: Usually encountered singly or in small flocks. In flight, underwing black, and black tail often obscured by white undertail-coverts. VOICE: Generally silent except for whistling greeting calls and bill-clapping at nest site. HABITAT: Marshes, streams or ponds in open forest, and freshwater swamp forest. DISTRIBUTION: Resident in S Sumatra, Java, Bali, the Philippines, Sulawesi and the Lesser Sundas.

6 STORM'S STORK *Ciconia stormi* 75–91cm FIELD NOTES: Usually forages alone or in pairs. In flight, shows black underwing and tail, the latter often covered by white undertail-coverts. VOICE: A short series of sibilant whistles and a *karau*; bill-clapping occurs at nesting sites. HABITAT: Freshwater peat-swamp forest, rivers, streams and pools in forests. DISTRIBUTION: Resident in Sumatra and Borneo; vagrant in Java.

7 GREATER ADJUTANT *Leptoptilos dubius* 120–150cm FIELD NOTES: In non-breeding adults, wings are more uniform slate black. In flight, underwing paler grey than Lesser Adjutant, and shows a small white triangle in axillary area. Flies with neck drawn back. VOICE: Generally silent. HABITAT: Marshes and pools in or near open dry forests, swamp forest, paddyfields and various open areas. DISTRIBUTION: Vagrant in Sumatra.

8 LESSER ADJUTANT *Leptoptilos javanicus* 110–120cm FIELD NOTES: Usually encountered singly or in small flocks. In flight, blackish underwing shows a small white triangle in the axillary area. Flies with neck drawn back. VOICE: During display, utters a series of high-pitched squeaks and cow-like moos. HABITAT: Marshes, forest pools, freshwater swamp forest, mangroves and mudflats. DISTRIBUTION: Resident in Sumatra, Java, Bali and Borneo.

9 SARUS CRANE *Antigone antigone* 156–176cm FIELD NOTES: In flight from below, shows black primaries; flies with outstretched neck and legs protruding well beyond tail. Juvenile has rusty head and upper neck, upperparts tinged rufous. VOICE: A loud trumpeting. HABITAT: Watery areas such as marshes, paddyfields, lakes and rivers. DISTRIBUTION: Formerly bred in Luzon in the Philippines; slight possibility of vagrants occurring.

90 PETRELS

1 CAPE PETREL (PINTADO PETREL, CAPE PIGEON) *Daption capense* 38–40cm
FIELD NOTES: Unmistakable. Flies with rapid, shallow, stiff wing-beats interspersed with short glides. Follows ships and fishing boats. Normally occurs in large flocks. VOICE: Generally silent. HABITAT: Pelagic. DISTRIBUTION: Vagrant in the Banda Sea.

2 TAHITI PETREL *Pseudobulweria rostrata* 39cm FIELD NOTES: Stout bill, long body. Flight usually low over water, on loose wing-beats. Solitary, rarely follows ships or fishing boats. VOICE: Generally silent. HABITAT: Pelagic. DISTRIBUTION: Scarce visitor to the Philippines, Moluccas and Lesser Sundas.

3 BONIN PETREL *Pterodroma hypoleuca* 30cm FIELD NOTES: Typical fast, bounding 'gadfly' flight – beating wings to gain height, followed by long glides and wide, banking arcs. Tends not to follow ships. VOICE: Generally silent. HABITAT: Pelagic. DISTRIBUTION: Possible vagrant in the N Philippines.

4 HAWAIIAN PETREL *Pterodroma sandwichensis* 43cm FIELD NOTES: Typical 'gadfly' flight (see previous species). Usually solitary. VOICE: Generally silent. HABITAT: Pelagic. DISTRIBUTION: Vagrant in the Philippines and N Moluccas.

5 KERMADEC PETREL *Pterodroma neglecta* 38cm FIELD NOTES: White at base of primaries on upperwing is diagnostic. Typical 'gadfly' flight (see Bonin Petrel). Solitary, does not follow ships or boats. VOICE: Generally silent. HABITAT: Pelagic. DISTRIBUTION: Vagrant in the N Philippines.

6 BARAU'S PETREL *Pterodroma baraui* 38cm FIELD NOTES: Generally solitary, rarely follows ships. Typical flight of the genus, beating wings to gain height, followed by long glides and wide, banking arcs. VOICE: Silent. HABITAT: Pelagic. DISTRIBUTION: Vagrant off Sumatra.

7 BULWER'S PETREL *Bulweria bulwerii* 26–28cm FIELD NOTES: Generally flies low over water in an erratic, buoyant manner, much like a large storm petrel. Tail wedge-shaped when fanned. Solitary or in pairs. Does not generally follow ships. VOICE: Usually silent. HABITAT: Pelagic. DISTRIBUTION: Regular visitor off Borneo; rare visitor off the W Philippines, NE Sulawesi, N Moluccas, the Banda Sea and the Lesser Sundas.

8 JOUANIN'S PETREL *Bulweria fallax* 31cm FIELD NOTES: Solitary, does not follow ships. Flies close to the water with distinctly bowed wings. VOICE: Silent. HABITAT: Pelagic. DISTRIBUTION: Vagrant off S Sumatra.

intermediate

light

5

dark

1

2

3

4

6

7

8

91 PRION; SHEARWATERS; STORM PETRELS

1 ANTARCTIC PRION *Pachyptila desolata* 27cm FIELD NOTES: Flies with a fast, erratic, zigzagging action. Gregarious, often seen in large flocks. Rarely follows ships or boats. VOICE: Silent. HABITAT: Pelagic. DISTRIBUTION: Accidental vagrant in S Java.

2 STREAKED SHEARWATER (WHITE-FACED SHEARWATER)
Calonectris leucomelas 48cm FIELD NOTES: Sometimes shows a pale crescent at base of tail. Flight can appear lazy, although it is actually quite fast, with dynamic small albatross-like soaring in strong winds. Follows fishing boats and often occurs in large flocks. VOICE: Generally silent. HABITAT: Pelagic. DISTRIBUTION: Regular migrant to the seas of the region.

3 FLESH-FOOTED SHEARWATER (PALE-FOOTED SHEARWATER)
Ardenna carneipes 40–45cm FIELD NOTES: Flight consists of lazy wing-flaps, followed by long glides on stiff wings. Occurs singly or in small groups, attracted to fishing boats. VOICE: Generally silent. HABITAT: Pelagic. DISTRIBUTION: Vagrant off the W and N coasts of Sumatra.

4 WEDGE-TAILED SHEARWATER *Ardenna pacifica* 41–46cm FIELD NOTES: Slow wing-flaps followed by short glides; has a more bounding flight in strong winds. Often found around fishing boats. VOICE: Generally silent. HABITAT: Pelagic. DISTRIBUTION: Regular in the region's seas.

5 WILSON'S STORM PETREL *Oceanites oceanicus* 15–19cm FIELD NOTES: Has yellow webs between toes, visible only at close range. Often dangles feet and 'dances' on sea surface while feeding. Attracted to fishing vessels. VOICE: A rapid 'chattering', occasionally uttered while feeding. HABITAT: Pelagic. DISTRIBUTION: Regular in the seas off Sumatra, Java, Bali and Wallacea.

6 WHITE-FACED STORM PETREL *Pelagodroma marina* 18–21cm FIELD NOTES: Forages in a series of swinging bounces, dangling feet at each bounce, so it looks like it is walking on water. In flight, feet project well beyond tail; at close range, yellow webs may be seen. Attracted to fishing vessels. VOICE: Usually silent. HABITAT: Pelagic. DISTRIBUTION: Probably a regular migrant off Sumatra and the W Lesser Sundas.

7 SWINHOE'S STORM PETREL (SWINHOE'S PETREL) *Oceanodroma monorhis* 19–20cm FIELD NOTES: Feeds erratically, with a bounding flight and hovering on shallow wing-beats to pick prey from sea surface. Tends not to follow ships. VOICE: Silent. HABITAT: Pelagic. DISTRIBUTION: Probably a regular migrant in the Sunda Straits and off the Moluccas.

8 MATSUDAIRA'S STORM PETREL (SOOTY STORM PETREL)
Oceanodroma matsudairae 24–25cm FIELD NOTES: Holds wings in a shallow 'V' while dipping down to pick food from sea surface; also feeds by landing on water. Often follows ships. VOICE: Generally silent. HABITAT: Pelagic. DISTRIBUTION: Regular passage migrant to Wallacea; vagrant off Borneo and probably the Philippines and Sulawesi.

dark morph

pale morph

92 PITTAS

1 SCHNEIDER'S PITTA *Hydrornis schneideri* 21–23cm FIELD NOTES: Forages on the forest floor, turning over leaves in search of prey. VOICE: A low, soft, prolonged, tremulous, double-noted whistle, the first note rising and the second falling. HABITAT: Primary mountain forest with dense undergrowth and tree-fall clearings, or forest edges. DISTRIBUTION: Endemic to Sumatra.

2 GIANT PITTA *Hydrornis caeruleus* 25–29cm FIELD NOTES: Forages on the ground among leaf litter, feeding on snails, earthworms, frogs, small snakes and large insects; uses rocks and stones to smash snail shells. VOICE: A slow, mournful *hwoo-er*; a soft, repeated *wheer*; and a falling *pheeeeeeoou*. HABITAT: Bamboo and broadleaved evergreen forest. DISTRIBUTION: Resident in Borneo; formerly resident in Sumatra, but now possibly extinct there.

3 MALAYAN BANDED PITTA *Hydrornis irena* 21–24cm FIELD NOTES: Forages on the ground, scratching about much like a chicken. Formerly considered a race of Javan Banded Pitta. VOICE: A short, repeated *pouw* or *poww*, and a whirring *kirrr* or *pprrr*. HABITAT: Broadleaved evergreen and secondary forest. DISTRIBUTION: Resident in Sumatra.

4 JAVAN BANDED PITTA *Hydrornis guajanus* 20–23cm FIELD NOTES: Forages on the forest floor using long hops with stops to pick over leaves in search of food. Formerly considered conspecific with Malayan and Bornean banded pittas. VOICE: Similar to previous species, but higher in pitch. HABITAT: Primary forest and old secondary forest. DISTRIBUTION: Endemic to Java and Bali.

5 BORNEAN BANDED PITTA *Hydrornis schwaneri* 20–23cm FIELD NOTES: Forages on the forest floor, turning over leaf litter in search of food. This and the previous two species were formerly considered conspecific. VOICE: A repeated *pow pow pow* and *whrr whrr whrr*, also an explosive *pauk* and a gentle *kur-kur* or *purr*. HABITAT: Forested slopes and hills, and lowland forest on limestone hills. DISTRIBUTION: Endemic to Borneo.

6 BLUE-HEADED PITTA *Hydrornis baudii* 16–17cm FIELD NOTES: Forages among leaf litter in search of worms, insects and arthropods. VOICE: A soft, descending *ppor-wi-iil* or *ppor-or*; female utters a drawn-out *hwee-ouu* when alarmed. HABITAT: Primary lowland forest and old secondary forest; also logged forest, often with a river nearby. DISTRIBUTION: Endemic to Borneo.

7 SULA PITTA *Erythropitta dohertyi* 16–18cm FIELD NOTES: Forages on the forest floor, hopping with pauses to pick over leaves in search of insects, worms, snails, etc. Formerly considered a race of the Philippine Pitta (Plate 93). VOICE: A trisyllabic phrase, followed by a brief pause and then a descending series of five drawn-out notes that decrease in volume. HABITAT: Lowland evergreen forest and degraded, selectively logged forest. DISTRIBUTION: Endemic to the Sula and Banggai islands.

8 WHISKERED PITTA *Erythropitta kochi* 22–23cm FIELD NOTES: Usually seen on or near the ground, often near wild pig diggings. Calls from an exposed perch or from the top of a small tree. VOICE: A monotonous, deep, mournful *haaawwww haaww haaww haaww haaw-r* or *goow-goow-goow-goow-goo*. HABITAT: Montane and submontane forest, usually with dense undergrowth, and high-elevation mossy forest with *Rhododendron* or fern understorey. DISTRIBUTION: Endemic to Luzon in the N Philippines.

93 PITTAS

1 PHILIPPINE PITTA (RED-BELLIED PITTA) *Erythropitta erythrogaster* 16–17cm
FIELD NOTES: Usually seen on or near the ground. Generally shy and inconspicuous, unless calling. Calls from an exposed rock, stump or high in a tree. Immature generally dull brown, with a paler throat and bluish-tinged wings and tail. VOICE: Two long, hollow, owl-like whistled notes, the first ascending and wavering, and the second descending. HABITAT: Forests and secondary growth. DISTRIBUTION: Endemic to the Philippines.

2 SOUTH MOLUCCAN PITTA *Erythropitta rubrinucha* 16–17cm FIELD NOTES: Formerly considered a race of the Philippine Pitta; actions presumed to be similar. VOICE: Presumed to be similar to Philippine Pitta. HABITAT: Tropical moist lowland forests. DISTRIBUTION: Endemic to Buru and Seram in the S Moluccas.

3 NORTH MOLUCCAN PITTA *Erythropitta rufiventris* 16–17cm FIELD NOTES: Formerly considered a race of the Philippine Pitta; actions prseumed to be similar. VOICE: Presumed to be similar to Philippine Pitta. HABITAT: Subtropical and moist lowland forest. DISTRIBUTION: Endemic to the N Moluccas.

4 SULAWESI PITTA *Erythropitta celebensis* 16–17cm FIELD NOTES: Formerly considered a race of the Philippine Pitta; actions presumed to be similar. VOICE: Presumed to be similar to Philippine Pitta. HABITAT: Subtropical and tropical moist lowland forests and plantations. DISTRIBUTION: Endemic to Sulawesi and the Togian Islands.

5 SIAU PITTA (SIAO PITTA) *Erythropitta palliceps* 16–17cm FIELD NOTES: Formerly considered a race of the Philippine Pitta; actions presumed to be similar. VOICE: Presumed to be similar to Philippine Pitta. HABITAT: Subtropical and tropical moist lowland forest, also secondary forest. DISTRIBUTION: Endemic to Siau, Tahulandang and Ruang islands.

6 SANIGHE PITTA *Erythropitta caeruleitorques* 16–17cm FIELD NOTES: Formerly considered a race of the Philippine Pitta; actions presumed to be similar. VOICE: Presumed to be similar to Philippine Pitta. HABITAT: Subtropical and tropical moist lowland forest. DISTRIBUTION: Endemic to the Sangihe Islands.

7 GARNET PITTA *Erythropitta granatina* 15–16cm FIELD NOTES: Forages on the ground, among leaf litter and around fallen branches and logs; occasionally searches on logs. Juvenile generally dull brown with dull blue on wings and tail; nape reddish. VOICE: A drawn-out, monotone whistle that increases in volume; when agitated, utters a purring *prrr prrr prrr*. HABITAT: Primary and logged lowland forests. DISTRIBUTION: Resident in Sumatra and Borneo.

8 GRACEFUL PITTA *Erythropitta venusta* 18cm FIELD NOTES: Forages on the ground or on fallen logs. Juvenile plain dark brown, head stripe buffy. VOICE: A low, mournful whistle. HABITAT: Moist, dark highland forest, with dense understorey and ravines. DISTRIBUTION: Endemic to Sumatra.

9 BLACK-CROWNED PITTA *Erythropitta ussheri* 15–16cm FIELD NOTES: Forages by probing in leaf litter, or on damp ground or fallen logs. Formerly considered a race of Garnet Pitta. VOICE: Similar to Garnet Pitta but more prolonged. HABITAT: Lowland primary and logged forest. DISTRIBUTION: Endemic to Borneo.

1 BLUE-BANDED PITTA *Erythropitta arquata* 15cm FIELD NOTES: Little recorded information; presumed to forage on the ground, feeding on ants and other insects. Juvenile generally brownish, mottled grey-brown and buffish on side of head and throat. VOICE: A monotonous, fluty whistle. HABITAT: Forests with bamboo and many fallen trees. DISTRIBUTION: Endemic to Borneo.

2 HOODED PITTA *Pitta sordida* 16–19cm FIELD NOTES: Feeds on the ground; often perches on vines or branches while singing. Juvenile duller, underparts dirty buff, lacks red vent. *P. s. cucullata* (2b) is a migrant to Sumatra and Java. VOICE: A loud *whew-whew*. HABITAT: Primary riverine forest, secondary forest with thick understorey or scrub, wet or dry forests, and various plantations. DISTRIBUTION: Resident in, and winter visitor to, Sumatra, Java, Borneo, the Philippines and Sulawesi.

3 IVORY-BREASTED PITTA *Pitta maxima* 22–28cm FIELD NOTES: Usually encountered singly, in pairs or occasionally in groups. Tends to spend more time off the ground than most pittas. Juvenile like adult but duller. VOICE: A distinctive, mournful *wu-whoouw*, repeated constantly. HABITAT: Undisturbed and selectively logged hill forest on limestone, with an understorey of palms or dense thickets of spiny rattan; also occurs in damp primary lowland forest. DISTRIBUTION: Endemic to the N Moluccas.

4 AZURE-BREASTED PITTA *Pitta steerii* 19cm FIELD NOTES: Forages on the ground, on boulders and on fallen logs. Juvenile resembles adult but duller, with mottling on throat and a greyish-green tinge to upper breast and flanks. VOICE: An explosive *whirp whirp whirp whirp whirp*, also a loud, repeated *kweioo*. HABITAT: Forests with thick undergrowth on limestone, also degraded forest. DISTRIBUTION: Endemic to the C and S Philippines.

5 FAIRY PITTA *Pitta nympha* 19cm FIELD NOTES: Forages on the ground among leaf litter. Juvenile much duller, with white spots on wing-coverts. VOICE: A clear, whistled *kwah-he-kwa-wu*; when alarmed, also a *kriaih* or *kahei-kahei*. HABITAT: Mixed dipterocarp forest and primary forest. DISTRIBUTION: Rare winter visitor to Borneo.

6 MANGROVE PITTA *Pitta megarhyncha* 20cm FIELD NOTES: Forages in muddy areas around mangrove roots and on nearby drier ground. Juvenile duller, crown barred blackish. VOICE: A loud *tae-laew* or *wieuw-wieuw*. HABITAT: Mangroves. DISTRIBUTION: Resident in Sumatra; vagrant in Borneo.

7 BLUE-WINGED PITTA *Pitta moluccensis* 18cm FIELD NOTES: Forages on the ground, hopping like a thrush. Juvenile duller and lacks the red belly and vent. VOICE: A loud, clear *taew-laew taew-laew* or *yeeow-yeeow yeeow-yeeow*, repeated every few seconds; when alarmed, utters a harsh *skyeew*. HABITAT: Primary and mixed deciduous forest, secondary growth, bamboo and mangroves; also parks and gardens on migration. DISTRIBUTION: Winter visitor to Sumatra and Borneo; vagrant in the Philippines.

8 ELEGANT PITTA *Pitta elegans* 19cm FIELD NOTES: Occurs singly or in pairs. Shy and retiring, best located by calls. Juvenile duller. *P. e. vigorsii* (8b) occurs in the E Lesser Sundas and S Moluccas. VOICE: A *kwweee-kwill*; variations have been noted on individual islands, such as a *ka-wha-kil* on Sumba, *kwuwik-kwk* in the Sula Islands and *perriew-priew* in the Banggai Islands. HABITAT: Various forest types, including humid primary forest, dry monsoon forest, forest edges, and degraded and selectively logged forest. DISTRIBUTION: Resident in the Lesser Sundas, Moluccas, Sula and Sangihe islands, and islands in the Flores Sea.

95 BROADBILLS

1 DUSKY BROADBILL *Corydon sumatranus* 25–29cm FIELD NOTES: Often in small, noisy flocks in the upper storey; sits quietly before making short sallies to pick insects off branches or foliage. VOICE: Shrill, upward-inflected whistles, *hi-ky-ui ky-ui ky-ui* or *ky-ee ky-ee ky-ee…*; also utters a shrill, falling *pseeoo* and a high *tsiu*. HABITAT: Primary lowland and hill forests. DISTRIBUTION: Resident in Sumatra and Borneo.

2 BLACK-AND-RED BROADBILL *Cymbirhynchus macrorhynchos* 20–24cm FIELD NOTES: Unobtrusive; sits motionless for long periods. VOICE: An accelerating series of *parnk* notes and grating cicada-like notes; also various churrings, melodious whistles and a monotonous, repeated *tyook*. When alarmed, utters a rapid *pip-pip-pip-pip…* HABITAT: Lowland forests and forest edges near water, freshwater swamp forest and mangroves. DISTRIBUTION: Resident in Sumatra and Borneo.

3 BANDED BROADBILL *Eurylaimus javanicus* 21–23cm FIELD NOTES: Often encountered in small, slow-moving parties in the mid-storey. VOICE: A sharp *wheeoo*, followed by a frantic, rising series of notes; also a nasal *whee-u*, a falling *kyeeow*, a rolling *keowrr* and a yelping *keek-eek-eek*. HABITAT: Various forest types, often near streams and rivers. DISTRIBUTION: Resident in Sumatra, Java and Borneo.

4 BLACK-AND-YELLOW BROADBILL *Eurylaimus ochromalus* 13–15cm FIELD NOTES: Usually encountered in small groups foraging in the middle to upper storey. Generally sits quietly before making short sallies to capture insects from foliage. VOICE: A rapid, frantic series of notes, starting slowly and then gradually gaining speed; also a *kyeeow* and *keowrr*. HABITAT: Various forest types, from lowlands to hills. DISTRIBUTION: Resident in Sumatra and Borneo.

5 MINDANAO WATTLED BROADBILL (WATTLED BROADBILL) *Sarcophanops steerii* 16–17cm FIELD NOTES: Forages in the middle and lower forest levels, singly, in pairs or in small flocks. Usually seen making short sallies to glean insects or capture them in flight. Sometimes a part of mixed-species feeding flocks. VOICE: A plaintive whistle. HABITAT: Rainforest, and dipterocarp, mixed dipterocarp and hillside secondary forest; occasionally mangroves and scrub forest. DISTRIBUTION: Endemic to Mindanao in the S Philippines.

6 VISAYAN WATTLED BROADBILL (VISAYAN BROADBILL) *Sarcophanops samarensis* 16–17cm FIELD NOTES: Formerly considered a race of the previous species; actions similar. VOICE: An insect-like *tik tik t-rrrrrrrr*. HABITAT: Primary forest, often near limestone outcrops. DISTRIBUTION: Endemic to Samar, Leyte and Bohol in the C Philippines.

7 SILVER-BREASTED BROADBILL *Serilophus lunatus* 18cm FIELD NOTES: Forages in pairs or small groups, gleaning prey from branches or foliage; also makes short aerial sallies after flying insects. VOICE: A soft, musical *chir-r-r-r*; also a squeaky *ki-uu*. HABITAT: Open hill forests, along streams and rivers. DISTRIBUTION: Resident in Sumatra.

8 LONG-TAILED BROADBILL *Psarisomus dalhousiae* 28cm FIELD NOTES: Encountered in small, loose parties; forages by gleaning or making short sallies after flying insects. VOICE: A loud, sharp *tseeay-tseeay-tseeay-tseeay…*, *pseew-pseew-pseew-pseew…* or *piu-piu-piu-piu*. HABITAT: Primary and secondary forests. DISTRIBUTION: Resident in Sumatra and Borneo.

9 GREEN BROADBILL *Calyptomena viridis* 18cm FIELD NOTES: Quiet; forages mainly in the lower levels and understorey, and has a preference for fruiting figs. VOICE: A soft, bubbling trill that increases in tempo; also a frog-like, bubbling *oo-turr*. HABITAT: Lowland primary forest. DISTRIBUTION: Resident in Sumatra and Borneo.

10 HOSE'S BROADBILL *Calyptomena hosii* 20cm FIELD NOTES: Forages at lower levels, singly or in pairs, or in small parties at fruiting trees. VOICE: A soft, dove-like cooing. HABITAT: Hill and submontane forests. DISTRIBUTION: Endemic to Borneo.

11 WHITEHEAD'S BROADBILL *Calyptomena whiteheadi* 25cm FIELD NOTES: Feeds in fruiting trees, singly, in pairs or sometimes in noisy groups. Occasionally joins mixed-species foraging flocks. VOICE: A loud, screeching *eek eek eek*, a *wark wark wark* and woodpecker-like rattles. HABITAT: Montane forest and forest edges. DISTRIBUTION: Endemic to Borneo.

96 HONEYEATERS

1 DARK-EARED MYZA Myza celebensis 17cm FIELD NOTES: Feeds at flowering trees and gleans from vines, branches and foliage, mainly in the canopy. Usually seen singly or in pairs. VOICE: A series of twittering squeaks, or a thin, shrill *pst* or *pst-pst*; also a sharp, harsh *tsreet*. HABITAT: Montane forest. DISTRIBUTION: Endemic to Sulawesi.

2 WHITE-EARED MYZA Myza sarasinorum 20cm FIELD NOTES: Active and conspicuous. Feeds at flowers and gleans arthropods from plants. M. s. chionogenys (2b) occurs in NC and SC Sulawesi. VOICE: Calls include a high-pitched *kik* or *kuik*, a nasal *tuck* and 3–5 wheezy, high-pitched notes, given while feeding; song consists of a series of high-pitched squeaks. HABITAT: Upper montane forests. DISTRIBUTION: Endemic to Sulawesi.

3 DRAB MYZOMELA Myzomela blasii 11–12cm FIELD NOTES: Forages in the crowns of tall flowering trees; inconspicuous. VOICE: Undescribed. HABITAT: Lowland to montane forest. DISTRIBUTION: Endemic to the S Moluccas.

4 DUSKY MYZOMELA Myzomela obscura 13cm FIELD NOTES: Forages singly or in mixed-species groups, from the sub-stage to mid-storey. M. o. rubrotincta (main illustration) occurs on Obi and Bisa islands; M. o. simplex (4b) occurs on Halmahera and satellite islands. VOICE: A thin, high *sut-sit sut-sit sut-sit*. HABITAT: Primary and tall secondary forest and forest edges. DISTRIBUTION: Resident in the N Moluccas.

5 CRIMSON-HOODED MYZOMELA Myzomela kuehni 11cm FIELD NOTES: Forages from dense undergrowth up to the canopy, singly, in pairs or as part of mixed-species feeding parties. VOICE: A high-pitched, down-slurred *tsiew tsiew...*; also a thin, insect-like *tsii-tsii*. HABITAT: Lowland monsoon forest, tall secondary woodland, overgrown cultivation, subcoastal scrub and gardens. DISTRIBUTION: Endemic to Wetar in the E Lesser Sundas.

6 SUMBA MYZOMELA Myzomela dammermani 11cm FIELD NOTES: Generally encountered singly, in pairs and in small groups. Forages mainly in the canopy and mid-storey. VOICE: Unrecorded. HABITAT: Primary forest; favours deciduous forest and forest edges. DISTRIBUTION: Endemic to Sumba in the W Lesser Sundas.

7 BANDA MYZOMELA Myzomela boiei 9–12cm FIELD NOTES: Seen singly, in pairs and sometimes in small parties; otherwise little recorded information. M. b. annabellae (7b) occurs in the E Lesser Sundas. VOICE: Unrecorded. HABITAT: Primary closed forest and tall secondary forest, secondary woodland, lightly wooded farmland, selectively logged forest and mangroves. DISTRIBUTION: Endemic to the S Moluccas and E Lesser Sundas.

8 SULAWESI MYZOMELA Myzomela chloroptera 9–12cm FIELD NOTES: Favours foraging in flowering trees in the canopy or mid-storey. Usually found alone, in pairs or in small flocks; often part of mixed-species feeding parties. M. c. batjanensis (8b) occurs in the Bacan Islands in the N Moluccas. VOICE: A loud, repeated *peeeew*, a *treeu tree*, a fast *tuweedu*, and a brief, high-pitched warble or twittering. HABITAT: Primary montane and tall secondary and moss forest. DISTRIBUTION: Endemic to Sulawesi, the Sula Islands, and the Bacan Islands in the N Moluccas.

9 WAKOLO MYZOMELA Myzomela wakoloensis 9–12cm FIELD NOTES: Seen singly, in pairs or in small groups; also forages with mixed-species parties in flowering trees. M. w. elisabethae (9b) occurs on Seram in the S Moluccas. VOICE: Undescribed. HABITAT: Primary and tall secondary forest, and mangroves. DISTRIBUTION: Endemic to Buru and Seram in the S Moluccas.

10 RED-RUMPED MYZOMELA (BLACK-BREASTED MYZOMELA)
Myzomela vulnerata 10–11cm FIELD NOTES: Active forager among flowering trees in the canopy or mid-storey, singly or in pairs. VOICE: A weak insect-like *sit-sit-sit...*, also a rapidly repeated *tipa-tipa-tipa...* HABITAT: Secondary monsoon forest and scrub, and primary forest. DISTRIBUTION: Endemic to Timor in the E Lesser Sundas.

1

2

2b
chionogenys

3

4
rubrotincta

4b
simplex

♀
6

♂

5

♂
7b
annabellae

♀
7

♂

8b
batjanensis

♀

elisabethae

8
♂

9b

♂

♀
9

10

♂

97 HONEYEATERS

1 SCALY-CROWNED HONEYEATER *Lichmera lombokia* 13–15cm
FIELD NOTES: Forages in flowering trees from the sub-stage to the canopy; alone, in pairs or in small parties; also forms part of mixed-species feeding flocks. VOICE: A series of rapidly repeated, chattering notes. HABITAT: Primary and degraded forest, forest edges, lightly wooded cultivation and scrub. DISTRIBUTION: Endemic to the W Lesser Sundas.

2 OLIVE HONEYEATER *Lichmera argentauris* 13–16cm FIELD NOTES: Feeds in flowering trees, singly, in pairs or in small groups. VOICE: A harsh *zhip*. HABITAT: Coastal *Casuarina* trees, coconut palms and scrub. DISTRIBUTION: Resident in the Moluccas.

3 INDONESIAN HONEYEATER *Lichmera limbata* 15cm FIELD NOTES: Noisy and aggressive. An active, acrobatic forager in flowering trees and shrubs. Usually seen alone, in pairs or in small groups. VOICE: A variety of loud, staccato notes, rapid whistles and harsh chatters. HABITAT: Monsoon woodland, secondary growth, mangroves, scrub, lightly wooded cultivation and gardens. DISTRIBUTION: Resident in Bali and the Lesser Sundas.

4 SCALY-BREASTED HONEYEATER *Lichmera squamata* 14–15cm FIELD NOTES: Noisy and conspicuous. Forages at flowering trees, also gleans prey from the underside of leaves. VOICE: A down-slurred *chirrup*, an upslurred *chirrup* or *chisip*, a whistled *tsi-tsi-tsi*, a seesawing *whitcheo whitcheo whitcheo…* and a loud, descending trill. HABITAT: Coastal and lowland secondary monsoon woodland, mangroves, lightly wooded cultivation, coconut plantations and villages with scattered trees. DISTRIBUTION: Endemic to the SE Moluccas and E Lesser Sundas.

5 BURU HONEYEATER *Lichmera deningeri* 15–16cm FIELD NOTES: Usually seen singly or in pairs; may associate with Wakolo Myzomela (Plate 96) when feeding at *Rhododendron* flowers or other flowering plants. VOICE: A soft *kew-kew-kew*. HABITAT: Primary and selectively logged and disturbed forest, tall secondary forest and scrub. DISTRIBUTION: Endemic to Buru in the S Moluccas.

6 SERAM HONEYEATER *Lichmera monticola* 14–17cm FIELD NOTES: Usually encountered in small flocks foraging in flowering trees and shrubs. VOICE: A repeated *tshoek tschoek tschoek*, very like the call of a European Blackbird (*Turdus merula*). HABITAT: Montane forest and montane heath forest. DISTRIBUTION: Endemic to Seram in the S Moluccas.

7 YELLOW-EARED HONEYEATER (FLAME-EARED HONEYEATER)
Lichmera flavicans 12–14cm FIELD NOTES: Forages at flowers in the upper mid-storey, alone or in pairs. VOICE: A series of short, very rapid, bubbling whistled notes, and a soft, nasal *bzz*. Other phrases include an *ik-a-blik*, a *ze-plerk* and a *klook-klook*; also utters a harsh, chortling song that includes various bell-like phrases. HABITAT: Lowland to montane forests, riparian woodland, secondary growth, open *Eucalyptus* forest and forest edges. DISTRIBUTION: Endemic to Timor in the E Lesser Sundas.

8 BLACK-NECKLACED HONEYEATER *Lichmera notabilis* 13–15cm
FIELD NOTES: Occurs singly, in pairs or in mixed-species feeding flocks; forages at flowers in tree canopies and in vine tangles. VOICE: Unrecorded. HABITAT: Lowland monsoon forest, coastal scrub, overgrown cultivation, tall secondary woodland and gardens. DISTRIBUTION: Endemic to Wetar in the E Lesser Sundas.

98 HONEYEATERS; FRIARBIRDS

1 STREAK-BREASTED HONEYEATER *Meliphaga reticulata* 15–16cm
FIELD NOTES: Noisy. Favours feeding at the flowers of *Eucalyptus* trees, singly, in pairs or in small groups. VOICE: A series of plaintive, upslurred *wheep* notes, starting quickly and then slowing; also a rapidly repeated, high-pitched *wik-wik-wik…* or *week-week-week*, and a lower-pitched *work-work*. HABITAT: Primary and secondary deciduous and evergreen forest, degraded forest, scrub and semi-cultivated areas, urban gardens and mangroves. DISTRIBUTION: Endemic to Seram and Timor in the Lesser Sundas.

2 WHITE-STREAKED FRIARBIRD *Melitograis gilolensis* 23cm FIELD NOTES: Feeds at flowering trees and shrubs, also gleans for invertebrate prey; usually seen singly, in pairs or in small groups. VOICE: An unmusical note, moderately high to high in pitch; also a harsh, rasping note. HABITAT: Lowland and montane forest, forest edges, remnant forest in grasslands and cultivation, selectively logged forest, regrowth forest, mangroves and coconut plantations. DISTRIBUTION: Endemic to the N Moluccas.

3 TIMOR FRIARBIRD *Philemon inornatus* 24cm FIELD NOTES: Noisy, conspicuous and aggressive. Forages in the canopy, alone, in pairs or in small groups. VOICE: Song is a medley of moderately loud notes, including a rapid series of *t-chika-wook* notes; also utters a series of seesawing notes that often precedes the song. HABITAT: Primary and secondary monsoon forest, open woodland, open scrub and, occasionally, lightly wooded cultivation. DISTRIBUTION: Endemic to Timor in the E Lesser Sundas.

4 GREY FRIARBIRD *Philemon kisserensis* 25cm FIELD NOTES: Little recorded information; actions presumed to be similar to the previous species. Formerly considered to be conspecific with the Little Friarbird (*P. citreogularis*) of Australia and New Guinea. HABITAT: Primary and secondary monsoon forest, open woodland, open scrub and, occasionally, lightly wooded cultivation. DISTRIBUTION: Endemic to islands off E Timor in the Lesser Sundas.

5 DUSKY FRIARBIRD *Philemon fuscicapillus* 30cm FIELD NOTES: Usually encountered singly or in pairs foraging in the canopy of tall trees. VOICE: Unrecorded. HABITAT: Primary and logged forest, secondary growth and coconut plantations. DISTRIBUTION: Endemic to the N Moluccas.

6 BLACK-FACED FRIARBIRD *Philemon moluccensis* 31–37cm FIELD NOTES: Noisy and aggressive; forages in the middle to upper levels of trees, singly or in pairs. VOICE: Calls include a loud, fluid *yio-wheea*, a short *ka wha* and a hard *kawah*. HABITAT: Lowland and montane forest, monsoon forest, secondary forest and plantations. DISTRIBUTION: Endemic to Buru in the S Moluccas.

7 TANIMBAR FRIARBIRD *Philemon plumigenis* 31–37cm FIELD NOTES: Occurs singly and in pairs, foraging in the middle to upper levels of trees. Noisy, aggressive and conspicuous. VOICE: A loud duet: first bird gives a *seeow*, followed by bubbling bugle from second bird. HABITAT: All types of wooded areas, including plantations, selectively logged forests and mangroves. DISTRIBUTION: Endemic to Tanimbar in the E Lesser Sundas and the Kai Islands in the S Moluccas.

8 SERAM FRIARBIRD *Philemon subcorniculatus* 35cm FIELD NOTES: Forages in the upper levels of forests, singly, in pairs or in small groups. Noisy and conspicuous. VOICE: An explosive *pprow* or *prrt*; also a loud *gock* or *geck*, and single loud, nasal notes. HABITAT: Forest, forest edges, mangroves and coastal coconut plantations. DISTRIBUTION: Endemic to Seram in the S Moluccas.

9 HELMETED FRIARBIRD *Philemon buceroides* 32–36cm FIELD NOTES: Forages in flowering and fruiting trees, singly, in pairs or in small parties. Noisy, conspicuous and aggressive. VOICE: A series of low-pitched, nasal notes. HABITAT: All types of wooded areas, including around human habitation. DISTRIBUTION: Resident in the Lesser Sundas.

99 FAIRY-BLUEBIRDS; LEAFBIRDS

1 ASIAN FAIRY-BLUEBIRD *Irena puella* 25cm FIELD NOTES: Forages in the tops of trees, especially those in fruit. Keeps on the move, hopping from branch to branch and flying from tree to tree. *I. p. crinigera* (1b) occurs in Sumatra. VOICE: A percussive, liquid *weet-weet be-quick peepit whats-it*, usually repeated every few seconds. In flight, utters a sharp *chichichichik*. HABITAT: Broadleaved evergreen forest and, occasionally, mixed deciduous forest. DISTRIBUTION: Resident in Sumatra, Java, Borneo and Palawan in the W Philippines.

2 PHILIPPINE FAIRY-BLUEBIRD *Irena cyanogastra* 23–28cm FIELD NOTES: Forages in fruiting canopy trees, alone or in small loose groups. VOICE: A snapping, whip-like *weep-weep pul paaawwww*; also a repeated, fluty *hu wee-u whip-tip hu wee-u*, the *whip* emphasised and the *tip* quiet. HABITAT: Tall lowland to mid-elevation forest and forest edges. DISTRIBUTION: Endemic to the Philippines.

3 BLUE-WINGED LEAFBIRD *Chloropsis cochinchinensis* 16–18cm FIELD NOTES: Acrobatic searcher of insects, fruit and nectar; often a member of mixed-species feeding parties. *C. c. viridinucha* (3b) resides in Borneo; *C. c. moluccensis* (3c) occurs in Sumatra and on its satellite islands, and on the Natuna Islands. VOICE: Various sweet, musical notes; also mimics other species. HABITAT: Deciduous and broadleaved evergreen forests, forest edges and secondary growth. DISTRIBUTION: Resident in Sumatra, Java and Borneo.

4 BORNEAN LEAFBIRD *Chloropsis kinabaluensis* 17cm FIELD NOTES: Forages alone, in pairs or in small groups; feeds in the canopy of fruiting trees. VOICE: A high-pitched twittering and a rapidly repeated *chit chit chit*. HABITAT: Mature and well-regenerated lower and upper montane forest. DISTRIBUTION: Endemic to Borneo.

5 GREATER GREEN LEAFBIRD *Chloropsis sonnerati* 20–23cm FIELD NOTES: Frequents the middle to upper storey, singly or in pairs; sometimes forms part of mixed-species feeding parties. VOICE: Musical whistles, interspersed with brief chattering notes; also indulges in mimicry. HABITAT: Lowland evergreen forest, peat-swamp forest, well-grown secondary forest and, occasionally, tall mangroves. DISTRIBUTION: Resident in Sumatra, Java, Bali and Borneo.

6 SUMATRAN LEAFBIRD *Chloropsis media* 17–19cm FIELD NOTES: Reported feeding on figs in the tree canopy, otherwise little recorded information. VOICE: Songs of captive birds recorded as loud and richly melodic. HABITAT: Lowland evergreen and secondary forest, plantations and orchards. DISTRIBUTION: Endemic to Sumatra.

7 LESSER GREEN LEAFBIRD *Chloropsis cyanopogon* 16–19cm FIELD NOTES: Forages in the tree canopy, singly, in pairs or as part of mixed-species feeding parties. VOICE: A loud, varied sequence of rich warbling phrases, including deep, mellow notes. HABITAT: Broadleaved evergreen forest, open forest, and forest edges and clearings. DISTRIBUTION: Resident in Sumatra and Borneo.

8 BLUE-MASKED LEAFBIRD *Chloropsis venusta* 14cm FIELD NOTES: Forages in the canopy, usually in pairs, although also recorded in small groups. VOICE: Undescribed. HABITAT: Mature lowland and lower montane forest, forest edges and clearings. DISTRIBUTION: Endemic to Sumatra.

9 YELLOW-THROATED LEAFBIRD *Chloropsis palawanensis* 15–17cm FIELD NOTES: Hard to see, best located by call. Forages in the canopy, singly or as part of a mixed-species feeding party. VOICE: A warbled *zo-o zo-o* and a rhythmic *twick err treet*. HABITAT: Lowland evergreen forest edges and secondary growth. DISTRIBUTION: Endemic to the W Philippines.

10 PHILIPPINE LEAFBIRD *Chloropsis flavipennis* 18–19cm FIELD NOTES: Forages in the canopy, singly or in pairs. Usually difficult to see, best located by calls. VOICE: A whistled *chick weeeeep* and a whistled *chick-ur-treet*. HABITAT: Lowland evergreen forest and secondary growth, and forest edges. DISTRIBUTION: Endemic to the S Philippines.

100 GERYGONES; FLYROBIN; SHRIKES

1 GOLDEN-BELLIED GERYGONE *Gerygone sulphurea* 10–11cm FIELD NOTES: Makes short aerial sorties to capture disturbed insects, also gleans insects from leaves in the tree canopy or mid-storey. VOICE: Various high-pitched whistles, a rising *chu-whee* and a long series of wheezy *whiz* notes. HABITAT: Mangroves, coastal scrub, freshwater swamp forest, plantations, parks and gardens. DISTRIBUTION: Resident in Sumatra, Java, Bali, Borneo, the Philippines, Sulawesi and the Lesser Sundas.

2 PLAIN GERYGONE *Gerygone inornata* 10cm FIELD NOTES: Active gleaner in the mid-storey and lower canopy; often forms part of mixed-species feeding parties. VOICE: A melodious, descending 16–18 paired notes, *poo-pii, pee-pee, po-po, po-pu,* likened to a rapid peal of bells. HABITAT: Lowland and montane primary and secondary monsoon forest, woodland scrub and mangroves. DISTRIBUTION: Endemic to the Lesser Sundas.

3 RUFOUS-SIDED GERYGONE *Gerygone dorsalis* 10cm FIELD NOTES: Usually seen in pairs gleaning from foliage in the mid-storey and vine tangles. VOICE: A series of semi-trilled level-pitched notes, also a jangle of unhurried, slightly warbled notes. HABITAT: Coastal and lowland forest, secondary forest, forest edges, partially cleared areas, lightly wooded cultivation and mangroves. DISTRIBUTION: Resident in the SE Moluccas, E Lesser Sundas and islands in the Flores Sea.

4 GOLDEN-BELLIED FLYROBIN (TANIMBAR FLYROBIN) *Microeca hemixantha* 12cm FIELD NOTES: Usually uses exposed branches or overhead wires to launch short sallies to capture flying insects; also forages with mixed-species feeding parties. VOICE: A medley of 12–14 sweet, warbled notes. HABITAT: Mangroves, forest, forest edges and open woodland. DISTRIBUTION: Endemic to the E Lesser Sundas.

5 TIGER SHRIKE (THICK-BILLED SHRIKE) *Lanius tigrinus* 17cm FIELD NOTES: Perches in cover more than most shrikes. Captures insect prey from leaves and branches. VOICE: Calls include a repeated *tcha* and a sharp *tchik.* HABITAT: Open forest, forest edges and clearings. DISTRIBUTION: Winter visitor to Sumatra, Java, Bali and Borneo; vagrant in the Philippines and Sulawesi.

6 BROWN SHRIKE *Lanius cristatus* 18cm FIELD NOTES: Uses a prominent perch to launch aerial sallies to capture prey on or near the ground. Grey-headed race *L. c. lucionensis* (6b) winters in the Philippines and Sulawesi, and in Borneo along with the nominate race. VOICE: A harsh *chr-r-r-ri.* HABITAT: Forest edges, scrub and open cultivation. DISTRIBUTION: Widespread winter visitor or casual vagrant to the region, except in the E Lesser Sundas.

7 MOUNTAIN SHRIKE *Lanius validirostris* 20–23cm FIELD NOTES: Generally found singly or in pairs. Dives down, from an exposed perch, to capture insect prey from or near the ground. *L. v. tertius* (7b) occurs on mountains in Mindoro. VOICE: A series of harsh, loud, whistled *piaaoo* or *chaaoo* notes. HABITAT: Montane forest clearings, open secondary growth, forest edges and scrub in grassland. DISTRIBUTION: Endemic to the Philippines.

8 LONG-TAILED SHRIKE *Lanius schach* 24cm FIELD NOTES: Noisy, restless and aggressive. Hawks insects from an exposed perch. *L. s. nasutus* (8b) is resident in the Philippines and a vagrant in Borneo; *'fuscatus'* morph (8c) may occur as a winter visitor to Borneo. VOICE: A metallic warbler whose repertoire may include mimicry; calls include a harsh *tchick,* and a scolding *chaak-chaak* when alarmed. HABITAT: Open wooded country, open country with scrub and scattered trees, forest edges and plantations. DISTRIBUTION: Resident in Sumatra, Java, Bali, the Philippines and the Lesser Sundas; resident in, and winter visitor to, Borneo.

9 STEPPE GREY SHRIKE *Lanius pallidirostris* 25cm FIELD NOTES: Perches prominently on bushes, rocks or wires, from where sallies are made to capture prey on or near the ground. VOICE: Calls include a repeated *kwi-wide, sheenk-sheenk* or *shihk-shihk.* HABITAT: Open country with scattered bushes. DISTRIBUTION: Vagrant in Borneo.

1

2

3

4

5
♂   ♀

6
6b
lucionensis

7b
tertius

7

8b
nasutus

8

8c
'*fuscatus*'

9

101 WHISTLERS

1 HYLOCITREA (YELLOW-FLANKED WHISTLER) *Hylocitrea bonensis* 14–15cm
FIELD NOTES: Inconspicuous. Forages in the mid-storey and understorey, singly, in pairs or
as part of mixed-species feeding flocks. *H. b. bonthaina* (1b) is found on Mt Lompobattang
in SW Sulawesi. VOICE: Thin, high-pitched buzzy notes; also utters a loud, piping call.
HABITAT: Mountain forest, especially moss forest. DISTRIBUTION: Endemic to Sulawesi.

2 MAROON-BACKED WHISTLER *Coracornis raveni* 15cm FIELD NOTES: Shy and
skulking. Usually seen in pairs or singly, foraging from the sub-stage to the lower mid-
storey. VOICE: A repeated, loud, explosive whip-crack call. HABITAT: Montane forests.
DISTRIBUTION: Endemic to Sulawesi.

3 SANGIHE SHRIKE-THRUSH *Coracornis sanghirensis* 17–19cm FIELD NOTES: Forages
in the middle and upper storey, also in dense rattan undergrowth and occasionally on the
ground. VOICE: Song is loud and consists of repeated ten-second-long phrases; also a lisping
chweep chweep. HABITAT: Lower montane primary forest and well-established secondary
forest. DISTRIBUTION: Endemic to Sangihe Island, north of Sulawesi.

4 MANGROVE WHISTLER *Pachycephala cinerea* 17cm FIELD NOTES: Unobtrusive
and sluggish; gleans insects from branches and trunks. Juvenile has rusty edges to wing-
coverts and secondaries. VOICE: A loud, whistled *oo-oo-oo-oo chew-it* or similar; in W
Philippines, utters a whistled *peeee pur-purr chiaoonkk* or *peee pur chiaoonkk*, the last note
ending abruptly. HABITAT: Mangroves and nearby vegetation, forest, riverine vegetation,
plantations and wooded gardens. DISTRIBUTION: Resident in Sumatra, Java, Bali, Borneo,
the W Philippines and Lombok in the W Lesser Sundas.

5 ISLAND WHISTLER *Pachycephala phaionota* 16cm FIELD NOTES: Skulking. Forages in
the shady understorey, singly or in pairs. VOICE: A loud *weet-chuw-weeEEee*, busy *chup* calls
and nasal notes. HABITAT: Mangroves, coastal woodland, beach scrub, secondary scrub and
plantations. DISTRIBUTION: Resident in the Moluccas.

6 WHITE-VENTED WHISTLER *Pachycephala homeyeri* 16–17cm FIELD NOTES: An
inconspicuous bird. Generally occurs singly or as part of mixed-species feeding parties.
P. h. winchelli (6b) occurs in the WC Philippines. VOICE: Various whistles, including
oo-wichee, *yump*, *yump-wit* and *u-wichee-u…*; also a high-pitched *wheeu tu tu tu* or similar.
HABITAT: Forests, from sea-level to mountains. DISTRIBUTION: Resident in the Philippines
and islands off NE Borneo.

7 GREEN-BACKED WHISTLER *Pachycephala albiventris* 16cm FIELD NOTES: Shy,
foraging quietly in the canopy or understorey; seen singly, in pairs or as a member of
mixed-species feeding groups. VOICE: A loud, metallic *peee* or *peee-wit*, repeated frequently.
HABITAT: Forests, from lowlands to high mountains. DISTRIBUTION: Endemic to the Philippines.

8 BORNEAN WHISTLER *Pachycephala hypoxantha* 16cm FIELD NOTES: Forages in the
middle to upper canopy, often as part of mixed-species feeding parties. Captures prey by
gleaning or during fly-catching sallies. VOICE: A whistled *dee-dee-dee-dee-dit*, the last note
like a whip-crack. HABITAT: Montane forests. DISTRIBUTION: Endemic to Borneo.

9 SULPHUR-VENTED WHISTLER *Pachycephala sulfuriventer* 14–15cm
FIELD NOTES: Encountered singly, in pairs or as part of mixed-species feeding parties;
forages mainly in the mid-storey, on trunks or large branches. VOICE: A whistled
wiwiwiwiwiwiuWHIT that decreases in pitch and increases in volume; also a short,
staccato *wheeu tu tu tu*. HABITAT: Primary and secondary forest and forest edges.
DISTRIBUTION: Endemic to Sulawesi.

10 YELLOW-BELLIED WHISTLER *Pachycephala philippinensis* 15–16cm
FIELD NOTES: An inconspicuous bird. Forages from the understorey to the canopy, singly,
in pairs or as part of mixed-species feeding flocks. *P. p. apoensis* (10b) occurs in the EC
and S Philippines. VOICE: A repeated, rising *peeeeeup*; also gives a forceful *hu-i-yu wit weeu*.
HABITAT: Forests, from sea-level to mountains. DISTRIBUTION: Endemic to the Philippines.

1 GREY WHISTLER *Pachycephala simplex* 15–16cm FIELD NOTES: Forages in the mid-storey and canopy, mainly gleaning from foliage or branches. Often forms part of mixed-species feeding flocks. VOICE: A series of five whistled notes, the first two brief and the last three disyllabic. HABITAT: Lowland monsoon forest. DISTRIBUTION: Resident in the Kai Islands in the SE Moluccas.

2 FAWN-BREASTED WHISTLER *Pachycephala orpheus* 14cm FIELD NOTES: Occurs singly or in pairs, foraging from the understorey to the mid-storey. VOICE: A series of 10–16 clear, whistled notes, beginning softly and then increasing in volume and speed, the notes at the end running together before ending in a sharp, explosive double note. HABITAT: Monsoon forest, secondary growth, beach and hill scrub, and mangroves. DISTRIBUTION: Endemic to the Lesser Sundas.

3 RUSTY-BREASTED WHISTLER *Pachycephala fulvotincta* 16–19cm FIELD NOTES: Usually seen singly or in pairs. Forages mainly in the middle levels, although may sing from the canopy. *P. f. fulviventris* (3b) occurs on Sumba in the Lesser Sundas; *P. f. everetti* (3c) resides on Jampea, Kalaotoa and Madu islands south of Sulawesi. Formerly considered a race of the Australian Golden Whistler (*P. pectoralis*). VOICE: Loud, clear whistles. HABITAT: Primary and secondary forest, scrub, wooded cultivation and, occasionally, mangroves. DISTRIBUTION: Resident in Java, Bali, the Lesser Sundas and islands south of Sulawesi.

4 YELLOW-THROATED WHISTLER *Pachycephala macrorhyncha* 16–19cm FIELD NOTES: Formerly considered a race of the Australian Golden Whistler (*P. pectoralis*). Actions presumed to be similar to the previous species. *P. m. fuscoflava* (4b) occurs on Tanimbar in the E Lesser Sundas; *P. m. compar* (4c) resides on Leti and Moa in the E Lesser Sundas. VOICE: Loud, clear whistles. HABITAT: Presumed to be similar to the previous species. DISTRIBUTION: Resident in the Lesser Sundas, Moluccas and Banggai Islands east of Sulawesi.

5 BLACK-CHINNED WHISTLER *Pachycephala mentalis* 16–19cm FIELD NOTES: Presumed to be similar to the previous two species. Formerly considered a race of the Australian Golden Whistler (*P. pectoralis*). VOICE: Loud, clear whistles. HABITAT: Presumed to be similar to the previous two species. DISTRIBUTION: Resident in the N Moluccas.

6 BARE-THROATED WHISTLER *Pachycephala nudigula* 19–20cm FIELD NOTES: Usually encountered singly. Very vocal; its calls are one of the characteristic sounds of montane forests in Flores. VOICE: A complex, beautiful, random series of loud, clear notes, including trilled whistles, bell-like bugles, squawks and squeaks. HABITAT: Primary and tall secondary moist hill and montane forest. DISTRIBUTION: Endemic to the W Lesser Sundas.

7 WALLACEAN WHISTLER *Pachycephala arctitorquis* 14cm FIELD NOTES: Forages in the upper or middle levels of trees, singly or in pairs. VOICE: A slowly accelerating series of five upslurred whistles, ending with a high *whee*; also a rising and falling, loud *chitchuwit* and a *chuuuu-wit*, followed by two short notes and then nine disyllabic notes. HABITAT: Mangroves, forest, forest edges, plantations and gardens. DISTRIBUTION: Resident in the E Lesser Sundas and S Moluccas.

8 DRAB WHISTLER *Pachycephala griseonota* 14–16cm FIELD NOTES: Forages from the understorey to the canopy, singly, in pairs or as part of a mixed-species feeding group. Best located by its calls. *P. g. lineolata* (8b) occurs in the Sula Islands. VOICE: A loud, prolonged, cheery warble; also six staccato notes with an explosive finish. HABITAT: Primary and tall secondary forest, selectively logged forest and lightly wooded cultivation. DISTRIBUTION: Endemic to the Moluccas and the Sula Islands.

9 CINNAMON-BREASTED WHISTLER *Pachycephala johni* 14–16cm FIELD NOTES: Forages from the understorey up to the canopy, sometimes in mixed-species feeding parties. Formerly considered a race of the previous species. VOICE: Presumed to be similar to the previous species. HABITAT: Primary and tall secondary forest and lightly wooded cultivation. DISTRIBUTION: Endemic to Obi Island in the N Moluccas.

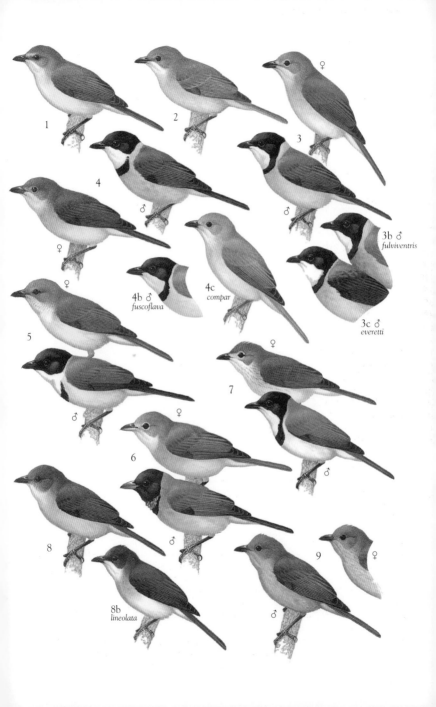

3b ♂
fulviventris

4b ♂
fuscoflava

4c
compar

3c ♂
everetti

8b
lineolata

103 CROWS

1 SLENDER-BILLED CROW *Corvus enca* 43–47cm FIELD NOTES: Generally encountered in small flocks feeding in, or flying above, the canopy. VOICE: Variable, including a high-pitched *ahk-ahk-ahk*, a nasal *werk-werk-werk* and a *whaaa-whaaa-whaaa*. HABITAT: Forests, forest edges and secondary growth. DISTRIBUTION: Resident in Sumatra, Java, Bali, Borneo, the Philippines, Sulawesi, the Sula Islands and the S Moluccas.

2 VIOLET CROW *Corvus violaceus* 40–42cm FIELD NOTES: Usually found in pairs or small parties; often raids ripening maize fields. Formerly considered a race of the previous species. VOICE: Short nasal barks, given singly or in a 2–3-note series. HABITAT: Forests, semi-open country and farmland. DISTRIBUTION: Endemic to Seram.

3 HOUSE CROW (INDIAN HOUSE CROW) *Corvus splendens* 40cm FIELD NOTES: Bold, very sociable and usually seen in small flocks. VOICE: A flat, dry *kaaa-kaaa*. HABITAT: Often common around ports; also occurs in villages, towns and cultivated areas. DISTRIBUTION: Resident in NW Borneo.

4 PIPING CROW *Corvus typicus* 19–20cm FIELD NOTES: Shy and very nervous, flying away with noisy, swooshing wing-beats. Regularly occurs in small parties. VOICE: A raucous, shrill screech; also three rising whistles followed by a crowing sound, and a variety of creaking and trilling notes. HABITAT: Forest edges and open woodland with clearings. DISTRIBUTION: Endemic to C and S Sulawesi.

5 BANGGAI CROW *Corvus unicolor* 39cm FIELD NOTES: Little information, known only from two old specimens. Possibly a secretive bird of forested hills. VOICE: Unknown. HABITAT: Presumed to be hill forest. DISTRIBUTION: Endemic to the Banggai Islands off Sulawesi.

6 LONG-BILLED CROW *Corvus validus* 46–48cm FIELD NOTES: Usually occurs in pairs or small parties, seen mainly in the tree canopy; often calls from the topmost branches. VOICE: A loud, short, dry, croaked *cruk… cruk… cruk… cruk*. HABITAT: Forests. DISTRIBUTION: Endemic to the N Moluccas.

7 FLORES CROW *Corvus florensis* 40cm FIELD NOTES: Usually seen singly or in pairs, occasionally found in small groups; frequents the canopy or subcanopy. VOICE: A high-pitched, downward-inflected, rasping *cwaaa, cawaraa* or *waak*; also a popping or gurgling *pol-ok* or *burr-ok*. HABITAT: Primary, tall secondary, and disturbed moist and semi-deciduous lowland and hill forest; occasionally in relict patches of forest and lightly wooded areas. DISTRIBUTION: Endemic to Flores Island in the W Lesser Sundas.

8 LARGE-BILLED CROW *Corvus macrorhynchos* 41–49cm FIELD NOTES: Seen singly, in pairs or in small groups. Feeds on both carrion and live prey. VOICE: A hoarse *kyarrh kyarrh, kyearh kyearh, kaaa-kaaa* or *weerrk weerrk weerk*. HABITAT: Open forest and woodland, mangroves, open country and near human habitation. DISTRIBUTION: Resident in Sumatra, Java, Bali, the Philippines and the Lesser Sundas. Rare visitor to Borneo.

9 TORRESIAN CROW *Corvus orru* 39cm FIELD NOTES: Occurs singly, in pairs or in small flocks. Regularly scavenges at road-kills. VOICE: 8–14 nasal *uk* notes, ending with an *uk-ohw*; also a variety of harsh cawing or *uk* notes. HABITAT: Open coastal areas, lightly wooded cultivation, and woodland near villages or towns. DISTRIBUTION: Resident in the N Moluccas and E Lesser Sundas.

104 JAYS; MAGPIES; TREEPIES

1 CRESTED JAY *Platylophus galericulatus* 31–33cm FIELD NOTES: Generally encountered in pairs or small parties, foraging in the low to middle canopy. *P. g. coronatus* (1b) occurs on Sumatra and Borneo. VOICE: An excited, staccato, chattering rattle; also a single *chik*, usually delivered while foraging in foliage. HABITAT: Broadleaved evergreen forests. DISTRIBUTION: Resident in Sumatra, Java and Borneo.

2 BLACK MAGPIE *Platysmurus leucopterus* 39–41cm FIELD NOTES: Usually found in pairs or small parties. Forages in trees from the lower to upper canopy. While perched, repeatedly bobs and bows head. The race on Borneo lacks white in the wing. VOICE: Noisy, varied vocabulary, including a loud, discordant *keh-eh-eh-eh-eh*, a bell-like *tel-ope* and a *kontingka-longk*; also utters a xylophone-like *tok-tok terlingk-klingk-klingk…*, a repeated *kip* and a high-pitched mewing. HABITAT: Lowland forest, swamp woodland, secondary forest and forest edges. DISTRIBUTION: Resident in Sumatra and Borneo.

3 GREEN MAGPIE (COMMON GREEN MAGPIE) *Cissa chinensis* 37–39cm FIELD NOTES: Inconspicuous, its presence usually given away by its whistled calls. Generally forages low down in shrubbery or in the forest understorey. Post-breeding, forms small flocks that are often part of mixed-species feeding parties. VOICE: Loud and variable shrieks, whistles and chatterings. HABITAT: Broadleaved evergreen and mixed deciduous forests. DISTRIBUTION: Resident in Sumatra and Borneo.

4 BORNEAN GREEN MAGPIE *Cissa jefferyi* 32cm FIELD NOTES: Often part of mixed-species foraging flocks. Sometimes feeds on the ground around mossy tree trunks. VOICE: Hash whistles and chatterings; also an incisive, rapid *swe-swi-swee-swi-swe sweet* or similar. HABITAT: Montane forests. DISTRIBUTION: Endemic to Borneo.

5 JAVAN GREEN MAGPIE *Cissa thalassina* 31–33cm FIELD NOTES: Hunts in the lower levels of forests, in small, noisy groups. VOICE: Unrecorded, presumed to be as other green magpies. HABITAT: Foothill and montane forest, occasionally lowland forest and adjacent cultivated areas. DISTRIBUTION: Endemic to Java.

6 BORNEAN TREEPIE *Dendrocitta cinerascens* 40cm FIELD NOTES: Noisy and conspicuous; sociable, usually encountered in small parties foraging in the canopy. VOICE: A variable bell-like *choing*, also a harsh *shraank*. HABITAT: Montane forests, preferring foothill and valley forests with clearings and cultivation; also secondary scrub jungle and bamboo thickets. DISTRIBUTION: Endemic to Borneo.

7 SUMATRAN TREEPIE *Dendrocitta occipitalis* 40cm FIELD NOTES: Forages in small, noisy parties in the forest canopy. VOICE: Bell-like calls, presumed to be much like those of the previous species. HABITAT: Mountain and foothill forests, favouring open forest with plantations and bamboo thickets. DISTRIBUTION: Endemic to Sumatra.

8 RACKET-TAILED TREEPIE *Crypsirina temia* 31–33cm FIELD NOTES: Scarce. Generally found singly, in pairs or in small parties. Agile forager in shrubbery, the lower canopy and tall understorey. VOICE: Foraging parties utter a high-pitched, gruff, ringing *chu*; also gives a rasping *churg-churg, grasp-grasp* or *chrrrk-chrrrk churrrk*. HABITAT: Forests, secondary growth, scrub forest and cultivation. DISTRIBUTION: Resident in Java and Bali.

105 STANDARDWING; PARADISE CROW; BRISTLEHEAD; WOODSWALLOWS; RAIL-BABBLER; MAGPIE-LARK

1 WALLACE'S STANDARDWING *Semioptera wallacii* 23–26cm FIELD NOTES: Away from display leks, usually seen singly or in pairs; may also form part of mixed-species feeding parties. Males display with flamboyant flights, branch-hopping and static poses. VOICE: Advertising call consists of a series of loud, upslurred, nasal *wark* notes. HABITAT: Primary and selectively logged lowland and hill forest. DISTRIBUTION: Endemic to the N Moluccas.

2 PARADISE CROW *Lycocorax pyrrhopterus* 40–44cm FIELD NOTES: Secretive, best located by its calls; usually encountered foraging in fruiting trees, singly, in pairs or, occasionally, in small parties. VOICE: A distinctive, low *wu-wuk* or *woo-up krek*, and a loud *wu-wnk* or *krek-kek*; also a barked or croaked *ekk*. HABITAT: Primary and tall secondary forest, scrub bordering cultivation, lightly wooded cultivation, coconut plantations and orchards. DISTRIBUTION: Endemic to the N Moluccas.

3 BORNEAN BRISTLEHEAD *Pityriasis gymnocephala* 26cm FIELD NOTES: Usually seen in parties of 5–12 birds foraging in the middle level of trees; often forms part of mixed-species feeding flocks. Female has patchy red flanks, also sometimes shown by male. In flight, shows a white wing-bar on primaries. VOICE: Various peculiar snorts and whistles, and strange nasal wheezes; also utters a *pit-pit-peeoo*, interspersed with a crow-like chatter. HABITAT: Primary and secondary lowland forest, especially peat-swamp forest. DISTRIBUTION: Endemic to Borneo.

4 WHITE-BREASTED WOODSWALLOW *Artamus leucorynchus* 19cm FIELD NOTES: Gregarious, groups often perching together on bare treetop branches or wires, from where aerial sallies are made after flying insects. VOICE: A chattering that includes mimicry; calls include a rasping *wek-wek-wek*, a sharp *pirt pirt* and a *git*, *geet* or *geet geet*. HABITAT: Open wooded country, forest clearings, open areas with scattered trees, plantations and near human habitation. DISTRIBUTION: Widespread in the region.

5 IVORY-BACKED WOODSWALLOW *Artamus monachus* 20cm FIELD NOTES: Encountered in pairs or flocks of up to 20 birds. Perches on exposed branches in forest clearings or open areas close to forests, from where short sallies are made after flying insects; also hawks insects and soars above unbroken forests. VOICE: A series of monosyllabic notes, more metallic and penetrating than those of the previous species. HABITAT: Forest, forest edges and forest clearings. DISTRIBUTION: Endemic to Sulawesi and the Sula Islands.

6 BLACK-FACED WOODSWALLOW *Artamus cinereus* 18cm FIELD NOTES: Occurs singly, in pairs or in small flocks. Perches on low branches, fences, posts and overhead wires, from where it makes aerial sallies after flying insects; also hawks insects while in soaring flight. Tends to fly lower than other woodswallows. VOICE: A drawn-out *tchiff-tchiff-tchiff* contact call and a soft, twittering song that often includes mimicry. HABITAT: Open woodland, shrubland and cultivation. DISTRIBUTION: Resident in the E Lesser Sundas.

7 RAIL-BABBLER *Eupetes macrocerus* 29cm FIELD NOTES: Forages on the forest floor. Walks with a nodding head, much like a chicken; also dashes over ground and fallen branches in pursuit of invertebrates. VOICE: A long, drawn-out, monotonous whistle. HABITAT: Broadleaved evergreen forest. DISTRIBUTION: Resident in Sumatra and Borneo.

8 MAGPIE-LARK *Grallina cyanoleuca* 26cm FIELD NOTES: Occurs singly, in pairs or in small groups. Forages mainly on the ground, but also perches on trees, from where occasional sallies are made after flying insects. VOICE: A duet: first bird utters a *tee-hee*, followed by second bird giving a *pee-o-wee* or *pee-o-wit*. Also gives a liquid, mellow *cloop cloop cloop* or *clue-weet clue-weet*, and an emphatic *pee pee pee* when alarmed. HABITAT: Damp grassland, paddyfields, swampy areas and savannah. DISTRIBUTION: Resident in the E Lesser Sundas and SE Moluccas.

106 ORIOLES

1 OLIVE-BROWN ORIOLE *Oriolus melanotis* 25cm FIELD NOTES: Usually best located by its calls. Occurs singly or in pairs, foraging from the mid-storey to the canopy. Female is a visual mimic of Helmeted Friarbird (Plate 98). *O. m. finschi* (1b) occurs on Wetar and Atauro islands. VOICE: A variable, liquid, musical, three-syllable yodel, *ti-ti-lu-i*; also a harsh, nasal scolding call. HABITAT: Remnant patches of monsoon forest, secondary monsoon forest, open woodland, partially wooded cultivation and mangroves. DISTRIBUTION: Endemic to the Lesser Sundas.

2 BLACK-EARED ORIOLE *Oriolus bouroensis* 23–32cm FIELD NOTES: Forages alone or in pairs, often in the company of Black-faced Friarbirds (Plate 98); as the oriole is a visual mimic of the latter, it is difficult to separate the two. VOICE: Said to mimic the Black-faced Friarbird, but not certainly recorded. Possibly a fluid *yio-wheea*. HABITAT: Lowland and montane forest, deciduous monsoon forest, secondary woodland, mangroves and lightly wooded cultivation. DISTRIBUTION: Endemic to Buru in the S Moluccas.

3 TANIMBAR ORIOLE *Oriolus decipiens* 23–32cm FIELD NOTES: Forages alone or in pairs. Formerly considered a race of Black-eared Oriole. A visual mimic of the Tanimbar Friarbird (Plate 98). VOICE: A rich, loud, clear, down-slurred musical note; also a clear, pure whistle, low at first and rising at the end. HABITAT: Moist montane and lowland forests, and mangroves. DISTRIBUTION: Endemic to Tanimbar in the E Lesser Sundas.

4 DUSKY-BROWN ORIOLE *Oriolus phaeochromus* 26cm FIELD NOTES: Forages in the crowns of tall trees, singly, or sometimes in small flocks or as part of mixed-species feeding parties. A visual mimic of the Dusky Friarbird (Plate 98). VOICE: A liquid *k k-wheeou*, repeated at eight-second intervals. HABITAT: Primary and mature secondary lowland and hill forest, and in cultivated land. DISTRIBUTION: Endemic to Halmahera in the N Moluccas.

5 GREY-COLLARED ORIOLE *Oriolus forsteni* 31–32cm FIELD NOTES: Occurs singly, in pairs, or sometimes as a member of mixed-species feeding parties; forages in the lower canopy and mid-storey of tall trees. A visual mimic of the Seram Friarbird (Plate 98). VOICE: Calls include 3–4 ascending, liquid, musical notes and a fluty *whee-who*. HABITAT: Primary lowland and montane forest. DISTRIBUTION: Endemic to Seram in the S Moluccas.

6 GREEN ORIOLE *Oriolus flavocinctus* 25–30cm FIELD NOTES: Favours the canopy. Forages alone, in pairs or in small groups. VOICE: A loud, bubbling *yok-yok-yoddle*, a clear *peek-kwwek*, a harsh *scarab* and a soft, warbling sub-song. HABITAT: Monsoon forest and, occasionally, lightly wooded cultivation. DISTRIBUTION: Resident in the E Lesser Sundas.

7 OLIVE-BACKED ORIOLE *Oriolus sagittatus* 27cm FIELD NOTES: Occurs singly, in pairs or in small family parties. Noisy – usually heard before it is seen. Forages in the leafy canopy on arthropods and fruit. VOICE: A rolling, mellow, repeated *olly*, *olly-ole*, *urry*, *orry-ole* or *olio*; also utters a harsh, scolding note. HABITAT: Open woodland, wooded cultivation and forest edges. DISTRIBUTION: Vagrant in the E Lesser Sundas.

8 DARK-THROATED ORIOLE *Oriolus xanthonotus* 20–21cm FIELD NOTES: Generally forages from the mid-storey to the canopy; sometimes forms part of mixed-species feeding flocks, otherwise usually seen singly or in pairs. VOICE: A melodious, fluty *tu-u-liu* or *peu-peu-peu-poh*, the last note a descending rasp. Call is a high-pitched, piping *kyew*, *pheeu* or *ti-u*. HABITAT: Primary and tall secondary forest, secondary growth and forest edges. DISTRIBUTION: Resident in Sumatra, Java, Borneo and the W Philippines.

107 ORIOLES; FIGBIRDS

1 PHILIPPINE ORIOLE *Oriolus steerii* 20–21cm FIELD NOTES: Forages singly, in pairs and, occasionally, in mixed-species feeding flocks, usually in the canopy. *O. s. cinereogenys* (1b) resides in the Sulu Archipelago. VOICE: A trumpeted, high-pitched *per-jek* that speeds up and is repeated; also utters a trumpeting *eeerk eeerk eeerk* and a *hooooo-op*. HABITAT: Forests, forest edges and secondary growth. DISTRIBUTION: Endemic to the Philippines, apart from in the north.

2 WHITE-LORED ORIOLE *Oriolus albiloris* 20–21cm FIELD NOTES: Formerly considered a race of the previous species; actions presumed to be similar. VOICE: A slightly mournful *chow-wooooo* and a rapid, staccato *chup-chup-chup*. HABITAT: Forest, forest edges and secondary growth. DISTRIBUTION: Endemic to the N Philippines.

3 ISABELA ORIOLE *Oriolus isabellae* 20–21cm FIELD NOTES: Very rare. Forages from the mid-storey to the canopy, singly, in pairs or in small groups, and as part of mixed-species feeding parties. VOICE: Unrecorded. HABITAT: Lowland rainforests, especially thick bamboo; also secondary growth and forest edges. DISTRIBUTION: Endemic to the N Philippines.

4 BLACK-NAPED ORIOLE *Oriolus chinensis* 27cm FIELD NOTES: Arboreal, attracted to fruit-bearing trees, singly, in pairs or in mixed-species feeding parties. *O. c. celebensis* (4b) occurs on Sulawesi and islands off the N coast; *O. c. melanisticus* (4c) resides on the Talaud Islands. VOICE: A liquid, fluty *luwee - wee - wee-leeow* or similar; also an upslurred *wheeeip*. HABITAT: Open woodland, plantations, mangroves, parks and gardens. DISTRIBUTION: Resident in Sumatra, Java, Bali, the Philippines, Sulawesi, the Sula Islands, the W Lesser Sundas, the Talaud Islands and Mayu Island in the N Moluccas; vagrant in Borneo.

5 BLACK-HOODED ORIOLE *Oriolus xanthornus* 25cm FIELD NOTES: Mainly arboreal, foraging singly or in pairs high in trees; occasionally descends to pick insects off the ground. Sometimes joins mixed-species feeding parties. VOICE: A melodious, fluty *why-you* or *why-you-you*, often interspersed with harsh *cheeahs* and *kwaaks*. HABITAT: Mangrove, riverine and coastal forest, open forest, secondary forest and cultivation. DISTRIBUTION: Resident in Borneo; winter visitor to N and E Sumatra.

6 BLACK ORIOLE *Oriolus hosii* 21cm FIELD NOTES: Forages on fruits, berries and invertebrates in the canopy, singly, in pairs or in small groups. VOICE: Clear whistles with a downward inflection. HABITAT: Montane forest and mossy transitional forest. DISTRIBUTION: Endemic to Borneo.

7 BLACK-AND-CRIMSON ORIOLE *Oriolus cruentus* 23–25cm FIELD NOTES: Forages singly or in pairs from the understorey to the canopy; regularly joins mixed-species feeding parties. VOICE: A short, melodious call and a hard *kek kreo* or *ee-oo*; also utters a cat-like *keeeeu* and a strained *hhsssu*. HABITAT: Broadleaved evergreen forest. DISTRIBUTION: Resident in Sumatra, Java and Borneo.

8 TIMOR FIGBIRD (GREEN FIGBIRD) *Sphecotheres viridis* 26cm FIELD NOTES: Forages in fruiting trees and shrubs, singly, in pairs or in groups, and with other fruit-eating species. Often calls from an exposed position in the treetops. VOICE: A burred, metallic trill, consisting of two very brief phrases. HABITAT: Primary and tall secondary monsoon forest, remnant forest patches, woodland, wooded cultivation, mangroves and scrub. DISTRIBUTION: Endemic to the E Lesser Sundas.

9 WETAR FIGBIRD *Sphecotheres hypoleucus* 26cm FIELD NOTES: Little recorded information; actions presumed to be similar to the previous species. VOICE: A muted series of harsh, chirpy, nasal and unmusical notes. HABITAT: Primary and secondary deciduous monsoon forest, woodland and lightly wooded scrub. DISTRIBUTION: Endemic to Wetar in the E Lesser Sundas.

10 AUSTRALASIAN FIGBIRD *Sphecotheres vieilloti* 27–30cm FIELD NOTES: Feeds mainly in fruiting trees, often in flocks of 20 or so birds. VOICE: High-pitched, descending whistles and a short, weak, rustling trill. Song consists of 3–5 simple whistles, the final note with a strong down-slur. HABITAT: Coastal secondary forest and adjacent cultivation. DISTRIBUTION: Resident in the Kai Islands in the SE Moluccas.

108 CUCKOO-SHRIKES

1 SUNDA CUCKOO-SHRIKE *Coracina larvata* 26–27cm FIELD NOTES: Frequents the canopy, singly or in pairs; sometimes found in mixed-species feeding flocks. *C. l. melanocephala* (1b) occurs in Sumatra. VOICE: A harsh, ringing *eeooo-eeooo-eeooo*, a *shreeok* and a curious loud, wheezy song. HABITAT: Montane forests. DISTRIBUTION: Resident in Sumatra, Java and Borneo.

2 JAVAN CUCKOO-SHRIKE *Coracina javensis* 28cm FIELD NOTES: Forages singly or in pairs at the top of tall trees or at the edge of forest clearings. VOICE: A loud, piercing, whistled *pee-eeo-pee-eeo* and a *tweer* or *twee-eet*. HABITAT: Open forest, forest edges and clearings, and savannah. DISTRIBUTION: Endemic to Java and Bali.

3 SLATY CUCKOO-SHRIKE *Coracina schistacea* 31cm FIELD NOTES: Usually forages singly or in pairs, 10m or higher in trees. VOICE: A series of slightly down-slurred, nasal, whistled notes; also short, unmusical, slightly metallic notes. HABITAT: Primary and selectively logged lowland forest, degraded forest, secondary forest, lightly wooded cultivation, lightly wooded swampland and tall mangrove forest. DISTRIBUTION: Endemic to the Banggai and Sula islands.

4 WALLACEAN CUCKOO-SHRIKE *Coracina personata* 30–35cm FIELD NOTES: Quietly forages in the canopy and at the tops of isolated trees, alone, in pairs or in threes. *C. p. alfrediana* (4b) occurs on Lembata and Alor in the W Lesser Sundas; *C. p. sumbensis* (4c) resides on Sumba in the W Lesser Sundas; *C. p. pollens* (4d) occurs on the Kai Islands in the SE Moluccas. VOICE: A long, drawn-out *weeeer*, a series of piping whistles, 2–3 upslurred buzzy notes and nasal squabbling notes. HABITAT: Primary lowland and hill monsoon forest and woodland; also secondary woodland, scrub and savannah. DISTRIBUTION: Endemic to the Lesser Sundas and SE Moluccas.

5 MOLUCCAN CUCKOO-SHRIKE *Coracina atriceps* 32–35cm FIELD NOTES: Often noisy and conspicuous. Forages in the upper tree levels, singly, in pairs or in threes. *C. a. magnirostris* (5b) occurs in the N Moluccas. VOICE: A harsh, staccato, dry chattering, given alternately by two individuals. HABITAT: Primary lowland and hill forest, tall secondary and selectively logged forest, coastal *Casuarina* groves and woodland, lightly wooded cultivation and, occasionally, mangroves. DISTRIBUTION: Endemic to the Moluccas.

6 BURU CUCKOO-SHRIKE *Coracina fortis* 35cm FIELD NOTES: Very little information; said to be unobtrusive. VOICE: Unrecorded. HABITAT: Lowland, montane and monsoon forest, and disturbed areas. DISTRIBUTION: Endemic to Buru in the S Moluccas.

7 BLACK-FACED CUCKOO-SHRIKE *Coracina novaehollandiae* 32–35cm FIELD NOTES: Generally seen singly or in small groups, usually perching on exposed branches; on alighting, repeatedly folds wings. *C. n. subpallida* (7b) is a non-breeding visitor to the Lesser Sundas and Kai Islands in the SE Moluccas. VOICE: A nasal, plaintive *plee-urk*; also a creaky, nasal purring note, often given in flight. HABITAT: Open forest, forest edges, clearings and secondary growth, savannah woodland and urban gardens. DISTRIBUTION: Non-breeding visitor to Sulawesi, the Sula Islands, the Lesser Sundas and the Moluccas.

8 STOUT-BILLED CUCKOO-SHRIKE *Coracina caeruleogrisea* 33–37cm FIELD NOTES: Forages slowly and deliberately along large branches in upper levels of trees, usually in pairs or small parties. VOICE: A slightly musical, harsh *shhhy yun-eshhhyuway*; also a soft, mewing slur, a short *chirp*, a soft rasp and harsh buzzy notes. HABITAT: Forest, forest edges, tall secondary growth and disturbed areas. DISTRIBUTION: Vagrant, or perhaps overlooked resident, on Halmahera in the N Moluccas.

1b ♂
melanocephala

4b ♂
alfrediana

4c ♂
sumbensis

4d ♂
pollens

5b ♂
magnirostris

7b
subpallida

109 CUCKOO-SHRIKES

1 CERULEAN CUCKOO-SHRIKE *Coracina temminckii* 30–31cm
FIELD NOTES: Generally encountered in pairs or small groups foraging in the mid-storey or crown of tall trees; often calls from high bare branches. VOICE: A drawn-out, nasal, rasping *sssssschu*, which is sometimes preceded by 2–3 dry, staccato notes; also utters a whistled *pi pi pi pi pi* and a short, high-pitched flight note. HABITAT: Primary and tall secondary hill and montane forest, and occasionally pine plantations. DISTRIBUTION: Endemic to Sulawesi.

2 BAR-BELLIED CUCKOO-SHRIKE *Coracina striata* 28cm FIELD NOTES: Noisy and conspicuous, often seen flying over forest clearings or between ridges, generally in small groups or as part of mixed-species feeding flocks. *C. s. difficilis* (2b) resides in the W Philippines; *C. s. sumatrensis* (2c) occurs in Sumatra and Borneo; *C. s. kochii* (2d) occurs in the S Philippines. VOICE: A clear, whinnying *kliu-kliu-kliu* or shrill *kriiu-kriiu*, also a harsh *klee kleep* and a rising *see-up*. HABITAT: Lowland forest, including mangroves, plantations and secondary growth. DISTRIBUTION: Resident in Sumatra, Borneo and the Philippines.

3 PIED CUCKOO-SHRIKE *Coracina bicolor* 31cm FIELD NOTES: Usually seen in pairs or small groups foraging in the dense leafy canopy. Best located by call. VOICE: A loud, ringing series of 3–5 trisyllabic notes followed by 4–8 louder single whistles, often preceded by several rasping notes. HABITAT: Primary lowland and hill forest, forest edges and clearings, scrub and mangroves. DISTRIBUTION: Endemic to Sulawesi and adjacent islands.

4 WHITE-RUMPED CUCKOO-SHRIKE *Coracina leucopygia* 25–29cm
FIELD NOTES: Generally seen in pairs or small groups; forages in the canopy, but will venture to the ground to collect food. Regularly perches on exposed branches at the top of trees and shrubs. VOICE: A series of jangling notes; also weak, nasal, chattering notes. HABITAT: Open wooded areas, lightly wooded cultivation, secondary woodland, scrub with trees and swamp forest. DISTRIBUTION: Endemic to Sulawesi.

5 WHITE-BELLIED CUCKOO-SHRIKE *Coracina papuensis* 22–29cm
FIELD NOTES: Occurs singly, in pairs or in small groups; forages from the mid-storey to the canopy, feeding by gleaning or making short aerial sallies. Often perches on the branches of dead trees; has an exaggerated wing-flicking habit while perched. *C. p. hypoleuca* (5b) occurs in the E Lesser Sundas and SE Moluccas. VOICE: A high-pitched, nasal, squealing *wheo-eeyu* or *witchew*. HABITAT: Forest edges, secondary forest, lightly wooded cultivation, scrub with scattered trees, mangroves and coconut plantations. DISTRIBUTION: Resident in the Moluccas and E Lesser Sundas.

6 HALMAHERA CUCKOO-SHRIKE *Coracina parvula* 25cm FIELD NOTES: Generally found in pairs, foraging in the canopy or perched at the top of dead trees, from where sallies are made after flying insects. VOICE: A series of rapidly repeated staccato, chattering notes, slowing and descending before tailing off. HABITAT: Primary and selectively logged hill forest. DISTRIBUTION: Endemic to Halmahera in the N Moluccas.

7 PYGMY CUCKOO-SHRIKE *Coracina abbotti* 20cm FIELD NOTES: Forages sluggishly in the crowns of tall trees and nuthatch-like on thick branches; usually encountered singly or in pairs, occasionally in small groups or as part of mixed-species feeding parties. VOICE: Song consists of two quiet notes followed by a four-note warble; calls include a high-pitched descending *thip* and a sharp *tseet*, given in flight. HABITAT: Montane forest. DISTRIBUTION: Endemic to Sulawesi.

8 BLACKISH CUCKOO-SHRIKE *Coracina coerulescens* 25–26cm
FIELD NOTES: Generally occurs in small groups or mixed-species feeding parties; forages in the canopy or upper understorey of forests or secondary growth. VOICE: A loud, harsh *peeeeeuuuu* or *peeeeeuuu peeuu-tip-tip-peeuu…*, the latter snapping and almost twittering; also utters a harsh, twittering *tip-tip-tip-tip*. HABITAT: Subtropical or tropical moist lowland forest and secondary growth. DISTRIBUTION: Endemic to the Philippines.

110 CUCKOO-SHRIKES

1 COMMON CICADABIRD *Coracina tenuirostris* 24–27cm FIELD NOTES: Inconspicuous forager in the dense leafy crowns of tall trees, best located by its voice. Generally seen alone or in pairs. *C. t. grayi* (1b) occurs in the N Moluccas; *C. t. pelingi* (1c) is found in the Banggai Islands. VOICE: A jumbled cicada-like *ch-ch-ch*, followed by a down-slurred nasal note. HABITAT: Primary, secondary and selectively logged forest and forest edges. DISTRIBUTION: Resident in S Sulawesi and islands off Sulawesi, the Moluccas and the Lesser Sundas.

2 SUMBA CICADABIRD *Coracina dohertyi* 20–24cm FIELD NOTES: Usually occurs in pairs, or sometimes alone or in threes. Forages in the mid-storey and the lower canopy of large trees. VOICE: Song consists of three grating cicada-like notes; also utters a harsh, rasping *queep*. HABITAT: Primary and tall secondary evergreen forest, monsoon forest and *Casuarina* woodland. DISTRIBUTION: Endemic to the W Lesser Sundas.

3 SULA CICADABIRD *Coracina sula* 20–24cm FIELD NOTES: Usually seen singly, in pairs or in small groups, often forming part of mixed-species feeding parties. Forages mainly in the lower storeys of forests, up to 15m or so from the ground. VOICE: A series of short, explosive metallic notes, given at the rate of 2–3 per second. HABITAT: Primary forest, woodland, plantations and scrub. DISTRIBUTION: Endemic to the Sula Islands.

4 KAI CICADABIRD *Coracina dispar* 21–25cm FIELD NOTES: Generally seen alone or in pairs. Active forager, mainly from the mid-storey to the lower canopy, gleaning from the underside of leaves. VOICE: A repeated, unmusical, down-slurred note; also utters a single *chuk*. HABITAT: Forest, forest edges and secondary woodland. DISTRIBUTION: Endemic to the SE Moluccas and E Lesser Sundas.

5 SULAWESI CICADABIRD *Coracina morio* 23–25cm FIELD NOTES: Occurs in pairs or small groups, and as part of mixed-species feeding parties; forages in the canopy and subcanopy. *C. m. talautensis* (5b) occurs in the Talaud Islands. VOICE: A slow sequence of buzzy, nasal, ringing cicada-like notes, alternating with a clear descending whistle; also piercing, excited *ki* or *ke* calls, a rapid nasal chatter and a low-pitched *chup*. HABITAT: Primary and tall secondary lowland, hill and montane forest, forest edges, small forest patches and secondary growth. DISTRIBUTION: Endemic to Sulawesi.

6 BLACK-BIBBED CICADABIRD *Coracina mindanensis* 23cm
FIELD NOTES: Inconspicuous forager, mainly in the canopy; occurs singly, in small groups or as part of mixed-species feeding parties. *C. m. elusa* (6b) occurs in Mindoro. VOICE: No information. HABITAT: Forest and secondary growth. DISTRIBUTION: Endemic to the Philippines.

7 PALE CICADABIRD *Coracina ceramensis* 24–25cm FIELD NOTES: Often seen in mixed-species feeding parties foraging in the dense foliage of the crowns of tall trees; gleans from branches and the underside of leaves. VOICE: A rapid, dry chatter and a short, staccato *tick*; in flight, utters a distinctive nasal chatter. HABITAT: Forests, including selectively logged forest, secondary growth and, occasionally, mangroves. DISTRIBUTION: Endemic to the S Moluccas.

8 LESSER CUCKOO-SHRIKE *Coracina fimbriata* 19–21cm FIELD NOTES: Forages in the canopy, often with mixed-species feeding parties; also occurs singly or in pairs. VOICE: A repeated, loud *whit-it-it-chui-choi…*; also a rapid series of *whit* notes and a squeaky, nasal *wherrh* when alarmed. HABITAT: Forest, secondary growth, peat-swamp forest and cultivation. DISTRIBUTION: Resident in Sumatra, Java, Bali and Borneo.

1 ♀

1 ♂

1c *pelingi* ♀

1b *grayi* ♀

1b *grayi* ♂

2 ♀

2 ♂

3 ♀

3 ♂

4 ♀

4 ♂

5b *talautensis* ♀

5 ♀

5 ♂

6b *elusa* ♂

6 ♀

6 ♂

7 ♀

7 ♂

8 ♀

8 ♂

111 CUCKOO-SHRIKES; TRILLERS

1 McGREGOR'S CUCKOO-SHRIKE *Coracina mcgregori* 21cm FIELD NOTES: Often seen in groups or mixed-species feeding flocks; forages in the canopy and understorey, and at forest edges. VOICE: A rasping or snapping *chu chu chu zwheeeeeeet-zhuuuuuuuu*, likened to the sound made while tuning a radio; also a *zwheeet zwheeet zwheeet*. HABITAT: Mossy montane forest and forest edges. DISTRIBUTION: Endemic to Mindanao in the S Philippines.

2 WHITE-WINGED CUCKOO-SHRIKE *Coracina ostenta* 25cm FIELD NOTES: Usually found in small flocks or as part of mixed-species feeding parties, foraging in the canopy or at forest edges. VOICE: A loud, downward-inflected *schiirp* or *pi-ieu*; also gives a *chu chu chu chu pi-ieuu ki chu*. HABITAT: Lowland and mid-montane forest, forest edges and secondary forest. DISTRIBUTION: Endemic to the WC Philippines.

3 BLACK-AND-WHITE TRILLER *Lalage melanoleuca* 21–22cm FIELD NOTES: Generally encountered in the canopy or at forest edges, singly or as part of mixed-species feeding parties; often noisy. *L. m. minor* (3b) occurs in the E and S Philippines. VOICE: A loud *cha-chi cha-chi cha-chi…* or *ka-choo ka-choo ka-choo*; also a staccato *chi chi chi chi*. HABITAT: Forest and forest edges. DISTRIBUTION: Endemic to the Philippines.

4 PIED TRILLER *Lalage nigra* 18cm FIELD NOTES: Usually occurs singly, in pairs or in small parties. Forages at all levels and occasionally hunts on the ground in short grass. VOICE: Various nasal chuckles, *chaka-chevu* or similar; also a rattling *wheek chechechecheche-chuk*, and a *kew kew* followed by 2–8 *kyhek* or *chack* notes. HABITAT: Open woodland, forest edges, cultivation, plantations, coastal woodland, parks and gardens. DISTRIBUTION: Resident in Sumatra, Java, Borneo and the Philippines.

5 WHITE-SHOULDERED TRILLER *Lalage sueurii* 18cm FIELD NOTES: Usually conspicuous. Forages singly, in pairs or in small groups, on the ground in short grass or on bare areas. Perches on isolated trees, and on fence posts and stumps. VOICE: A harsh, rattling series of rapid, staccato notes that almost run together; song consists of twelve clear, rapidly repeated musical notes. HABITAT: Woodland, savannah, open forest, mangroves, overgrown or lightly wooded cultivation, scrub and gardens. DISTRIBUTION: Resident in E Java, Bali, the Lesser Sundas and Sulawesi.

6 WHITE-RUMPED TRILLER *Lalage leucopygialis* 19cm FIELD NOTES: Forages from near the ground to the crowns of small or large trees, singly, in pairs or in small groups. VOICE: A loud, swelling series of rapid, hard, clear chattering notes. HABITAT: Forest edges, heavily disturbed forest, secondary forest, lightly wooded cultivation and mangroves. DISTRIBUTION: Endemic to Sulawesi and the Togian and Sula islands.

7 RUFOUS-BELLIED TRILLER *Lalage aurea* 18–20cm FIELD NOTES: Usually found singly, in pairs or in small groups; forages from the mid-storey to the canopy. VOICE: A series of seven staccato, piping notes. HABITAT: Primary and secondary logged forest, forest edges, open secondary forest, scrub, coastal woodland and mangroves. DISTRIBUTION: Endemic to the N Moluccas.

8 WHITE-BROWED TRILLER *Lalage moesta* 18–19cm FIELD NOTES: Forages, singly or in pairs, from the mid-storey to the canopy; feeds by gleaning from leaves and taking small fruits. VOICE: Muted, unmusical, staccato *nit nit* notes. HABITAT: Secondary forest, mangroves, low open forest and, occasionally, tall forest. DISTRIBUTION: Endemic to the Tanimbar Islands in the E Lesser Sundas.

9 VARIED TRILLER *Lalage leucomela* 17–20cm FIELD NOTES: Forages mainly in the canopy, in pairs or threes; inconspicuous. Feeds by gleaning from leaves or branches; occasionally makes short aerial sallies after flying insects. VOICE: A series of loud, harsh *s-teeu* notes, given at the rate of about two notes per second. HABITAT: Monsoon forest, secondary woodland and lightly wooded cultivation. DISTRIBUTION: Resident in the Kai Islands in the SE Moluccas.

112 MINIVETS; FLYCATCHER-SHRIKES

1 ASHY MINIVET *Pericrocotus divaricatus* 18cm FIELD NOTES: Usually occurs in small flocks, foraging in the outer branches of the tree canopy; also a regular member of mixed-species feeding parties. VOICE: A jangling, metallic trill, usually uttered in flight. HABITAT: Various woodlands, open areas with scattered trees, plantations and mangroves. DISTRIBUTION: Winter visitor to Sumatra, Borneo and the Philippines; vagrant in Sulawesi.

2 SMALL MINIVET *Pericrocotus cinnamomeus* 16cm FIELD NOTES: Generally occurs in restless, noisy flocks, flitting about in the foliage at the top of trees in search of insects; also makes short fly-catching sallies. VOICE: A constantly repeated *tswee-swee* and a high-pitched *tsch-tsch-tsch-tsch* contact call is given between flock members. HABITAT: Open forest, mangroves, cultivated areas and gardens. DISTRIBUTION: Resident in Java and Bali; possible vagrant in Borneo.

3 FIERY MINIVET *Pericrocotus igneus* 15–16cm FIELD NOTES: Often occurs in small groups or as a member of mixed-species feeding parties; forages in the tree canopy. VOICE: A thin, rising, musical *swee-eet*. HABITAT: Forests, forest edges, clearings, woodlands, scrub and, occasionally, mangroves. DISTRIBUTION: Resident in Sumatra, Borneo and Palawan in the W Philippines.

4 FLORES MINIVET (LITTLE MINIVET) *Pericrocotus lansbergei* 16cm FIELD NOTES: Occurs in pairs or in small groups, and regularly a member of mixed-species feeding parties; feeds by gleaning and hover-gleaning from horizontal perches in the mid-storey. VOICE: Quiet, trilling calls. HABITAT: Open parkland-type forest with sparse understorey; also primary, tall secondary and riverine forests. DISTRIBUTION: Endemic to Sumbawa and Flores in the Lesser Sundas.

5 GREY-CHINNED MINIVET *Pericrocotus solaris* 17–19cm FIELD NOTES: Gleans invertebrates from foliage in the forest canopy, or makes aerial sorties after flying insects. Occurs in groups and often mixes with other foraging species. Birds in Borneo have a slightly paler grey throat. VOICE: A repeated *tzeep-zip* and a slurred *swirrrririt*; also a soft *trip* or stronger *trii-ti*. HABITAT: Montane forests. DISTRIBUTION: Resident in W Sumatra and N Borneo.

6 SUNDA MINIVET *Pericrocotus miniatus* 19cm FIELD NOTES: Forages in the canopy in small or large flocks. VOICE: A hard, shrill *chee-chee-chee* and a drawn-out, loud *tsree-ee*. HABITAT: Montane forest and forest edges, occasionally in cultivated areas. DISTRIBUTION: Endemic to Sumatra and Java.

7 SCARLET MINIVET *Pericrocotus speciosus* 20–22cm FIELD NOTES: Gregarious; regularly a member of mixed-species foraging flocks. Feeds by gleaning or hovering to take invertebrates from foliage, and makes short aerial sallies to catch flying insects. VOICE: A loud, piercing *sweep-sweep-sweep-sweep*, *swee-et sweet-e* or *twii-it twii-it* and similar. HABITAT: Forests and wooded areas. DISTRIBUTION: Resident in Sumatra, Java, Bali, Borneo, the Philippines and Lombok in the W Lesser Sundas.

8 BLACK-WINGED FLYCATCHER-SHRIKE *Hemipus hirundinaceus* 13–15cm FIELD NOTES: Usually seen in pairs or small parties hovering to snatch insects from terminal foliage or making short aerial sallies to take flying insects. Often part of mixed-species foraging flocks. VOICE: A coarse *tu-tu-tu-tu hee-heetee-teet* and a *hee-too-weet*, interspersed with a high *cheet-weet-weet-weet* and a *dee-dit-do*. HABITAT: All types of lowland forest, including secondary growth and coastal forest. DISTRIBUTION: Resident in Sumatra, Java, Bali and Borneo.

9 BAR-WINGED FLYCATCHER-SHRIKE *Hemipus picatus* 15cm FIELD NOTES: Usually found in small flocks, often mixing with other species. Makes fly-catching sallies from regularly used perches; also gleans from foliage or occasionally takes prey from the ground. VOICE: A sharp *chisik* or *chir-up*; also a high-pitched trilling. HABITAT: Lowland, hill and mountain forests. DISTRIBUTION: Resident in Sumatra and Borneo.

113 FANTAILS

1 MINDANAO BLUE FANTAIL *Rhipidura superciliaris* 16cm FIELD NOTES: Forages in the understorey, often as part of mixed-species feeding parties. Best located by its distinctive call. VOICE: A repeated, rapid, ascending *woo-woo-woo-woo-woo…*; also a sharp, raspy *whickkk whickkk* call note. HABITAT: Shady areas of forests, also forest edges. DISTRIBUTION: Endemic to the S Philippines.

2 VISAYAN BLUE FANTAIL *Rhipidura samarensis* 16cm FIELD NOTES: Formerly considered a race of the previous species; actions presumed to be similar. VOICE: No information; presumed to be similar to the previous species. HABITAT: Forests and forest edges. DISTRIBUTION: Endemic to the C Philippines.

3 BLUE-HEADED FANTAIL *Rhipidura cyaniceps* 18cm FIELD NOTES: Conspicuous and noisy. Forages in the understorey, usually in small parties or as part of mixed-species feeding flocks. VOICE: A sharp, metallic, staccato *chip-chip-chip-chip chip chip* that slows and is interspersed with sharp *chick* notes. HABITAT: Primary oak and pine forests, and heavily disturbed secondary growth. DISTRIBUTION: Endemic to the N Philippines.

4 TABLAS FANTAIL *Rhipidura sauli* 18cm FIELD NOTES: Formerly considered conspecific with the previous species; actions presumed to be similar. VOICE: Probably similar to the previous species. HABITAT: Mature and semi-mature lowland forest. DISTRIBUTION: Endemic to Tablas Island in the C Philippines.

5 VISAYAN FANTAIL *Rhipidura albiventris* 18cm FIELD NOTES: Actions presumed to be similar to Blue-headed Fantail, with which it was formerly considered conspecific. VOICE: Presumed to be similar to Blue-headed Fantail. HABITAT: All types of woodland. DISTRIBUTION: Endemic to the C Philippines.

6 RUFOUS-TAILED FANTAIL *Rhipidura phoenicura* 17cm FIELD NOTES: Forages close to the ground in the dense understorey; often joins mixed-species feeding parties. VOICE: Song rendered as *he-tee-tee-tee--oh-weet*. HABITAT: Mature forests with dense thickets and bushes. DISTRIBUTION: Endemic to Java.

7 BLACK-AND-CINNAMON FANTAIL *Rhipidura nigrocinnamomea* 16cm FIELD NOTES: Conspicuous, actively flitting through the forest understorey, singly, in pairs or as part of mixed-species feeding parties. *R. n. hutchinsoni* (7b) occurs in NW and E Mindanao VOICE: A sharp *squeek* or *chick*, likened to the sound of a squeaky toy. HABITAT: Mid-montane and montane forest. DISTRIBUTION: Endemic to Mindanao in the Philippines.

8 WHITE-THROATED FANTAIL *Rhipidura albicollis* 17–21cm FIELD NOTES: Restless forager, often working up and around the main trunk of a tree or nearby branches; also makes short fly-catching sallies. Often part of mixed-species foraging flocks. Tail often fanned and held erect. VOICE: A series of 4–8 thin, high-pitched, descending notes, often followed by a series of ascending notes. HABITAT: Open secondary forest on hills and mountains, and forest edges. DISTRIBUTION: Resident in Sumatra and Borneo.

9 WHITE-BELLIED FANTAIL *Rhipidura euryura* 18cm FIELD NOTES: Active feeder on small flying insects; seen singly or in pairs, and often forms part of mixed-species foraging parties. Regularly fans and sways tail. VOICE: An excited, squeaky *cheet-cheet*. HABITAT: Montane forest. DISTRIBUTION: Endemic to Java.

7b
hutchinsoni

114 FANTAILS

1 MALAYSIAN PIED FANTAIL *Rhipidura javanica* 17–20cm FIELD NOTES: Constantly on the move in vegetation, interspersed with fly-catching sallies; reported to follow domestic animals or monkeys feeding on disturbed insects. Occurs singly, in pairs or in small groups, and joins mixed-species feeding parties. VOICE: A high-pitched, squeaky *chee-chee-wee-weet*; also various squeaky chattering and squawking calls. HABITAT: Open wooded areas, secondary forest, mangroves and gardens. DISTRIBUTION: Resident in Sumatra, Java, Bali, Borneo and Lombok in the W Lesser Sundas.

2 PHILIPPINE PIED FANTAIL *Rhipidura nigritorquis* 19cm FIELD NOTES: Conspicuous and noisy; occurs alone or in pairs. Continuously fans tail. Formerly considered conspecific with the previous species. VOICE: A metallic chime-like *pip pip chop siitt chop why-su-weet*, repeated several times a minute. HABITAT: Early secondary growth, bamboo thickets, mangroves, parks and gardens. DISTRIBUTION: Endemic to the Philippines.

3 SPOTTED FANTAIL *Rhipidura perlata* 17–18cm FIELD NOTES: Active forager in the middle and upper storey; makes regular sallies after flying insects. Regular member of mixed-species feeding flocks. VOICE: A melodious *chilip pechilip-chi*. HABITAT: Primary and old secondary forest with tall trees. DISTRIBUTION: Resident in Sumatra and Borneo; possible vagrant in Java.

4 WILLIE WAGTAIL *Rhipidura leucophrys* 21cm FIELD NOTES: Searches for insects on or near the ground; regularly runs around flashing wings and tail, presumably to flush insects. VOICE: A variable phrase of squeaky, whistled notes that rise and then fall; gives a harsh, rattling chatter when alarmed. HABITAT: Grassy areas, beaches, mangroves, cultivation and urban areas. DISTRIBUTION: Resident in the Moluccas; vagrant in Borneo.

5 BROWN-CAPPED FANTAIL *Rhipidura diluta* 16–17cm FIELD NOTES: Forages in the dense understorey, singly, in pairs, in small groups or in mixed-species feeding parties. Frequently fans or wags tail from side to side. VOICE: A series of sweet and unmusical, discordant, staccato notes; also utters a high-pitched *chingk*. HABITAT: Primary and degraded forest, mangroves, bamboo thickets, coastal savannah and shrubland with grass cover. DISTRIBUTION: Endemic to the W Lesser Sundas.

6 NORTHERN FANTAIL *Rhipidura rufiventris* 16–19cm FIELD NOTES: Conspicuous, often perching upright when at rest. Favours open areas in the mid-storey. Plumage very variable; includes the following races: *R. r. bouruensis* (6b), found on Buru; *R. r. finitima* (6c), from the Watubela Islands; *R. r. obiensis* (6d), from Obi; *R. r. tenkatei* (6e) from Rote. It is possible that all of the above and some of the other races will be given full species status. VOICE: A series of halting, high, piping notes that alternates up and down and accelerates slightly, or variants of this. HABITAT: Primary and secondary forest, forest edges, lightly wooded cultivation, open scrub and mangroves. DISTRIBUTION: Resident in the Moluccas and E Lesser Sundas.

7 CINNAMON-TAILED FANTAIL *Rhipidura fuscorufa* 18cm FIELD NOTES: Forages by gleaning and by making aerial sallies; active, constantly fanning tail. Regular member of mixed-species feeding parties. VOICE: Song consists of short, discordant, whistled notes, interspersed with a high-pitched cheep. HABITAT: Forest, forest edges and mangroves. DISTRIBUTION: Endemic to the Lesser Sundas.

8 RUSTY-BELLIED FANTAIL *Rhipidura teysmanni* 14cm FIELD NOTES: Active forager from the mid-storey to the lower canopy, singly, in pairs or as part of mixed-species feeding parties. Reported following malkohas to capture disturbed insects. VOICE: A rising and falling series of 3–5 subdued, high-pitched notes, interspersed with *churr* and *tzic* notes. HABITAT: Hill and montane forest; occasionally in selectively logged lowland forest. DISTRIBUTION: Endemic to Sulawesi and the Sula Islands.

9 TAWNY-BACKED FANTAIL *Rhipidura superflua* 14cm FIELD NOTES: Usually occurs singly or in pairs; forages in the understorey. VOICE: A short, quiet series of tinkling notes. HABITAT: Hill and montane forest, and forest edges. DISTRIBUTION: Endemic to Buru in the S Moluccas.

115 FANTAILS; IORAS; PHILENTOMAS; WOODSHRIKE

1 STREAK-BREASTED FANTAIL *Rhipidura dedemi* 13–14cm FIELD NOTES: Very conspicuous and a regular member of mixed-species foraging parties. Little other information. VOICE: Attractive, rapidly repeated, medium-pitched musical notes. HABITAT: Forest undergrowth in lowland and montane forest. DISTRIBUTION: Endemic to Seram in the S Moluccas.

2 LONG-TAILED FANTAIL *Rhipidura opistherythra* 17cm FIELD NOTES: Shy and skulking; often part of mixed-species foraging flocks. VOICE: Song consists of a series of high-pitched squeaky notes; calls are short, unmusical repeated notes. HABITAT: Primary and secondary forest, forest edges and, occasionally, mangroves. DISTRIBUTION: Endemic to the Tanimbar Islands in the E Lesser Sundas.

3 RUFOUS FANTAIL *Rhipidura rufifrons* 15–18cm FIELD NOTES: Forages from the ground to the upper canopy; feeds by searching foliage, fly-catching and, occasionally, hover-gleaning. VOICE: Calls include chips, buzzes and scolding notes. DISTRIBUTION: Resident in the N Moluccas.

4 ARAFURA FANTAIL *Rhipidura dryas* 16–17cm FIELD NOTES: Often joins mixed-species feeding parties foraging from the ground to the canopy, favouring mainly the understorey to lower middle levels. VOICE: Song consists of piping and bubbling notes and a jangle of short notes. HABITAT: Mangroves, coastal woodland, monsoon woodland, primary and secondary lowland, hill and montane forest, and forest edges. DISTRIBUTION: Resident in the Lesser Sundas, S Moluccas and islands in the Flores Sea.

5 GREEN IORA *Aegithina viridissima* 12–15cm FIELD NOTES: Feeds on invertebrates in canopy foliage, in pairs or small parties, and as part of mixed-species foraging groups. VOICE: A high-pitched *itsu tsi-tu tsi-tu*, a chattering *tit-teeer* and a subdued *chititititit*. HABITAT: Primary and tall secondary forest and forest edges. DISTRIBUTION: Resident in Sumatra and Borneo.

6 COMMON IORA *Aegithina tiphia* 14cm FIELD NOTES: Acrobatic forager in the canopy, often making darting sallies to capture passing insects. Usually alone or in pairs; non-breeders often join mixed-species feeding parties. VOICE: Various strident, unmusical, whistling and whining songs. HABITAT: Open forest, mangroves, peat-swamp forest, secondary growth, plantations, parks and gardens. DISTRIBUTION: Resident in Sumatra, Java, Bali, Borneo and the W Philippines.

7 MAROON-BREASTED PHILENTOMA *Philentoma velata* 19–21cm FIELD NOTES: Often sits motionless for long periods. Movements generally sluggish, but will make sallies after flying insects; frequents the middle to upper storey. VOICE: A clear, bell-like *phu phu phu phu phu…*, a strong, clear *chut-ut chut-up chut-ut…* and a grating, metallic *churr*. HABITAT: Broadleaved evergreen lowland and lower montane primary forest, logged forest and secondary forest. DISTRIBUTION: Resident in Sumatra, Java and Borneo.

8 RUFOUS-WINGED PHILENTOMA *Philentoma pyrhoptera* 16–17cm FIELD NOTES: Sluggish. Frequents the lower to mid-storey; also occurs in low undergrowth and on the ground. Five percent occur as blue morph. VOICE: A mellow, piping *tu-tuuuuu* or *wee toooo*, and harsh, scolding notes. HABITAT: Primary and secondary forest, and peat-swamp, heath and logged forest. DISTRIBUTION: Resident in Sumatra and Borneo.

9 LARGE WOODSHRIKE *Tephrodornis virgatus* 23cm FIELD NOTES: Occurs in small parties in treetops; feeds by gleaning large insects from leaves, branches and sometimes the ground, or by making aerial sallies after flying insects. VOICE: A ringing *kew-kew-kew-kew* and a harsh *chreek-chreek-chreek…* HABITAT: Primary, secondary and plantation forests in lowlands and hills. DISTRIBUTION: Resident in Sumatra, Java and Borneo.

116 PARADISE FLYCATCHERS

1 CERULEAN PARADISE FLYCATCHER *Eutrichomyias rowleyi* 18cm
FIELD NOTES: Forages mainly in the canopy and subcanopy in small groups of 2–5 birds, and occasionally joins mixed-species feeding flocks. Feeds by fly-catching and snatching or gleaning from vegetation. Tail often raised and sometimes fanned. VOICE: Calls include a loud, rasping *chew chew chew chew chew chew*; a single *tuk*; a loud, descending, trilled *chreechreechreechree*; and a high, fizzing *streeeeee*. The song may be a wispy whistle of thin notes. HABITAT: Broadleaved tropical hill rainforest; favours sheltered forest in valleys. DISTRIBUTION: Endemic to Sangihe Island north of Sulawesi.

2 BLYTH'S PARADISE FLYCATCHER *Terpsiphone affinis* 20cm; male with tail 45cm FIELD NOTES: Generally hunts from a perch in lower part of tree canopy, usually in pairs. Females in the Lesser Sundas are tinged rufous below. VOICE: A clear, rolling *chu-wu-wu-wu-wu-wu…*, a loud *chee-tew*, a *zhee* and a whistled *whit-it* or *pop-it*. HABITAT: Primary and secondary lowland and hill monsoon forest, open woodland and lightly wooded cultivation. DISTRIBUTION: Resident in Sumatra, Java, Borneo and the W Lesser Sundas.

3 JAPANESE PARADISE FLYCATCHER *Terpsiphone atrocaudata* 18cm; male with tail 45cm FIELD NOTES: Hunts from a perch low in the canopy. Noisy and conspicuous in Batan. *T. a. periophthalmica* (3b) breeds in the Batan Islands. VOICE: Calls include a *tee chee chee* and a querulous *jouey*. HABITAT: Forest, forest edges and mangroves. DISTRIBUTION: Resident in the Batan Islands in the N Philippines; non-breeding visitor to Sumatra and the Philippines; vagrant in Borneo.

4 RUFOUS PARADISE FLYCATCHER *Terpsiphone cinnamomea* 21–22cm; male with tail 30–31cm FIELD NOTES: Forages singly, in pairs and in mixed-species feeding parties. *T. c. unirufa* (4b) occurs in the N Philippines. VOICE: A continuous series of 30 or more strident *schweet* whistles, and a harsh, raspy *tre-chee*. On the Talaud Islands, song consists of an indistinct *swik* followed by a rapid series of muted *wik-wik-wik* notes; also an upslurred *whik-whik-whik-whik*. HABITAT: Forest and secondary growth in lowlands and hills; on the Talaud Islands also found in remnant patches of monsoon forest and scrub mixed with secondary woodland. DISTRIBUTION: Resident in the Philippines and the Talaud Islands north of Sulawesi.

5 BLUE PARADISE FLYCATCHER *Terpsiphone cyanescens* Male 22cm, female 19cm FIELD NOTES: Forages from the ground up to 15m or so. Little other information. VOICE: A loud, staccato trill, lasting about four seconds and repeated several times per minute; also utters a mild *chh-chh-chh* or similar. HABITAT: Primary lowland forest and secondary growth. DISTRIBUTION: Endemic to the W Philippines.

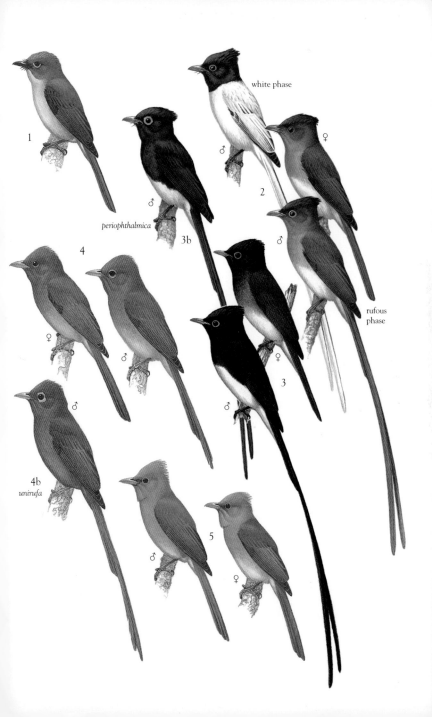

117 MONARCH FLYCATCHERS

1 BLACK-NAPED MONARCH *Hypothymis azurea* 16cm FIELD NOTES: Active. Gleans insects from foliage, and hover-gleans or makes aerial sallies. VOICE: A ringing *wii-wii-wii-wii-wii-wii*; also a high-pitched, rasping *sweech-which* or *che-chwe*. HABITAT: Primary lowland, hill, secondary and peat-swamp forest, and forest edges. DISTRIBUTION: Resident in Sumatra, Java, Bali, Borneo, the Philippines and the W Lesser Sundas.

2 SHORT-CRESTED MONARCH *Hypothymis helenae* 14cm FIELD NOTES: Generally seen alone, in pairs or as part of mixed-species foraging parties. *H. h. agusanae* (2b) occurs in the EC and SE Philippines. VOICE: A rapid, high-pitched, metallic *pi-pi-pi-pi-pi-pi-pi-pi* that increases in volume; also utters a rasping *tzeet-zip-zip* or *swee-sip*. HABITAT: Forest understorey; little other information. DISTRIBUTION: Endemic to the Philippines.

3 CELESTIAL MONARCH *Hypothymis coelestis* 15–16cm FIELD NOTES: Forages in the middle and upper canopy, singly or in mixed-species feeding flocks. VOICE: A loud, ringing *pwee pwee pwee* and a repeated, raspy *pee-chittt*. HABITAT: Lowland forest, forest edges and secondary growth. DISTRIBUTION: Endemic to the Philippines.

4 PALE-BLUE MONARCH *Hypothymis puella* 15–17cm FIELD NOTES: Occurs singly, in pairs or in small groups. Forages mainly by gleaning from leaves, from the sub-stage to middle levels and, occasionally, to the lower canopy. Often sits in an upright position. VOICE: Song consists of a series of whistled notes, including a *s-si-si SI-SI-SII*, a bubbling *whiwhiwhiwhiwhi...* and an upslurred *sweei-sweei-sweei...* HABITAT: Lowland, hill and secondary forest, scrub and lightly wooded cultivation. DISTRIBUTION: Endemic to Sulawesi and the Sula and Banggai islands.

5 ISLAND MONARCH *Monarcha cinerascens* 16–19cm FIELD NOTES: Forages singly, in pairs or in small groups, from near the ground to the canopy, feeding mainly by gleaning. Noisy. VOICE: A rapid, loud, slurred *weeweeweeweeweewee...*; calls include harsh, scolding chatters, followed by a jangle of squeaky, twittering notes. HABITAT: Lowland forest and scrub. DISTRIBUTION: Widespread in Wallacea.

6 WHITE-NAPED MONARCH *Carterornis pileatus* 14–15cm FIELD NOTES: Active. Feeds by gleaning or hover-gleaning in the canopy or mid-storey, generally in small groups or mixed-species flocks. *C. p. castus* (6b) resides in the E Lesser Sundas and S Moluccas. VOICE: A series of semi-musical, nasal, squabbling and chattering notes, followed by a single harsh, down-slurred note. HABITAT: Lowland and hill forest, selectively logged forest and forest edges. DISTRIBUTION: Endemic to the Moluccas and E Lesser Sundas.

7 MOLUCCAN FLYCATCHER *Myiagra galeata* 14cm FIELD NOTES: Usually encountered in pairs or mixed-species feeding parties. Forages mainly in the canopy, or lower down when in mixed flocks. Often raises crown feathers and shivers tail. *M. g. buruensis* (7b) occurs on Buru. VOICE: A loud, whistled *teu-teu-teu-teu-teu-teu...*, and calls with rapid, unmusical *wik* notes. HABITAT: Primary and secondary lowland and hill forest, logged forest, forest edges, forest patches in cultivation, mangroves and coconut groves. DISTRIBUTION: Endemic to the Moluccas.

8 BROAD-BILLED FLYCATCHER *Myiagra ruficollis* 15cm FIELD NOTES: Forages from the middle to lower storeys, usually alone or in pairs. Captures prey by gleaning or aerial sallies. *M. r. fulviventris* (8b) occurs on the Tanimbar Islands. VOICE: A musical *weeoo weeoo weeoo*, interspersed with a *chwik chwik chwik*; calls include a harsh, raspy *zzzt* or *zsh-wit* and a nasal *bzzzsh*. HABITAT: Mangroves, deciduous forest, secondary monsoon forest and lightly wooded cultivation. DISTRIBUTION: Resident in the Lesser Sundas and small islands in the Flores Sea.

9 SHINING FLYCATCHER *Myiagra alecto* 16–17cm FIELD NOTES: Usually encountered in pairs, foraging in dense thickets. VOICE: Song consists of a series of clear, trilled, whistled notes; calls include a loud, long, down-slurred, rasping note. HABITAT: Mangroves, forest edges, secondary growth and scrub. DISTRIBUTION: Resident in the N Moluccas and the Tanimbar Islands in the E Lesser Sundas.

118 MONARCH FLYCATCHERS

1 BLACK-BIBBED MONARCH *Symposiachrus mundus* 16cm FIELD NOTES: Occurs singly, in pairs or in small groups; also joins mixed-species feeding parties. Actively gleans from the underside of leaves. When excited, cocks and fans tail. VOICE: Song consists of a series of well-spaced whistled *swih* notes, increasing in volume and accelerating, followed by a series of high, rising notes that run together; also utters harsh, drawn-out notes. HABITAT: Primary semi-evergreen forest and mangroves. DISTRIBUTION: Endemic to the E Lesser Sundas.

2 SPECTACLED MONARCH *Symposiachrus trivirgatus* 14–16cm FIELD NOTES: Forages from the sub-stage to the lower canopy, singly or in pairs; also joins mixed-species feeding parties. VOICE: A series of harsh, muted, rasping notes, a churring *prrrrt* and a melodious *whit*. HABITAT: Primary and secondary forest, forest edges and, occasionally, mangroves. DISTRIBUTION: Endemic to the Lesser Sundas and S Moluccas.

3 MOLUCCAN MONARCH *Symposiachrus bimaculatus* 14–16cm FIELD NOTES: Singles or pairs forage from the sub-stage to the lower canopy; also forms part of mixed-species feeding groups. VOICE: A series of rapid, rasping, slightly nasal, staccato, disyllabic notes, often with an ascending or descending whistle; also various harsh, nasal, squabbling notes. HABITAT: Primary and secondary forest. DISTRIBUTION: Endemic to the N Moluccas.

4 FLORES MONARCH *Symposiachrus sacerdotum* 15–16cm FIELD NOTES: Forages singly, in pairs or in small mixed-species feeding parties. VOICE: An upward-inflected whistle; also buzzing notes, a nasal *schr schr schr* followed by a flute-like whistle, and a scolding *sjay-sjay*. HABITAT: Primary moist semi-evergreen hill forest, and old secondary and partially degraded forest. DISTRIBUTION: Endemic to Flores in the Lesser Sundas.

5 WHITE-TIPPED MONARCH *Symposiachrus everetti* 14cm FIELD NOTES: Noisy. Forages in pairs or occasionally in small groups; also in mixed-species feeding parties. Frequently cocks and half-fans tail. VOICE: A slightly tremulous, plaintive whistle; also harsh, scolding notes. HABITAT: Forests, scrub and mangroves with scattered large trees. DISTRIBUTION: Endemic to Jampea Island in the Flores Sea.

6 BLACK-TIPPED MONARCH *Symposiachrus loricatus* 18cm FIELD NOTES: Forages in the understorey and in secondary growth, alone or in pairs. VOICE: A rich, descending *teoow teoow teoow*. HABITAT: Lowland and submontane primary forest, shrubby secondary growth, open areas with tall trees, edges of logged areas and cultivation. DISTRIBUTION: Endemic to Buru in the S Moluccas.

7 BLACK-CHINNED MONARCH *Symposiachrus boanensis* 16cm FIELD NOTES: Very rare. Occurs singly, in twos or in threes, and a regular member of mixed-species feeding parties. Active forager in undergrowth near the ground. Frequently fans tail. VOICE: A clear *tjuuu tjuuu*, immediately followed by a soft, monotonous, fading, buzzing trill. HABITAT: Remnant patches of dense semi-evergreen secondary forest in gorges and valleys in foothills. DISTRIBUTION: Endemic to Boano in the S Moluccas.

8 WHITE-TAILED MONARCH *Symposiachrus leucurus* 15–16cm FIELD NOTES: Gleans from leaves in the mid-storey, alone, in pairs and in mixed-species feeding parties. VOICE: A series of four clear, descending, high-pitched whistles; a series of slow, dry, rasping, double-note scolding calls and a series of staccato, slightly musical, harsh chattering notes. HABITAT: Primary and secondary coastal lowland monsoon forest, hill forest and lightly wooded cultivation. DISTRIBUTION: Endemic to the Kai Islands in the S Moluccas.

119 DRONGOS

1 CROW-BILLED DRONGO *Dicrurus annectans* 28cm FIELD NOTES: Favours tall undergrowth and lower tree branches; makes fly-catching sallies from a hidden perch. VOICE: Loud, musical whistles, chatterings and churrs. HABITAT: Forest, plantations, wooded gardens, secondary growth, coastal shrubs and mangroves. DISTRIBUTION: Winter visitor to Sumatra, Java, Borneo and very rarely to coastal Philippines.

2 BRONZED DRONGO *Dicrurus aeneus* 24cm FIELD NOTES: Arboreal, mainly in treetops; makes fly-catching sallies after flying insects. Often a member of mixed-species foraging parties. VOICE: Loud, clear, musical whistles. HABITAT: Broadleaved evergreen, semi-evergreen and deciduous forests, forest edges and secondary growth. DISTRIBUTION: Resident in Sumatra and Borneo.

3 HAIR-CRESTED DRONGO *Dicrurus hottentottus* 32cm FIELD NOTES: Arboreal. Takes insects, mainly by fly-catching sorties; also feeds on nectar. Generally noisy and active, alone, in pairs or in small groups. White-eyed *D. h. leucops* (3b) occurs in Sulawesi; *D. h. striatus* (3c) is found in the S Philippines. VOICE: Calls include a loud *chit-wiii*, a single *wiii*, a *tsit-wit* and a *tsit-wit wuu*. HABITAT: Forest, forest edges, lightly wooded areas, scrub woodland and mangroves. DISTRIBUTION: Resident in Java, Bali, Borneo, the Philippines, Sulawesi, the Banggai and Sula islands, and Obi Island in the Moluccas.

4 SUMATRAN DRONGO *Dicrurus sumatranus* 29cm FIELD NOTES: Preys on insects by making fly-catching sallies or searching branches and foliage. Regularly joins mixed-species feeding parties. VOICE: A melodious *tee-tiyeeah* and harsh notes. HABITAT: Submontane and lower montane dry primary and tall secondary forest, and forest edges. DISTRIBUTION: Endemic to Sumatra.

5 TABLAS DRONGO *Dicrurus menagei* 35–36cm FIELD NOTES: Captures prey by hawking, and by foraging in foliage and on trunks. Favours the mid-canopy, often near streams. VOICE: A rasping, cicada-like call, a rasping *dzak-tess-k* and a *tsee-ik*. HABITAT: Mature closed-canopy forest and forest clearings. DISTRIBUTION: Endemic to Tablas in the C Philippines.

6 WALLACEAN DRONGO *Dicrurus densus* 28–38cm FIELD NOTES: Occurs singly, in pairs and occasionally in small groups. Perches in the under-canopy, from where sallies are made to catch passing insects. On Sumba, often seen in the company of Crab-eating Macaques (*Macaca fascicularis*). VOICE: A series of scratchy and high- or low-pitched grinding notes, and short phrases of chopped percussive notes, twittery and liquid, starting with a harsh, rapid churr. HABITAT: Primary and tall secondary forest, open woodland, lightly wooded cultivation and mangroves. DISTRIBUTION: Endemic to the SE Moluccas and Lesser Sundas.

7 SPANGLED DRONGO *Dicrurus bracteatus* 30–32cm FIELD NOTES: Usually encountered singly, in pairs and occasionally in small groups; also joins mixed-species feeding flocks. Favours the mid-storey and canopy; feeds by hawking flying insects from an exposed perch, and sometimes eats fruit. VOICE: A penetrating, long, nasal, high-pitched upslur. Duets with a collection of disjointed phrases, including a fluid *dew-dew-dew*, a vibrating *krrreeow* and a strident *chu-chu-seee-chu*, the latter apparently sounding like a mixture of frog and bird tones. HABITAT: Lowland and hill forest, forest edges, and secondary and littoral woodland. DISTRIBUTION: Resident in the Moluccas.

1

2

3

3b
leucops

3c
striatus

4

5

6

7

120 DRONGOS

1 SULAWESI DRONGO *Dicrurus montanus* 28cm FIELD NOTES: Usually encountered singly, in pairs or as part of mixed-species foraging parties. VOICE: A duet: first bird utters a harsh, grating *trrsh-trrsrh-trrrsh*, second bird answers with a soft, low-pitched *twuu* or *tee-twuu*. Calls include a siren-like note, loud, whistled upslurs and repeated upslurs given in flight. HABITAT: Hill and montane forest. DISTRIBUTION: Endemic to Sulawesi.

2 BLACK DRONGO *Dicrurus macrocercus* 30cm FIELD NOTES: Uses a prominent perch to make fly-catching sallies; captures prey in the air or pounces on insects on the ground. VOICE: Calls include a harsh *ti-tui*, a rasping *jeez*, a *cheece* or *cheece-cheece-chichuk*. HABITAT: Open country, cultivation, scrub and roadsides. DISTRIBUTION: Resident in Java and Bali; non-breeding visitor to Sumatra and Borneo.

3 GREATER RACKET-TAILED DRONGO *Dicrurus paradieus* 30cm, with tail up to 65cm FIELD NOTES: Makes swooping sallies after insects or small vertebrates; also gleans insects from foliage and takes nectar from flowering trees. Regularly joins mixed-species foraging parties. VOICE: Calls include a monotonous *kit-kit-kit-kit-kit…*, loud churrs, melodious bell-like notes and whistles. Song consists of loud, jangling notes, staccato notes, and strident whistles followed by a nasal sound. HABITAT: Primary, secondary and swamp forests, and mangroves. DISTRIBUTION: Resident in Sumatra, Java, Bali and Borneo.

4 LESSER RACKET-TAILED DRONGO *Dicrurus remifer* 25cm, with tail up to 40cm FIELD NOTES: Favours the forest canopy, from where bold, dashing pursuits are made after flying insects. Usually seen singly or in pairs, and often part of mixed-species feeding parties. VOICE: A large range of loud, metallic, musical whistles; also mimics the calls of other bird species. HABITAT: Dense lowland and montane rainforest, secondary forest and forest edges. DISTRIBUTION: Resident in Sumatra and W Java.

5 BALICASSIAO *Dicrurus balicassius* 26–27cm FIELD NOTES: Noisy and conspicuous. Usually seen in small groups, and sometimes in mixed-species feeding parties. Uses an exposed perch to make sallies after flying insects. *D. b. mirabilis* (5b) occurs in the C Philippines. VOICE: A mixture of clear and screechy whistles, interspersed with *chuck*, *chunk* or similar; often mimics other forest species. HABITAT: Subtropical or tropical moist lowland forest, and sometimes forest edges. DISTRIBUTION: Endemic to the Philippines.

6 ASHY DRONGO *Dicrurus leucophaeus* 30cm FIELD NOTES: Occurs singly or in pairs, and sometimes in small, noisy parties. Makes fly-catching sorties from exposed perches at the tops of trees or low down and at forest edges; sometimes uses overhead wires. Paler race *D. l. stigmatops* (6b) occurs in N Borneo. VOICE: Variable; includes a *chink-churr-tree*, and a loud, clear *tjuur-urr-tjuu* or *wie-piet wie-piet*; also mimics other bird calls. HABITAT: Forest clearings, forest edges, secondary growth, mangroves and coastal scrub. DISTRIBUTION: Resident in Sumatra, Java, Bali, Borneo, the Philippines and Lombok in the W Lesser Sundas.

5b
mirabilis

6b
stigmatops

121 WHISTLING THRUSHES; FRUITHUNTER; THRUSHES

1 SHINY WHISTLING THRUSH *Myophonus melanurus* 24–29cm FIELD NOTES: Shy. Forages on, or close to, the forest floor, often near running water; usually alone or in pairs. VOICE: A high-pitched screech; little other information. HABITAT: Primary mossy hill and montane forest with rivers and streams. DISTRIBUTION: Endemic to Sumatra.

2 JAVAN WHISTLING THRUSH *Myophonus glaucinus* 24–27cm FIELD NOTES: Forages on the ground and in lower storeys. Regularly fans tail. VOICE: Song consists of a series of loud, clear whistles; calls include a screeching, a pleasant whistled note and, when alarmed, an *ooweet-ooweet-teet* followed by a *truuu-truuu*, *cheet* or *tee-ee-eet… tee-ee-ee-eet*. HABITAT: Montane forest with dark caves and crevices. DISTRIBUTION: Endemic to Java and Bali.

3 SUMATRAN WHISTLING THRUSH (BROWN-WINGED WHISTLING THRUSH) *Myophonus castaneus* 25cm FIELD NOTES: Generally forages in the middle and upper levels of trees, especially those in fruit; occasionally on rocks in streams. Regularly fans tail. VOICE: A grating *waach*; little other information. HABITAT: Hill and montane forest, mainly alongside watercourses. DISTRIBUTION: Endemic to Sumatra.

4 BORNEAN WHISTLING THRUSH *Myophonus borneensis* 25cm FIELD NOTES: Forages on the ground among leaf litter. Frequently flicks tail open, like a fan. VOICE: Calls include a long, drawn-out whistle, a screech, a high-pitched ringing whistle and a long chittering. HABITAT: Hill and montane forest, near rocky cliffs or streams. DISTRIBUTION: Endemic to Borneo.

5 BLUE WHISTLING THRUSH *Myophonus caeruleus* 32cm FIELD NOTES: Generally seen feeding from rocks in strong-flowing forest waterways, dipping to collect food from the water surface. VOICE: Song consists of a disjointed string of melodious, high-pitched human-like whistles; sometimes includes mimicry. Calls include a far-carrying *tzeet-tze-tze-tzeet*, *tzeet-tzuit-tzuit-zuit* or *ee-ee-ee*. HABITAT: Lowland and hill forest, with rocky outcrops and rivers. DISTRIBUTION: Resident in Sumatra and Java.

6 FRUITHUNTER (BLACK-BREASTED FRUITHUNTER) *Chlamydochaera jefferyi* 22–23cm FIELD NOTES: Usually seen in small, wandering groups and mixed-species parties. Forages in the mid-storey and on the ground in leaf litter. VOICE: A quiet, high-pitched *seep*. HABITAT: Tall montane forest at lower altitudes and nearby gardens. DISTRIBUTION: Endemic to Borneo.

7 BLUE ROCK THRUSH *Monticola solitarius* 20cm FIELD NOTES: Forages on the ground or drops onto prey from a low perch; occasionally makes short aerial sorties after flying insects. VOICE: A loud, fluty, melodic *chu sree chur tee tee wuchi-trr-trrt-tri*; may also include some mimicry. Calls include a deep *chak-chak*, a plaintive *see* and a *wit-wit*. HABITAT: Open rocky areas, cliffs, cultivation, roadsides and urban areas. DISTRIBUTION: Resident in the Batan Islands in the N Philippines; winter visitor to Sumatra, Borneo, the Philippines, Sulawesi and the Moluccas.

8 SULAWESI THRUSH *Cataponera turdoides* 20–25cm FIELD NOTES: Usually encountered alone or in small groups; occasionally joins mixed-species foraging parties. Hops along horizontal branches searching for prey in epiphytic growth. *C. t. abditiva* (8b) occurs in NC Sulawesi. VOICE: A chatter and a pleasant melody of notes, generally given at dawn or dusk. HABITAT: Montane evergreen forest and moss forest with dense undergrowth. DISTRIBUTION: Endemic to Sulawesi.

122 THRUSHES

1 ISLAND THRUSH *Turdus poliocephalus* 21–25cm FIELD NOTES: Generally shy, mostly foraging on the ground among leaf litter in dense cover. Plumage very variable, with many races described (around 50 worldwide); the following are a selection of those found in this region: *T. p. deningeri* (main illustration), in Seram in the S Moluccas; *T. p. thomassoni* (1b), in Luzon in the Philippines; *T. p. malindangensis* (1c), in Mindanao in the Philippines; *T. p. whiteheadi* (1d), in E Java; *T. p. erythropleurus* (1e), from Christmas Island; *T. p. javanicus* (1f), in C Java; *T. p. mindorensis* (1g), found in Mindoro in the Philippines; *T. p. indrapurae* (1h), found in SC Sumatra; *T. p. seebohmi* (1i), in N Borneo; *T. p. fumidus* (1j), found in W Java. VOICE: A subdued melody of flute-like whistles; calls include a *chook-chook*, a rapid, chattering *tchick-tchick-tchick* or *tchick-chink-chink*, and a *tchook-tchook-toaweet-oweet-toaweetoweet* when excited or alarmed. HABITAT: Montane forest. DISTRIBUTION: Resident throughout the region.

2 PALE THRUSH *Turdus pallidus* 22–23cm FIELD NOTES: Shy and wary, foraging mainly on the ground or in fruiting trees. VOICE: Various double or triple whistles; calls include a *chook*, a *tuck-tuck*, a thin *tsee* or *tsee-ip*, and a *think-think* when alarmed. HABITAT: Open areas, copses, scrub, cultivation and gardens. DISTRIBUTION: Rare winter visitor to the N Philippines.

3 EYEBROWED THRUSH *Turdus obscurus* 22cm FIELD NOTES: Often seen in small to large flocks. Forages on the ground and in fruiting bushes and trees. VOICE: A soft *chuk*, a hard *tack-tack* and a *shree*; in flight, gives a *dzee*. HABITAT: Open forest, forest edges, mangroves and gardens. DISTRIBUTION: Winter visitor to Sumatra, Java, Bali, Borneo and the Philippines; vagrant in Sulawesi and the Lesser Sundas.

4 BROWN-HEADED THRUSH *Turdus chrysolaus* 23cm FIELD NOTES: Feeds low down, in or near the cover of bushes, or at all levels in fruiting trees. VOICE: A repeated *krurr krurr krr-zee* or *kiron kiron tsee*, and a *chuck-chuck-chuck*; in flight or when alarmed, gives a thin *zeeee*. HABITAT: Forests, secondary growth or in the open near cover. DISTRIBUTION: Winter visitor to the Philippines.

5 JAPANESE THRUSH *Turdus cardis* 22cm FIELD NOTES: Usually shy, feeding on the ground or in fruiting trees. VOICE: Song consists of a series of fluty trills and whistles; calls include a thin *tsweee* or *tsuuu*. HABITAT: Mixed or deciduous woodland with brush or scrub, thickets, edges of cultivation and large gardens. DISTRIBUTION: Vagrant in Borneo.

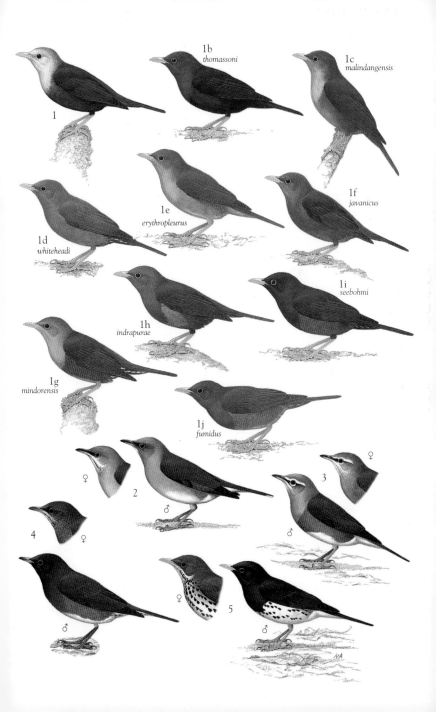

1b *thomassoni*

1c *malindangensis*

1

1e *erythropleurus*

1f *javanicus*

1d *whiteheadi*

1i *seebohmi*

1h *indrapurae*

1g *mindorensis*

1j *fumidus*

♀

2 ♂

3 ♀

♂

4 ♀

♂

5 ♀

♂

123 THRUSHES

1 SCALY THRUSH *Zoothera dauma* 27cm FIELD NOTES: Forages on the ground, usually in thick cover, moving with a nervous, jerky gait. VOICE: A soft, monotonous whistle and a thin, short *tzeet*. HABITAT: Mainly broadleaved evergreen forest. DISTRIBUTION: Resident in Sumatra, Java, Bali and Lombok in the W Lesser Sundas; winter visitor to the Philippines; vagrant in Borneo.

2 FAWN-BREASTED THRUSH *Zoothera machiki* 21–22cm FIELD NOTES: Skulks in dense scrub, although regularly forages in the open on the forest floor, along streams, on forest roads and in recently burnt areas; usually alone. VOICE: Unknown. HABITAT: Lowland monsoon and gallery forest, degraded and secondary forest, forest edges and scrub. DISTRIBUTION: Endemic to the Tanimbar Islands in the E Lesser Sundas.

3 SUNDA THRUSH *Zoothera andromedae* 25cm FIELD NOTES: Extremely shy and skulking. Forages on the ground or in low, dense cover; flees to perch in the mid-storey when disturbed. VOICE: Undescribed. HABITAT: Hill forest and montane mossy forest. DISTRIBUTION: Resident in Sumatra, Java, Bali, the Philippines and the Lesser Sundas.

4 EVERETT'S THRUSH *Zoothera everetti* 23cm FIELD NOTES: Forages on the ground, often in moist areas and near streams; quickly disappears into thick undergrowth if disturbed. White face markings are variable. VOICE: A soft, musical song; little other information. HABITAT: Submontane deciduous forest. DISTRIBUTION: Endemic to N Borneo.

5 GEOMALIA *Zoothera heinrichi* 28–30cm FIELD NOTES: Shy and secretive. Forages on the ground, among decaying vegetation in thick undergrowth. VOICE: An intermittent, thin, high-pitched, insistent whistle. HABITAT: Primary montane forest with thick undergrowth. DISTRIBUTION: Endemic to Sulawesi.

6 SIBERIAN THRUSH *Geokichla sibirica* 22cm FIELD NOTES: Secretive, feeding on the ground or in fruiting trees. VOICE: A weak *tseee*, a soft *zit* and a gruff squawk when alarmed. HABITAT: Hill and montane forests. DISTRIBUTION: Winter visitor to Sumatra and W Java; vagrant in Bali and Borneo.

7 SLATY-BACKED THRUSH *Geokichla schistacea* 16–17cm FIELD NOTES: Forages mainly on or near the forest floor; when disturbed, often flees to a perch in the subcanopy. Usually seen alone, in pairs or in small groups. VOICE: An exquisite melody of eight clear, sweet notes, the first drawn out and upslurred, followed by six short, alternating up-and-down notes that end with a long, upslurred, high-pitched whistle; also gives a thin *tsee*. HABITAT: Primary and secondary lowland forest. DISTRIBUTION: Endemic to the Tanimbar Islands in the E Lesser Sundas.

8 BURU THRUSH *Geokichla dumasi* 17cm FIELD NOTES: Forages on the ground. Little recorded information. VOICE: Calls with a high *pthhhhhh*. HABITAT: Primary lower montane rainforest. DISTRIBUTION: Endemic to Buru in the S Moluccas.

9 SERAM THRUSH *Geokichla joiceyi* 17cm FIELD NOTES: Forages on the ground, in deep undergrowth, usually alone or in pairs. VOICE: Calls with a thin *tseep*. HABITAT: Montane rainforest. DISTRIBUTION: Endemic to Seram in the S Moluccas.

1 CHESTNUT-CAPPED THRUSH *Geokichla interpres* 17–19cm FIELD NOTES: Shy; usually seen singly or in pairs. Forages on the ground up to the mid-storey. VOICE: Rising, flute-like whistles, interspersed with chirrups, transcribed as *see it-tu-tu tyuu*. Calls include a harsh *tac* and a high-pitched, falling *tsi-i-i-i*. HABITAT: Broadleaved evergreen forest. DISTRIBUTION: Resident in Sumatra, Java, Borneo, the Philippines and the W Lesser Sundas.

2 CHESTNUT-BACKED THRUSH *Geokichla dohertyi* 16–18cm FIELD NOTES: Generally seen singly; occasionally occurs in small groups at fruiting trees, otherwise forages on the ground. VOICE: 3–7 mellow, sweet whistles, interspersed with more complex phrases; calls include a thin whistle and a high-pitched, squeaky whistle. HABITAT: Primary hill and montane forest. DISTRIBUTION: Endemic to the Lesser Sundas.

3 ENGGANO THRUSH *Geokichla leucolaema* 16–19cm FIELD NOTES: Little information; presumed to be similar to the Chestnut-capped Thrush, with which it was formerly considered conspecific. VOICE: Song said to resemble a juvenile begging call. HABITAT: Rainforest. DISTRIBUTION: Endemic to Enggano Island off SW Sumatra.

4 RED-BACKED THRUSH *Geokichla erythronota* 20cm FIELD NOTES: Shy and secretive, foraging mainly on the ground in shady forest areas, usually singly. G. *e. kabaena* (4b) occurs on Kabaena Island off SE Sulawesi. VOICE: A thin, high-pitched, upslurred note; song consists of a series of liquid notes. HABITAT: Tropical lowland and mid-elevation broadleaved evergreen forest. DISTRIBUTION: Endemic to Sulawesi.

5 RED-AND-BLACK THRUSH *Geokichla mendeni* 20cm FIELD NOTES: Formerly considered a race of the previous species; actions and habits presumed to be similar. VOICE: Unrecorded. HABITAT: Selectively logged forest. DISTRIBUTION: Endemic to the Banggai and Sula islands.

6 ORANGE-HEADED THRUSH *Geokichla citrina* 20–23cm FIELD NOTES: Shy. Forages on the ground in thick vegetation and forest undergrowth; also feeds in fruiting trees and bushes. VOICE: A loud, clear series of lilting phrases; calls include a soft *chuk* and a screeching *kreeee* or *teer-teer-teer*. HABITAT: Broadleaved evergreen forest, forest edges, secondary growth and thickets. DISTRIBUTION: Resident in Java, Bali and Borneo; vagrant in Sumatra.

7 ASHY THRUSH *Geokichla cinerea* 19cm FIELD NOTES: Forages on or near the ground, usually in open patches. VOICE: A wheezy, up-and-down *wheeezizizizi zizizizi*. HABITAT: Primary, secondary and selectively logged forests, forests with limestone outcrops, remnant ridgetop forest patches, mossy forest and forest with an open understorey dominated by rattans. DISTRIBUTION: Endemic to the N Philippines.

8 ORANGE-SIDED THRUSH *Geokichla peronii* 19–22cm FIELD NOTES: Usually encountered singly or in pairs. Small groups gather in fruiting trees, otherwise forages mainly on the ground, with occasional forays into the mid-level or canopy. VOICE: Beautiful, rich, clear whistled notes, interspersed with occasional short, harsh notes and long, high-pitched notes. HABITAT: Closed-canopy monsoon forest and degraded forest patches. DISTRIBUTION: Endemic to the E Lesser Sundas.

125 SHORTWINGS; RUBYTHROAT; REDSTARTS; BLUE ROBINS

1 WHITE-BROWED SHORTWING *Brachypteryx montana* 14cm FIELD NOTES: Skulking; forages on the ground. Actions much like a European Robin (*Erithacus rubecula*). *B. m. floris* (1b) occurs in Flores in the Lesser Sundas; *B. m. erythrogyna* (1c) is found in N Borneo; *B. m. andersoni* (1d) occurs in Luzon in the Philippines. VOICE: Variable; generally starts slowly with a few single notes, speeds to a plaintive babble and then ends abruptly, or similar. Calls include a hard *tack*, and a *tt-tt-tt* when alarmed. HABITAT: Dense undergrowth and thickets in forests. DISTRIBUTION: Resident in Sumatra, Java, Borneo, the Philippines and Flores in the Lesser Sundas.

2 LESSER SHORTWING *Brachypteryx leucophris* 13cm FIELD NOTES: Often holds tail erect while foraging among dead leaves on the forest floor. VOICE: A single note followed by a melodious, sibilant warble with a jumbled finish of buzzy and rich musical notes; calls include a thin whistle and a harsh *tack*. HABITAT: Dense, damp undergrowth in humid forests. DISTRIBUTION: Resident in Sumatra, Java, Bali and the Lesser Sundas.

3 GREAT SHORTWING *Heinrichia calligyna* 17–18cm FIELD NOTES: Very shy. Hops along the ground foraging among leaf litter, moss and lichen, and around small stones. *H. c. picta* (3b) occurs in SE Sulawesi; *H. c. simplex* (3c) is found in N Sulawesi. VOICE: Song consists of three loud, clear, upslurred disyllabic whistles, ending with a shrill, high-pitched note. HABITAT: Primary montane forest, with rocky gullies and overgrown stream sides. DISTRIBUTION: Endemic to Sulawesi.

4 SIBERIAN RUBYTHROAT *Calliope calliope* 15cm FIELD NOTES: Shy, skulks in dense vegetation. Tends to be more exposed if singing. Often cocks tail. VOICE: Calls include a loud *chak-chak*, a falling *ee-uk* and a plaintive *chee-wee*. Song is a varied, loud, sustained warbling, interspersed with harsh notes. HABITAT: Scrub thickets, forest edges, grassy areas with bushes, and marshes. DISTRIBUTION: Winter visitor to the Philippines; vagrant in Borneo.

5 SIBERIAN BLUE ROBIN *Larvivora cyane* 14cm FIELD NOTES: Shivers tail while foraging on the ground or in low cover; reported to run and hop like a small crake. VOICE: Calls include a subdued *tak*, a louder *se-ic* and, when alarmed, a *chuck-chuck-chuck*. HABITAT: Forests and secondary growth. DISTRIBUTION: Winter visitor to Sumatra, Borneo and rare in the Philippines.

6 RED-FLANKED BLUETAIL (ORANGE-FLANKED BUSH ROBIN)
Tarsiger cyanurus 14cm FIELD NOTES: Forages on the ground and in low cover. Flicks tail downwards. VOICE: Calls include a deep, croaking *tok-tok-tok* and a mournful *pheeou*. HABITAT: Broadleaved evergreen forest. DISTRIBUTION: Vagrant in Borneo.

7 DAURIAN REDSTART *Phoenicurus auroreus* 15cm FIELD NOTES: Forages in trees and bushes, often in the manner of a flycatcher. Shivers tail. VOICE: Calls include a *tsip*, a rapid *titititik* and a *teck-teck*. HABITAT: Bushy areas, forest edges, cultivation and gardens. DISTRIBUTION: Vagrant in the Philippines.

8 LUZON WATER REDSTART *Phoenicurus bicolor* 14–15cm FIELD NOTES: Often seen in small groups perching on stream-side rocks and feeding on invertebrates at the water's edge. VOICE: A fairly loud, repeated *seep*. HABITAT: Clear, fast-flowing, rocky-sided mountain streams and rivers running through montane forests. DISTRIBUTION: Endemic to the N Philippines.

9 SUNDA BLUE ROBIN (SUNDA ROBIN) *Myiomela diana* 15cm FIELD NOTES: Forages in undergrowth; little other information. VOICE: A simple 2–5-note melancholic, sweet warble. HABITAT: Montane forests with undergrowth. DISTRIBUTION: Endemic to Sumatra and Java.

126 MAGPIE-ROBINS; SHAMAS; COCHOAS

1 PHILIPPINE MAGPIE-ROBIN *Copsychus mindanensis* 19–20cm FIELD NOTES: Noisy. Regularly flicks and fans tail when perched. VOICE: Melodious, repetitive, clear whistles. HABITAT: Secondary growth, cultivated areas, scrub and bamboo thickets. DISTRIBUTION: Endemic to the Philippines.

2 ORIENTAL MAGPIE-ROBIN *Copsychus saularis* 20cm FIELD NOTES: Pumps cocked tail while hopping along ground to feed on worms and insects. *C. s. pluto* (2b) occurs in NE and SE Borneo. VOICE: Variable musical warbling, alternating with churrs and sliding whistles; calls include a clear, rising whistle and a harsh *che-e-e-e-h* when alarmed. HABITAT: Secondary growth, mangroves, cultivation, parks and gardens. DISTRIBUTION: Resident in Sumatra, Java, Bali and Borneo.

3 WHITE-RUMPED SHAMA *Copsychus malabaricus* 25cm FIELD NOTES: Usually forages on the ground or in low cover. Wings make a clicking sound when flying over open ground. VOICE: Rich, melodious phrases, including mimicry; when alarmed, utters a harsh *tshak*. HABITAT: Undergrowth and edges of primary and secondary lowland and hill forests. DISTRIBUTION: Resident in Sumatra, Java and Borneo.

4 WHITE-CROWNED SHAMA *Copsychus stricklandii* 25cm FIELD NOTES: Generally forages on the ground or in low cover. Apparently hybridises over a large area with the previous species – perhaps better treated as a race of the latter? *C. s. barbouri* (4b) occurs on Marutua Island off E Borneo. VOICE: Reported as being similar to White-rumped Shama. HABITAT: Lowland and hill primary forest. DISTRIBUTION: Endemic to N Borneo.

5 WHITE-BROWED SHAMA *Copsychus luzoniensis* 17–18cm FIELD NOTES: Forages in forest undergrowth, close to the ground. Best located by its calls. *C. l. superciliaris* (5b) occurs in the C Philippines. VOICE: A pleasant series of melodious phrases, including gurgles and whistles, rising and falling, and often finishing on a high note. HABITAT: Primary forest and secondary growth. DISTRIBUTION: Endemic to the N Philippines.

6 WHITE-VENTED SHAMA *Copsychus niger* 18–22cm FIELD NOTES: Occurs singly or in pairs; best located by its loud song. VOICE: Various repeated, loud, melodious, rising and falling phrases. HABITAT: Lowland forest, forest edges, secondary growth and scrub. DISTRIBUTION: Endemic to Palawan in the W Philippines.

7 BLACK SHAMA *Copsychus cebuensis* 20cm FIELD NOTES: Forages on or close to the ground in the understorey. Secretive; best located by its calls. VOICE: A long series of melodious, rising and falling whistles. HABITAT: Primary forest, dense scrub, thickets and bamboo groves. DISTRIBUTION: Endemic to Cebu in the Philippines.

8 RUFOUS-TAILED SHAMA *Copsychus pyrropygus* 25cm FIELD NOTES: Sits still for long periods; regularly cocks tail. Forages on the ground and in trees, gleans from leaves and the ground. VOICE: Song is a loud, whistled *whi-iii whi-iii whi-uuu*; call is a scolding *tchurr*. HABITAT: Lowland and hill primary broadleaved evergreen forest. DISTRIBUTION: Resident in Sumatra and Borneo.

9 SUMATRAN COCHOA *Cochoa beccarii* 28cm FIELD NOTES: Mainly seen in the middle and upper storeys – look for short flights between perches. Forages for fruit in tall trees and possibly also searches for invertebrates on the forest floor. VOICE: A long, thin, high, mournful whistle; in flight, also gives a *sip*. HABITAT: Lower montane forest. DISTRIBUTION: Endemic to Sumatra.

10 JAVAN COCHOA *Cochoa azurea* 23cm FIELD NOTES: Often sits silently for long periods or moves about quietly, making detection difficult – watch for short flights from perch to perch. Favours fruiting forest trees. VOICE: A thin, high, whistled *siiiit*; calls include a scolding *cet-cet-cet*, usually given when alarmed. HABITAT: Lower and upper tropical montane rainforest. DISTRIBUTION: Endemic to Java.

127 CHATS; WHEATEAR; FORKTAILS

1 SIBERIAN STONECHAT *Saxicola maurus* 13cm FIELD NOTES: Sits on a prominent perch in order to make frequent sallies to capture insects from or near the ground, and occasionally makes aerial fly-catching sorties. VOICE: A variable, scratchy series of twittering and warbling notes; calls include a hard *chack* and a thin *hweet*. HABITAT: Open areas with scrub and cultivation. DISTRIBUTION: Vagrant in Borneo.

2 PIED BUSHCHAT (PIED STONECHAT) *Saxicola caprata* 13–14cm
FIELD NOTES: Feeding actions similar to Siberian Stonechat. VOICE: Song is a brisk, whistled *chip-chepee-chewee-ch* or similar; calls include a plaintive *chep-chep-hee* and a scolding *chuh*. HABITAT: Open areas with scrub or scattered trees, grassland and cultivation. DISTRIBUTION: Resident in Java, Bali, the Philippines, Sulawesi and the Lesser Sundas; vagrant in Borneo.

3 WHITE-BELLIED BUSHCHAT *Saxicola gutturalis* 15–17cm FIELD NOTES: Usually seen in pairs; gleans and makes short sallies after insects. Favours the canopy or tall understorey shrubs, and sings from dense canopy of tall trees. *S. g. luctuosus* (3b) occurs on Semau Island. VOICE: A series of sweet, unhurried phrases; calls include a *tchk-tchk*. HABITAT: Remnant patches of monsoon forest, monsoon woodland and secondary growth. DISTRIBUTION: Endemic to the E Lesser Sundas.

4 WHEATEAR (NORTHERN WHEATEAR) *Oenanthe oenanthe* 14–16cm
FIELD NOTES: Forages in a stop–start fashion: little runs, interspersed with short stops to pick up prey or to look about. Regularly flicks wings and tail. In flight, shows white rump and white outer tail bases. VOICE: Calls include a hard *chak* and a *wheet*, or these combined as *wheet-chak-chak*. HABITAT: Open areas, managed grassland and cultivated fields. DISTRIBUTION: Vagrant in Borneo and the Philippines.

5 BORNEAN FORKTAIL *Enicurus borneensis* 28cm FIELD NOTES: Actions and habits similar to the following species, with which it is often considered conspecific. VOICE: A shrill double whistle. HABITAT: Rocky streams in montane primary forest. DISTRIBUTION: Endemic to Borneo.

6 WHITE-CROWNED FORKTAIL *Enicurus leschenaulti* 25–28cm FIELD NOTES: Forages on rocks or along the water's edge; when disturbed, disappears into nearby forest cover. Juvenile browner and lacks the white crown. VOICE: An elaborate series of sweet, high-pitched whistles; calls include a harsh *tssee or tssee-chit-chit-chit*. HABITAT: Fast-flowing rivers and streams in dense forest. DISTRIBUTION: Resident in Sumatra, Java, Bali and Borneo.

7 CHESTNUT-NAPED FORKTAIL *Enicurus ruficapillus* 18–25cm FIELD NOTES: Wary; searches for food along stream edges and on rocks in water. VOICE: Utters a series of thin, shrill whistles and a high *dir-tee*. HABITAT: Rivers, streams and waterfalls. DISTRIBUTION: Resident in Sumatra and Borneo.

8 SUNDA FORKTAIL *Enicurus velatus* 16cm FIELD NOTES: Little information; presumably similar to other forktails. VOICE: A hard, shrill *chee* or *hie-tie-tie*. HABITAT: Boulder-strewn rivers and fast-flowing streams in hill and mountain forests. DISTRIBUTION: Endemic to Sumatra and Java.

1 RUFOUS-BROWED FLYCATCHER *Anthipes solitaris* 12–13cm FIELD NOTES: Spends long periods in the lower storey, resting on a shady perch. Makes short aerial fly-catching forays, and collects insects from the ground. VOICE: A thin, tremulous *three-blind-mice*. Calls include a thin *tseep*, a sharp *tchik* and a harsh churring. HABITAT: Broadleaved evergreen forest. DISTRIBUTION: Resident in Sumatra.

2 YELLOW-RUMPED FLYCATCHER *Ficedula zanthopygia* 13cm FIELD NOTES: Forages in tree foliage or undergrowth, and often makes sallies after flying insects. VOICE: A dry, rattling *tr-r-r-rt*. HABITAT: Forest, forest edges and scrub. DISTRIBUTION: Winter visitor to Sumatra; vagrant in Java, Bali and Borneo.

3 NARCISSUS FLYCATCHER *Ficedula narcissina* 13–14cm FIELD NOTES: Makes fly-catching sallies from middle storey or canopy; also forages in bushy undergrowth and low vegetation. VOICE: Calls include a soft *tink-tink*. HABITAT: Open woodland, selectively logged forest, cultivation with scattered trees, scrub and mangroves. DISTRIBUTION: Winter visitor to Borneo and the Philippines.

4 MUGIMAKI FLYCATCHER *Ficedula mugimaki* 13cm FIELD NOTES: Unobtrusive forager in the middle and upper canopy. Often flicks and spreads tail. VOICE: Calls include a soft, rattled *trrrr*. HABITAT: Forest and forest edges. DISTRIBUTION: Winter visitor to Sumatra, Java, Bali, Borneo, the Philippines and Sulawesi; vagrant in the N Moluccas.

5 TANIMBAR FLYCATCHER *Ficedula riedeli* 11–12cm FIELD NOTES: Forages in the forest understorey and bamboo. Formerly considered a race of the Rufous-chested Flycatcher. VOICE: Presumed to be similar to the Rufous-chested Flycatcher. HABITAT: Lowland and lower montane forest. DISTRIBUTION: Endemic to the Tanimbar Islands in the E Lesser Sundas.

6 RUFOUS-CHESTED FLYCATCHER *Ficedula dumetoria* 11–12cm FIELD NOTES: Forages low down in dense vegetation, often near streams; regularly catches insects in flight. VOICE: A distinctive high-pitched, rising and falling *sii wi-sii si-wi-si-ii si-wi-oo*; calls include a soft *sst-sst*. HABITAT: Lowland to lower montane primary forest, with bamboo and understorey. DISTRIBUTION: Resident in Sumatra, Java, Borneo and the W Lesser Sundas.

7 BUNDOK FLYCATCHER *Ficedula luzoniensis* 11–13cm FIELD NOTES: Secretive, foraging in the forest understorey. Formerly considered to be a race of the Snowy-browed Flycatcher. *F. l. nigrorum* (7b) occurs on Negros and Panay in the C Philippines. VOICE: Little information; may be similar to the following species. HABITAT: Montane forest. DISTRIBUTION: Endemic to the Philippines.

8 SNOWY-BROWED FLYCATCHER *Ficedula hyperythra* 11–13cm FIELD NOTES: Forages low down in scrub and thickets; runs along the ground much like a shortwing. *F. h. pallidipectus* (8b) occurs in the Bacan Islands in the N Moluccas. VOICE: A thin *sip* and an upslurred *seep*; song is a wheezy, shrill *tsit-sit-si-sii tsi-sii-swrri* or *tsi-sit-i*. HABITAT: Hill and montane forest. DISTRIBUTION: Widespread in the region, except the Philippines.

9 RUFOUS-THROATED FLYCATCHER *Ficedula rufigula* 11–12cm FIELD NOTES: Generally forages on the ground in dense rattan thickets, usually in pairs. VOICE: An up-and-down *si-si-si* or *swee-wee-seee*; calls include a quick *chik* and a staccato chattering. HABITAT: Primary lowland and hill forest, and swamp forest. DISTRIBUTION: Endemic to Sulawesi.

10 CINNAMON-CHESTED FLYCATCHER *Ficedula buruensis* 11–12cm FIELD NOTES: Inconspicuous. Favours the shady parts of dense forest understorey. VOICE: A buzzing, nasal *tup tup tezeeew*. HABITAT: Lowland and hill forest. DISTRIBUTION: Endemic to the S Moluccas.

7b ♂
nigrorum

8b ♂
pallidipectus

129 FLYCATCHERS

1 LITTLE SLATY FLYCATCHER *Ficedula basilanica* 12–13cm FIELD NOTES: Usually secretive, foraging on the ground and in tangled understorey; best detected by its calls. *F. b. samarensis* (1b) occurs in the EC Philippines. VOICE: A series of chattering whistles, sometimes ending in a trill. Calls include a soft, whistled *pee-pawww pee-pee-hi-hi*. HABITAT: Primary forest and secondary growth. DISTRIBUTION: Endemic to the Philippines.

2 DAMAR FLYCATCHER *Ficedula henrici* 12–13cm FIELD NOTES: Generally seen alone or in pairs. Uses an exposed branch to make drops onto insects; also gleans prey. VOICE: A far-carrying whistle. HABITAT: Lush evergreen forest. DISTRIBUTION: Endemic to Damar Island in the E Lesser Sundas.

3 PALAWAN FLYCATCHER *Ficedula platenae* 11–12cm FIELD NOTES: Shy and secretive, favouring dense tangles of rattan and climbing bamboo; usually alone. VOICE: A varied, raspy, high-pitched *zee-zawww, zawwp-zeeepp, zee zeet zeeett* or *zeee-zawwwpppp*, followed by a short chatter. HABITAT: Lowland primary forest and secondary growth. DISTRIBUTION: Endemic to Palawan in the W Philippines.

4 SUMBA FLYCATCHER *Ficedula harterti* 11cm FIELD NOTES: Shy and secretive. Forages in the forest undergrowth, usually alone or in pairs. Continuously pumps tail. VOICE: A mournful series of three descending, whistled notes, followed by a sharp *zip*; calls include an insect-like, buzzing *tszzz*, a *chik-ik* and a *chikikikikiki*. HABITAT: Primary and secondary forest, forest edges, bushy thickets and secondary growth. DISTRIBUTION: Endemic to Sumba Island in the Lesser Sundas.

5 CRYPTIC FLYCATCHER *Ficedula crypta* 11–12cm FIELD NOTES: Secretive, usually favouring undergrowth and secondary growth; occurs singly or in pairs. VOICE: A series of high-pitched phrases. HABITAT: Submontane primary moss forest and secondary growth. DISTRIBUTION: Endemic to Mindanao in the S Philippines.

6 LOMPOBATTANG FLYCATCHER *Ficedula bonthaina* 10–11cm FIELD NOTES: Frequents the dense forest understorey, on or close to the ground. VOICE: Unknown. HABITAT: Primary montane moss forest. DISTRIBUTION: Endemic to S Sulawesi.

7 FURTIVE FLYCATCHER *Ficedula disposita* 11–12cm FIELD NOTES: Favours dense climbing bamboo in the forest understorey. Secretive; usually seen alone or in pairs. VOICE: A faint, high-pitched, whistled *wan he, wau he hu, he haaww* or *he-u-heee*, repeated every 4–5 seconds; also utters a sharp, repeated *zeet zeet*. HABITAT: Dense lowland secondary forest. DISTRIBUTION: Endemic to Luzon in the N Philippines.

8 TAIGA FLYCATCHER (RED-THROATED FLYCATCHER) *Ficedula albicilla* 11–12cm FIELD NOTES: Forages among foliage; makes occasional sallies after flying insects, when white outer tail bases are prominent. VOICE: A buzzing *drrrrt* and a harsh *zree*. HABITAT: Open forest, forest edges, plantations, parks and gardens. DISTRIBUTION: Winter visitor to Borneo; vagrant in the Philippines.

9 LITTLE PIED FLYCATCHER *Ficedula westermanni* 11–12cm FIELD NOTES: Forages in treetops, constantly on the move; also makes short sallies after flying insects. VOICE: Variable, including a flute-like *sueep* or *seeeup*, interspersed with a rapid, vibrating trill, and *tee-dee* notes followed by a long warbling; calls include a mellow *tweet*, a low *chur*, and a high note followed by soft, trilled *trrrt* notes. HABITAT: Mossy, *Casuarina* and other forest; may use more open woodlands post-breeding. DISTRIBUTION: Widespread resident in the region.

10 BLACK-BANDED FLYCATCHER *Ficedula timorensis* 11cm FIELD NOTES: Shy and elusive, favouring dense undergrowth. Feeds by snatching or sallying for insects. Generally seen singly or in pairs. VOICE: A soft, low-pitched *buzz-buzz-buzz*, often repeated and sometimes interspersed with a short, piercing, descending whistle; song consists of a series of muted, high-pitched disyllabic whistles, repeated every 2–3 seconds. HABITAT: Monsoon hill forest with limestone boulders and rocky scree slopes. DISTRIBUTION: Endemic to Timor in the Lesser Sundas.

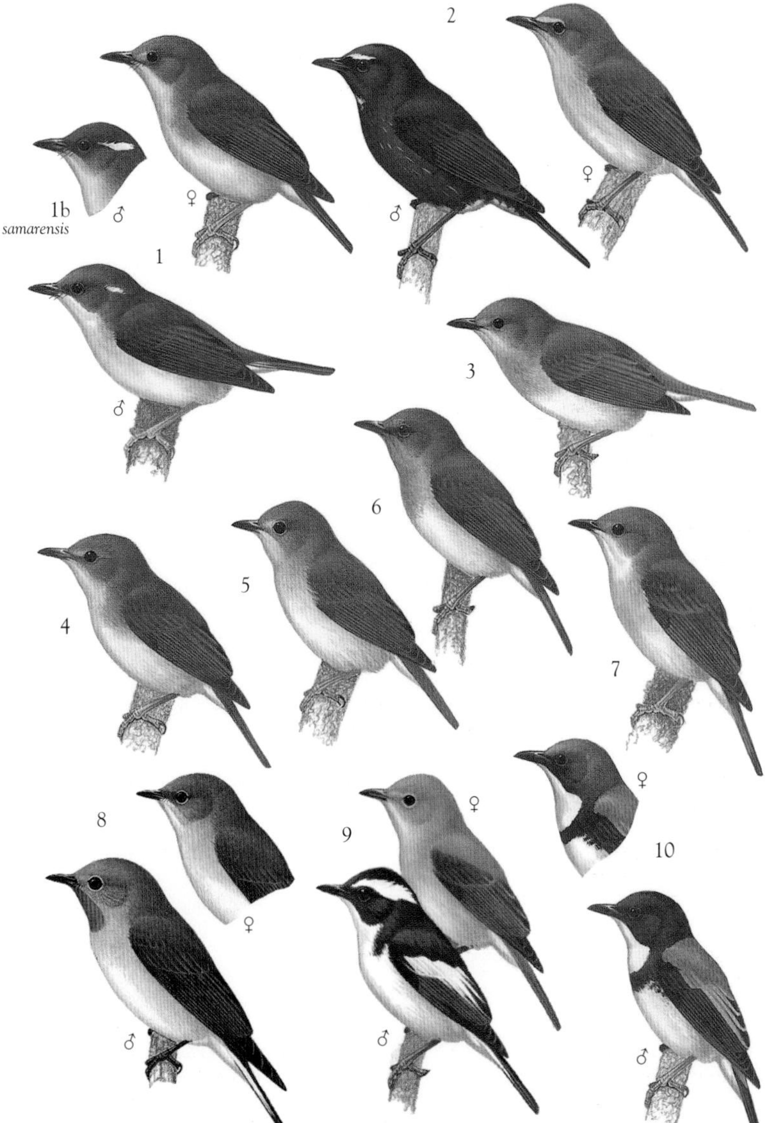
2
♀
♂
♀
♂
1b
samarensis
1
♂
3
6
4
5
7
♀
8
9
♀
10
♀
♂
♂
♂

1 WHITE-THROATED JUNGLE FLYCATCHER *Vauriella albigularis* 16–17cm
FIELD NOTES: Forages in the forest understorey. Unobtrusive. VOICE: A series of very high-pitched, almost inaudible phrases, interspersed with low churring notes; calls include a high-pitched, rapid, rising and accelerating *ti-ti-ti-ti-tip*. HABITAT: Lowland, lower montane and secondary forest. DISTRIBUTION: Endemic to the WC Philippines.

2 SLATY-BACKED JUNGLE FLYCATCHER *Vauriella goodfellowi* 17–18cm
FIELD NOTES: Usually alone or in pairs, sitting quietly in the forest understorey. VOICE: A series of up to sixteen high-pitched, rapidly repeated *tsi* notes, which rises and then levels out, before accelerating and then descending at the end. HABITAT: Montane forest. DISTRIBUTION: Endemic to the S Philippines.

3 EYEBROWED JUNGLE FLYCATCHER *Vauriella gularis* 15cm FIELD NOTES: Occurs alone, in small groups or in mixed-species feeding parties. Forages low down or on the ground. Inquisitive. VOICE: A churring call, and a sharp *prrrt* when alarmed. HABITAT: Montane forest. DISTRIBUTION: Endemic to Borneo.

4 WHITE-BROWED JUNGLE FLYCATCHER *Vauriella insignis* 16–20cm
FIELD NOTES: Very secretive, foraging in the understorey and in shady lower levels of trees. VOICE: Thin, high-pitched phrases. HABITAT: Primary montane moss forest and secondary forest close to primary oak forest. DISTRIBUTION: Endemic to the N Philippines.

5 GREY-STREAKED FLYCATCHER *Muscicapa griseisticta* 14cm FIELD NOTES: Usually alone; makes rapid dashes after flying insects, frequently returning to the same treetop perch. VOICE: Calls include a loud *chipee*, *tee-tee* or *zeet zeet zeet*. HABITAT: Open woodland, forest edges and clearings, and grassy areas with trees. DISTRIBUTION: Winter visitor to N Borneo, the Philippines, and Wallacea except the W Lesser Sundas.

6 SULAWESI STREAKED FLYCATCHER *Muscicapa sodhii* 12–14cm
FIELD NOTES: Makes sallies after flying insects from a perch in the understorey or higher. Occasionally seen in mixed-species foraging parties. VOICE: Thin, high whistles, chirps, twitters, trills and buzzy notes. HABITAT: Primary lowland and submontane broadleaved evergreen forests. DISTRIBUTION: Endemic to Sulawesi.

7 ASHY-BREASTED FLYCATCHER *Muscicapa randi* 12–13cm FIELD NOTES: Forages low down in the understorey or lower levels at forest edges or clearings. Usually alone or in pairs. VOICE: A high-pitched, repeated *wee-tit* and a longer *zeeeeee-tip-tip-zee zizizizi*. HABITAT: Montane and selectively logged forest. DISTRIBUTION: Endemic to the Philippines.

8 DARK-SIDED FLYCATCHER *Muscicapa sibirica* 13cm FIELD NOTES: Makes darting dashes to capture insects from a prominent perch. VOICE: A tinkling *chi-up-chi-up-chi-up*. HABITAT: Submontane and montane forest. DISTRIBUTION: Winter visitor to Sumatra, Java and Borneo; vagrant in the Philippines.

9 ASIAN BROWN FLYCATCHER *Muscicapa dauurica* 13cm FIELD NOTES: Sallies for insects from a prominent perch. VOICE: Calls include a soft rattling, a short *tzi* and a soft *churr*. HABITAT: Open forest, secondary growth, parks and gardens. DISTRIBUTION: Winter visitor to Sumatra, Java, Borneo, the Philippines and Sulawesi.

10 BROWN-STREAKED FLYCATCHER *Muscicapa williamsoni* 14cm FIELD NOTES: Makes fly-catching sallies from a prominent perch. Resident race (not depicted) is generally darker. VOICE: A squeaky whistle; calls include a thin *tzi* and a harsh, slurred *cheititit*. HABITAT: Broadleaved evergreen forest. DISTRIBUTION: Resident in, and winter visitor to, Borneo.

11 SUMBA BROWN FLYCATCHER *Muscicapa segregata* 13cm FIELD NOTES: Forages in the understorey and lower levels of trees; often sits unobtrusively for long periods. VOICE: A jumbled series of rapid, high-pitched, whistled, trilled and harsh notes, often ending with a trill. HABITAT: Lowland primary forest, secondary forest and forest edges. DISTRIBUTION: Endemic to Sumba in the W Lesser Sundas.

12 FERRUGINOUS FLYCATCHER *Muscicapa ferruginea* 12–13cm FIELD NOTES: Catches insects in sweeping aerial pursuits, returning to a favourite or nearby perch. VOICE: A shrill *tsit-tittu-titt* and a soft, trilling *si-si-si*. HABITAT: Lowland and lower montane mature and secondary forest. DISTRIBUTION: Winter visitor to Sumatra, Java, Borneo and the Philippines.

131 FLYCATCHERS

1 BLUE-AND-WHITE FLYCATCHER *Cyanoptila cyanomelana* 17cm
FIELD NOTES: Forages in the canopy; also visits lower levels to glean insects from foliage or branches, and makes fly-catching sorties from a prominent perch. VOICE: Calls include a harsh *tchk-tchk* and a soft *tic* or *tac*. HABITAT: Primary and secondary lowland and submontane forest, coastal woodland and scrub. DISTRIBUTION: Winter visitor to Sumatra, Java, Borneo, N Sulawesi and the Philippines.

2 TURQUOISE FLYCATCHER *Eumyias panayensis* 14cm FIELD NOTES: Usually seen singly or in pairs; regularly joins mixed-species feeding parties. Captures prey by sallying or gleaning. *E. p. nigrimentalis* (2b) occurs in the N Philippines; *E. p. nigriloris* (2c) is found in the S Philippines. VOICE: Song is a monotonous warble, consisting of about 20 notes. HABITAT: Submontane forest, forest clearings and edges. DISTRIBUTION: Resident in the Philippines, Sulawesi, the Sula Islands and the Moluccas.

3 VERDITER FLYCATCHER *Eumyias thalassinus* 15–17cm FIELD NOTES: Makes aerial sallies after flying insects from an exposed perch in the canopy or at forest edges. VOICE: A pleasant, trilled *p-p-pwe… p-p-pwe… pe-tititi-wu-pitititi-weu*; calls include a short, plaintive *pseeut* and a dry *tze-ju-jui*. HABITAT: Lowland and submontane forest, forest clearings and edges. DISTRIBUTION: Resident in Sumatra and Borneo.

4 INDIGO FLYCATCHER *Eumyias indigo* 14cm FIELD NOTES: Forages low down, often in dark undergrowth. Captures small invertebrates by gleaning or by making short aerial sallies; also feeds on small berries. Occurs singly, in pairs or in mixed-species parties. *E. i. ruficrissa* (4b) resides in Sumatra. VOICE: A squeaky, ringing *fee-foo-fu-fee-fee-fee* or *chit chwit choo wee tooo*; calls include a harsh, rattling *turrr-tur*, and a *tzit-tzit-tzit* when alarmed. HABITAT: Submontane and montane forest. DISTRIBUTION: Resident in Sumatra, Java and Borneo.

5 STREAK-BREASTED FLYCATCHER (STREAK-BREASTED JUNGLE FLYCATCHER) *Eumyias additus* 15cm FIELD NOTES: An active flycatcher; little other information. VOICE: Unreported. HABITAT: Lowland, montane and selectively logged forest, and forest edges. DISTRIBUTION: Endemic to Buru in the S Moluccas.

6 RUSSET-BACKED JUNGLE FLYCATCHER *Cyornis oscillans* 13–15cm
FIELD NOTES: Forages in thick undergrowth and up to the middle levels of forest trees; pounces on insects or pursues them in flight. Usually seen singly or in mixed-species feeding parties. May raise and spread tail while perched. *C. o. stresemanni* (6b) occurs on Sumba. VOICE: A loud series of jumbled, high-pitched, slightly staccato notes. Calls include a harsh *tak* or *chek*. HABITAT: Primary hill and montane semi-evergreen forest. DISTRIBUTION: Endemic to the Lesser Sundas.

7 BROWN-CHESTED JUNGLE FLYCATCHER *Cyornis brunneatus* 15cm
FIELD NOTES: Frequents the lower canopy and bushes; captures insects in flight or forages among leaf litter on the forest floor. VOICE: A series of loud, descending whistles; calls include harsh churrs. HABITAT: Semi-evergreen and mixed deciduous forest, mangroves and scrub. DISTRIBUTION: Vagrant in Borneo.

8 GREY-CHESTED JUNGLE FLYCATCHER *Cyornis umbratilis* 15cm
FIELD NOTES: Forages from the undergrowth up to the middle canopy; occasionally makes aerial sallies after insects. Cocks and spreads tail. VOICE: A thin, sweet, descending *si ti-tu-ti tlooeeu*; calls include a scolding *churr-churr-churr*, a *trrrt it it it* and a clicking *tchk-tchk*. HABITAT: Lowland primary and secondary forest, peat-swamp forest and plantations. DISTRIBUTION: Resident in Sumatra and Borneo.

2b *nigrimentalis*

2c *nigriloris*

4b *ruficrissa*

6b *stresemanni*

1 HENNA-TAILED JUNGLE FLYCATCHER *Cyornis colonus* 14cm
FIELD NOTES: Occurs singly, in pairs or in small groups. Unobtrusive. Little other information. VOICE: A jumble of shrill, sweet, clear, high-pitched notes, including single rising notes, hurried descending whistles and trills, and alternate high and low notes. HABITAT: Lowland primary, secondary and degraded forest; also in selectively logged forest. DISTRIBUTION: Resident in Sulawesi and the Sula Islands.

2 RUFOUS-TAILED JUNGLE FLYCATCHER *Cyornis ruficauda* 15cm
FIELD NOTES: Forages in the understorey and along forest edges; occasionally hawks insects from a low perch. VOICE: A series of up to three repeated, high-pitched *chirr* notes or a more musical *cheep cheep chirr*, sometimes followed by a buzzing note or a trill. HABITAT: Lowland and lower montane forests and forest clearings. DISTRIBUTION: Resident in Borneo and the Philippines.

3 FULVOUS-CHESTED JUNGLE FLYCATCHER *Cyornis olivaceus* 15cm
FIELD NOTES: Usually found in the lower and middle storey. Makes sallies after flying insects. Occasionally cocks and fans tail. VOICE: A rapid series of short phrases, alternating in pitch, consisting of musical, scratchy, tinkling and churring notes; calls include a low *tchuck-tchuck*, a *trrt* and a harsh *tac*. HABITAT: Lowland broadleaved primary and secondary forest, plantations and forest edges. DISTRIBUTION: Resident in Sumatra, Java, Bali and Borneo.

4 MATINAN FLYCATCHER (MATINAN BLUE FLYCATCHER) *Cyornis sanfordi* 14–15cm FIELD NOTES: Inconspicuous. Frequents the undergrowth and lower to middle levels of forests, making fly-catching sallies after insects; usually alone or in mixed-species foraging flocks. VOICE: A series of rapid, thin, clear or subdued notes, varying in pitch. HABITAT: Primary hill and montane broadleaved evergreen forest. DISTRIBUTION: Endemic to N Sulawesi.

5 BLUE-FRONTED FLYCATCHER (BLUE-FRONTED BLUE FLYCATCHER) *Cyornis hoevelli* 15cm FIELD NOTES: Forages from the undergrowth to the middle levels of forest trees, gleaning insects from foliage. Usually seen singly, in pairs or, occasionally, in mixed-species feeding parties. Inconspicuous; best located by its calls. VOICE: A pleasant, rich sequence of 10–20 notes; also a medley of 4–5 discordant notes and a loud *tsat-tsat-tsat*. HABITAT: Montane rainforest and moss forest. DISTRIBUTION: Endemic to Sulawesi.

6 WHITE-TAILED FLYCATCHER *Cyornis concretus* 18cm FIELD NOTES: Forages low down in undergrowth or lower branches of forest trees; often spreads tail to reveal white panels. *C. c. everetti* (6b) occurs in Borneo, male lacks white in tail. VOICE: A variable series of penetrating, sibilant whistles; calls include a soft *pweee* and a harsh *scree*. HABITAT: Primary lowland, hill and montane forest. DISTRIBUTION: Resident in Sumatra and Borneo.

7 TIMOR BLUE FLYCATCHER *Cyornis hyacinthinus* 16cm FIELD NOTES: Frequents the lower to middle levels of trees. Sallies after flying insects, frequently returning to the same high perch. *C. h. kuehni* (7b) occurs on Wetar. VOICE: A monotonous, rapid series of babbled rising and falling notes; calls include a short, subdued bubbling. HABITAT: Remnant patches of primary and secondary monsoon forest and woodland, hillside shrubbery, and borders of degraded forests and plantations. DISTRIBUTION: Endemic to the E Lesser Sundas.

8 RÜCK'S BLUE FLYCATCHER *Cyornis ruckii* 17cm FIELD NOTES: Little information; known only from two specimens collected in 1917 and 1918. VOICE: Unrecorded. HABITAT: Logged lowland forest. DISTRIBUTION: Endemic to NE Sumatra.

133 FLYCATCHERS

1 BLUE-BREASTED BLUE FLYCATCHER *Cyornis herioti* 15cm
FIELD NOTES: Encountered singly, in pairs or in mixed-species foraging parties, from the understorey to mid-levels of forest trees. *C. h. camarinensis* (1b) occurs in S Luzon and the Catanduanes. VOICE: A whistled *seeeep wheeu* or *seeeep seeeep wheeu*, interspersed with chattering and buzzy notes. HABITAT: Lowland and submontane primary and selectively logged forest. DISTRIBUTION: Endemic to the N Philippines.

2 PALE BLUE FLYCATCHER *Cyornis unicolor* 18cm FIELD NOTES: Makes aerial sorties after flying insects, and forages among the foliage in the middle and upper storeys of trees. VOICE: Song is rich and melodious, very thrush-like; gives a soft *tr-r-r-r* when alarmed. HABITAT: Primary and secondary broadleaved lowland, hill and lower montane forest. DISTRIBUTION: Resident in Sumatra, Java and Borneo.

3 HILL BLUE FLYCATCHER *Cyornis banyumas* 15cm FIELD NOTES: Unobtrusive; hawks insects from a low perch. VOICE: A short, metallic, descending trill; calls include a harsh *tac* and a scolding *trrt-trrt-trrt*. HABITAT: Submontane forest with dense undergrowth. DISTRIBUTION: Resident in Java and Borneo.

4 PALAWAN BLUE FLYCATCHER *Cyornis lemprieri* 16cm FIELD NOTES: Usually encountered singly or in pairs. Forages in the forest understorey. VOICE: A soft, pleasant, descending and then rising *de do da da do de*, and a *da de do poy*. HABITAT: Lowland and submontane dry primary and secondary forest. DISTRIBUTION: Endemic to the W Philippines.

5 BORNEAN BLUE FLYCATCHER *Cyornis superbus* 15cm FIELD NOTES: Usually seen alone or in pairs. Fly-catches from a low perch, and hovers to pick insects from branches. VOICE: A high-pitched *hiu-te-hie*. HABITAT: Submontane primary and secondary forest; occasionally lower forests. DISTRIBUTION: Endemic to Borneo.

6 LARGE-BILLED BLUE FLYCATCHER (SUNDA BLUE FLYCATCHER)
Cyornis caerulatus 14cm FIELD NOTES: Forages by fly-catching from a low, exposed perch; generally seen in pairs. VOICE: A thin, metallic, rising and falling *si-si-tiuuuw*. HABITAT: Lowland mixed dipterocarp forest. DISTRIBUTION: Resident in Sumatra and Borneo.

7 MALAYSIAN BLUE FLYCATCHER *Cyornis turcosus* 13–14cm FIELD NOTES: Makes aerial pursuits of insects from a low perch. VOICE: A soft, whistled *diddle diddle dee diddle dee*; calls include a harsh *chrrk*, and a hard *tik-tk-tk* when alarmed. HABITAT: Primary lowland and secondary forest, often near rivers or streams in Sumatra. DISTRIBUTION: Resident in Sumatra and Borneo.

8 TICKELL'S BLUE FLYCATCHER *Cyornis tickelliae* 14cm FIELD NOTES: Forages from undergrowth up to middle levels; regularly makes sallies to capture flying insects, and occasionally hovers to pick insects from foliage. Flicks tail, often while giving a sharp call. VOICE: Song consists of a short, metallic trill of 6–10 notes, first descending and then ascending; calls include a harsh *tac* or *kak*, a *tik-tik* and a sharp, churring *trrt-trrt*. HABITAT: Lowland and submontane open, dry forest and woodland. DISTRIBUTION: Vagrant in Sumatra.

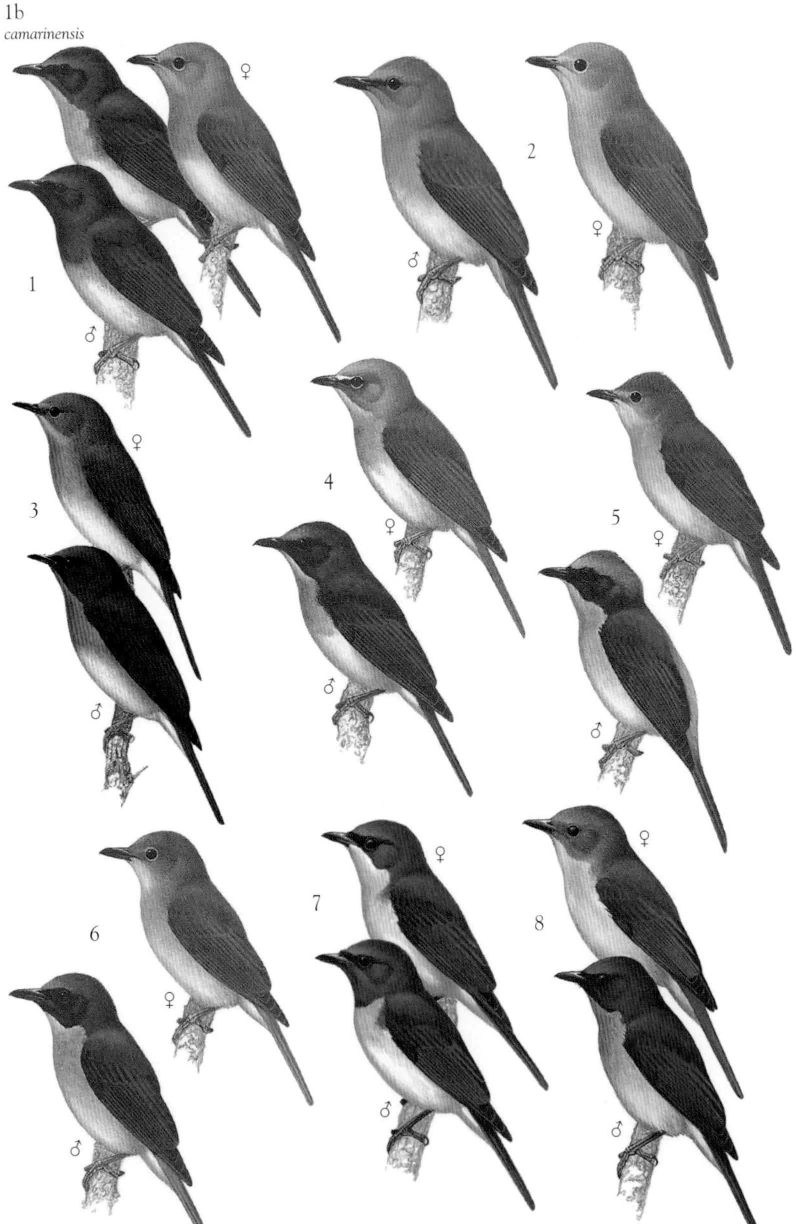
1b
camarinensis
1
♂
♀
2
♂
♀
3
♀
♂
4
♀
♂
5
♀
♂
6
♀
♂
7
♀
♂
8
♀
♂

1 SULAWESI BLUE FLYCATCHER *Cyornis omissus* 14–15cm FIELD NOTES: Often seen in roadside vegetation at dawn, otherwise favours understorey and mid-storey of forest trees. Usually encountered singly, in pairs or occasionally as part of mixed-species feeding parties. Formerly considered a race of the Mangrove Blue Flycatcher. VOICE: A short, weak 4–5-note warble, or a clear, whistled 4–6-note warble followed by 3–4 loud, clear whistles. HABITAT: Hill, lower montane and tall secondary forest, and montane secondary scrub. DISTRIBUTION: Endemic to Sulawesi.

2 MANGROVE BLUE FLYCATCHER *Cyornis rufigastra* 14–15cm FIELD NOTES: Forages low down, and frequently sallies out from a secluded perch to capture passing insects. *C. r. kalaoensis* (2b) occurs on Kalao Island; *C. r. philippinensis* (2c) is found in the WC and S Philippines. VOICE: A slow, low, short, metallic trill, first descending and then ascending; calls include a repeated dry *psst* and a sharp, staccato *chi-chik-chik-chik*. HABITAT: Mangroves, coastal forest, scrub and overgrown edges of plantations. DISTRIBUTION: Resident in Sumatra, Java, Borneo, the Philippines and the Selayar Islands in the Flores Sea.

3 TANAHJAMPEA BLUE FLYCATCHER *Cyornis djampeanus* 14–15cm FIELD NOTES: Formerly considered a race of the Mangrove Blue Flycatcher; actions presumed to be similar. VOICE: Unknown. HABITAT: Closed-canopy forest. DISTRIBUTION: Endemic to Jampea Island in the Flores Sea.

4 LARGE NILTAVA *Niltava grandis* 21cm FIELD NOTES: Skulks in dark undergrowth. Occasionally pursues insects in flight, although normally less agile than most flycatchers; sometimes feeds on the ground. VOICE: A whistled *do ray ray me* or *uu-uu-du-di*; calls include a nasal *dju-ee*, a loud *trr-k trr-k* and a harsh rattle. HABITAT: Hill and montane forest. DISTRIBUTION: Resident in Sumatra.

5 RUFOUS-VENTED NILTAVA (SUMATRAN NILTAVA) *Niltava sumatrana* 15cm FIELD NOTES: Forages on the ground, in dense undergrowth and in the lower to middle storeys of forest trees. VOICE: A monotonous series of clear, undulating whistles, and a series of rapid, scratchy, slurred notes; calls include a hard *chik*. HABITAT: Montane broadleaved evergreen forest. DISTRIBUTION: Resident in Sumatra

6 PYGMY BLUE FLYCATCHER (PYGMY FLYCATCHER) *Muscicapella hodgsoni* 10cm FIELD NOTES: Active, leaf warbler-like forager in the foliage of trees, usually in pairs or alone; also joins mixed-species feeding parties. Often flicks wings and cocks tail. VOICE: A high-pitched *tzzit-che-che-che-heeee* or similar; calls include a feeble *tsip*, *tip* or *tup* and a low *churr*. HABITAT: Dense montane broadleaved forest. DISTRIBUTION: Resident in Sumatra and Borneo.

7 GREY-HEADED FLYCATCHER (GREY-HEADED CANARY-FLYCATCHER) *Culicicapa ceylonensis* 12–13cm FIELD NOTES: Actively flits between branches, foliage and vines; also makes acrobatic sallies to capture insects. Frequently flicks tail while perched. VOICE: Variable, including a loud, squeaky *tit-titu- whee*, a *chilup chilli chilli* and a *saw-see-saw-see-saw*; calls include a soft *pit - pit - pit* and a rattling *churru*. HABITAT: Primary and tall secondary lowland and hill forest, riverine forest, forest fragments, forest edges and cultivation. DISTRIBUTION: Resident in Sumatra, Java, Bali, Borneo and the Lesser Sundas.

8 CITRINE FLYCATCHER (CITRINE CANARY-FLYCATCHER) *Culicicapa helianthea* 11–12cm FIELD NOTES: Favours the mid-storey and lower canopy, and the tops of secondary-growth shrubbery; feeds by fly-catching or gleaning from foliage. Occurs singly, in pairs and in mixed-species foraging parties. VOICE: A series of 4–5 loud, clear notes of varying pitch or with rising and falling buzzing phrases, such as *tsu-si-tchu-si-si* or *sweet su sweet*, finished with a short trill; calls include a *tsu-tsu tswee*, a long, nasal, staccato trill and a *speet*. HABITAT: Lowland to montane forest, forest edges, secondary growth and edges of cultivation. DISTRIBUTION: Resident in the Philippines, Sulawesi, and the Banggai and Sula islands.

1

2

2b ♂
kalaoensis

♀

♂

♂

2c
philippinensis

♂

3

♀

4

♀

5

♀

♂

♂

♂

6

♀

7

8

♂

135 STARLINGS

1 TANIMBAR STARLING *Aplonis crassa* 20cm FIELD NOTES: Occurs singly, in pairs or in flocks of up to 200 birds, regularly seen in the crowns of flowering or fruiting trees. Immature dull brown, pale below with dark streaking. VOICE: Repeated piping, metallic notes; flocks utter a jumbled cacophony of piping, metallic calls. HABITAT: Wooded areas, including secondary forest and woodland edges. DISTRIBUTION: Endemic to the Tanimbar Islands in the E Lesser Sundas.

2 MOLUCCAN STARLING *Aplonis mysolensis* 20cm FIELD NOTES: Gregarious. Generally occurs in small or large groups, often seen high in fruiting trees. Immature brownish black above, and pale buff below, heavily streaked darker. VOICE: An unmusical, nasal, slurred whistle, often uttered by flocks; also various chattering and squealing notes. HABITAT: Mangroves, coastal woodland, primary lowland and hill forest, degraded forest, forest edges, cultivated areas and urban areas. DISTRIBUTION: Resident in the Banggai and Sula islands and the Moluccas.

3 VIOLET-HOODED STARLING *Aplonis circumscripta* 21–26cm FIELD NOTES: Formerly considered a race of the Metallic Starling; habits and actions presumed to be similar. VOICE: Unknown; presumed to be similar to Metallic Starling. HABITAT: Forest edges, lightly wooded cultivation, disturbed forest, secondary woodland, mangroves and plantations. DISTRIBUTION: Endemic to the Tanimbar Islands in the E Lesser Sundas.

4 ASIAN GLOSSY STARLING *Aplonis panayensis* 20cm FIELD NOTES: Mainly arboreal. Gregarious, breeding and roosting communally. Immature dark above, and greyish white below with dark streaking. VOICE: A series of metallic squeaks. HABITAT: Forest edges, secondary growth, coastal forest, plantations and urban areas. DISTRIBUTION: Resident in Sumatra, Java, Bali, Borneo, the Philippines and Sulawesi.

5 METALLIC STARLING *Aplonis metallica* 21–26cm FIELD NOTES: Gregarious, usually seen in small to large, noisy flocks, often in the company of Moluccan Starlings. Favours the crowns of flowering or fruiting trees. Immature dark above, and pale below, lightly streaked dark. VOICE: A loud, unmusical, down-slurred note; also harsh notes, including a coarse *squeeow*. HABITAT: Lightly wooded cultivation, disturbed forest, plantations, mangroves, secondary woodland and forest edges. DISTRIBUTION: Resident in the Sula Islands, the E Lesser Sundas and the Moluccas.

6 SHORT-TAILED STARLING *Aplonis minor* 18cm FIELD NOTES: Gregarious; forages in small flocks, with larger concentrations at fruiting trees. Immature brownish green above and on breast, buffy below with dark streaks. VOICE: Calls include a plaintive *seep*, a slurred, metallic *chilanc* and short chattering notes. HABITAT: Forest, forest edges and, occasionally, cultivation and villages. DISTRIBUTION: Resident in Java, Bali, the S Philippines, Sulawesi and the Lesser Sundas.

7 CHESTNUT-CHEEKED STARLING *Agropsar philippensis* 16–18cm FIELD NOTES: Mainly arboreal. Gregarious, roosting communally; often mixes with other starling species. VOICE: Calls include an *airr* or *tshairr*, and a penetrating *tshick* when alarmed; flight call is a melodious *chrueruchu*. HABITAT: Secondary growth, open areas with trees, cultivation and gardens. DISTRIBUTION: Winter visitor to Borneo and the Philippines; vagrant in Sulawesi and the N Moluccas.

8 DAURIAN STARLING (PURPLE-BACKED STARLING) *Agropsar sturninus* 17cm FIELD NOTES: Gregarious, roosting communally; often associates with other starling species. Resting flocks often sit on exposed dead treetop branches, preening. VOICE: Calls include loud cracking sounds and a soft *prrp*, given in flight. HABITAT: Coastal forest, forest edges, secondary growth, open areas with trees, cultivation and gardens. DISTRIBUTION: Winter visitor to Sumatra and Java; vagrant in Borneo.

136 STARLINGS; MYNAS

1 RED-BILLED STARLING (SILKY STARLING) *Spodiopsar sericeus* 22cm
FIELD NOTES: Gregarious, often in large flocks. Forages on the ground and in trees.
VOICE: Song is sweet and melodious; flocks make chattering calls. HABITAT: Cultivated areas with scattered trees, scrub and gardens. DISTRIBUTION: Vagrant in the Philippines.

2 WHITE-CHEEKED STARLING *Spodiopsar cineraceus* 22cm FIELD NOTES: Gregarious. Forages mostly on the ground. VOICE: A monotonous, creaking *chir-chir-chay-cheet-cheet…* HABITAT: Open country, cultivation and open woodland. DISTRIBUTION: Vagrant in the N Philippines.

3 WHITE-SHOULDERED STARLING *Sturnia sinensis* 17cm FIELD NOTES: Usually gregarious. Forages in trees and on the ground. VOICE: A harsh *kaar* and a soft *preep* flight call. HABITAT: Open areas with scattered trees, scrub, cultivation and urban areas. DISTRIBUTION: Vagrant in Borneo and the Philippines.

4 ASIAN PIED STARLING (PIED MYNA) *Gracupica contra* 22–25cm
FIELD NOTES: Forages predominantly on the ground, usually in pairs or small parties, with larger flocks at communal roosts. VOICE: A prolonged series of shrill churrs with a few croaking and buzzing notes, sometimes including mimicry of other birds; calls include a loud *staar-staar*, a shrill *shree-shree*, and various chuckles, warbles and whistles. HABITAT: Open, usually moist areas with scattered trees, cultivation and urban areas. DISTRIBUTION: Resident in Sumatra, Java and Bali.

5 BLACK-WINGED STARLING *Acridotheres melanopterus* 22–24cm
FIELD NOTES: Forages mostly on the ground, usually in flocks of 3–10 birds. *A. m. tertius* (5b) occurs in Bali and Lombok; *A. m. tricolor* (not depicted), found in SE Java, has a greyish back and black secondary coverts. VOICE: Calls include a downward-inflected *cha cha cha*, a throaty *tok* or *chok*, a harsh *kaar kaar*, a drawn-out *kreeer* and a *kishaa kishaa*; also various whistles and squeaks. HABITAT: Cultivated areas, fallow fields, grazing land, lawns and orchards; formerly in primary and secondary monsoon forest, forest edges and woodland. DISTRIBUTION: Endemic to Java, Bali and Lombok in the W Lesser Sundas.

6 COMMON MYNA *Acridotheres tristis* 23cm FIELD NOTES: Very tame. In flight, shows bold white primary patches. VOICE: A querulous *kwerrh* and many gurgling and chattering notes; when alarmed, utters a harsh *chake-chake*. Song is a tuneless mixture of gurgling and whistled phrases. HABITAT: Around human habitation, open areas and cultivation. DISTRIBUTION: Introduced to Borneo.

7 JAVAN MYNA *Acridotheres javanicus* 24–25cm FIELD NOTES: Forages mainly on the ground in pairs or small groups, and larger flocks occur where food is plentiful. In flight, shows white patches at base of primaries. VOICE: Very similar to Common Myna. HABITAT: Open country, cultivation and urban areas. DISTRIBUTION: Resident in Sumatra, Java and Bali; introduced to Borneo.

8 PALE-BELLIED MYNA (SULAWESI MYNA) *Acridotheres cinereus* 25cm
FIELD NOTES: Usually encountered in small flocks of 3–10 birds foraging on the ground; often around feeding cattle. VOICE: A random variety of dry, unmusical, nasal, squeaky rattles and whistles. HABITAT: Dry, fallow paddyfields, cattle pastures, lightly wooded cultivation and urban areas. DISTRIBUTION: Endemic to Sulawesi; introduced to Borneo and the Lesser Sundas.

9 CRESTED MYNA *Acridotheres cristatellus* 25cm FIELD NOTES: Usually found in flocks, foraging on the ground. Roosts communally. In flight, shows a white flash at base of primaries. VOICE: Similar to Common Myna, but song is more whistled. HABITAT: Open areas, scrub, cultivation and urban areas. DISTRIBUTION: Introduced to Borneo and the Philippines.

137 MYNAS

1 BALI MYNA *Leucopsar rothschildi* 25cm FIELD NOTES: Mainly arboreal. Usually occurs in pairs; roosts communally. Immature has greyer back and cinnamon-tinged wings. VOICE: Loud, harsh whistles and chattering notes. HABITAT: Open woodland with a grassy understorey. DISTRIBUTION: Endemic to Bali.

2 SULAWESI CRESTED MYNA (SULAWESI MYNA) *Basilornis celebensis* 23–27cm FIELD NOTES: Usually seen in pairs or small groups. Forages in the canopy, especially in fruiting trees. Perches on exposed branches in early morning or late afternoon. VOICE: Calls consist mainly of high-pitched whistles and drawn-out nasal notes; also utters brief squeaks and *chip* notes. HABITAT: Lowland, hill and riverine primary forest, disturbed forest, forest edges, secondary woodland, lightly wooded cultivation and remnant patches of forest in cultivation. DISTRIBUTION: Endemic to Sulawesi.

3 HELMETED MYNA *Basilornis galeatus* 24–25cm FIELD NOTES: Generally seen in pairs; small flocks occur in fruiting tees. VOICE: A booming *poo poo poop*, repeated every few seconds. HABITAT: Primary, selectively logged and degraded forest, tall secondary forest, overgrown, lightly wooded cultivation and tall mangroves. DISTRIBUTION: Endemic to the Banggai and Sula islands.

4 LONG-CRESTED MYNA *Basilornis corythaix* 24–26cm FIELD NOTES: Noisy. Favours fruiting trees. Occurs singly, in pairs or in small groups, and often mixes with Moluccan Starlings (Plate 135) in garden areas. Regularly rests on exposed branches. VOICE: Calls include a series of five piercing, rising whistles and various ascending and descending nasal notes, interspersed with occasional short, piping notes. HABITAT: Tall secondary forest, forest edges, gardens in hill forests and overgrown, lightly wooded cultivation. DISTRIBUTION: Endemic to Seram in the S Moluccas.

5 APO MYNA *Basilornis mirandus* 28–30cm FIELD NOTES: Occurs singly, in pairs or in small groups. Favours perching on high, exposed branches. VOICE: Various tinkling and metallic notes, interspersed with snapping, gurgling and squeaky notes. HABITAT: Montane forest and forest edges. DISTRIBUTION: Endemic to Mindanao in the S Philippines.

6 WHITE-NECKED MYNA *Streptocitta albicollis* 42–50cm FIELD NOTES: Generally seen in pairs or small groups; also joins mixed-species foraging parties. Regularly perches, conspicuously, on dead tree branches. Black-billed race *S. a. torquata* (6b) occurs in N Sulawesi. VOICE: A clear, whistled *towee*, 2–3 twangy, nasal notes, a drawn-out rasping and a penetrating *keee* alarm call. HABITAT: Primary and secondary lowland and hill forest, swamp forest, forest edges, wooded bushland, and isolated thickets and groups of trees. DISTRIBUTION: Endemic to Sulawesi.

7 BARE-EYED MYNA *Streptocitta albertinae* 42–45cm FIELD NOTES: Usually seen in pairs, occasionally alone or in trios. Tends to favour the mid- to upper levels of tall trees. VOICE: Call recalls the sound made by a squeaky gate, consisting of a descending series of five notes. HABITAT: Degraded, selectively logged and open forest, lightly wooded cultivation and lightly wooded swamps. DISTRIBUTION: Endemic to the Sula Islands.

8 COLETO *Sarcops calvus* 26–28cm FIELD NOTES: Usually seen in pairs, with larger groups occurring in fruiting trees. Frequently seen perched at the top of dead trees. Black-backed race *S. c. melanonotus* (8b) occurs in the S Philippines. VOICE: A metallic click, followed by a high-pitched *kliing-kliing*; also chiming notes mixed with mechanical gurgles and splutters, likened to the warming up of an orchestra. HABITAT: Forest, forest edges, secondary growth, clearings with isolated trees and coconut groves. DISTRIBUTION: Endemic to the Philippines.

6b
torquata

8b
melanonotus

138 MYNAS; GROSBEAK STARLING; RHABDORNIS

1 HILL MYNA (COMMON HILL MYNA) *Gracula religiosa* 25–29cm
FIELD NOTES: Arboreal, generally encountered in pairs or small groups in the exposed tops of tall trees. In flight, shows white patches at base of primaries. *G. r. venerata* (1b) occurs in the Lesser Sundas. VOICE: Various *chip* notes, soft *um* sounds, whispered whistles, and many other types of whistles, croaks and wails. HABITAT: Broadleaved evergreen and deciduous forest, forest edges and clearings. DISTRIBUTION: Resident in Sumatra, Java, Bali and Borneo.

2 NIAS HILL MYNA *Gracula robusta* 32cm FIELD NOTES: Usually found in small flocks. In flight, shows a white patch at base of primaries. Formerly considered conspecific with the Hill Myna. VOICE: Said to be an excellent mimic of human speech; no other information. HABITAT: Hill forests. DISTRIBUTION: Endemic to islands off NW Sumatra.

3 ENGGANO HILL MYNA *Gracula enganensis* 27cm FIELD NOTES: In flight, shows a white patch at base of primaries. Actions presumably much like those of Hill Myna, with which it has been considered conspecific. VOICE: Unreported; probably much like Hill Myna. HABITAT: Forested areas. DISTRIBUTION: Endemic to Enggano Island off SW Sumatra.

4 FIERY-BROWED MYNA (FIERY-BROWED STARLING) *Enodes erythrophris* 27cm FIELD NOTES: Forages in the canopy, in pairs or in small groups. Often perches on high, exposed branches. Can be quite acrobatic when searching for food. VOICE: A metallic *pik, tik, tsiit, sip* or *ssii*; also a rapid, sharp, hard *tik-tik-tt-tt-tt*, and a high-pitched *peeep* interspersed with various guttural notes. HABITAT: Mature forest, tall secondary forest, selectively logged forest and forest edges. DISTRIBUTION: Endemic to Sulawesi.

5 GROSBEAK STARLING *Scissirostrum dubium* 17–21cm FIELD NOTES: Gregarious, foraging in noisy flocks at forest edges. Breeds colonially. VOICE: Calls include a whistled *wrriu*, given by feeding groups; also a loud, clear, high-pitched *swee*, a nasal chatter and a liquid *chiruip* flight note. HABITAT: Forest edges, lightly wooded country and plantations. DISTRIBUTION: Endemic to Sulawesi and the Banggai Islands.

6 STRIPE-BREASTED RHABDORNIS *Rhabdornis inornatus* 15–19cm
FIELD NOTES: Tends to forage in small groups, in the middle and upper canopy of forest trees. Active, searching among branches with hops, jumps and stretches; also makes sallies after passing insects. May join mixed-species feeding parties. VOICE: A high-pitched *tzit* or *tzit-tzit-tzit-tzit-tzit*. HABITAT: Submontane and montane forest. DISTRIBUTION: Endemic to the C and S Philippines.

7 GRAND RHABDORNIS *Rhabdornis grandis* 16–18cm FIELD NOTES: Forages after insects and small fruits by hopping and jumping along branches. Usually seen singly or in small groups; also joins mixed-species feeding flocks. Often perches at the top of dead trees. VOICE: A high-pitched *zip zip zeet zip*, some notes more trilled. HABITAT: Mid- and high-elevation primary and secondary dipterocarp and hardwood forest. DISTRIBUTION: Endemic to the N Philippines.

8 STRIPE-HEADED RHABDORNIS *Rhabdornis mystacalis* 15–16cm
FIELD NOTES: Occurs in active groups from the mid-storey to the canopy, hopping and jumping in search of food, or by making short fly-catching sorties. Often a member of mixed-species feeding parties. VOICE: An unmusical, high-pitched *tsee tsee wick-tsee*, the first two notes hardly audible; also a series of *zeet* notes, uttered when perched or feeding. HABITAT: Forest, forest edges and clearings. DISTRIBUTION: Endemic to the Philippines.

139 NUTHATCHES; TITS

1 VELVET-FRONTED NUTHATCH *Sitta frontalis* 12–13cm FIELD NOTES: Forages from the understorey to the canopy. *S. f. corallipes* (1b) occurs in Borneo. VOICE: Song is a rattling *sit-sit-sit…* Calls include a hard *chat*, *chip* or *chlit* and a thin *sip*. HABITAT: Broadleaved evergreen, semi-evergreen, mixed deciduous and mixed oak and pine forests. DISTRIBUTION: Resident in Sumatra, Java, Borneo and the W Philippines.

2 SULPHUR-BILLED NUTHATCH *Sitta oenochlamys* 12–13cm FIELD NOTES: Forages on main tree trunks and nearby branches in the upper tree levels. VOICE: Calls include a *chit*, a thinner *sit* or *sit-sit-sit-sit…*, a squeaky *snii* and a winding rattle. HABITAT: Pine and evergreen forests, forest edges and clearings, remnant patches of forest and secondary growth. DISTRIBUTION: Endemic to the Philippines.

3 BLUE NUTHATCH *Sitta azurea* 13–14cm FIELD NOTES: Forages mainly in the upper storey on trunks and large branches. VOICE: A short *chit* or *chi-chit*, a *chit-chit-chit*, a *chir-ri-rit* or a trilling *tititititititiik*, a mellow *tup*, a squeaky *zhe* or *zhe-zhe* and a nasal *kneu*. HABITAT: Lower montane forest and tall upper montane forest. DISTRIBUTION: Resident in Sumatra and Java.

4 ELEGANT TIT *Pardaliparus elegans* 11–12cm FIELD NOTES: Usually encountered in pairs or small flocks; an active forager from the middle levels to the canopy. *P. e. bongaoensis* (4b) occurs in the Sulu Islands; *P. e. mindanensis* (4c) is found in Mindanao; *P. e. albescens* (4d) resides in the C Philippines. VOICE: Variable; includes a *tweet chuck-z-chuck-z-chuck-z*, a monotonous *sweet sweet sweet sweet…*, a *chi-bow sweet-zee-sweet-zee-sweet-zee* and a faster *swee-zee-swee-swee-zee-zoo*. HABITAT: Dense primary evergreen forest, edges of secondary forest and scattered trees at the edges of cultivation. DISTRIBUTION: Endemic to the Philippines.

5 PALAWAN TIT *Pardaliparus amabilis* 12cm FIELD NOTES: Active forager in the middle storey and canopy. VOICE: Very vocal; calls include a harsh *chuwi-chuwi-chuwi…*, a *wichi-wichi-wichi-wichi* or similar, simple accelerating rattles, a musical *tui-tui-tui-tui…* and a silvery, descending trill. HABITAT: Forest, forest edges, wooded fringes of swamps and secondary growth. DISTRIBUTION: Endemic to Palawan in the W Philippines.

6 CINEREOUS TIT *Parus cinereus* 13–14cm FIELD NOTES: Active from low levels to the treetops. VOICE: A rapidly repeated *chew-a-ti chew-a-ti chew-a-ti* or similar; calls include a harsh *tcha-tcha-tcha-tcha* and a ringing *pink-pink-pink*. HABITAT: Open forest, forest edges, mangroves, lightly wooded cultivation and gardens. DISTRIBUTION: Resident in Sumatra, Java, Bali and the W Lesser Sundas.

7 WHITE-FRONTED TIT *Sittiparus semilarvatus* 13–14cm FIELD NOTES: Forages in the middle storey and the canopy of tall trees. *S. s. nehrkorni* (7b) occurs on Mindanao; *S. s. snowi* (7c) is found in NE Luzon. VOICE: Calls include a sharp, high *psit*, a plaintive, rolling *tsuit*, a high-pitched *tsi-tsi-tsi-tsi-tsi* and a *tseeeh tsi-tsi-tsi-tsi-tsi-tsi-ts ts ts*. HABITAT: Forest, forest edges, remnant forest patches, secondary growth and, occasionally, scrub. DISTRIBUTION: Endemic to the Philippines.

8 SULTAN TIT *Melanochlora sultanea* 20–21cm FIELD NOTES: Acrobatic forager in foliage of trees and bushes. VOICE: Song consists of a mellow, whistled *piu-piu-piu-piu-piu* or similar; calls include a rattling *chi-dip tri-trip* and a fast, squeaky *tria-tria-tria*, *tcheery-tcheery-tcheery* or *squear-squear-squear*. HABITAT: Broadleaved evergreen, semi-evergreen and mixed deciduous forest. DISTRIBUTION: Possibly a rare resident in Sumatra (6–10 birds seen in 1938, and one very old specimen collected in the 19th century and now lost).

9 PYGMY BUSHTIT *Psaltria exilis* 8–9cm FIELD NOTES: Active; forages in small flocks, often low down. VOICE: A high-pitched *si*, *sisi* or *silililili*; also a high-pitched, grating *srrr* and a soft *chip*, *tchip* or *sip*, these sometimes combining to make longer phrases. HABITAT: Montane forest, forest edges and plantations. DISTRIBUTION: Endemic to Java.

140 SWALLOWS; MARTINS

1 SAND MARTIN (COLLARED SAND MARTIN) *Riparia riparia* 12cm
FIELD NOTES: Gregarious; regularly associates with other swallow species. Rapid, light flight, usually low over water or the ground. VOICE: A harsh *tschr*, and a *schrrp* when excited. HABITAT: Lakes, rivers and marshes; also over open country on migration. DISTRIBUTION: Winter visitor to the Philippines and Borneo.

2 SWALLOW (BARN SWALLOW) *Hirundo rustica* 18cm FIELD NOTES: Gregarious, often in large flocks. Agile; flies with twists and turns to capture flying insects. Regularly perches on overhead wires or exposed branches. Immatures lack the long outer tail feathers. Rusty race *H. r. saturata* (2b) noted in Borneo and the N Philippines. VOICE: Calls include a *vit-vit*, and a *chir-chir* when agitated. HABITAT: Open country, usually not far from water and human habitation. DISTRIBUTION: Winter visitor throughout the area.

3 PACIFIC SWALLOW *Hirundo tahitica* 13cm FIELD NOTES: Fast flight, with frequent swerving, gliding and banking. VOICE: A twittering *twsit-twsit-twsit*; calls include a *titswwe* and a low *swoo*. HABITAT: Coastal areas, over forests and in open country; often associated with human habitation and bridges. DISTRIBUTION: Resident in the region.

4 RED-RUMPED SWALLOW *Cecropis daurica* 16–17cm FIELD NOTES: Flight is generally slow and graceful, with much gliding and soaring. Immatures lack the longer outer tail feathers. VOICE: Calls include a mewing, an aggressive *krr* and a *djuit* contact note. HABITAT: Open country, lightly wooded areas, rocky gorges and cliffs. DISTRIBUTION: Scarce winter visitor to Sumatra and Borneo.

5 STRIATED SWALLOW *Cecropis striolata* 19cm FIELD NOTES: Flight is slow and buoyant, usually low over the ground or around cliffs. Immatures lack the longer outer tail feathers. VOICE: A soft twittering; calls include a drawn-out *quitsch*, a *pin* and a repeated *chi-chi-chi*. HABITAT: Open areas, often near water, cliffs and river gorges. DISTRIBUTION: Resident in Sumatra, Java, Bali, Borneo, the Philippines and the Lesser Sundas.

6 TREE MARTIN *Petrochelidon nigricans* 13cm FIELD NOTES: Flight is swift, with frequent twists and turns; often hawks for insects over water. Usually in groups of 10–30 birds. VOICE: A short, thin, high-pitched twittering; a low-pitched twitter or chatter; and a high-pitched, repeated, hard, nasal *zzit* or *tsweet*. HABITAT: Open areas, including grasslands, airfields and paddyfields, also open woodland. DISTRIBUTION: Resident or winter visitor to the Lesser Sundas and Moluccas.

7 FAIRY MARTIN *Petrochelidon ariel* 11cm FIELD NOTES: Generally in small groups; often mixes with other swallow species. Flight is slow and fluttery, usually high up. VOICE: Calls include a short *chrrr* or *prrrt-prrrt*. HABITAT: Open woodland and open country, usually near water. DISTRIBUTION: Vagrant in the Lesser Sundas.

8 ASIAN HOUSE MARTIN *Delichon dasypus* 12cm FIELD NOTES: Flight contains frequent gliding, swooping and banking, often at great height. VOICE: A shrill contact call. HABITAT: Valleys and gorges in mountain, hill and coastal areas; also near human habitation. DISTRIBUTION: Winter visitor or vagrant to N Sumatra, Java, Borneo and the Philippines.

141 BULBULS

1 STRAW-HEADED BULBUL *Pycnonotus zeylanicus* 29cm FIELD NOTES: Usually encountered in small groups, foraging from the ground up to the canopy. VOICE: A melodious, rich warbling; utters a weak chattering and gurgling while foraging. HABITAT: Forests, often near streams and rivers. DISTRIBUTION: Resident in Greater Sundas.

2 CREAM-STRIPED BULBUL *Pycnonotus leucogrammicus* 17–18cm FIELD NOTES: Forages on fruit and insects in the middle storey or subcanopy. Usually seen singly or in pairs, occasionally in small groups; regular member of mixed-species feeding flocks. VOICE: A *tree-troo-troo*. HABITAT: Hill and montane evergreen forest, forest edges and secondary growth. DISTRIBUTION: Endemic to Sumatra.

3 SPOT-NECKED BULBUL *Pycnonotus tympanistrigus* 16cm FIELD NOTES: Usually seen in pairs or small groups; sometimes joins mixed-species foraging parties. Tends to favour the middle storey and canopy. VOICE: A disyllabic *tdip-diew*; also a repeated, emphatic *jret-jret-jtry*. HABITAT: Evergreen forest, forest edges and secondary growth. DISTRIBUTION: Endemic to Sumatra.

4 BLACK-AND-WHITE BULBUL *Pycnonotus melanoleucos* 18cm FIELD NOTES: Most often encountered in the forest canopy, although also ventures to forage among low fruiting shrubs. VOICE: Generally quiet; occasionally utters a tuneless *pet-it*, *tee-too* or similar, and a longer *cherlee-chlee-chlee-chee-chee*. HABITAT: Broadleaved evergreen forest and forest edges. DISTRIBUTION: Resident in Sumatra and Borneo.

5 BLACK-HEADED BULBUL *Pycnonotus atriceps* 18cm FIELD NOTES: Usually found in pairs or small parties foraging in trees or bushes. Plumage variable; normal, intermediate and grey shown; the grey birds on Maratua Island, off E Borneo, are sometimes considered a full species (*P. hodiernus*). VOICE: The song is a disjointed series of rising and falling *tink* notes; calls include an emphatic *chew* or *chewp*. HABITAT: Lowland primary and secondary forest and wooded gardens. DISTRIBUTION: Resident in Sumatra, Java, Borneo and the W Philippines.

6 RUBY-THROATED BULBUL *Pycnonotus dispar* 17–20cm FIELD NOTES: Forages for fruits and insects; little other information. VOICE: A *tee-tee-wheet-wheet*, *whit-wheet-wit* or *hii-tii-hii-tii-wiit*, or other permutations of these notes. HABITAT: Open woodland, shrubby areas and plantations. DISTRIBUTION: Endemic to Sumatra, Java and Bali.

7 BORNEAN BULBUL *Pycnonotus montis* 17–18cm FIELD NOTES: Often perches in the open at forest edges. Forages in fruiting trees, making regular aerial sallies after passing insects. VOICE: A constantly repeated *yek yek*, also a whistled *grrrt grrrt*. HABITAT: Evergreen forest, secondary forest and shrubby regrowth of abandoned cultivation. DISTRIBUTION: Endemic to Borneo.

8 GREY-BELLIED BULBUL *Pycnonotus cyaniventris* 16–17cm FIELD NOTES: Usually keeps to the canopy, in pairs or small parties. Agile, often hanging tit-like to gather berries. VOICE: A sweet *pi-pi-pwi… pi-pi-pwi…*, a trilled, bubbling *pi-pi-pi-pi-pi-pi-pi* and a subdued *wit-wit-wit*. HABITAT: Primary and secondary forest, forest edges by clearings, roads and rivers. DISTRIBUTION: Resident in Sumatra and Borneo.

9 SCALY-BREASTED BULBUL *Pycnonotus squamatus* 14–16cm FIELD NOTES: Usually found in the forest canopy, singly or in small groups; sometimes in larger gatherings in fruiting trees. VOICE: Calls include a high-pitched *wit* or *tit*, a thin *tree*, a persistent *trrip trip* and a pretty trill. HABITAT: Submontane primary and secondary forest. DISTRIBUTION: Resident in Sumatra, Java and Borneo.

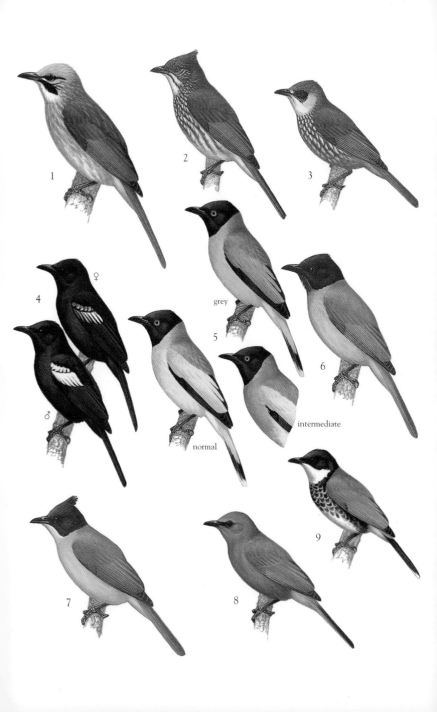

142 BULBULS

1 RED-WHISKERED BULBUL *Pycnonotus jocosus* 20cm FIELD NOTES: Usually found singly, in pairs or in small parties. Juveniles lack the red cheek-patch. VOICE: Variable musical phrases; calls include a rolling *prroop* and a harsh, raspy *bzeep*. HABITAT: Open forest, scrub, cultivation, parks and gardens. DISTRIBUTION: Introduced to Sumatra and possibly Borneo.

2 SOOTY-HEADED BULBUL *Pycnonotus aurigaster* 19–21cm FIELD NOTES: Usually seen in small, noisy flocks. Forages on the ground and in trees or bushes. VOICE: A chatty *whi-wi-wiwi-wiwi, u whi hi hu* or *wh-i-i-wi*; also a *chook chook*. HABITAT: Open wooded or bushy areas, forest edges, secondary growth, parks and gardens. DISTRIBUTION: Resident in Java and Bali, expanding to Sumatra and Borneo.

3 PUFF-BACKED BULBUL *Pycnonotus eutilotus* 20–22cm FIELD NOTES: Forages in trees after fruits and insects, usually singly or in pairs; sometimes joins mixed-species feeding parties. Note white tips on undertail. VOICE: A loud, high-pitched, quavering warble. HABITAT: Lowland and hill primary forest, peat swamp forest, secondary growth and forest edges. DISTRIBUTION: Resident in Sumatra and Borneo.

4 BLUE-WATTLED BULBUL *Pycnonotus nieuwenhuisii* 18cm FIELD NOTES: Little information; known from only two specimens. Possibly a hybrid. VOICE: Unknown. HABITAT: Lowland dipterocarp forest in Borneo and low shrubbery in Sumatra. DISTRIBUTION: Resident in Sumatra and Borneo.

5 YELLOW-WATTLED BULBUL *Pycnonotus urostictus* 19cm FIELD NOTES: Occurs singly, in pairs or in small parties; favours fruiting trees. VOICE: A variable, loud, trisyllabic, whistled *wee-we-weeee* or *wee-eeee-ee*; also high-pitched, squeaky whistles and longer, more complicated whistles ending with a *wee-eeee-ee*. HABITAT: Open woods, secondary growth and forest edges. DISTRIBUTION: Endemic to the Philippines.

6 ORANGE-SPOTTED BULBUL *Pycnonotus bimaculatus* 20cm FIELD NOTES: Generally seen alone or in small parties; favours open glades and forest edges. VOICE: Various loud, harsh songs, including a *toc-toc-toc-toroc*, a clear *chewlk-chewlk-chewlk* or *chuk-chuk-chooh-chewlewlewlew*; also utters a sharp *tik*. HABITAT: Montane forest edges, tall secondary growth, scrub and elfin forest near mountain summits. DISTRIBUTION: Endemic to Sumatra, Java and Bali.

7 ACEH BULBUL *Pycnonotus snouckaerti* 20–21cm FIELD NOTES: Favours small scrubby clearings dominated by ferns and high grasses. Formerly considered a race of the previous species. VOICE: Song similar to the previous species, but with a more metallic or dry, reedy quality. HABITAT: Submontane forests with clearings. DISTRIBUTION: Endemic to N Sumatra.

8 FLAVESCENT BULBUL *Pycnonotus flavescens* 22cm FIELD NOTES: Usually seen singly or in pairs, in the canopy of montane forest and in shrubby growth above the tree line. VOICE: A short five-note song and a harsh chatter. HABITAT: Tall bushes, thickets and clearings in forested hills and mountains. DISTRIBUTION: Resident in N Borneo.

9 YELLOW-VENTED BULBUL *Pycnonotus goiavier* 20–21cm FIELD NOTES: Forages singly, in pairs or in small parties. Occasionally makes fly-catching sallies from an exposed perch. VOICE: Song consists of a series of variable choppy notes; calls are cheerful and loud, including a bubbling *chic-chic-chic, tiddloo-tiddloo-tiddloo* or *tid-liu tid-liu tid-liu* and similar. HABITAT: Open areas, secondary growth, cultivation, roadsides and gardens. DISTRIBUTION: Resident in Sumatra, Java, Bali, Borneo, the Philippines and the W Lesser Sundas.

10 OLIVE-WINGED BULBUL *Pycnonotus plumosus* 20–21cm FIELD NOTES: Generally seen foraging low down, singly, in pairs or in small groups. Often joins other bulbuls in fruiting trees. VOICE: Various soft chirping and liquid phrases; calls include a throaty *whip-whip* and a purring *wrrh-wrrh-wrrh*. HABITAT: Lowland forest, secondary growth, forest edges, degraded forest and coastal scrub. DISTRIBUTION: Resident in Sumatra, Java, Bali and Borneo.

143 BULBULS

1 ASHY-FRONTED BULBUL *Pycnonotus cinereifrons* 19–20cm FIELD NOTES: Favours fruiting trees. Usually seen singly or in pairs, and sometimes in small groups; often a member of mixed-species feeding parties. Formerly considered to be a race of the Olive-winged Bulbul (Plate 142). VOICE: A bubbling, repeated *chop wit chu do-de-do-de-du*; calls are presumed to be much like those of the Olive-winged Bulbul, including a *whip-whip* and a purring *wrrh wrrh wrrh*. HABITAT: Open country, forest edges and secondary growth. DISTRIBUTION: Endemic to Palawan in the W Philippines.

2 CREAM-VENTED BULBUL *Pycnonotus simplex* 18cm FIELD NOTES: Occurs singly, in pairs or as part of mixed-species foraging flocks. Favours fruiting trees. VOICE: A subdued, quavering *whi-whi-whi-whi…*, interspersed with a low *pru-pru prr* and *prr-pru*; also harsh call notes and short phrases such as *quik chop, quik-plik chop* and a longer *bee-quik* or *pee dee kew*. HABITAT: Broadleaved evergreen forest, forest edges and secondary growth. DISTRIBUTION: Resident in Sumatra, Java and Borneo.

3 ASIAN RED-EYED BULBUL *Pycnonotus brunneus* 19cm FIELD NOTES: Arboreal, mainly in the lower and middle storeys; usually seen singly, in pairs or as part of mixed-species feeding parties in fruiting trees. VOICE: A high-pitched, bubbling, rising *pri-pri-pri-pri-pri-pit-pit*; also brief trills and a strident *chirrup* or *whit-it*. HABITAT: Broadleaved forest, forest edges, secondary growth and scrub. DISTRIBUTION: Resident in Sumatra and Borneo.

4 SPECTACLED BULBUL *Pycnonotus erythropthalmos* 16–18cm FIELD NOTES: Usually encountered singly or in pairs, often in the forest understorey or in fruiting trees with other bulbul species. VOICE: A high-pitched, mechanical *pip-pippidi* or *wip-wip-wi i i i*; also short phrases, such as *willy-nilly, pippi-dippi* or *willy-nilly-no*. HABITAT: Primary and mature secondary lowland forest, swamp forest and secondary growth. DISTRIBUTION: Resident in Sumatra and Borneo.

5 FINSCH'S BULBUL *Alophoixus finchii* 16–17cm FIELD NOTES: Forages mainly in the middle storey, or lower if trees or bushes are in fruit. VOICE: A simple *choi-choi-chong-choi choi-choi*; calls include a subdued *wek* or *twut*, a loud, nasal *hwuiikt* and a grating *scree*. HABITAT: Lowland, hill and submontane forest, and secondary growth. DISTRIBUTION: Resident in Sumatra and Borneo.

6 OCHRACEOUS BULBUL *Alophoixus ochraceus* 19–22cm FIELD NOTES: Usually encountered in loose, noisy parties feeding in fruiting trees and shrubs. VOICE: Song consists of warbled sequences and chattering notes; calls include a harsh *chrrt-chrrt-chrrt-chrrt… chik-chik-chik-chik* or *chi-it-chit-it-chit-it-chitit*, all often preceded by a fluty, nasal *eeyi* or *iiwu*. HABITAT: Montane broadleaved evergreen forest and tall secondary forest with bamboo. DISTRIBUTION: Resident in Sumatra and Borneo.

7 GREY-CHEEKED BULBUL *Alophoixus bres* 21–22cm FIELD NOTES: Noisy. Generally seen singly, in pairs or in small groups foraging in fruiting trees and shrubs. VOICE: Variable; song consists of a mournful *whi-u wiu iwi*, followed by a high-pitched *ii-wi-tchiu-tchiu* or similar, interspersed with scolding or rattling notes. HABITAT: Hill and montane broadleaved evergreen forest, forest edges and secondary growth. DISTRIBUTION: Resident in Sumatra, Java, Bali and Borneo.

8 PALAWAN BULBUL *Alophoixus frater* 21–22cm FIELD NOTES: Formerly considered a race of the previous species; actions presumed to be similar. VOICE: A loud *chip-pu chu-chu-chu-chu cha-wheeet* or similar. HABITAT: Forest, forest edges and secondary growth. DISTRIBUTION: Endemic to Palawan in the W Philippines.

9 YELLOW-BELLIED BULBUL *Alophoixus phaeocephalus* 20–21cm FIELD NOTES: Generally seen singly, in pairs or in small parties. Frequents the lower storeys, regularly descending to feed on the ground, although soon returning to lower branches. VOICE: A subdued, buzzy *whi-ee whi-ee whi-ee* or a rasping *cherrit-berrit*, and a variety of grating notes. HABITAT: Lowland and hill primary forest. DISTRIBUTION: Resident in Sumatra and Borneo.

144 BULBULS

1 NORTHERN GOLDEN BULBUL *Thapsinillas longirostris* 21–22cm
FIELD NOTES: Usually encountered in small groups, foraging for fruit and invertebrates.
VOICE: Emphatic husky, chattering notes, often accelerating into a repetitive, loud, melodious phrase; also utters a meandering sequence of clipped notes and a lorikeet-like *twe-twe* call. HABITAT: Primary and secondary forest, from lowlands to montane areas; also secondary growth, plantations and scrub at the edge of disturbed forest.
DISTRIBUTION: Endemic to the Togian, Banggai and Sula islands and the N Moluccas.

2 SERAM GOLDEN BULBUL *Thapsinillas affinis* 22–24cm FIELD NOTES: Forages from the understorey to the subcanopy, and occasionally feeds among leaf litter on the forest floor. Joins mixed-species feeding parties. VOICE: A mournful series of sweet minor-key notes, essentially slow and leisurely, occasionally interspersed with harsh *chrek* or *kruk* notes; also utters a raucous, parakeet-like *ki-ki-ki-ki-kreee-kreee-kreee-kre kr kr kr.*
HABITAT: Forests, from sea-level to submontane areas. DISTRIBUTION: Endemic to Seram in the S Moluccas.

3 BURU GOLDEN BULBUL *Thapsinillas mysticalis* 22–24cm FIELD NOTES: Formerly considered conspecific with the previous species; actions presumed to be similar.
VOICE: Begins with a series of *kek-kek* notes, followed by a series of upslurred or warbled, whistled notes. HABITAT: Broadleaved evergreen forest and light woodland.
DISTRIBUTION: Endemic to Buru in the S Moluccas.

4 HOOK-BILLED BULBUL *Setornis criniger* 20cm FIELD NOTES: Noisy. Forages in the middle storey and lower growth, in pairs or small parties. VOICE: A harsh *carrrk* or *currrk*, and a harsh *chow-cho cho.* HABITAT: Lowland primary forest, stunted ridgetop forest and abandoned plantations. DISTRIBUTION: Resident in Sumatra and Borneo.

5 HAIRY-BACKED BULBUL *Tricholestes criniger* 16–17cm FIELD NOTES: Usually encountered in pairs in the lower or middle storeys. Forages for fruit or invertebrates, and often makes short sallies to take flying insects. Unassuming but can be inquisitive.
VOICE: A scratchy, chattering warble, interspersed with a quavering *whirrrh*; calls include a high-pitched, rising *whiiii.* HABITAT: Primary, secondary and coastal forest and mangroves.
DISTRIBUTION: Resident in Sumatra and Borneo.

6 BUFF-VENTED BULBUL *Iole crypta* 20–21cm FIELD NOTES: Forages in the canopy and middle storey, sometimes descending to lower levels to feed in fruiting shrubs.
VOICE: Calls include a musical *cherrit*, a *whe-ic* and a flatter *whirr.* HABITAT: Broadleaved evergreen forest, forest edges and secondary growth. DISTRIBUTION: Resident in Sumatra and Borneo.

7 SULPHUR-BELLIED BULBUL *Iole palawanensis* 18cm FIELD NOTES: Occurs singly, in pairs or in small groups. VOICE: Calls include a *chirrup*, *chirrrup-chi* or *chip.*
HABITAT: Evergreen forest, forest edges and secondary growth. DISTRIBUTION: Endemic to Palawan in the W Philippines.

8 STREAKED BULBUL *Ixos malaccensis* 23cm FIELD NOTES: Forages mainly in the canopy, singly or in pairs; occasionally makes sorties after flying insects. VOICE: A high-pitched, descending *chiri-chiri-chu*, or a longer *ka-jee ka-jee ka-jee jueee* that sometimes runs into a delicate, descending trill; calls include harsh, loud rasping or rattling notes.
HABITAT: Lowland and hill primary and secondary forest. DISTRIBUTION: Resident in Sumatra and Borneo.

145 BULBULS; MALIA

1 SUNDA BULBUL *Ixos virescens* 20cm FIELD NOTES: Sluggish forager in the middle storey and the canopy, singly, in pairs or in small, noisy groups. *I. v. sumatranus* (1b) occurs in W Sumatra. VOICE: Calls include a *chiit-chiit* and a sharp *twink*. HABITAT: Evergreen montane forest, forest edges and secondary growth. DISTRIBUTION: Endemic to Sumatra and Java.

2 CINEREOUS BULBUL *Hemixos cinereus* 20–21cm FIELD NOTES: Forages in the middle storey, canopy and forest edges. *H. c. connectens* (2b) occurs in Borneo. VOICE: A brief, sweet *beelee-bear beelee burlee*; calls include a loud, ringing *tree-tree-tree*, a whining *whear*, a sharp *chiap* and a whistled *wheesh-wheesh*. HABITAT: Montane broadleaved evergreen forest and secondary growth. DISTRIBUTION: Resident in Sumatra and Borneo.

3 PHILIPPINE BULBUL *Hypsipetes philippinus* 22cm FIELD NOTES: Usually seen singly or in pairs, and sometimes occurs in small parties. Forages from the understorey to the canopy. VOICE: Variable, including a rising and falling *deut doo doo doo da-leee-eut*. HABITAT: Broadleaved evergreen forest, forest edges, shrubby clearings, secondary growth, cultivated areas with trees and coconut groves. DISTRIBUTION: Endemic to the Philippines.

4 MINDORO BULBUL *Hypsipetes mindorensis* 22cm FIELD NOTES: Formerly considered a race of the previous species; actions and habits presumed to be similar. VOICE: A teetering *we-to we-to we-to-to*. HABITAT: Presumed to be similar to the previous species. DISTRIBUTION: Endemic to Mindoro in the N Philippines.

5 VISAYAN BULBUL *Hypsipetes guimarasensis* 22cm FIELD NOTES: Actions presumed to be similar to the Philippine Bulbul, with which it was formerly considered conspecific. VOICE: A *deut deut deut*, which accelerates into a complex series of musical notes. HABITAT: Presumed to be similar to Philippine Bulbul. DISTRIBUTION: Endemic to the WC Philippines.

6 ZAMBOANGO BULBUL *Hypsipetes rufigularis* 24cm FIELD NOTES: Forages in the middle and upper levels of trees, usually in small groups. VOICE: A *chigur-chigur-chigur-chigur-chigur* and a faster *chli-chli-chli…*; calls include a *chuk*, a *tweer* and a *choik*. HABITAT: Forest and forest edges. DISTRIBUTION: Endemic to W Mindanao and Basilan in the Philippines.

7 STREAK-BREASTED BULBUL *Hypsipetes siquijorensis* 26–27cm FIELD NOTES: Forages at all forest levels, usually in small groups. *H. s. cinereiceps* (7b) occurs on the islands of Tablas and Romblon. VOICE: A strident *whit pu whit tooer whit whee-er* or *pu-er whit pu-er* are both reputed to be given by the Tablas/Romblon race. HABITAT: Forest, forest edges, secondary growth and clearings. DISTRIBUTION: Occurs on Cebu, Tablas and Romblon.

8 BROWN-EARED BULBUL *Hypsipetes amaurotis* 28cm FIELD NOTES: Noisy and conspicuous; usually in groups or in mixed-species flocks. Forages at all forest levels, in forest corridors and in secondary-growth patches. VOICE: A harsh *pee-yuk* and a descending, accelerating *pee-yuk p-uk p-uk…*. HABITAT: Deciduous, mixed and evergreen forest. DISTRIBUTION: Resident in the islands of the N Philippines.

9 YELLOWISH BULBUL *Hypsipetes everetti* 24–26cm FIELD NOTES: Generally forages from the understorey to the middle storey, in small groups or in mixed-species flocks. *H. e. catarmanensis* (9b) occurs on Camiguin Island. VOICE: A long *peeeee* or *peeeeee-yuk*; song is a melodious *doo dee-dee-dee-dee-dee dee-boy-aay dee-boy-aaaay*. The Camiguin race utters a rising and falling *wee wee wo wee wee-wee wo*, followed by a *wu-wu-wu-wu* or stuttering *tu-tu-tu-tu*. HABITAT: Forest, forest edges and secondary growth. DISTRIBUTION: Endemic to the Philippines.

10 MALIA *Malia grata* 28–29cm FIELD NOTES: Usually occurs in small, noisy, active parties, foraging from the ground to the lower canopy. *M. g. stresemanni* (10b) occurs in CE Sulawesi. VOICE: Group calls include a repeated, high-pitched whistle, accompanied by a harsh, rapid *tsut-sut KA-KA* and a cacophony of guttural, warbling notes, along with rapid, harsh chattering or grating calls. HABITAT: Primary montane forest and, occasionally, disturbed forest. DISTRIBUTION: Endemic to Sulawesi.

1   1b
     sumatranus

2   2b
     connectens

3

4

5

6

7   7b
     cinereiceps

8

9   9b
     catarmanensis

10b
stresemanni

10

146 CISTICOLAS; PRINIAS; TESIAS; STUBTAILS

1 ZITTING CISTICOLA *Cisticola juncidis* 10–12cm FIELD NOTES: Best located while singing from an exposed perch or during song-flight. Forages on or close to the ground. VOICE: A simple *zit-zit-zit-zit-zit…*; calls include a *tew* and a *tsipp-tsipp-tsipp* or *tick tick tick…* HABITAT: Grassland, marshes and rice paddies. DISTRIBUTION: Resident in Sumatra, Java, Bali, the Philippines, Sulawesi and the Lesser Sundas.

2 BRIGHT-HEADED CISTICOLA (GOLDEN-HEADED CISTICOLA) *Cisticola exilis* 10cm FIELD NOTES: Sings from an exposed perch or in flight. Forages on the ground or in tangled vegetation. VOICE: Buzzy or wheezy notes, followed by a loud, liquid *scrrrrr plook* or similar. Calls include a scolding *squee* or *speeee*. HABITAT: Tall marshland vegetation, grassland with scattered bushes, rice paddies and scrub. DISTRIBUTION: Resident in Sumatra, Java, Bali, SW Borneo, the Philippines, Sulawesi, the Lesser Sundas and the S Moluccas.

3 BROWN PRINIA *Prinia polychroa* 16cm FIELD NOTES: Keeps to thick cover; if disturbed, tends to creep away through vegetation. VOICE: A loud *twee-ee-ee-ee-eet* or *chook-chook-chook*. HABITAT: Grassland with low scrub, cultivation, open forest with low shrubby growth. DISTRIBUTION: Resident in Java.

4 HILL PRINIA *Prinia superciliaris* 17cm FIELD NOTES: Noisy and active in grass and low vegetation. VOICE: A loud, piercing *cho-ee cho-ee cho-ee*. HABITAT: Scrub, low vegetation, and grass in submontane and montane forests. DISTRIBUTION: Resident in Sumatra.

5 BAR-WINGED PRINIA *Prinia familiaris* 13cm FIELD NOTES: Forages from the ground to the treetops, usually alone or in pairs; post-breeding, occurs in noisy parties of up to fifteen birds. VOICE: A loud, high-pitched *chweet-chweet-chweet*. HABITAT: Mangroves, secondary growth, plantations, parks and shrubby gardens. DISTRIBUTION: Endemic to Sumatra, Java and Bali.

6 YELLOW-BELLIED PRINIA *Prinia flaviventris* 13cm FIELD NOTES: Restless forager among grasses. Sings from an exposed perch or in a song-flight. VOICE: A weak, harsh *schink-schink-schink*, a bubbling *tidli-tidli-u* and a soft mewing. Bornean birds utter a *sen-si-lak* or similar. HABITAT: Reedy swamps, tall grassland and scrub. DISTRIBUTION: Resident in Sumatra, Java and Borneo.

7 PLAIN PRINIA *Prinia inornata* 10–11cm FIELD NOTES: Often in small, active parties, foraging low down in vegetation. Calls from grass stems or bushes. VOICE: A shrill *chee-cheerrrrrr-roowet* or *cheerrrrlet*. HABITAT: Long grass, reeds, marshes and cultivation. DISTRIBUTION: Resident in Java.

8 JAVAN TESIA *Tesia superciliaris* 7cm FIELD NOTES: Forages on or close to the forest floor; favours dense undergrowth, thickets in clearings and forest edges. VOICE: A loud, explosive, fast song of about fifteen notes. HABITAT: Montane forest. DISTRIBUTION: Endemic to W Java.

9 RUSSET-CAPPED TESIA *Tesia everetti* 9–10cm FIELD NOTES: Active. Forages on the ground, in undergrowth, the understorey and among creepers on tree trunks. VOICE: A loud, staccato series of ascending and other whistled notes, alternating up and down the scale. HABITAT: Damp forest, degraded woodland, secondary forest and scrub. DISTRIBUTION: Endemic to Sumbawa and Flores in the Lesser Sundas.

10 TIMOR STUBTAIL *Urosphena subulata* 10cm FIELD NOTES: Forages in leaf litter and around roots, fallen trees or branches. VOICE: A thin, high-pitched, slightly rising whistle. HABITAT: Primary and tall monsoon forest and hillside scrub. DISTRIBUTION: Endemic to the E Lesser Sundas.

11 BORNEAN STUBTAIL *Urosphena whiteheadi* 10cm FIELD NOTES: Creeps about mouse-like in thick undergrowth and on the ground. Usually alone. VOICE: A drawn-out, high-pitched, quiet, bat-like, squeaky *tzi-tzi-tzeeee*. HABITAT: Montane forest. DISTRIBUTION: Endemic to Borneo.

147 BUSH WARBLERS

1 JAPANESE BUSH WARBLER *Horornis diphone* 18cm FIELD NOTES: Inconspicuous forager in thick foliage. VOICE: Calls include a dry *tchet-tchet-tchet* and a rattling *trrt*. HABITAT: Bamboo thickets and brush. DISTRIBUTION: Winter visitor to the N Philippines.

2 ORIENTAL BUSH WARBLER (MANCHURIAN BUSH WARBLER) *Horornis borealis* 15cm FIELD NOTES: Forages in thick foliage. Much taxonomic confusion with this and the previous species, with which it is often considered conspecific. VOICE: Calls similar to those of the previous species. HABITAT: Bamboo thickets and brush. DISTRIBUTION: Winter visitor to the N Philippines.

3 PHILIPPINE BUSH WARBLER *Horornis seebohmi* 12cm FIELD NOTES: Forages on or near ground, in thick cover; usually alone. VOICE: A rhythmic *pee chap chop*, *pee chap chop chi* or *do doooooor dor-pro-dee-dor-pee*; calls include a repeated *chekk*. HABITAT: Open deciduous and pine forest, with understorey, thickets and low vegetation. DISTRIBUTION: Endemic to the N Philippines.

4 TANIMBAR BUSH WARBLER *Horornis carolinae* 12–13cm FIELD NOTES: Forages in dense undergrowth, alone or as part of mixed-species groups. VOICE: A drawn-out whistle, followed by a short, jumbled warble; calls include a soft *cherr* or *chuck*. HABITAT: Primary and monsoon forest, secondary woodland, bamboo, scrub and forest edges. DISTRIBUTION: Endemic to the Tanimbar Islands in the E Lesser Sundas.

5 SUNDA BUSH WARBLER *Horornis vulcanius* 12–13cm FIELD NOTES: Forages alone or in pairs in thick undergrowth or on the ground. *H. v. oreophilus* (5b) occurs in N Borneo. VOICE: A rising and falling *chee-heeoow cheeoow-wee-ee-eet*; calls include a sharp, repeated *trr-trr*. HABITAT: Stunted montane forest, with dense undergrowth, ferns or tall grasses. DISTRIBUTION: Resident in Sumatra, Java, Bali, Borneo, the W Philippines and the Lesser Sundas.

6 BENGUET BUSH WARBLER *Locustella seebohmi* 14cm FIELD NOTES: Little information; presumed to have the typical skulking behaviour of the genus. VOICE: A metallic zipping sound. HABITAT: Steep, grassy valleys. DISTRIBUTION: Endemic to the N Philippines.

7 JAVAN BUSH WARBLER *Locustella montis* 14–15cm FIELD NOTES: Hops around on low branches or on boulder-strewn slopes. *L. m. timorensis* (7b), formerly considered a full species, occurs on Timor. VOICE: A monotonously repeated *klpklpzeeep*. HABITAT: Bushes and grassy areas at forest edges, and cleared slopes with scattered trees and scrub. DISTRIBUTION: Resident in Java, Bali and Timor in the Lesser Sundas.

8 LONG-TAILED BUSH WARBLER *Locustella caudata* 16–18cm FIELD NOTES: Forages alone or in pairs, on or close to the ground; when disturbed, runs for cover like a rodent. VOICE: A high-pitched, insect-like *to-to-zeeee*, *trp trp twzzz*, *zeeeuuu* or *zeee-zuuu*. HABITAT: Forest undergrowth and dense secondary growth in forest clearings. DISTRIBUTION: Endemic to the Philippines.

9 FRIENDLY BUSH WARBLER *Locustella accentor* 15cm FIELD NOTES: Forages on or close to the ground, alone or in pairs. Often follows people in the forest, picking up disturbed invertebrates. VOICE: A repeated *dzhee-dzhee-zeeeeee-ah* or *trrp trrrp trzzzzz*. HABITAT: Damp, dark rainforest undergrowth with moss-covered dead tree trunks or branches. DISTRIBUTION: Endemic to Sabah in N Borneo.

10 CHESTNUT-BACKED BUSH WARBLER *Locustella castanea* 14–15cm FIELD NOTES: Occurs singly or in pairs; forages on or close to the ground, gleaning insects from foliage and twigs. *L. c. disturbans* (10b) is found on Buru in the S Moluccas. VOICE: A buzzy, rising and falling three-note trill, repeated at five-second intervals; calls include a *tsp* or (on Seram) a soft, repeated *zit-oh-zit*. HABITAT: Dense undergrowth, vines and tangles in montane forest, edges of upland grassland and forest edges. DISTRIBUTION: Resident in Sulawesi and the S Moluccas.

148 GRASSHOPPER WARBLERS; GRASSBIRDS; REED WARBLERS

1 LANCEOLATED WARBLER *Locustella lanceolata* 12cm FIELD NOTES: Secretive; tends to forage in low vegetation or on the ground. VOICE: A continual thin, pulsing reeling; calls include a loud, urgent *chirr-chirr*, an explosive *tzht-tzht-tzht* and a repeated *pit*. HABITAT: Scrub, grass and weedy vegetation, often in marshy areas. DISTRIBUTION: Winter visitor to Sumatra, W Java, Borneo and the Philippines; vagrant in the N Moluccas.

2 PALLAS'S GRASSHOPPER WARBLER *Locustella certhiola* 13–14cm FIELD NOTES: Creeps mouse-like among tall grasses and reeds, and in thick cover. VOICE: A high-pitched twittering that leads into a ringing *che-che-che-che-che*; calls include a repeated *pwit* and a rapid *tiktiktiktik*. HABITAT: Tall grasses, reeds and tangled vegetation in marshes or other wetlands. DISTRIBUTION: Winter visitor to Sumatra, Java and Borneo.

3 GRAY'S GRASSHOPPER WARBLER *Locustella fasciolata* 16–18cm FIELD NOTES: Secretive, foraging in deep cover or among grass stems. VOICE: Song is rich and fluty, starting softly, then getting louder and finishing with a rapid, falling-away *u-chic-toi-tu-tee-chee*; calls include a trilling *cherr-cherr* and a *tschrrok*. HABITAT: Thickets, forest edges and tall grass. DISTRIBUTION: Winter visitor to the Philippines, Sulawesi, the Sula Islands and the Moluccas.

4 MIDDENDORFF'S GRASSHOPPER WARBLER *Locustella ochotensis* 13–15cm FIELD NOTES: Skulking, foraging in or under low cover. VOICE: A *drrt-chrit-chrit-chit-cherwee-cherwee-cherwee*; calls with a quiet *chit*. HABITAT: Damp scrub, grassland and marshes with emergent vegetation. DISTRIBUTION: Winter visitor to Borneo and the Philippines; vagrant in Sulawesi.

5 STRIATED GRASSBIRD *Megalurus palustris* 24–26cm FIELD NOTES: Forages in reeds and bushes. VOICE: A strong, rich warble, and a subdued whistle followed by a loud *wheeechoo*; calls include an explosive *pwit* and a harsh *chat*. HABITAT: Tall, damp grassland, reed-beds and scrub. DISTRIBUTION: Resident in Java, Bali, Borneo and the Philippines.

6 TAWNY GRASSBIRD *Megalurus timoriensis* 22–24cm FIELD NOTES: Skulking; often uses the tops of grass stems as a look-out. VOICE: Song contains ascending and descending, rattling, ringing notes. Calls include a *tsip*, *chir-up* or *threr-up*. HABITAT: Reed-beds and grassland with scattered trees and shrubs. DISTRIBUTION: Resident in the Philippines, Sulawesi, the Lesser Sundas and the S Moluccas.

7 BUFF-BANDED THICKETBIRD *Buettikoferella bivittata* 18–19cm FIELD NOTES: Skulks low down in dense thickets. VOICE: A staccato *zi-ka-cheet* or *tswi-chit*, a harsh, descending trill and a high-pitched rattle. HABITAT: Patches of monsoon forest, secondary woodland and scrub. DISTRIBUTION: Endemic to Timor in the E Lesser Sundas.

8 STREAKED REED WARBLER (SPECKLED REED WARBLER) *Acrocephalus sorghophilus* 13cm FIELD NOTES: Forages low down in vegetation, climbs reed stems and sings from a prominent perch. VOICE: A series or rasping, churring notes. HABITAT: Reed-beds and boggy grassland, often near water. DISTRIBUTION: Winter visitor to Luzon, Negros and Bohol in the Philippines.

9 BLACK-BROWED REED WARBLER *Acrocephalus bistrigiceps* 12cm FIELD NOTES: Shy and skulking, foraging in thick cover. VOICE: Short phrases, interspersed with rasping and churring notes; calls include a soft *dzak* and a harsh *chur*. HABITAT: Emergent vegetation near marshes or watery areas. DISTRIBUTION: Rare winter visitor or vagrant to N Sumatra.

10 CLAMOROUS REED WARBLER *Acrocephalus stentoreus* 18cm FIELD NOTES: Clambers low down among reed stems or in bushes. VOICE: Variable; generally a loud combination of grating, chattering, squeaky and sweet notes. Calls include a harsh *chack* and a low *churr*. HABITAT: Riverside, lakeside and pondside reed-beds, riverside scrub and paddyfields. DISTRIBUTION: Resident in W Java, S Borneo, the Philippines and Wallacea.

11 ORIENTAL REED WARBLER *Acrocephalus orientalis* 18cm FIELD NOTES: Clambers among reed stems or in bushes. VOICE: Deep, guttural churring and croaking, interspersed with warbling phrases; calls include a quiet *krak*, a *chichikarr* and a hoarse *si-si-si-si*. HABITAT: Reed-beds and scrub, usually not far from water. DISTRIBUTION: Winter visitor to Sumatra, Borneo, the Philippines, Sulawesi and Wallacea.

149 TAILORBIRDS

1 MOUNTAIN TAILORBIRD *Phyllergates cuculatus* 11–12cm FIELD NOTES: Elusive. Forages in low thickets; sometimes makes aerial sallies after flying insects. Juvenile has a grey forehead, crown and nape. *P. c. riedeli* (1b) is found in N Sulawesi; *P. c. dumasi* (1c) resides on Buru and Seram in the S Moluccas. VOICE: A thin, high-pitched *pee-pee-peeeeeeee-pee-pee* or variations on this theme. Calls include a dry, descending trill, a low, buzzy *kiz-ki*, a thin *trit* and a nasal chatter. HABITAT: Bushy thickets and undergrowth in broadleaved evergreen forest. DISTRIBUTION: Widespread resident, but patchily distributed over much of the region.

2 RUFOUS-HEADED TAILORBIRD *Phyllergates heterolaemus* 11cm FIELD NOTES: Usually seen in pairs or small parties, foraging in thick, tangled vegetation; occasionally shows itself when flitting out after a passing insect. VOICE: A high-pitched *tee-tee lee-oot tee-lee-leee*; when alarmed, utters a rapid, trilled *trip-p-p-p-p-p-p-p-p*, often repeated continuously. HABITAT: High-elevation forest and secondary scrub. DISTRIBUTION: Endemic to Mindanao in the S Philippines.

3 COMMON TAILORBIRD *Orthotomus sutorius* 10–14cm FIELD NOTES: Forages in cover or on the ground under cover; often seen in pairs. Breeding males develop long central tail feathers. VOICE: A loud, monotonous *te-chee-te-chee-te-chee* and a single *twee*. HABITAT: Light forest, secondary forest and bushy gardens. DISTRIBUTION: Resident in Java.

4 RUFOUS-FRONTED TAILORBIRD *Orthotomus frontalis* 12cm FIELD NOTES: Forages in low undergrowth. VOICE: A drawn-out *de de drer-r-r-rw*, likened to a bouncing table-tennis ball. HABITAT: Lowland forest, forest edges and clearings with rank secondary growth. DISTRIBUTION: Endemic to the EC and S Philippines.

5 PHILIPPINE TAILORBIRD *Orthotomus castaneiceps* 13cm FIELD NOTES: Noisy. Forages in low, tangled undergrowth, usually near the ground. VOICE: A *twee-pee twee-doo* and a more complex series of similar notes. HABITAT: Lowland forest, forest edges, clearings with secondary growth and dense, tangled undergrowth. DISTRIBUTION: Endemic to the C Philippines.

6 TRILLING TAILORBIRD *Orthotomus chloronotus* 13cm FIELD NOTES: Formerly considered a race of the previous species; actions are similar. VOICE: A bubbly, pulsing *tuuut tuuutt p-p-p-p*; calls include a scolding *speeee*. HABITAT: Lowland forest, especially forest edges and clearings with secondary growth and associated tangled undergrowth. DISTRIBUTION: Endemic to N Luzon in the Philippines.

7 GREY-BACKED TAILORBIRD *Orthotomus derbianus* 11cm FIELD NOTES: Keeps hidden while foraging in thick undergrowth. VOICE: A loud, pulsing *chew-ee-peee*, *twee-purrr* or simple *purr*, and a buzzing *eeeeh eeeeh eeeeh*. HABITAT: Lowland secondary forest, forest edges and clearings with tangled undergrowth. DISTRIBUTION: Endemic to S Luzon in the Philippines.

8 RUFOUS-TAILED TAILORBIRD *Orthotomus sericeus* 12–14cm FIELD NOTES: Shy and skulking; keeps to dense foliage, usually alone or in pairs. VOICE: A variety of loud, rapid, disyllabic notes; calls include a harsh *terr-terr*, a wheezy *tzee-tzee-tzee*, a sharp *twip-twip-twip* and a scolding *speee-speee-speee*. HABITAT: Forest edges, overgrown clearings, shrubby cultivation and overgrown gardens. DISTRIBUTION: Resident in Sumatra, Borneo and the W and SW Philippines.

150 TAILORBIRDS

1 DARK-NECKED TAILORBIRD *Orthotomus atrogularis* 11–12cm FIELD NOTES: Shy and unobtrusive. Forages in low vegetation, but works up to higher levels. *O. a. humphreysi* (1b) occurs in NE Borneo. VOICE: A high-pitched, shivery *pirra pirra…* and a trilled *kri-kri-kri*; on Borneo, also said to utter a high, clear *dweet-dweet dweet-dweet*. HABITAT: Primary and secondary forest, secondary growth, forest edges, bushy thickets and gardens. DISTRIBUTION: Resident in Sumatra and Borneo.

2 OLIVE-BACKED TAILORBIRD *Orthotomus sepium* 12cm FIELD NOTES: Active forager from the understorey to the canopy. VOICE: Various single notes, rhythmically repeated monotonously, such as *chew-chew-chew…* or *turr-turr-tsee-weet --- tsee-weet*; also utters a quavering nasal call and a loud, trilled *tree-yip*. HABITAT: Inland secondary forest, forest edges, bamboo thickets and bushy edges of cultivation. DISTRIBUTION: Endemic to Java, Bali and Lombok in the W Lesser Sundas.

3 ASHY TAILORBIRD *Orthotomus ruficeps* 11–12cm FIELD NOTES: Occurs in pairs or in small parties, foraging from the undergrowth up to the canopy. VOICE: A repeated *chip-wee chip-wee…* or similar; calls include a *trrree-yip*, a plaintive *cho-choee*, a spluttering *prrrt*, a rolling *prit-u* and a harsh *thieu*. HABITAT: Secondary forest, bamboo thickets, mangrove swamps, coastal scrub, peat-swamp forest and roadside vegetation. DISTRIBUTION: Resident in Sumatra, Java and Borneo.

4 YELLOW-BREASTED TAILORBIRD *Orthotomus samarensis* 12cm FIELD NOTES: Shy forager in dense undergrowth, usually in pairs; rarely comes into the open. VOICE: A long, descending, stuttering trill that slows, levels out and then becomes a monotonous throbbing, transcribed as *dededede-de-de-de-de-dep-dep-dep-deep-deep-deep-deeup-deeup-deeup…* HABITAT: Dense forest undergrowth in lowlands and forest edges; sometimes found along watercourses, gullies and dry streambeds. DISTRIBUTION: Endemic to the EC Philippines.

5 BLACK-HEADED TAILORBIRD *Orthotomus nigriceps* 12cm FIELD NOTES: Shy and elusive forager in dense undergrowth, rarely appearing in the open. VOICE: A long, descending, stuttering trill, very similar to that of the previous species but more metallic and ringing; also utters an agitated, descending *ssiirrrrpppppp* and a ringing *key-e ei*. HABITAT: Dense forest undergrowth in lowlands. DISTRIBUTION: Endemic to the SE Philippines.

6 WHITE-EARED TAILORBIRD *Orthotomus cinereiceps* 12–13cm FIELD NOTES: Usually seen in pairs foraging in dense undergrowth; rarely seen in the open. VOICE: Similar to that of the two previous species, but less explosive, transcribed as *dededede-dep-dep-deep-deeup deee-up deee-up deee-up deee-up*; also utters an agitated *chat-chat-chat-chat-chat*. HABITAT: Dense, tangled undergrowth in lowland forest clearings or forest edges. DISTRIBUTION: Endemic to W Mindanao in the Philippines

151 LEAF WARBLERS

1 ARCTIC WARBLER *Phylloscopus borealis* 12–13cm FIELD NOTES: Active, agile, mainly arboreal forager; frequently flicks wings and tail. Often part of mixed-species feeding parties. VOICE: A shivering trill, interspersed with call notes; calls include a husky *dzit*, *dz-dzit* or *chizzick*. HABITAT: Open woodland, secondary and selectively logged forest, forest edges, monsoon woodland, mangroves and wooded gardens. DISTRIBUTION: Winter visitor to the region.

2 JAPANESE LEAF WARBLER *Phylloscopus xanthodryas* 12–13cm
FIELD NOTES: Formerly considered a race of the previous species; actions and habits are similar. VOICE: Calls similar to those of the previous species. HABITAT: Woodlands, secondary forest and mangroves. DISTRIBUTION: Winter visitor to the region.

3 YELLOW-BROWED WARBLER *Phylloscopus inornatus* 11–12cm FIELD NOTES: Active forager at all tree levels; picks prey from foliage, hovers to glean insects from outer leaves or makes fly-catching sallies to capture flying insects. VOICE: Calls include a high *tswe-eeet* or *tsweet*. HABITAT: Woodland, secondary growth, parks and gardens. DISTRIBUTION: Vagrant in Sumatra and Borneo.

4 RADDE'S WARBLER *Phylloscopus schwarzi* 13–14cm FIELD NOTES: Skulking; movements are quite slow. Forages in thick vegetation or on the ground under dense undergrowth. Frequently flicks wings and tail. VOICE: Calls include a *chek* and a *pwit*. HABITAT: Low vegetation in open forests, forest clearings and edges, and scrub and tall grass in open areas. DISTRIBUTION: Vagrant in the Philippines.

5 DUSKY WARBLER *Phylloscopus fuscatus* 11–12cm FIELD NOTES: Skulking. Active forager in thick vegetation or among low branches of trees. VOICE: Calls include a sharp *chac* or *chett*, likened to two pebbles being tapped together. HABITAT: Open areas with low bushes, often near water. DISTRIBUTION: Vagrant in the Philippines.

6 EASTERN CROWNED WARBLER *Phylloscopus coronatus* 12–13cm
FIELD NOTES: Active forager at all levels. VOICE: A rising *pitschu-pitsch-wii* or a longer *tuweeu tuweeu tuweeu tsu-eet tsu-eet-tzaa*; calls include a soft *phit phit* or a harsher *dwee*. HABITAT: Mixed and evergreen forest, forest edges, low trees, bushes and mangroves. DISTRIBUTION: Winter visitor or vagrant to Sumatra and Java.

7 IJIMA'S LEAF WARBLER *Phylloscopus ijimae* 12cm FIELD NOTES: Often makes fly-catching sorties, otherwise a typical active forager in foliage. VOICE: Calls include a loud *twee* and a thin *phi-phi-phi*. HABITAT: Deciduous and mixed subtropical evergreen forest, forest edges, bamboo and tangled scrub. DISTRIBUTION: Vagrant in the Philippines.

8 PHILIPPINE LEAF WARBLER *Phylloscopus olivaceus* 11–13cm FIELD NOTES: Forages alone or as part of mixed-species feeding parties; picks insects from the outer foliage of bushes or trees. VOICE: A frequently repeated, short, sharp *prrrr-chi*. HABITAT: Lowland and middle-elevation forest and forest edges. DISTRIBUTION: Endemic to the Philippines.

9 MOUNTAIN LEAF WARBLER *Phylloscopus trivirgatus* 10–11cm
FIELD NOTES: Favours the middle level and canopy, feeding on insects picked from among foliage or by hovering to take them from outer leaves. Forages alone, in pairs or in small groups, and as part of mixed-species flocks. *P. t. kinabaluensis* (9b) is found in N Borneo. VOICE: An unmusical *tisiwi-tsuwiri-swit* or faster *tsee-chee-chee-weet*; calls include a *cheecheechee* or a jangling *tersiwit*. HABITAT: Submontane and montane forest, and forest edges. DISTRIBUTION: Resident in Sumatra, Java, Bali, Borneo and the W Lesser Sundas.

1

2

3

4

5

6

7

8

9

9b
kinabaluensis

152 LEAF WARBLERS; WARBLERS

1 NEGROS LEAF WARBLER *Phylloscopus nigrorum* 10–11cm FIELD NOTES: Regularly seen in flocks, gleaning from leaves and branches. Formerly considered conspecific with the Mountain Leaf Warbler (Plate 151). VOICE: Variable, including an explosive *chi-chi-chi-chi-pa-aw*, a *chi-cherru* and a *sweet sweet chu*. HABITAT: Submontane and montane forest. DISTRIBUTION: Endemic to the Philippines.

2 LEMON-THROATED LEAF WARBLER *Phylloscopus cebuensis* 11–12cm
FIELD NOTES: Forages alone or in mixed-species feeding parties. VOICE: A loud, repeated *chi-chi-oo* or *chip chi-u*. HABITAT: Lowland forest and forest edges. DISTRIBUTION: Endemic to the WC and N Philippines.

3 TIMOR LEAF WARBLER *Phylloscopus presbytes* 11cm FIELD NOTES: Occurs singly, in small groups or in mixed-species flocks; forages in the middle level and the canopy, gleaning insects from leaves. VOICE: A short, rapid, staccato jangle of sweet, high-pitched notes; in Flores, gives a short, high-pitched, rising and falling warble. HABITAT: Lowland and hill semi-evergreen forest and woodland; birds on Flores occur in primary and slightly degraded montane forest, secondary scrub and *Casuarina* forest. DISTRIBUTION: Endemic to the Lesser Sundas.

4 SULAWESI LEAF WARBLER *Phylloscopus sarasinorum* 11cm FIELD NOTES: Gleans and hover-gleans from foliage in the mid-storey and canopy, alone, in pairs, or in small groups; also joins mixed-species feeding parties. VOICE: A weak, variable, rapid series of high-pitched, repetitive warbles and trills. HABITAT: Montane moss forest and forest edges. DISTRIBUTION: Endemic to Sulawesi.

5 ISLAND LEAF WARBLER *Phylloscopus maforensis* 10–11cm FIELD NOTES: Active, gleaning from leaves in the mid-storey and the crowns of small trees. Found singly, in pairs, in small groups or in mixed-species feeding flocks. VOICE: A rapid series of sweet, sibilant, tinkling notes or a sweet, melodious warble. HABITAT: Hill and montane primary and secondary forest. DISTRIBUTION: Resident in the Moluccas.

6 YELLOW-BREASTED WARBLER *Seicercus montis* 9–10cm FIELD NOTES: Forages mainly in foliage of the understorey or mid-canopy at forest edges; feeds by gleaning, hovering or fly-catching. Regular member of mixed-species feeding parties. Birds on the Lesser Sundas lack the yellow rump. VOICE: A very high-pitched, rising and then fading *zizizizizizi-azuuuu*, interspersed with *chit chit* notes. HABITAT: Subtropical humid forest with a well-developed understorey and stands of bamboo. DISTRIBUTION: Resident in Sumatra, Borneo, Palawan in the Philippines and the Lesser Sundas.

7 CHESTNUT-CROWNED WARBLER *Seicercus castaniceps* 9–10cm
FIELD NOTES: Forages in the upper canopy. Flicks wings and tail. VOICE: A very high-pitched *see see see-see-see-see-see*; calls include a quiet *chik* and a *chee-chee*. HABITAT: Subtropical humid montane forests. DISTRIBUTION: Resident in Sumatra.

8 SUNDA WARBLER *Seicercus grammiceps* 10cm FIELD NOTES: Active forager in the understorey and lower canopy of forest edges; post-breeding, often found in mixed-species feeding groups. *S. g. sumatrensis* (8b) occurs on Sumatra. VOICE: A ringing, high-pitched *chee-chee-chechee*; calls with a buzzing *turrr*. HABITAT: Subtropical humid montane forest with a well-developed understorey. DISTRIBUTION: Endemic to Sumatra, Java and Bali.

9 YELLOW-BELLIED WARBLER *Abroscopus superciliaris* 9cm FIELD NOTES: Forages mainly in the understorey, gleaning or making short fly-catching sorties; frequently flicks wings. VOICE: A sweet, high *dee-dee-dir-rit-tit-dewwt*; also a continuous twittering. HABITAT: Undergrowth, especially bamboo in submontane and montane forest. DISTRIBUTION: Resident in Sumatra, Java and Borneo.

153 GROUND WARBLERS; WREN-BABBLERS

1 CORDILLERA GROUND WARBLER *Robsonius rabori* 20–22cm FIELD NOTES: Forages among leaf litter or wood debris by walking or hopping; also said to run through the forest like a small rail. Often cocks tail. VOICE: A variable, very high-pitched insect-like *tsui-ts sii uu ee, tsui-ts ssuuu ee, tit-tuuits ts ssu eeet* or similar. HABITAT: Lowland forest and secondary growth. DISTRIBUTION: Endemic to NC Luzon in the Philippines.

2 SIERRA MADRE GROUND WARBLER *Robsonius thompsoni* 20–22cm FIELD NOTES: Recently discovered. Forages on the ground, walking and running around in search of prey. VOICE: High-pitched and ventriloquial, therefore very difficult to locate. HABITAT: Forest with a dense understorey. DISTRIBUTION: Endemic to N Luzon in the Philippines.

3 BICOL GROUND WARBLER *Robsonius sorsogonensis* 20–22cm FIELD NOTES: Walks, runs or hops while foraging among leaves on the forest floor; often fans and cocks tail. VOICE: A high-pitched *tit ----tsuuuu-tsiiiiii*, and a *tssuit swïieeii, tssuu sit suuiee, tssiiuu sweeiieet* or *tit-tsuee-swiieet*. HABITAT: Broadleaved evergreen forest, forest edges, secondary growth and bamboo; has a liking for areas with limestone rocks or outcrops. DISTRIBUTION: Endemic to S Luzon in the Philippines.

4 SUMATRAN WREN-BABBLER *Rimator albostriatus* 13cm FIELD NOTES: Forages on the forest floor or on fallen trees or branches. VOICE: A short, clear, bell-like *puu* or *puh*; when excited, mixes these with a series of *whipu ip* or *whipu-wip* notes. Calls include a low *wrrrt, trrrp* or *trr h*. HABITAT: Lower montane oak and laurel forest. DISTRIBUTION: Endemic to W Sumatra.

5 BORNEAN WREN-BABBLER *Ptilocichla leucogrammica* 15–16cm FIELD NOTES: Usually seen in pairs or small groups foraging on the forest floor among leaf litter and rotting, fallen branches. VOICE: A mournful *doo-dee* or *doo-doo-dee*; calls include a spluttering *churr* or *prr prr*. HABITAT: Primary, secondary, logged, peat-swamp and upland heath forest. DISTRIBUTION: Endemic to Borneo.

6 STRIATED WREN-BABBLER *Ptilocichla mindanensis* 13–14cm FIELD NOTES: Found singly, in pairs or in small parties foraging in low vegetation or among leaf litter. *P. m. basilanica* (6b) occurs on Basilan Island off W Mindanao. VOICE: A descending *hi hi hi uu uu uu uu-u* and a penetrating *hiuu-hiuu-hiuu-hiuu…*; calls include a *trrr-t, trrr trrr* and a *wh rrp*. HABITAT: Primary and logged forest. DISTRIBUTION: Endemic to the Philippines.

7 FALCATED WREN-BABBLER *Ptilocichla falcata* 19–20cm FIELD NOTES: Forages by walking or hopping on the ground, or scrambling around in dense thickets and fallen trees. VOICE: A loud, mournful, undulating *hiuuu-huu oo* or similar. HABITAT: Primary broadleaved evergreen forest, often near streams; also bamboo forest. DISTRIBUTION: Endemic to Palawan in the W Philippines.

154 WREN-BABBLERS

1 STRIPED WREN-BABBLER *Kenopia striata* 14–15cm FIELD NOTES: Forages on or close to the ground among leaf litter and fallen branches. VOICE: A short, monotonous *chuuii, chiuuu* or *chi-uuu*; calls include a soft *pee-pee-pee*, a soft, frog-like *churrh-churrh-churrh* and short, twangy nasal notes. HABITAT: Broadleaved evergreen forest, lightly logged forest and upland heath forest. DISTRIBUTION: Resident in Sumatra and Borneo.

2 LARGE WREN-BABBLER *Napothera macrodactyla* 19cm FIELD NOTES: Forages singly, in pairs or in small parties, on or close to the ground; sings from higher perches. *N. m. beauforti* (2b) occurs in Sumatra. VOICE: Very variable, consisting of short, loud, clear, whistled phrases, repeated every few seconds. HABITAT: Broadleaved evergreen, selectively logged and bamboo forest. DISTRIBUTION: Resident in Sumatra and Java.

3 RUSTY-BREASTED WREN-BABBLER *Napothera rufipectus* 18–19cm FIELD NOTES: Forages on or near the ground, generally under dense vegetation cover. VOICE: A clear, piping *hi-hi-hi-hi-hi-huuuuh* or *ip ip ip ip ip ip-puuuuuh*; during duets, one bird utters a continuous *ip ip ip ip ip…*, while the second bird utters an undulating *hu wip ii* or *hu-wip ee*. HABITAT: Montane primary broadleaved evergreen forest and dense roadside vegetation in conifer plantations. DISTRIBUTION: Endemic to Sumatra.

4 BLACK-THROATED WREN-BABBLER *Napothera atrigularis* 18cm FIELD NOTES: Forages mainly on the ground among leaf litter, beneath tree roots and by probing in tree-trunk crevices. Usually found in small parties. VOICE: Duets, one bird giving a long series of clear, bell-like notes, while the second adds a slightly descending *iuuh-iuh-iuh… iuuh-uh-uh*; calls include a *we-ah we-ah we-ah* and a nasal, coarse *krar krar*. HABITAT: Lowland primary broadleaved evergreen forest, old secondary forest and logged forest. DISTRIBUTION: Endemic to Borneo.

5 MARBLED WREN-BABBLER *Napothera marmorata* 21–22cm FIELD NOTES: Shy and secretive, foraging on or near the ground, in undergrowth and often in damp areas. VOICE: A clear, whistled *puuu-chiiii, pyuuu-jhiiii, puuui-jhiiii, piuuu-whiiii, uuuu-jhiii* or a single *piuuu*. HABITAT: Lower montane broadleaved evergreen forest. DISTRIBUTION: Resident in Sumatra.

6 MOUNTAIN WREN-BABBLER *Napothera crassa* 14cm FIELD NOTES: Forages in low vegetation and sometimes at higher levels. Skulking but can be very tame. VOICE: A shrill, piping *hi-hi-hi hu hi, hi hi hi-hu-hi* or *hi-hi-hi hu hi-hu-hu*; during duets, one bird sings song while the second utters a repeated, descending *hii-hii-hiiu*. Calls include a quick *whit, whik* or *whiti chrrh*. HABITAT: Broadleaved evergreen forest, favouring dense, dark areas broken by steep slopes and rocky ravines; also forest edges, low bamboo, and densely vegetated banks and beds of small streams. DISTRIBUTION: Endemic to Borneo.

7 EYEBROWED WREN-BABBLER *Napothera epilepidota* 10–11cm FIELD NOTES: Generally seen in pairs or in small groups foraging on the forest floor among fallen leaves. VOICE: A thin, clear, falling *cheeeeu, cheeeoo* or *piiiiiu*, repeated at intervals of 2–5 seconds. Calls include a squeaky *chikachik-chikachik-chikachik* and *skreeti-skreeti*, and a *prrrt-prrrt-prrrt* or similar when alarmed; also a loud, rising *chyurk* and a low *pit pit pit*. HABITAT: Broadleaved evergreen, mixed dipterocarp, damp gallery, conifer and secondary forest, and in bamboo. DISTRIBUTION: Resident in Sumatra, Java and Borneo.

8 PYGMY WREN-BABBLER *Pnoepyga pusilla* 7–9cm FIELD NOTES: Usually seen alone or in pairs, foraging on the ground in well-shaded areas and moderately dense undergrowth. *P. p. timorensis* (8b) occurs on Timor VOICE: A descending *tseei - tss – tsu*, a *tss-tsip*, a *tss-drrii* and, on Timor, a *tsiee tsu tsii tssu*; calls include a sharp, sibilant *tchit* or *chit* and, on Timor, a rising *tss u u u u u u u u u-ssi-ssi*. HABITAT: Montane forest, tall secondary forest, scrub and, occasionally, roadside regrowth. DISTRIBUTION: Resident in Sumatra, Java and Flores and Timor in the Lesser Sundas.

2b
beauforti

1

2

3

4

5

6

7

8

8b
timorensis

155 SCIMITAR BABBLER; BABBLERS

1 BAGOBO BABBLER *Leonardina woodi* 19–20cm FIELD NOTES: Very secretive. Forages on or close to the forest floor. VOICE: A very high-pitched, tinkling *seeeeep seepseep seep*, repeated every 4–5 seconds. HABITAT: Primary broadleaved evergreen and montane evergreen forest, forest edges, ridgetop forest and transition (lowland/montane) forest. DISTRIBUTION: Endemic to the S Philippines.

2 CHESTNUT-BACKED SCIMITAR BABBLER *Pomatorhinus montanus* 19–21cm FIELD NOTES: Usually forages in undergrowth and the lower middle storey, singly, in pairs or in small parties; also joins mixed-species feeding flocks. VOICE: A quick *wu-pwi*, followed by a second bird uttering a *wu-pu pu pu pu pu pu*; on Java, first bird gives a *hu-wi* or *wihu-wi*, and the second follows with a low *wupup-wupup-wupup-wupup*. HABITAT: Broadleaved evergreen forest. DISTRIBUTION: Resident in Sumatra, Java, Bali and Borneo.

3 SULAWESI BABBLER *Trichastoma celebense* 15–16cm FIELD NOTES: Forages mainly on or near the ground with mouse-like actions. *T. c. finschi* (3b) occurs in SW Sulawesi. VOICE: A loud, cheerful phrase of 2–5 liquid, fluty, melancholy whistles, sometimes answered, presumably by female, with a down-slurred *kiew kiew kiew*. HABITAT: Primary forest, secondary woodland and thickets at forest edges. DISTRIBUTION: Endemic to Sulawesi.

4 WHITE-CHESTED BABBLER *Trichastoma rostratum* 15–17cm FIELD NOTES: Forages on or near the ground, and on roots, rocks or branches at the water's edge. VOICE: Variable, including a repeated, high-pitched *wi-ti-ti*, *chui-chwi-chew* or *chr chr oo-iwee*; calls with harsh rattles. HABITAT: Riverine broadleaved evergreen forest, secondary and freshwater peat-swamp forest, and sometimes mangroves. DISTRIBUTION: Resident in Sumatra and Borneo.

5 FERRUGINOUS BABBLER *Trichastoma bicolor* 16–18cm FIELD NOTES: Forages mainly in the lower to middle storey, in pairs or loose parties. VOICE: Various jolly phrases and a repeated, loud, sharp *u-wit* or *u-wee*; calls include an explosive *wit* and dry, rasping notes. HABITAT: Primary and secondary forest. DISTRIBUTION: Resident in Sumatra and Borneo.

6 ABBOTT'S BABBLER *Malacocincla abbotti* 15–17cm FIELD NOTES: Forages among leaf litter, alone or in pairs. VOICE: A series of 3–4 rich, fluty, liquid, whistled notes; calls include a mewing, a purring and an explosive *cheu* interspersed with nervous *wer* notes. HABITAT: Mangroves, coastal forest, riverside forest, secondary forest, forest edges and scrub. DISTRIBUTION: Resident in Sumatra, Java and Borneo.

7 HORSFIELD'S BABBLER *Malacocincla sepiaria* 15–17cm FIELD NOTES: Forages on the ground, in low vegetation and, occasionally, at higher levels. VOICE: A strident 3–4-note *wi-cho-teuu* or *tip top tiu*; Javan birds, give a plodding *wip-chup-chu--puiii*. HABITAT: Broadleaved evergreen forest, usually near water. DISTRIBUTION: Resident in Sumatra, Java, Bali and Borneo.

8 BLACK-BROWED BABBLER *Malacocincla perspicillata* 15–16cm FIELD NOTES: Known from only one specimen collected in the 1840s; actions presumed to be similar to the previous species. VOICE: Unrecorded. HABITAT: Lowland forest. DISTRIBUTION: Endemic to Banjarmasin in SE Borneo.

9 SHORT-TAILED BABBLER *Malacocincla malaccensis* 13–15cm FIELD NOTES: Forages on or close to the ground, usually in pairs. VOICE: A series of 6–7 loud, rich, descending, whistled notes, introduced by a dry trill; calls include a harsh, mechanical *chututututututut…*, interspersed with soft *yer* notes; also a *fit-zweet* or *fit-fit-zweet* and a repeated *pew*. HABITAT: Broadleaved evergreen forest, peat-swamp forest and secondary growth, thickets and scrub. DISTRIBUTION: Resident in Sumatra and Borneo.

10 ASHY-HEADED BABBLER *Malacocincla cinereiceps* 13cm FIELD NOTES: Often seen hopping on the ground or foraging in low vegetation, usually alone. VOICE: A series of 4–9 husky, nasal *jhew*, *chiew* or *jhew* notes, sometimes introduced by 1–4 stuttering notes. HABITAT: Lowland and mid-elevation forest, secondary growth and scrub. DISTRIBUTION: Endemic to the W Philippines.

156 BABBLERS

1 SUMATRAN BABBLER *Pellorneum buettikoferi* 15cm FIELD NOTES: Skulks in undergrowth or forages on the ground. VOICE: A loud, repeated *pwiy pii biyo* or *pii byopwiyu*. HABITAT: Primary and logged forest with undergrowth, and forest edges. DISTRIBUTION: Endemic to Sumatra.

2 TEMMINCK'S BABBLER *Pellorneum pyrrogenys* 15cm FIELD NOTES: Forages on the ground in undergrowth, although reported working up vines to the canopy, searching for insects. *P. p. canicapillus* (2b) occurs in N Borneo. VOICE: A shrill *witichew witichew witichew, wi-chu wi-chu* or single *chew*; also utters a skipping *tip ip ip ip ip-zrriiu*. HABITAT: Undergrowth and dense vegetation at the edge of clearings in lower montane and montane primary forest. DISTRIBUTION: Resident in Java and Borneo.

3 BLACK-CAPPED BABBLER *Pellorneum capistratum* 16–17cm FIELD NOTES: Walks or runs while foraging among leaf litter. *P. c. morrelli* (3b) occurs in N and E Borneo; *P. c. nigrocapitatum* (3c) is found in Sumatra. VOICE: A loud *ti-tuu* or *pi-tuu*; Bornean birds utter a thinner *ti-ii-uu* or *ti iiuu*, while Sumatran birds sing with a high-pitched *teeu*. Calls include a *yeryeryer*, a nasal *nwit-nwit-nwit* and a liquid, rising *pooeet*. HABITAT: Primary broadleaved evergreen forest, logged forest, peat-swamp forest, overgrown plantations, and bamboo and palm thickets. DISTRIBUTION: Resident in Sumatra, Java and Borneo.

4 MOUSTACHED BABBLER *Malacopteron magnirostre* 18cm FIELD NOTES: Forages mainly in the middle storey, in small flocks or mixed-species feeding groups; gleans from foliage and trunks. *M. m. cinereocapilla* (4b) occurs in Borneo. VOICE: A clear, sweet *tii-tu-ti-tu* or *ti-tiee-ti-ti-tu*; Bornean birds give a *doo-da-doo* followed by four descending notes. Calls include an explosive *whit*, interspersed with a buzzy *bzzii*. HABITAT: Primary broadleaved evergreen forest, peat-swamp forest, logged forest, and upland and old plantations. DISTRIBUTION: Resident in Sumatra and Borneo.

5 SOOTY-CAPPED BABBLER *Malacopteron affine* 15–17cm FIELD NOTES: Gleans insects from the foliage of small trees, bushes and vine tangles. VOICE: A series of 6–9 rising and falling whistles, sometimes introduced by scratchy or jumbled notes; calls include a sharp *which-it* or *pit-wit*. HABITAT: Broadleaved evergreen forest, swamp forest and forest edges, often with nearby water. DISTRIBUTION: Resident in Sumatra and Borneo.

6 SCALY-CROWNED BABBLER *Malacopteron cinereum* 14–16cm FIELD NOTES: Active and agile forager in the middle storey, often in parties. VOICE: Variable, transcribed as *dit-dit-dit-dit-dit-dit-du-du-du-du-du-du-phu-phu-phu-phu-w-wiwiwiwiwi-wi-wi-wi-wu* or similar; calls include a subdued *chit-chit* or *chreu-chreu*, and a shrill *chit*, *tcheu* or *titu*. HABITAT: Primary broadleaved evergreen forest, secondary growth, lowland forest and coastal forest. DISTRIBUTION: Resident in Sumatra, S Java and Borneo.

7 RUFOUS-CROWNED BABBLER *Malacopteron magnum* 18–20cm FIELD NOTES: Forages mainly in the middle storey and undergrowth, in pairs, small parties or as part of mixed-species flocks. VOICE: A three-part song, transcribed as *phu-phu-phu-phi chuwee-chuwee-chuwee-chuwu-chuwu chut-chut-chut-chut-chut*. HABITAT: Primary broadleaved evergreen, mixed dipterocarp, logged, upland heath and stunted ridgetop forest; also mangroves and abandoned plantations. DISTRIBUTION: Resident in Sumatra and Borneo.

8 MELODIOUS BABBLER *Malacopteron palawanense* 17–18cm FIELD NOTES: Forages in the middle and lower storeys, alone or in small parties; noted picking insects from dead leaves caught in bamboo canopy. VOICE: A loud series of mournful, clear, alternating, high and low whistles that increase in volume, accompanied by a *whit-whit-whit-whit* or *chi-chi-chi-chi-chi*. HABITAT: Lowland primary and old secondary evergreen forest, bamboo and forest edges. DISTRIBUTION: Endemic to Palawan in the W Philippines.

9 GREY-BREASTED BABBLER *Malacopteron albogulare* 14–16cm FIELD NOTES: Usually forages in the understorey, alone, in pairs or in small parties. VOICE: Long, subdued, discordant phrases calls include a persistent churring. HABITAT: Broadleaved evergreen and freshwater swamp forest. DISTRIBUTION: Resident in Sumatra and Borneo.

2b *canicapillus*

3b *morrelli*

3c *nigrocapitatum*

4b *cinereocapilla*

1 FLAME-TEMPLED BABBLER *Dasycrotapha speciosa* 13cm FIELD NOTES: Forages in undergrowth, understorey bushes, vine tangles and the middle storey. VOICE: A pleasant, slurred song that starts faintly and then gets louder; calls include a soft *yir, ju, chu* or *ju-jrrr*. HABITAT: Primary, secondary and degraded secondary forest, all with a thick understorey. DISTRIBUTION: Endemic to the WC Philippines.

2 MINDANAO PYGMY BABBLER *Dasycrotapha plateni* 10cm FIELD NOTES: Occurs from the middle storey up to the lower canopy; acrobatic forager, occasionally making fly-catching sallies. VOICE: Calls include a *tchik*, a *chik-chik-chik-chik-chik*, and a quiet *tsieu-tsieu...tsieu tsieu tsieu*. HABITAT: Primary and secondary forest, forest edges and secondary growth; also in fruiting trees in abandoned cultivation. DISTRIBUTION: Endemic to the S Philippines.

3 VISAYAN PYGMY BABBLER *Dasycrotapha pygmaea* 10cm FIELD NOTES: Forages in the middle storey or occasionally higher. VOICE: Unknown; may be similar to the previous species. HABITAT: Forest, forest edges and secondary growth. DISTRIBUTION: Endemic to the EC Philippines.

4 CHESTNUT-FACED BABBLER *Zosterornis whiteheadi* 15cm FIELD NOTES: Generally forages from low down up to the canopy; regularly seen in small groups of up to 30 birds or as part of mixed-species feeding parties. VOICE: A busy, twittering *chip chip chip chip*, interspersed with *pe-chu* notes. HABITAT: Forest, secondary growth, scrub, tangled high grass and small mountainside trees. DISTRIBUTION: Endemic to the N Philippines.

5 LUZON STRIPED BABBLER *Zosterornis striatus* 13–14cm FIELD NOTES: Forages slowly and methodically from the lower to upper storey. VOICE: High-pitched *tsi* notes, accelerating to a trill and ending with a *zeeep zep*; calls include a staccato, trilled *tiptiptiptiptiptip*. HABITAT: Primary, secondary, logged and bamboo forest, forest edges, secondary growth and overgrown clearings. DISTRIBUTION: Endemic to the N Philippines.

6 PANAY STRIPED BABBLER *Zosterornis latistriatus* 15cm FIELD NOTES: Generally forages low down. VOICE: An ascending, staccato, trilling *chi chi-chi-chi-chi...*, occasionally interspersed with sharp *tsik* notes or chattering. HABITAT: Montane evergreen and mossy forest. DISTRIBUTION: Endemic to the WC Philippines.

7 NEGROS STRIPED BABBLER *Zosterornis nigrorum* 14–15cm FIELD NOTES: Forages mainly in understorey bushes and trees. VOICE: A whistled *pli-hi pli-hy pli-hy* or *plea-he plea-he plea-he plea-he-plea-hu*; calls include a soft *tsip tsip*, a short *tzi* and a high *weeet*. HABITAT: Montane, secondary and degraded forest, forest edges, and adjacent plantations and bushes. DISTRIBUTION: Endemic to the WC Philippines.

8 PALAWAN STRIPED BABBLER *Zosterornis hypogrammicus* 14–15cm FIELD NOTES: Forages mainly in the canopy, gleaning insects from leaves. VOICE: A distinctive *zeep zeep zeep zeep*, also trills and bubbling notes. HABITAT: Montane evergreen forest. DISTRIBUTION: Endemic to the W Philippines.

9 GOLDEN-CROWNED BABBLER *Sterrhoptilus dennistouni* 13–14cm FIELD NOTES: Forages alone, in pairs or in small parties, usually fairly low down. VOICE: A noisy, fast *pilit-pilit-pilit poo poo poo poo poo wi-wi-wi-wi-prr-prr-prrt*, and a quiet *wit-wit, pi* or *pri-pri-pri*. HABITAT: Primary forest, logged and degraded forest, forest edges, bamboo and areas of tall grass. DISTRIBUTION: Endemic to the N Philippines.

10 BLACK-CROWNED BABBLER *Sterrhoptilus nigrocapitatus* 13–14cm FIELD NOTES: A slow, methodical, acrobatic forager in the lower branches of trees. *S. n. affinis* (10b) occurs in the N Philippines. VOICE: A level, descending *wi-wi-wi-wu-wiu-wiu* or similar; calls include a quiet *whit, whut* or *wue wue*. HABITAT: Undergrowth in forest and forest edges. DISTRIBUTION: Endemic to N and E parts of C Philippines.

11 RUSTY-CROWNED BABBLER *Sterrhoptilus capitalis* 14–15cm FIELD NOTES: Forages fairly low down. Acrobatic gleaner, although often sits motionless. VOICE: A soft, bubbling *whit whit chew-chew-chew*. HABITAT: Primary and logged forest, and forest edges. DISTRIBUTION: Endemic to the EC and S Philippines.

158 BABBLERS

1 RUFOUS-FRONTED BABBLER *Stachyridopsis rufifrons* 12cm FIELD NOTES: Lively forager in the undergrowth, usually in pairs, small groups or as part of mixed-species feeding parties. VOICE: A monotonous, piping *tuh tuh-tuh-tuh-tuh-tuh* or *pe pe-pe-pe-pe-pe*; calls include a short, rolling *wirrri*, a fast *wu-yu-yu-yu-yu-tu-yi*, and a soft *wit* or *wi* contact call. HABITAT: Hill and submontane forest with dense undergrowth and bamboo clumps in clearings and open forest. DISTRIBUTION: Resident in Sumatra and Borneo.

2 GOLDEN BABBLER *Stachyridopsis chrysaea* 10cm FIELD NOTES: Active, agile forager in tangled undergrowth and tree foliage. VOICE: A level-toned *tu tu-tu-tu-tu-tu-tu*, *chink chink-chink-chink-chink-chink* or similar; calls include a soft twittering, a *chirik-chirik* and a scolding *chrrrrrr*. HABITAT: Hill and montane forest. DISTRIBUTION: Resident in Sumatra.

3 WHITE-BREASTED BABBLER *Stachyris grammiceps* 12cm FIELD NOTES: Forages from the undergrowth to the middle levels, in small parties or in mixed-species flocks. VOICE: A loud, rattling trill that increases in volume; calls include a *chrr chrr*, a throaty *cheek-cheek*, a soft *tik* and *chup chup* flight notes. HABITAT: Primary lowland and hill forest, shrubs along forest trails and wooded streams. DISTRIBUTION: Endemic to Java.

4 GREY-THROATED BABBLER *Stachyris nigriceps* 12cm FIELD NOTES: Constantly on the move, foraging in small parties in low growth. VOICE: A rising, high-pitched, quavering *ti tsuuuuuuuueee* or similar; calls include a constant *chi chi chi*, and a scolding *chrrrt* or *chrrrrrr-rrr-rrt*. HABITAT: Primary and secondary evergreen broadleaved forest, low secondary scrub, bamboo in forest, forest clearings, forest edges and plantations. DISTRIBUTION: Resident in Sumatra and Borneo.

5 GREY-HEADED BABBLER *Stachyris poliocephala* 13–15cm FIELD NOTES: Forages on the ground, in undergrowth and in trees. VOICE: A clear, repeated *chit-tiwi-wioo-iwee* or *yit-uip-ui-wiee*, and a higher *chu-chi-chiee* or similar. Calls include a descending *dji-dji-dji-du*, a scolding *chrrrrttutut* and soft *tip-tip-tip* contact calls. HABITAT: Secondary evergreen forest, undergrowth and scrub. DISTRIBUTION: Resident in Sumatra and Borneo.

6 SPOT-NECKED BABBLER *Stachyris strialata* 15–17cm FIELD NOTES: Shy and skulking, foraging in undergrowth and on the ground. VOICE: A simple 2–3-note whistle; calls include a scolding *tirrrirrirr* and high-pitched *tip* notes. HABITAT: Hill and mountain forest, bamboo breaks, secondary growth and scrub. DISTRIBUTION: Resident in Sumatra.

7 WHITE-NECKED BABBLER *Stachyris leucotis* 14–15cm FIELD NOTES: Forages on or near the ground, singly, in pairs or in small groups, occasionally in the company of other small babblers. VOICE: A simple, whistled *uu-wi-u-wi*, *uu-wi-uwi-u* or *uui-wi-oi-wi*. HABITAT: Primary evergreen and logged forest. DISTRIBUTION: Resident in Sumatra and Borneo.

8 BLACK-THROATED BABBLER *Stachyris nigricollis* 15–16cm FIELD NOTES: Generally forages in low vegetation, sometimes in the company of other small babblers. VOICE: A well-spaced, monotonous, piping *pu-pu-pu-pu-pu-pu* or faster *pupupupupupupupupu*, followed by a low churring from a female; also a hollow *chu-chuwu-chu-chu-chu-chu*. Calls include a slow rattle, a harsh, descending *chi-chi-chew-chew* and a high *tchi-tchu*. HABITAT: Primary and secondary evergreen, swamp and, occasionally, tidal swamp forest, and overgrown plantations. DISTRIBUTION: Resident in Sumatra and Borneo.

9 WHITE-BIBBED BABBLER *Stachyris thoracica* 18cm FIELD NOTES: Forages in undergrowth and thickets, generally in small groups. *S. t. orientalis* (9b) occurs in C and E Java. VOICE: Calls include a low, pulsating *chr r r r r r…*, a shorter *chrr chrr chrr chrr* or an abrupt *chrrrp*. HABITAT: Broadleaved evergreen forest. DISTRIBUTION: Endemic to Java.

10 CHESTNUT-RUMPED BABBLER *Stachyris maculata* 17–19cm FIELD NOTES: Forages in the lower and middle storey, in noisy, busy groups. VOICE: Variable, including a persistent, loud *whup whup whup*, *wu wup-wwuhup-wup-wwuhup* or similar, often mixed with harsh trills and quiet conversational notes. HABITAT: Lowland forest. DISTRIBUTION: Resident in Sumatra and Borneo.

159 BABBLERS

1 CHESTNUT-WINGED BABBLER *Stachyris erythroptera* 12–14cm
FIELD NOTES: Forages in the middle storey in small parties. VOICE: A variable, mellow, quick, piping whistle of 7–10 notes, accompanied by low churrs, presumably uttered by the female. Calls include a scolding *trrrrrt-trrrrrt* and a soft *wip*. HABITAT: Broadleaved evergreen forest and secondary growth. DISTRIBUTION: Resident in Sumatra and Borneo.

2 CRESCENT-CHESTED BABBLER *Stachyris melanothorax* 13cm
FIELD NOTES: Forages in parties and occasionally with mixed-species groups. *S. m. baliensis* (2b) occurs in Bali. VOICE: A fast, rolling, piping trill, accompanied by harsh, low, churring calls. HABITAT: Dense thickets and scrub at forest edges, monsoon forest and wooded areas around villages. DISTRIBUTION: Endemic to Java and Bali.

3 PIN-STRIPED TIT-BABBLER *Macronus gularis* 11cm FIELD NOTES: Noisy. Forages in bushes or trees with tit-like actions; post-breeding, may occur in small parties. M. g. woodi (3b) occurs in the Philippines. VOICE: A monotonous *chunk chunk chunk, chu chu chu chu chu…* or similar HABITAT: Light and dense forest with bushes and undergrowth, bamboo and tall grass. DISTRIBUTION: Resident in Sumatra and the W Philippines.

4 BOLD-STRIPED TIT-BABBLER *Macronus bornensis* 12cm FIELD NOTES: Creeps around in dense undergrowth, in small parties. M. b. cagayanensis (4b) occurs on Mapun Island in the SW Sulu Sea. VOICE: Duets: male utters a *chuhu-chuhu-chuhu-chuhu*, while female utters a harsh, crackling *chuk uk uku*. Calls include a *chrr chrr chrr*, which may develop into a chatter, with an occasional explosive *chirrr*. HABITAT: Secondary forest, wooded riverbanks, coastal scrub and scrub jungle. DISTRIBUTION: Resident in Java and Borneo.

5 GREY-CHEEKED TIT-BABBLER *Macronus flavicollis* 13–14cm
FIELD NOTES: Forages in tangled vegetation in the lower and middle storey, usually in small groups. M. f. prillwitzi (5b) occurs on Kangean Island off NW Java. VOICE: A monotonous series of 4–25 bell-like notes, repeated after short phases. HABITAT: Open forest, secondary growth, dry forest patches and edges of beach forests. DISTRIBUTION: Endemic to Java.

6 BROWN TIT-BABBLER *Macronus striaticeps* 13cm FIELD NOTES: Forages in dense, tangled vegetation from the lower to middle storey, in small parties or as part of mixed-species groups. M. s. kettlewelli (6b) occurs in the Sulu Archipelago. VOICE: A chattering *we-chu-we-chu we-chu, pe-we-chu pe-we chu* or similar; calls include a quiet *jit* or *gug* and a distinctive *fshhht, fssstut-fssstut* or similar. HABITAT: Primary and secondary evergreen forest, logged forest, forest edges, secondary growth and scrub. DISTRIBUTION: Endemic to the Philippines.

7 FLUFFY-BACKED TIT-BABBLER *Macronus ptilosus* 16–17cm FIELD NOTES: Forages in the tree foliage, usually in pairs. VOICE: A repeated low, long, liquid *puh-puh-puh-puh-puh*, a slower *wuh wu-hu wu-hu wu-hu* or a *poop-poop… poop-poop*, often accompanied by a husky churring, presumably uttered by the female; calls include a *gertcha* and a harsh *ker*. HABITAT: Lowland forest and mangrove edges. DISTRIBUTION: Resident in Sumatra and Borneo.

8 VISAYAN MINIATURE BABBLER *Micromacronus leytensis* 7–8cm
FIELD NOTES: Forages from the undergrowth to the canopy, in small groups or mixed-species parties. VOICE: Unknown. HABITAT: Montane broadleaved evergreen forest and forest edges. DISTRIBUTION: Endemic to the EC Philippines.

9 MINDANAO MINIATURE BABBLER *Micromacronus sordidus* 7–8cm
FIELD NOTES: Little information; noted feeding in the canopy alongside groups of Mountain Leaf Warblers (Plate 151). VOICE: Unknown. HABITAT: Montane broadleaved evergreen forest. DISTRIBUTION: Endemic to the S Philippines.

10 CHESTNUT-CAPPED BABBLER *Timalia pileata* 15–17cm FIELD NOTES: Elusive, creeping through tangles of tall grass and bushes. VOICE: Husky phrases, ending with thin, metallic notes that fade at the end. Calls include a short *tzit*, a harsh *chrrt* and various chuntering notes. HABITAT: Tall grass, reeds, scrub and secondary growth, often along streams or tracks. DISTRIBUTION: Resident in W Java.

160 SHRIKE-BABBLERS; MESIA; CROCIAS; SIBIA; FULVETTAS; YUHINA; ERPORNIS

1 BLYTH'S SHRIKE-BABBLER *Pteruthius aeralatus* 14cm FIELD NOTES: Shuffles sideways along branches, searching among moss and lichen. VOICE: Variable, transcribed as *cha-chew cha-chew, cha-cha-chip cha-cha-chip, doo-du-dit-du-dit* or similar. Calls include a harsh grating and a short *pink*. HABITAT: Montane forest. DISTRIBUTION: Resident in Sumatra and Borneo.

2 PIED SHRIKE-BABBLER *Pteruthius flaviscapis* 14cm FIELD NOTES: Formerly considered conspecific with the previous species; actions presumed to be similar. This, the previous and the next species are not true babblers; the latest recommendation is to include them in the family Vireonidae. VOICE: A loud, strident, rhythmic series of notes with a short, weak introduction. HABITAT: Broadleaved evergreen forest and mixed evergreen–coniferous forest. DISTRIBUTION: Endemic to Java.

3 CHESTNUT-FRONTED SHRIKE-BABBLER (TRILLING SHRIKE-BABBLER) *Pteruthius aenobarbus* 11–12cm FIELD NOTES: Arboreal; sluggish forager in the canopy and mid-storey. VOICE: A monotonous *chip-chip-chip* or similar, and a tinny trill; calls include a buzzy *jer-jer-jer* and a sharp *pwit*. HABITAT: Broadleaved evergreen forest and forest edges. DISTRIBUTION: Resident in Java.

4 SILVER-EARED MESIA *Leiothrix argentauris* 15–17cm FIELD NOTES: Forages in bushes and trees, often in small parties. VOICE: A cheerful, descending *che tchu-tchu cher-it* or *che-chu chiwi chu u*; calls include a flat piping and a harsh chattering. HABITAT: Bushes and undergrowth in forest, forest edges, secondary growth and scrub. DISTRIBUTION: Resident in western side of Sumatra.

5 SPOTTED CROCIAS *Crocias albonotatus* 20cm FIELD NOTES: Generally seen in small groups or mixed-species foraging flocks feeding in the canopy or at forest edges. VOICE: A husky series of *jhew* or *jhrr* notes, and a series of repeated *whi tu* or *whi tui* notes. HABITAT: Broadleaved evergreen forest. DISTRIBUTION: Endemic to W Java.

6 LONG-TAILED SIBIA *Heterophasia picaoides* 28–35cm FIELD NOTES: Forages mainly in the canopy of tall trees, often in pairs or small flocks. VOICE: A rich, whistled six-note phrase; calls include a *tsip-tsip-tsip-tsip*, sometimes interspersed with rattles or trills. HABITAT: Broadleaved evergreen forest, forest edges, secondary growth and open scrub with large trees. DISTRIBUTION: Resident in Sumatra.

7 BROWN FULVETTA *Alcippe brunneicauda* 14–15cm FIELD NOTES: Forages in the lower middle storey and in low vegetation, in pairs or small parties. VOICE: A slow, high-pitched *hi-tu-tu ti-tu ti-tu* or similar; calls include a stressed *whit* and short, harsh rattles. HABITAT: Broadleaved evergreen forest, often near streams. DISTRIBUTION: Resident in Sumatra and Borneo.

8 JAVAN FULVETTA *Alcippe pyrrhoptera* 14–15cm FIELD NOTES: Forages in small parties or occasionally in mixed-species feeding flocks. VOICE: A loud, clear *ti-ti chi chi chew*; calls include an explosive *bhip* or *jesip*, and sometimes a loose rattle. HABITAT: Submontane and montane broadleaved evergreen forest. DISTRIBUTION: Endemic to W Java.

9 CHESTNUT-CRESTED YUHINA *Yuhina everetti* 14cm FIELD NOTES: Usually found in fast-moving flocks, foraging in the tops of small or large trees. VOICE: Calls include a low, quick *whit whit whit* or similar, and a rattling *chr r r r r t*; flocks produce a hurried chatter. HABITAT: Submontane and montane broadleaved evergreen forest, moss forest, forest edges and secondary growth. DISTRIBUTION: Endemic to Borneo.

10 WHITE-BELLIED ERPORNIS *Erpornis zantholeuca* 11–13cm FIELD NOTES: Forages with acrobatic tit-like actions in the lower canopy and high bushes. VOICE: A short, high-pitched, descending trill, sometimes rising, or rising and falling; calls include a nasal *nher-nher* or *jeer-jeer-jeer*, interspersed with chittering and dry trills. HABITAT: Broadleaved evergreen forest, secondary growth, logged forest, upland heath and overgrown plantations. DISTRIBUTION: Resident in NW Sumatra and Borneo.

161 LAUGHINGTHRUSHES

1 SUNDA LAUGHINGTHRUSH *Garrulax palliatus* 24–25cm FIELD NOTES: Forages in low vegetation or on the ground, usually in small flocks or in mixed-species feeding parties. VOICE: Group songs start gently, then speed up to a raucous, bubbling, tumbling chaos of screeching, chattering laughter, before easing into a series of repeated *wiku* notes or a flowing *wipiwuwipiwpiwu*. Contact calls include a *yo yo yo…*, *jieu jieu*, *yuk yuk*, *jup jup* or *jip*. HABITAT: Broadleaved evergreen forest and sometimes in secondary growth. DISTRIBUTION: Resident in Sumatra and Borneo.

2 RUFOUS-FRONTED LAUGHINGTHRUSH *Garrulax rufifrons* 27cm FIELD NOTES: Usually found in noisy groups or as part of mixed-species foraging flocks, feeding mainly in the understorey. VOICE: Calls include a repeated, subdued, harsh *kheh*, *queck* or *hii-tii hii-tii-tii…*; when agitated, utters a chuckling or tinkling *hi tu tu tu tu tu…* or *hihi hu hu hu hu hu hu…* HABITAT: Primary montane forest. DISTRIBUTION: Endemic to W Java.

3 SUMATRAN LAUGHINGTHRUSH (BLACK-AND-WHITE LAUGHINGTHRUSH) *Garrulax bicolor* 24–28cm FIELD NOTES: Noisy. Forages in groups in the middle and lower storeys, and occasionally feeds on the ground. VOICE: Starts with chattering notes, followed by loud, cackling, melodious laughter. HABITAT: Broadleaved evergreen forest. DISTRIBUTION: Endemic to Sumatra.

4 BLACK LAUGHINGTHRUSH *Garrulax lugubris* 25–27cm FIELD NOTES: Forages in pairs or small flocks, usually close to the ground. VOICE: A hollow, whooping *huup-huup-huup* and a rapid *okh-ohk-okh-okh-okh…*, accompanied by a harsh *awk* or *aak* notes. HABITAT: Broadleaved evergreen forest, forest edges and secondary growth. DISTRIBUTION: Resident in Sumatra.

5 BARE-HEADED LAUGHINGTHRUSH *Garrulax calvus* 25–26cm FIELD NOTES: Occurs in pairs or small parties, or sometimes in mixed-species foraging groups; favours the lower and middle storeys. Often acrobatic, hanging upside down in the manner of a giant tit. VOICE: A long series of flat, resonant *ooh* notes; in a duet, *ooh* notes are combined with comical *yow-yow* notes, transcribed as *ooh-yow-yow-yow ooh-yow-yow* or similar. HABITAT: Broadleaved evergreen forest and secondary growth. DISTRIBUTION: Endemic to Borneo.

6 CHESTNUT-CAPPED LAUGHINGTHRUSH (SPECTACLED LAUGHINGTHRUSH) *Garrulax mitratus* 22–24cm FIELD NOTES: Forages in pairs or small parties among creepers and thick foliage in the lower and middle storey. VOICE: A subdued, shrill *wi wu-wi-wu-wi*, *wi-wu-wi*, *wi-wu-wiu-wu-wi* or *wiu-wu-wui-wi erc*. Calls include a sibilant *ju-ju-ju-ju-ju* or *wi-jujujujuju*, and a cackling *wikakaka*. HABITAT: Broadleaved evergreen forest and forest edges. DISTRIBUTION: Resident in Sumatra.

7 CHESTNUT-HOODED LAUGHINGTHRUSH *Garrulax treacheri* 22–24cm FIELD NOTES: Forages from the ground to the canopy, in small parties or mixed-species feeding flocks. VOICE: A thin, high *chu-wu chwi-wi-wi-wi-wiee-wu* or similar; calls include harsh, scolding notes and a descending *ah-ah-ah-ah*. HABITAT: Broadleaved evergreen forest, disturbed and secondary forest, adjacent cultivation and forest edges. DISTRIBUTION: Endemic to Borneo.

1 MADANGA *Madanga ruficollis* 13cm FIELD NOTES: Little information. Last sightings were of birds in a mixed-species foraging flock; also recorded searching for food by climbing up and down trunks like a nuthatch. Recent DNA tests suggest this bird is related to the pipits! VOICE: Unrecorded. HABITAT: Montane forest. DISTRIBUTION: Endemic to Buru in the S Moluccas.

2 ORIENTAL WHITE-EYE *Zosterops palpebrosus* 9–11cm FIELD NOTES: Restless, agile forager among tree foliage and blossoms. Often part of mixed-species feeding parties. VOICE: Wispy, made up of slurred call notes; calls include a twittering *dzi-da-da* and a raspy, down-slurred *djeeeer*. HABITAT: Broadleaved evergreen, deciduous and swamp forest, secondary growth, mangroves, cultivation, parks and gardens. DISTRIBUTION: Resident in Sumatra, Java, Bali, Borneo and the W Lesser Sundas.

3 LOWLAND WHITE-EYE *Zosterops meyeni* 10–12cm FIELD NOTES: Noisy. Forages in groups or mixed-species flocks. VOICE: A *swit* or *swit-tzee* and a complicated series of twittering and wheezy notes. HABITAT: Forest, forest edges, bamboo thickets, scrub, cultivated areas and gardens. DISTRIBUTION: Endemic to the N Philippines.

4 ENGGANO WHITE-EYE *Zosterops salvadorii* 10cm FIELD NOTES: Seen foraging in small parties; little other information. VOICE: Reported as similar to that of the Oriental White-eye. HABITAT: Lowland wooded areas and coconut groves. DISTRIBUTION: Endemic to Enggano Island off SW Sumatra.

5 BLACK-CAPPED WHITE-EYE *Zosterops atricapilla* 9–10cm FIELD NOTES: Acrobatic forager in trees and bushes; regularly encountered in small flocks and as a member of mixed-species feeding flocks. VOICE: Calls include a trembling note and a loud, twinkling series of notes. HABITAT: Hill and lower montane forest, montane bush and alpine ericaceous meadows. DISTRIBUTION: Resident in Sumatra and Borneo.

6 EVERETT'S WHITE-EYE *Zosterops everetti* 11–12cm FIELD NOTES: Gregarious, usually in flocks of 5–20 individuals, although higher numbers reported; forages in treetops. VOICE: A series of 8–13 metallic, raspy, whistled notes and a series of sweet, weak, twittering notes; calls include a *tsee-tsee*, a metallic *spreet* or *peeet* and a buzzing *dzee* or *dzee-ap*. HABITAT: Evergreen forest. DISTRIBUTION: Resident in Borneo, the WC and S Philippines, and the Talaud Islands.

7 YELLOWISH WHITE-EYE (GOLDEN-GREEN WHITE-EYE) *Zosterops nigrorum* 10–12cm FIELD NOTES: Forages in noisy flocks of up 20 individuals or in mixed-species parties. *Z. n. aureiloris* (7b) occurs in N and NW Luzon. VOICE: A series of *pit-it tit, sit-it sit-it* or *sip-it sip-it* notes. HABITAT: Forest, forest edges, secondary growth, clearings and lower storeys of dipterocarp forest. DISTRIBUTION: Endemic to the C and N Philippines.

8 MOUNTAIN WHITE-EYE *Zosterops montanus* 11–12cm FIELD NOTES: Gregarious, often seen in small or large flocks foraging in the upper tree levels. *Z. m. obstinatus* (8b) resides on Seram, Ternate and Bacan in the Moluccas. VOICE: Variable; includes a warble in Java, a low, melodious song in Sumatra, and a *peet-peet* followed by a trill in Sulawesi. Contact calls are soft and high pitched. HABITAT: Primary montane forest, forest edges, secondary growth, *Casuarina* stands and wooded cultivation. DISTRIBUTION: Resident in Sumatra, Java, Bali, the Philippines and Wallacea.

9 CHRISTMAS WHITE-EYE *Zosterops natalis* 12–14cm FIELD NOTES: Forages from low levels to the canopy; gregarious. VOICE: A *yerr yerr weet yerr yerr tyerr weet…* Calls include twittering and chirping notes, a thin *ts-ee-sect… tsee-eet…*, a *tsirr-tsirr* when alarmed, and a scolding *cheeuw cheeuw cheeuw*. HABITAT: Woodland, shrubs, forest edges, and open country with trees and bushes. DISTRIBUTION: Endemic to Christmas Island.

163 WHITE-EYES

1 JAVAN WHITE-EYE *Zosterops flavus* 9–10cm FIELD NOTES: Arboreal; forages in tight gleaning groups of 10–40 individuals. VOICE: Calls include a *trrieew*, a short, soft *trrip* and a *wiwiwiwi* when alarmed. HABITAT: Mangroves, coastal forest edges, low waterside trees, groves, shrubby areas and gardens. DISTRIBUTION: Endemic to NW Java and S Borneo.

2 LEMON-BELLIED WHITE-EYE *Zosterops chloris* 11–12cm FIELD NOTES: Generally encountered in small flocks; restless forager at all levels. *Z. c. flavissimus* (2b) occurs on the Tukangbesi Islands off SE Sulawesi. VOICE: A mix of rich, beautiful, high-pitched, seesawing notes, along with short *si-si* notes, repeated, often monotonously. Calls include a *shilp* or *chiew*. HABITAT: Secondary forest and open woodland, scrub, mangroves, coastal woodland and thickets, cultivation and gardens. DISTRIBUTION: Resident in Sulawesi, the W Lesser Sundas and the Moluccas.

3 ASHY-BELLIED WHITE-EYE *Zosterops citrinella* 10–11cm FIELD NOTES: Active, foraging in the foliage of the outer canopy in small groups or as a member of mixed-species flocks. VOICE: A series of weak, high-pitched, twittering notes, interspersed with rapidly repeated warbles, trills and slurs; on Tanimbar, utters a series of rapid, up-and-down, loud, sweet, warbling notes. HABITAT: Primary and secondary forest, degraded forest, forest edges, open woodland, monsoon forest, mangroves, coastal woodland, cultivation and scrub. DISTRIBUTION: Endemic to the Lesser Sundas.

4 PEARL-BELLIED WHITE-EYE *Zosterops grayi* 13cm FIELD NOTES: Forages singly, in pairs and in mixed-species feeding parties in the middle storey. VOICE: A series of strident, squeaky, chattering notes interspersed with three sharp, high-pitched notes. Calls include a series of rapid, unmusical chattering or bubbling notes, and a *pipip* and *trrr*. HABITAT: Primary and secondary forest, open woodland and cultivated gardens. DISTRIBUTION: Kai Islands in the S Moluccas.

5 GOLDEN-BELLIED WHITE-EYE *Zosterops uropygialis* 12–13cm FIELD NOTES: Encountered in pairs or small parties; gleans and hover-gleans in the foliage of the canopy. VOICE: Calls include squeaky, nasal chatters; harsh, rasping squeaks; short, bubbling notes; and a mellow, nasal *chow*. HABITAT: Forest and cleared areas with scattered trees. DISTRIBUTION: Endemic to the Kai Islands in the S Moluccas.

6 PALE-BELLIED WHITE-EYE *Zosterops consobrinorum* 11–12cm FIELD NOTES: Forages mainly in the understorey and forest-edge thickets, and in the canopy of tall trees, usually in pairs, small groups or mixed-species flocks. VOICE: An attractive, pleasing song that lacks trilling notes. HABITAT: Remnant patches of lowland forest, forest edges, forest plantations, cultivation, scrub and gardens. DISTRIBUTION: Endemic to SE Sulawesi.

7 BLACK-RINGED WHITE-EYE *Zosterops anomalus* 12cm FIELD NOTES: Found singly, in pairs, in small groups or in mixed-species parties, from understorey vegetation to the canopy. VOICE: A muted series of teetering, chattering notes and a *chewchicheruit-chewticheru-i-uu rrr*; calls with a quivering whistle. HABITAT: Scrubby deforested hills, secondary forest, forest edges, orchards and gardens. DISTRIBUTION: Endemic to S Sulawesi.

8 YELLOW-RINGED WHITE-EYE (YELLOW-SPECTACLED WHITE-EYE) *Zosterops wallacei* 11–12cm FIELD NOTES: Forages in the middle and upper levels, singly, in pairs or in small flocks. VOICE: Variable: on Sumba, gives a descending, tinkling warble; on Komodo, utters a rapid series of warbled notes, starting with two short notes, a single upslurred whistle and a jumble of high-pitched sweet notes; on Flores, gives two short insect-like notes followed by a series of warbled, ascending and descending notes. HABITAT: Primary and secondary forest, forest edges, dry scrub and cultivation. DISTRIBUTION: Endemic to the W Lesser Sundas.

9 SANGIHE WHITE-EYE *Zosterops nehrkorni* 10–12cm FIELD NOTES: Forages in small parties in dense canopy and subcanopy foliage. VOICE: Thin, tinkling and trailing away; calls include a *swiit… swiit… swiit*. HABITAT: Primary broadleaved ridgetop forest, with dense *Pandanus*. DISTRIBUTION: Endemic to Sangihe Island.

164 WHITE-EYES

1 TOGIAN WHITE-EYE *Zosterops somadikartai* 11cm FIELD NOTES: Forages in dense, low shrubs, generally in pairs or small flocks. VOICE: A thin, sweet warble; moving flocks utter twittering chirrups. HABITAT: Low bushes near mangroves, coconut groves, secondary scrub in logged forest and gardens. DISTRIBUTION: Endemic to the Togian Islands in N Sulawesi.

2 SERAM WHITE-EYE *Zosterops stalkeri* 11cm FIELD NOTES: Occurs in small flocks or as part of mixed-species foraging parties; usually feeds in the forest undergrowth. VOICE: A series of rapidly repeated, sweet, tinkling notes, ending with a few ringing notes; also gives a rapid series of slightly rolling *swi* notes. HABITAT: Mid-montane secondary forest. DISTRIBUTION: Endemic to Seram in the S Moluccas.

3 BLACK-CROWNED WHITE-EYE *Zosterops atrifrons* 11–12cm FIELD NOTES: Forages from low down up to the canopy, in small groups or sometimes in much larger parties (100 or so recorded in Sulawesi). VOICE: Variable: a shrill warble, a rapid series of high-pitched sweet notes and a clear, high-pitched series of rolling, sweet, whistled notes. Calls include a double note followed by a descending and fading twitter, and a high-pitched *peee*, *tiu* or *teew*. HABITAT: Primary and secondary lowland and hill forest, logged and degraded forest, and forest edges. DISTRIBUTION: Resident in Sulawesi and the Banggai and Sula islands.

4 CREAM-THROATED WHITE-EYE *Zosterops atriceps* 12cm FIELD NOTES: Relatively skulking; forages in thickets, the middle storey or the canopy. *Z. a. dehaani* (4b) occurs on Morotai Island; *Z. a. fuscifrons* (4c) is found on Halmahera. VOICE: Thin, sweet, whistled notes, alternating up and down, then ending with 1–2 *tu-wit* notes; Halmahera birds give a louder version that lacks the end notes. HABITAT: Lowland and hill primary and secondary forest, forest edges and cultivation. DISTRIBUTION: Endemic to the N Moluccas.

5 AMBON WHITE-EYE *Zosterops kuehni* 12cm FIELD NOTES: Active forager in tree crowns, especially when in flower; occurs in pairs or small groups. VOICE: A musical warble; calls with a sibilant *teeu*. HABITAT: Lowland forest, remnant patches of secondary forest and woodland, lightly wooded cultivation, scrub and gardens. DISTRIBUTION: Endemic to Ambon and Seram in the S Moluccas.

6 BURU WHITE-EYE *Zosterops buruensis* 11–12cm FIELD NOTES: Forages in mixed-species flocks in dense foliage in the canopy or subcanopy. VOICE: While foraging, utters a quiet, quickly repeated *tsu-tsu-tsu-tsu-tsu*; also utters a *chewit chewit chewit*. HABITAT: Primary and selectively logged forest, secondary growth and scrub. DISTRIBUTION: Endemic to Buru in the S Moluccas.

7 RUFESCENT DARKEYE (BICOLOURED WHITE-EYE) *Tephrozosterops stalkeri* 12–13cm FIELD NOTES: Forages alone, in pairs or in mixed-species parties. VOICE: Unrecorded. HABITAT: Dense secondary growth at forest edges or in clearings, overgrown cultivation and scrub. DISTRIBUTION: Endemic to Seram in the S Moluccas.

8 MEES'S WHITE-EYE (GREY-THROATED WHITE-EYE) *Lophozosterops javanicus* 13cm FIELD NOTES: Mainly found in the canopy or high up in forest edges, in pairs, small flocks or as part of mixed-species groups. *L. j. elongatus* (8b) occurs in E Java and Bali; *L. j. frontalis* (8c) is found in W Java. VOICE: Song comprises melodious whistles and call notes; calls include a long, drawn-out, high cheeping, and a throaty *turr*, *teerrr-teerrr* or *chee-ee-wheet-chee-ee-weeeet*. HABITAT: Forest, dense secondary growth and neglected plantations. DISTRIBUTION: Endemic to Java and Bali.

9 STREAK-HEADED WHITE-EYE *Lophozosterops squamiceps* 12cm FIELD NOTES: Forages from the understorey to the canopy, in pairs or small groups, and as part of mixed-species flocks. *L. s. striaticeps* (9b) occurs in NC Sulawesi. VOICE: A repeated, warbled series of loud, clear, sweet, sibilant, high-pitched notes; also utters a harsh, chirruping trill. HABITAT: Primary montane forest, forest edges and secondary growth. DISTRIBUTION: Endemic to Sulawesi.

165 WHITE-EYES; HELEIAS; BLACKEYE

1 MINDANAO WHITE-EYE (BLACK-MASKED WHITE-EYE)

Lophozosterops goodfellowi 13–14cm FIELD NOTES: Forages at all levels of the forest, in small parties or mixed-species flocks. VOICE: A musical, whistled *tu-pik*, *chu-beer* or *su si deer*, often given together. HABITAT: Submontane and montane forest and forest edges. DISTRIBUTION: Endemic to Mindanao in the Philippines.

2 CREAM-BROWED WHITE-EYE (YELLOW-BROWED WHITE-EYE)

Lophozosterops superciliaris 13cm FIELD NOTES: Generally encountered foraging in small groups and occasionally in larger groups (over 50 noted on Flores), usually in the middle storey. VOICE: A rapid series of high-pitched, bubbling, trilled and warbled notes, occasionally interspersed with *tchee-tchee* notes; also utters a ringing *peu-peu*. HABITAT: Upper montane primary forest, semi-evergreen rainforest, *Casuarina* forest, logged and degraded forest, forest edges, thin secondary growth and scrub. DISTRIBUTION: Endemic to the W Lesser Sundas.

3 GREY-HOODED WHITE-EYE *Lophozosterops pinaiae* 14cm FIELD NOTES: Forages in the thick foliage of tree crowns and among dense arboreal epiphytes. Often a member of mixed-species foraging flocks. VOICE: Unknown. HABITAT: Montane forest. DISTRIBUTION: Endemic to Seram in the S Moluccas.

4 CRESTED WHITE-EYE *Lophozosterops dohertyi* 12cm FIELD NOTES: Favours the understorey and dense scrub, alone, in pairs or in small groups; also joins mixed-species feeding parties. VOICE: A moderately rapid series of fourteen clear, sweet whistles; also gives a soft *tsip-tsip*. HABITAT: Moist primary forest, degraded forest, tall secondary forest, lightly wooded cultivation and scrub. DISTRIBUTION: Endemic to the W Lesser Sundas.

5 PYGMY WHITE-EYE *Oculocincta squamifrons* 9–10cm FIELD NOTES: Fast-moving small groups forage in the crowns of tall trees, and in the middle level at forest edges. VOICE: A *chit-chit-chit* or high-pitched *tsee-tsee…* HABITAT: Hill and lower montane forest, forest edges, secondary growth, dense scrub and sandy forest with dwarf vegetation. DISTRIBUTION: Endemic to Borneo.

6 THICK-BILLED HELEIA (THICK-BILLED WHITE-EYE) *Heleia crassirostris* 13–14cm FIELD NOTES: Generally encountered in small groups, alone or in pairs, foraging from the understorey to the lower middle storey. Often joins mixed-species flocks. VOICE: A rapid series of loud whistles and trilled notes on an even pitch; calls include a deep, quiet *chup… chup…* HABITAT: Primary and degraded semi-evergreen rainforest and moist deciduous monsoon forest, forest edges and scrub. DISTRIBUTION: Endemic to the Lesser Sundas.

7 SPOT-BREASTED HELEIA (SPOT-BREASTED WHITE-EYE) *Heleia muelleri* 13–14cm FIELD NOTES: Usually found in pairs or compact, small groups; also joins mixed-species foraging flocks. VOICE: An unmusical rattle of 10–20 rapid, mechanical notes, initially rising and then falling; also gives a harsh, weak, grating noise. HABITAT: Primary and tall secondary monsoon and evergreen forest. DISTRIBUTION: Endemic to Timor in the Lesser Sundas.

8 MOUNTAIN BLACKEYE *Chlorocharis emiliae* 11–12cm FIELD NOTES: Forages from near the ground to treetops, in pairs or in small flocks. VOICE: A melodious *wit-a-wit wit wit wheer*. Calls include a twittering *twt-u*, *stweet-u* or *te-wio*; in flight, utters jangling notes and a stuttering *gujuguju*. HABITAT: Montane moss forest and stunted growth at higher elevations. DISTRIBUTION: Endemic to Borneo.

1 HORSFIELD'S BUSH LARK *Mirafra javanica* 14cm FIELD NOTES: Forages on the ground. Sings from a perch or in flight. VOICE: Variable short phrases; calls include an explosive *pitsi pitsi pitsipipipipi*. HABITAT: Grassland with bushes, dry marsh edges and dry paddyfields. DISTRIBUTION: Resident in Java, Bali, Borneo, the Philippines and the Lesser Sundas.

2 ORIENTAL SKYLARK *Alauda gulgula* 15–18cm FIELD NOTES: Forages on the ground. Short primary projection compared to the Skylark. VOICE: A mix of warbles, twitters and whistles; calls include a *baz-baz*, a *baz-terr* and a *twip*. HABITAT: Dry open country, grassland and dry paddyfields. DISTRIBUTION: Resident in the N Philippines.

3 SKYLARK (EURASIAN SKYLARK) *Alauda arvensis* 16–19cm FIELD NOTES: Forages on the ground. Long primary projection compared to the Oriental Skylark. VOICE: Calls include a liquid *chirrup* and a short *prryih*. HABITAT: Grassland, cultivated fields and coastal flats. DISTRIBUTION: Vagrant in Borneo.

4 RICHARD'S PIPIT *Anthus richardi* 17–20cm FIELD NOTES: Forages on the ground. Powerful, undulating flight; often hovers before landing. VOICE: Calls include a harsh *schreep* or *sherrreeep*, a *chup*, a subdued *chirp* and a *r-rump*. HABITAT: Open grassland. DISTRIBUTION: Winter visitor to Borneo.

5 PADDYFIELD PIPIT *Anthus rufulus* 15cm FIELD NOTES: Forages on the ground; often stands quite upright. VOICE: Calls include a loud *chep* or *chep-chep*, a thin *pipit* and a harsh *chwist*. HABITAT: Open country, grassland, paddyfields and farmland. DISTRIBUTION: Resident in Sumatra, Java, Bali, Borneo, the Philippines, Sulawesi and the Lesser Sundas.

6 PECHORA PIPIT *Anthus gustavi* 15cm FIELD NOTES: Skulking. Forages on the ground; tends to hover before landing. VOICE: A sharp *tsip*, *tsip-tsip* or *tsi-tsi-tsi-tsip*. HABITAT: Damp grassy areas and open woodland. DISTRIBUTION: Winter visitor to Borneo, the Philippines, Sulawesi, the Lesser Sundas and the N Moluccas.

7 RED-THROATED PIPIT *Anthus cervinus* 14–15cm FIELD NOTES: Forages on the ground, often in small flocks. Regularly perches on bushes, wires or fences. VOICE: A short *tew* and a longer, high-pitched *pseeeu*. HABITAT: Grassland, grassy edges of wetlands and stubble fields. DISTRIBUTION: Winter visitor to Borneo and the Philippines; vagrant Sulawesi.

8 OLIVE-BACKED PIPIT *Anthus hodgsoni* 14–15cm FIELD NOTES: Forages on the ground; also regularly perches in trees. Plain-backed race *A. h. yunnanensis* (8b) reported from the N Philippines. VOICE: A loud *teaze*, and a thin *teez* or *tseep*. HABITAT: Open forest, forest clearings, forest edges and wooded cultivations. DISTRIBUTION: Winter visitor to Borneo and the Philippines.

9 FOREST WAGTAIL *Dendronanthus indicus* 16–18cm FIELD NOTES: Runs or walks; sways tail and rear body from side to side. Flees to a perch in trees when alarmed. VOICE: A hard, shrill *pick* or *pick-pick*. HABITAT: Forest tracks, wooded cultivation and mangroves. DISTRIBUTION: Winter visitor to Sumatra, Java, Borneo and rarely to the Philippines.

10 WHITE WAGTAIL *Motacilla alba* 17–18cm FIELD NOTES: Walks or runs; wags tail up and down. *M. a. ocularis* (main illustration) occurs in Borneo and the Philippines; black-backed race *M. a. lugens* (10b) recorded from the Philippines. VOICE: A *ts-lee-wee*, *tslee-vit* or similar. HABITAT: Open areas, often near water. DISTRIBUTION: Winter visitor to Borneo and the Philippines.

11 EASTERN YELLOW WAGTAIL *Motacilla tschutschensis* 16–18cm FIELD NOTES: Forages on the ground. Both blue-headed and green-headed *M. t. taivana* (11b) birds occur. VOICE: A loud *pseeu* or *tsreep*. HABITAT: Damp and dry grassland, and dry paddyfields. DISTRIBUTION: Winter visitor to the region.

12 GREY WAGTAIL *Motacilla cinerea* 17–20cm FIELD NOTES: Constantly pumps rear body and tail. Often perches on branches overhanging water. VOICE: A high-pitched *zit-zit*, rapidly repeated when alarmed. HABITAT: Mountain streams, lowland watercourses, coastal areas and roadsides. DISTRIBUTION: Winter visitor to the region.

167 SUNBIRDS

1 PLAIN SUNBIRD *Anthreptes simplex* 13cm FIELD NOTES: Forages much like a leaf warbler, gleaning from leaves. VOICE: Metallic chips and trills, and a high-pitched *seep*. HABITAT: Forest, forest edges, scrub, coastal scrub and mangroves. DISTRIBUTION: Resident in Sumatra and Borneo.

2 BROWN-THROATED SUNBIRD *Anthreptes malacensis* 14cm FIELD NOTES: Forages singly or in pairs at all levels, gleaning from leaves and branches. *A. m. celebensis* (2b) occurs on Sulawesi. VOICE: A *sweet-sweet*, *swit-swit-sweet* or *wee-chew-chew-wee*; calls include a repeated *kelichap*, a hard *chip*, a drawn-out, high *siiewei* and a shrill *whiiu*. HABITAT: Forest edges, mangroves, freshwater swamp forest, secondary growth, coastal scrub, plantations and gardens. DISTRIBUTION: Resident in Sumatra, Java, Bali, Borneo, the Philippines, Sulawesi, and the Banggai and Sula islands.

3 GREY-THROATED SUNBIRD *Anthreptes griseigularis* 12–13cm FIELD NOTES: Formerly regarded as conspecific with the previous species; actions presumed to be similar. VOICE: Unknown. HABITAT: Forest, mangroves, plantations, scrub, groves and gardens. DISTRIBUTION: Endemic to the Philippines.

4 RED-THROATED SUNBIRD *Anthreptes rhodolaemus* 12cm FIELD NOTES: Gleans from foliage, usually in the canopy but also at lower levels. VOICE: A high-pitched *sit-sit-sit-see* or a slurred *sit-sit-sit-swe-er*; calls include various chirps and trills. HABITAT: Forest, forest edges, secondary growth, plantations and coastal vegetation. DISTRIBUTION: Resident in Sumatra and Borneo.

5 RUBY-CHEEKED SUNBIRD *Chalcoparia singalensis* 10–11cm FIELD NOTES: Forages mainly in the upper storey, probing flowers for nectar and gleaning from leaves. VOICE: A shrill, trilled *tirr-tititrirr tir tir* and a rapid, high *switi-ti-chi-chu tusi-tit swit-swit…*; calls include a shrill *seet-seet*, a *tweest-wit* and a soft *chi-wip*. HABITAT: Forest, secondary growth, coastal scrub and mangroves. DISTRIBUTION: Resident in Sumatra, Java and Borneo.

6 PURPLE-THROATED SUNBIRD *Leptocoma sperata* 9–10cm FIELD NOTES: Generally forages in pairs or, occasionally, in small groups. *L. s. henkei* (6b) occurs on N Luzon and islands off the N Philippines; *L. s. juliae* (6b) is found in W and S Mindanao and the Sulu Archipelago. VOICE: A metallic *spee-spit* or *pee-pit*. HABITAT: Lowland forest, secondary growth, mangroves, cultivation and gardens. DISTRIBUTION: Endemic to the Philippines.

7 VAN HASSELT'S SUNBIRD (MAROON-BELLIED SUNBIRD) *Leptocoma brasiliana* 10cm FIELD NOTES: Usually forages in treetops; hovers to take insects or water from foliage and nectar from flowers. VOICE: A series of discordant *psweet* notes; calls include a weak *chip chip*, a sharp *si-si-si*, an upslurred *psweet*, a *fut-chit* and short, high trills. HABITAT: Forest, forest edges, secondary growth, coastal scrub, cultivation and gardens. DISTRIBUTION: Resident in Sumatra, Java and Borneo.

8 BLACK SUNBIRD *Leptocoma aspasia* 11–12cm FIELD NOTES: Active, foraging by gleaning or hover-gleaning. Sometimes occurs in small groups. *L. a. talautensis* (8b) occurs in the Talaud Islands; *L. a. chlorolaema* (8c) resides in the Kai Islands; *L. a. grayi* (8d) is found in N Sulawesi. VOICE: A rapid, sweet, tinkling cadence; calls include a shrill *zi-zi-zi-zi-zi*, a down-slurred *swee*, and various high-pitched sibilant or harsh notes. HABITAT: Primary and secondary forest, forest edges, mangroves, scrub, village trees and gardens. DISTRIBUTION: Resident in Sulawesi and the Moluccas.

9 COPPER-THROATED SUNBIRD *Leptocoma calcostetha* 12–13cm FIELD NOTES: Forages mainly in mangroves, feeding on nectar and small invertebrates. VOICE: A high trill and a deep, melodious trill. HABITAT: Mangroves, coastal scrub, secondary growth and cultivation. DISTRIBUTION: Resident in Sumatra, Java, Borneo and the W Philippines.

2b
♀
celebensis

1
♀
♂

♀
2
♂

♀
3
♂

4
♀
♂

♀
5
♂

6
♀
♂

6c
juliae
♂

6b
henkei
♂

7
♀
♂

8b *talautensis*
♀
♂

8
♀
♂

9
♀
♂

8c
♂
chlorolaema

8d
♂
grayi

1 OLIVE-BACKED SUNBIRD *Cinnyris jugularis* 11–12cm FIELD NOTES: Feeds on invertebrates, nectar and small fruits. *C. j. teysmanni* (1b) occurs on islands in the Flores Sea; *C. j. aurora* (1c) is found in the W Philippines; *C. j. plateni* (1d) occurs in Sulawesi. VOICE: A feeble twittering; calls include a *chip* and a nasal *sweei*, and female utters a persistent *sweep*. HABITAT: Forest, forest edges, mangroves, coastal vegetation and scrub. DISTRIBUTION: Resident throughout the region.

2 APRICOT-BREASTED SUNBIRD *Cinnyris buettikoferi* 11cm FIELD NOTES: Forages singly or in pairs in the middle and upper storeys. VOICE: A long, sweet, high-pitched, tinkling warble and a *wee-chew wee-chew wee-chew wee-chew-wee*; in flight, utters a sharp, high *chee* or *sip*. HABITAT: Secondary forest, forest edges, cultivation and scrub. DISTRIBUTION: Endemic to Sumba in the Lesser Sundas.

3 FLAME-BREASTED SUNBIRD *Cinnyris solaris* 11cm FIELD NOTES: Favours foraging in flowering trees, singly, in pairs or in small groups. VOICE: Consists of 3–4 high-pitched, halting notes that go up and down the scale. HABITAT: Secondary forest, forest edges, woodland, plantations, *Eucalyptus* savannah, scrub and gardens. DISTRIBUTION: Endemic to the Lesser Sundas.

4 MAROON-NAPED SUNBIRD *Aethopyga guimarasensis* 9–10cm FIELD NOTES: Formerly considered a race of the Flaming Sunbird; actions presumed to be similar. VOICE: Presumed to be similar to that of the Flaming Sunbird. HABITAT: Forest, forest edges and secondary growth. DISTRIBUTION: Endemic to the WC Philippines.

5 FLAMING SUNBIRD *Aethopyga flagrans* 9–10cm FIELD NOTES: Forages alone, in pairs or in mixed-species flocks. VOICE: A repeated, short, high-pitched, rising *tsweet*. HABITAT: Forest, forest edges and secondary growth. DISTRIBUTION: Endemic to the N Philippines.

6 ELEGANT SUNBIRD *Aethopyga duyvenbodei* 12cm FIELD NOTES: Gleans insects from leaves and from spider webs; occurs in mixed-species flocks, in small groups, in pairs or alone. VOICE: A short insect-like trill, and a high trill of chipping notes; calls include a high-pitched, rasping *treek* or *tseeek*, and a *tit* or *tit-tit-tit-tit*. HABITAT: Mixed plantations near remnant forest patches, secondary forest, bamboo, tree ferns and scrub. DISTRIBUTION: Endemic to Sangihe Island.

7 LOVELY SUNBIRD *Aethopyga shelleyi* 10–11cm FIELD NOTES: Feeds on nectar, insects and grubs, in pairs, alone or as a member of mixed-species flocks. VOICE: A seesawing *zuep-ziip* that continues for several seconds. HABITAT: Forest, forest edges and cultivation with flowering trees. DISTRIBUTION: Endemic to the W Philippines.

8 HANDSOME SUNBIRD *Aethopyga bella* 9cm FIELD NOTES: Feeds on insects, grubs and nectar, singly, in pairs or in mixed-species foraging parties. VOICE: A rapid *sit-sit-sit-sit-tee-tee-tee* and a lower-pitched *tsit-tsit-tit-it*. HABITAT: Forest, forest edges, thickets and cultivation. DISTRIBUTION: Endemic to the Philippines.

1b *teysmanni*

1c *aurora*

1d *plateni*

1

♀

♂

♀

♂

2

♀

♂

3

♂

♀

4

♀

♂

♀

5

♂

6

♀

♂

7

♀

8

♂

♂

1 METALLIC-WINGED SUNBIRD *Aethopyga pulcherrima* 9–10cm FIELD NOTES: Forages alone, in small groups or as a member of mixed-species flocks. VOICE: Slow, well-spaced notes, followed by a trill and then a further series of slow, spaced notes. Calls include a repeated *squeak* and a repeated high-pitched *zeeeep*; also utters a sharp *see* or *see-see-tsik tsik*, which may turn into a rising trill. HABITAT: Forest, forest edges, secondary growth and plantain plantations. DISTRIBUTION: Endemic to the C and S Philippines.

2 LUZON SUNBIRD *Aethopyga jefferyi* 9–10cm FIELD NOTES: Formerly considered a race of the previous species; actions presumed to be similar. VOICE: Presumed to be similar to that of the Metallic-winged Sunbird. HABITAT: Forest, forest edges, secondary growth and plantations. DISTRIBUTION: Endemic to the N Philippines.

3 BOHOL SUNBIRD *Aethopyga decorosa* 9–10cm FIELD NOTES: Formerly considered a race of the Metallic-winged Sunbird; actions presumed to be similar. VOICE: Presumed to be similar to that of the Metallic-winged Sunbird. HABITAT: Forest, forest edges and plantations. DISTRIBUTION: Endemic to Bohol in the C Philippines.

4 WHITE-FLANKED SUNBIRD *Aethopyga eximia* 13cm FIELD NOTES: Favours flowering trees and vines in the lower and middle levels. Seen alone, in pairs or in small parties. VOICE: A clear, precise *tee-tee-tee-leet* or similar. HABITAT: Forest, forest edges, clearings and alpine scrub above the tree line. DISTRIBUTION: Endemic to Java.

5 CRIMSON SUNBIRD *Aethopyga siparaja* 10–11cm FIELD NOTES: Forages among the blossoms of trees and shrubs, alone, in pairs or occasionally in small groups. VOICE: A loud, chirping trill; calls include a *zit-zit* and a soft *siesiep-siepsiep*. HABITAT: Forest, secondary growth, cultivation, scrub and gardens. DISTRIBUTION: Resident in Sumatra, Java, Borneo and Sulawesi.

6 MAGNIFICENT SUNBIRD *Aethopyga magnifica* 15cm FIELD NOTES: Encountered singly, in pairs, in small groups or as part of mixed-species foraging parties; favours flowering trees. Formerly considered a race of the Crimson Sunbird. VOICE: Calls with a metallic *zit-zit*. HABITAT: Forest, secondary growth, cultivation and scrub. DISTRIBUTION: Endemic to the WC Philippines.

7 JAVAN SUNBIRD *Aethopyga mystacalis* 12cm FIELD NOTES: Forages in noisy pairs in the upper levels of forest trees, favouring mistletoe flowers. VOICE: A soft, ringing *tseep-tzeep cheet-cheet*. HABITAT: Lower montane forest, hill dipterocarp forest, secondary forest and forest edges. DISTRIBUTION: Endemic to Java.

8 TEMMINCK'S SUNBIRD *Aethopyga temminckii* 10cm (male with tail 13cm) FIELD NOTES: Forages mainly in the canopy, especially among mistletoe clumps. Occurs alone or in pairs, and occasionally found in small parties. VOICE: A soft *cheet-cheet* and a rhythmic *tit-ti tit-it tit-it tit-it…* HABITAT: Lowland, hill and lower montane forest, and mountain gardens. DISTRIBUTION: Resident in Sumatra and Borneo.

170 SUNBIRDS; SPIDERHUNTERS

1 GREY-HOODED SUNBIRD *Aethopyga primigenia* 10–11cm FIELD NOTES: Forages alone, in pairs or in mixed-species flocks; favours the flowers of banana plants. *A. p. diuatae* (1b) occurs on Mt Hilong-Hilong. VOICE: A repeated, high-pitched *pink-pink-pink*, level in pitch or ascending, and sometimes turning into a *see-see-see…*; also a *seck-seck*, repeated up to six times. HABITAT: Submontane and montane forest and forest edges. DISTRIBUTION: Endemic to Mindanao in the Philippines.

2 APO SUNBIRD *Aethopyga boltoni* 12cm FIELD NOTES: Active and noisy. Forages alone, in pairs or in mixed-species flocks, especially in flowering trees and shrubs. VOICE: An ascending, metallic *twip twip twip twit twit…*, repeated after a short pause; also gives a rapid, continuous, snapping *twit twit twit…* or *whit whit whit…*, which occasionally changes to a clear, whistled *whirp*. HABITAT: Montane forest. DISTRIBUTION: Endemic to Mindanao in the Philippines.

3 LINA'S SUNBIRD *Aethopyga linaraborae* 10–11cm FIELD NOTES: Forages in the middle and upper storey, alone, in pairs or in mixed-species flocks. VOICE: A long series of high-pitched, squeaky, twittering notes with repeated sequences. Calls include a high-pitched *suweet suweet suweet*, an upward-inflected *su-weet* or *tsoo-eet*, and a metallic *tip-tip-tip-tip…* HABITAT: Montane mossy forest. DISTRIBUTION: Endemic to E Mindanao in the Philippines.

4 PURPLE-NAPED SUNBIRD *Hypogramma hypogrammicum* 14–15cm FIELD NOTES: Forages mainly in the understorey, often flicking and fanning tail. It may soon be proved that this species is a spiderhunter? VOICE: A high, strong *sweet sweet sweet sweet*; calls include a strident *schewp*, *tsit-tsit*, *tchu* or *chip*. HABITAT: Broadleaved evergreen forest, freshwater swamp forest and secondary growth. DISTRIBUTION: Resident in Sumatra and Borneo.

5 LITTLE SPIDERHUNTER *Arachnothera longirostra* 13–16cm FIELD NOTES: Restless, acrobatic forager, mostly at lower levels; attracted to banana blossoms. VOICE: A monotonous, metallic *which-which*; calls include a harsh *cheep*, *chee-chee-chee* and a loud *sheep*, repeated up to 25 times. HABITAT: Broadleaved evergreen forest, forest edges, secondary growth, cultivation and gardens. DISTRIBUTION: Resident in Sumatra, Java, Bali and Borneo.

6 ORANGE-TUFTED SPIDERHUNTER *Arachnothera flammifera* 13–16cm FIELD NOTES: Formerly considered conspecific with the Little Spiderhunter; actions presumed to be similar. VOICE: Presumed to be similar to that of the previous species. HABITAT: Forest, forest edges, secondary growth and banana plantations. DISTRIBUTION: Endemic to the E and S Philippines.

7 PALE SPIDERHUNTER *Arachnothera dilutior* 13–16cm FIELD NOTES: Actions and habits presumed to be as the Little Spiderhunter, with which it was formerly considered conspecific. VOICE: Presumed to be similar to that of the Little Spiderhunter. HABITAT: Forest, forest edges, secondary growth and cultivation. DISTRIBUTION: Endemic to Palawan in the W Philippines.

8 THICK-BILLED SPIDERHUNTER *Arachnothera crassirostris* 16–17cm FIELD NOTES: Forages from the canopy down to the understorey, singly or in pairs; feeds on small invertebrates and nectar. VOICE: A hard, nasal *chit-chit* or *chissie-chissie*, also a *tch-tch* and a *chek-chek-chek* or similar. HABITAT: Forest, forest edges, secondary growth, banana plantations and gardens. DISTRIBUTION: Resident in Sumatra and Borneo.

171 SPIDERHUNTERS

1 LONG-BILLED SPIDERHUNTER *Arachnothera robusta* 21–22cm
FIELD NOTES: Forages mainly in the canopy. Solitary and aggressive. Often sings from a high perch. VOICE: A rising *choi choi choi choi…*; calls include a harsh *chuu-luut chuut-luut*, and a high-pitched *chit-chit-chit-chit* in flight. HABITAT: Forests, secondary growth and plantations. DISTRIBUTION: Resident in Sumatra, Java and Borneo.

2 SPECTACLED SPIDERHUNTER *Arachnothera flavigaster* 21–22cm
FIELD NOTES: Feeds on small invertebrates, nectar and small fruits. Forages in the middle and upper levels, singly or occasionally in pairs; small groups may occur in fruiting trees. VOICE: A high-pitched *chit-chit*, and an explosive *tak, cha-tak, cha-ta-tak* or variants. HABITAT: Open forest, secondary forest, secondary scrub, plantations and gardens. DISTRIBUTION: Resident in Sumatra, Java and Borneo.

3 YELLOW-EARED SPIDERHUNTER *Arachnothera chrysogenys* 17–18cm
FIELD NOTES: Acrobatic. Forages mainly in the canopy, searching for invertebrates in bark and broken branches; also feeds on nectar. Occurs in pairs, alone and occasionally in small groups. VOICE: A rough *chit* and a high-pitched *twit-twit-twit-twee-ee* flight call. HABITAT: Broadleaved evergreen forest, forest edges and secondary growth. DISTRIBUTION: Resident in Sumatra, Java and Borneo.

4 NAKED-FACED SPIDERHUNTER *Arachnothera clarae* 17cm FIELD NOTES: Noisy and conspicuous, seen singly and in pairs. Favours foraging among plantains. VOICE: A loud, raspy, repeated *serp-rp-rp-rp-rp-rp-rp*, an insect-like *seee*, a low, croaking *crrr*, a rapid *trrrik* and various rapid trills. HABITAT: Forest, forest edges and clearings, and scrub. DISTRIBUTION: Endemic to the Philippines.

5 GREY-BREASTED SPIDERHUNTER *Arachnothera modesta* 17–18cm
FIELD NOTES: Active. Forages at all forest levels, mostly in the low to middle storeys; occurs in pairs or alone. VOICE: A continuous *tee-chu*, the first note rising and the second falling. HABITAT: Broadleaved evergreen forest, secondary growth, cultivation and gardens. DISTRIBUTION: Resident in Sumatra and Borneo.

6 STREAKY-BREASTED SPIDERHUNTER *Arachnothera affinis* 21cm FIELD NOTES: Forages at higher levels in forest, alone or occasionally in pairs. VOICE: A *chee-wee-dee--weet… tee-ree chee chee-chur*, and piercing, ringing and raucous calls. HABITAT: Lower montane forest, forest edges and around plantations. DISTRIBUTION: Endemic to Java and Bali.

7 BORNEAN SPIDERHUNTER *Arachnothera everetti* 21cm FIELD NOTES: Feeds on the nectar of banana and Ginger (*Zingiber officinale*) flowers, and on small invertebrates. Occurs alone or in pairs. Formerly considered a race of the previous species. VOICE: Presumed to be similar to that of the previous species. HABITAT: Lowland, lower montane and submontane forest. DISTRIBUTION: Endemic to Borneo.

8 WHITEHEAD'S SPIDERHUNTER *Arachnothera juliae* 16–18cm
FIELD NOTES: Usually found foraging in the tops of trees, especially among orchid clusters and other flowers growing high up on tree trunks. Forages alone, in pairs or in small groups. VOICE: Calls include a loud shrieking, a prolonged twittering, a nasal *swee-urr*, a buzzing *erz dee erz*, a *tech-tech-wee* and a *tee-tee-swee-eee*; song is high pitched and squeaking. HABITAT: Hill dipterocarp forest, montane forest and forest edges. DISTRIBUTION: Endemic to Borneo.

172 FLOWERPECKERS

1 OLIVE-BACKED FLOWERPECKER *Prionochilus olivaceus* 9cm FIELD NOTES: Forages in the understorey, especially in flowering and fruiting trees. Often joins mixed-species feeding parties. *P. o. parsoni* (1b) occurs in the N Philippines. VOICE: A repeated, loud, precise *peeit* or *peeith*, a high-pitched *tsoo-eet* and a rattling trill. HABITAT: Forest, forest edges and secondary growth. DISTRIBUTION: Endemic to the Philippines.

2 YELLOW-BREASTED FLOWERPECKER *Prionochilus maculatus* 10cm FIELD NOTES: Forages in the middle to upper storey, in pairs or alone; favours flowering and fruiting trees. VOICE: A high-pitched *tswik*, a hoarse *tsweet-tsweet* and harsh, metallic, chittering calls. HABITAT: Lowland and hill dipterocarp, peat-swamp and secondary forest, forest edges and scrub. DISTRIBUTION: Resident in Sumatra and Borneo.

3 CRIMSON-BREASTED FLOWERPECKER *Prionochilus percussus* 10cm FIELD NOTES: Forages in the middle and lower storeys, especially in fruiting and flowering trees. VOICE: A *see-sik* and a fast *weg*. HABITAT: Primary, swamp and secondary forest, forest edges, old plantations and scrub. DISTRIBUTION: Resident in Sumatra, Java and Borneo.

4 PALAWAN FLOWERPECKER *Prionochilus plateni* 9cm FIELD NOTES: Forages at all levels, alone or occasionally in mixed-species flocks, usually in flowering and fruiting trees. VOICE: A repeated, high-pitched, metallic *seep-seep*. HABITAT: Forest, secondary growth, scrub and gardens. DISTRIBUTION: Endemic to the W Philippines.

5 YELLOW-RUMPED FLOWERPECKER *Prionochilus xanthopygius* 9cm FIELD NOTES: Forages at all levels; favours fruiting and flowering trees. VOICE: Calls include a *tsee-oo*, *ship-ship*, *ship-ship-ship* or *tsik-tsik*; also utters 7–9 descending notes and, in flight, a high-pitched chittering. HABITAT: Dipterocarp, peat-swamp, heath and secondary forest, forest edges, clearings and plantations. DISTRIBUTION: Endemic to Borneo.

6 SCARLET-BREASTED FLOWERPECKER *Prionochilus thoracicus* 9–10cm FIELD NOTES: Forages at all levels; sometimes climbs tree trunks, like a nuthatch. VOICE: A metallic, clicking twitter, a very high-pitched, insect-like *seek* and a harsh *chink*. HABITAT: Forest, forest edges, secondary growth and coastal vegetation. DISTRIBUTION: Resident in Sumatra and Borneo.

7 GOLDEN-RUMPED FLOWERPECKER *Dicaeum annae* 9–10cm FIELD NOTES: Favours the nectar, fruit and pollen of mistletoes; occurs singly, in pairs or in small groups. VOICE: A repeated, thin, level-pitched *see-see-see-see seeee seeee seeee*. HABITAT: Deciduous, semi-evergreen and secondary forest, woodland and cultivation. DISTRIBUTION: Endemic to the Lesser Sundas.

8 THICK-BILLED FLOWERPECKER *Dicaeum agile* 9–11cm FIELD NOTES: Restless, habitually twitching tail from side to side; attracted to flowering or fruiting trees and shrubs, especially if infested with mistletoes. VOICE: Utters 6–8 notes of differing pitches mixed with dry trills; calls include a sharp *chik-chik-chik-chik* and a rattling *titititiiili*. HABITAT: Forest and secondary growth. DISTRIBUTION: Resident in Sumatra, Java, Borneo and the Lesser Sundas.

9 STRIPED FLOWERPECKER *Dicaeum aeruginosum* 10–11cm FIELD NOTES: Forages in the canopy, mainly in fruiting and flowering trees, singly or in single-species or mixed-species groups. Wags tail from side to side. Formerly considered a race of the previous species. VOICE: Unrecorded. HABITAT: Forest, forest edges and secondary growth. DISTRIBUTION: Endemic to the Philippines.

10 SPECTACLED FLOWERPECKER *Dicaeum* sp. nov. 9–10cm FIELD NOTES: Recorded feeding among mistletoes. Newly discovered (2009). VOICE: A series of high-pitched, rising and falling *see see see* notes. HABITAT: Forest. DISTRIBUTION: Endemic to NE Borneo.

173 FLOWERPECKERS

1 BROWN-BACKED FLOWERPECKER *Dicaeum everetti* 10cm FIELD NOTES: Forages at all levels, feeding on spiders, insects and flowers, and possibly also nectar and fruits. VOICE: A sharp, metallic *chip-chip*. HABITAT: Coastal kerangas and secondary forest, and forest edges. DISTRIBUTION: Resident in Borneo.

2 WHISKERED FLOWERPECKER *Dicaeum proprium* 9cm FIELD NOTES: Forages in flowering and fruiting trees, especially those with mistletoe flowers and fruits. VOICE: Various raspy, snappy, insect-like notes; occasionally a series of notes such as *zaach-zee-peew*; and high, buzzy notes that sometimes run into a 'song'. HABITAT: Forest, forest edges and secondary growth. DISTRIBUTION: Endemic to Mindanao in the S Philippines.

3 YELLOW-VENTED FLOWERPECKER *Dicaeum chrysorrheum* 9–10cm FIELD NOTES: Active forager at all levels, attracted to mistletoes and small figs. Yellow rump. VOICE: Calls include a *zeet*, a repeated *chip-a-chip-tree*, a *zit-zit-zit* and various soft squeaks. HABITAT: Broadleaved evergreen, semi-evergreen and mixed deciduous forest, forest edges, secondary growth and gardens. DISTRIBUTION: Resident in Sumatra, Java, Bali and Borneo.

4 YELLOW-SIDED FLOWERPECKER *Dicaeum aureolimbatum* 8–9cm FIELD NOTES: Forages in pairs, singly or in small groups in flowering or fruiting trees. *D. a. laterale* (4b) occurs on Sangihe Island. VOICE: Calls include a *s-uit*, 5–6 dry, staccato *tuk* notes and a sharp, clear *zit-zit-zit…* HABITAT: Primary and tall secondary forest, forest edges, woodland, plantations and scrub. DISTRIBUTION: Endemic to Sulawesi.

5 OLIVE-CAPPED FLOWERPECKER *Dicaeum nigrilore* 9–10cm FIELD NOTES: Favours flowering and fruiting trees and mistletoes. *D. n. diuatae* (5b) is found in NE Mindanao. VOICE: A high-pitched, scratchy *zuti-zuti-zuti-zuti…*, repeated up to 15 times, a high *tseep-tseep* and a rapid, rising and falling, high-pitched trill. HABITAT: Submontane and montane forest. DISTRIBUTION: Endemic to Mindanao in the S Philippines.

6 FLAME-CROWNED FLOWERPECKER *Dicaeum anthonyi* 9–10cm FIELD NOTES: Forages at all levels, especially in flowering and fruiting trees. Occurs singly, in pairs and in mixed-species feeding parties. *D. a. kampalili* (6b) occurs in NC and SE Mindanao. VOICE: A high-pitched, sharp *srrreep*. HABITAT: Mossy forest and forest edges. DISTRIBUTION: Endemic to the N Philippines.

7 BICOLOURED FLOWERPECKER *Dicaeum bicolor* 9cm FIELD NOTES: Forages in the canopy, alone, in pairs, in small parties or in mixed-species flocks. Favours flowering and fruiting trees. VOICE: A *swip-swip…* that develops into a rapid trill and gets lower and slower. HABITAT: Forest, forest edges and secondary growth. DISTRIBUTION: Endemic to the Philippines.

8 CEBU FLOWERPECKER *Dicaeum quadricolor* 9cm FIELD NOTES: Attracted to flowering mistletoes, trees and vines, and fruiting trees. VOICE: A *seep-seep-seep tik tik tik tik*, a series of *tsip-tsip* or *trik-trik* notes that occasionally develops into a trill, a high, insect-like *see-ip* and a *sit-sit-sit*. HABITAT: Open and closed-canopy forest. DISTRIBUTION: Endemic to Cebu in the C Philippines.

9 RED-KEELED FLOWERPECKER *Dicaeum australe* 10cm FIELD NOTES: Forages mainly in the canopy, especially in fruiting and flowering trees and mistletoes. Occurs in small groups, in pairs and alone; also joins mixed-species feeding flocks. VOICE: A high-pitched, insect-like, trilling *suit-sui…* and a high, rising and falling *tik-tik* that evolves into a trill. HABITAT: Forest, forest edges, secondary growth, coconut groves and fruiting shrubs in open country. DISTRIBUTION: Endemic to the Philippines.

10 BLACK-BELTED FLOWERPECKER *Dicaeum haematostictum* 10cm FIELD NOTES: Forages alone or in pairs, small flocks or mixed-species feeding parties; favours fruiting and flowering trees and mistletoes. VOICE: A *seet-seet* that occasionally develops into a trill, a *chip*, rapid tinkling notes and a *chip-seet-seet* followed by a short trill. HABITAT: Forest, forest edges, secondary growth, cultivation, coconut groves and fruiting bushes in open country. DISTRIBUTION: Endemic to the WC Philippines.

1

2

3

4b
laterale

5b
diuatae

4

5

6

6b ♂
kampalili

♂

7
♀

8
♀

♂

9

10

♂

♀

174 FLOWERPECKERS

1 SCARLET-COLLARED FLOWERPECKER *Dicaeum retrocinctum* 10cm
FIELD NOTES: Favours flowering mistletoes and flowering and fruiting trees, generally in the higher levels; seen alone, in pairs or in small flocks, and also joins mixed-species flocks.
VOICE: A continuous *tipk-tipk-tipk-tipk* or *tip-chik zeet zeet zeet*. HABITAT: Closed-canopy forest, forest edges, secondary growth, coconut groves, cultivation and fruiting bushes in open country. DISTRIBUTION: Endemic to the WC Philippines.

2 ORANGE-BELLIED FLOWERPECKER *Dicaeum trigonostigma* 9cm
FIELD NOTES: Forages mainly in the tops of trees, especially those in flower or fruit.
D. t. xanthopygium (2b) is found in the N Philippines; *D. t. cinereigulare* (2c) occurs in the E and S Philippines; *D. t. dorsale* (2d) occurs in the WC Philippines. VOICE: A rising series of rapid, upslurred notes; calls include a *swit* or *swit-szee*, a drawn-out *zeeee*, a series of wheezy and twittering notes, a *zit-zit-zit*, a *chik-chik-chik* and a high-pitched *zeeeep-zeeeep*.
HABITAT: Forest glades and edges, secondary growth and gardens. DISTRIBUTION: Resident in Sumatra, Java, Bali, Borneo and the Philippines.

3 BUZZING FLOWERPECKER *Dicaeum hypoleucum* 8–9cm FIELD NOTES: Forages at all levels, feeding on fruits, nectar and pollen. Occurs singly, in pairs, in small parties or as part of mixed-species flocks. *D. h. obscurum* (3b) is found in C and S Luzon and Catanduanes. VOICE: A high-pitched, buzzing *bzeeeppp*, uttered singly or as a series, occasionally followed by a trilled *cheenjet*; also utters a metallic *chimp chimp*, which develops into a trill. HABITAT: Forest, forest edges, cultivation and scrub. DISTRIBUTION: Endemic to the Philippines.

4 PLAIN FLOWERPECKER *Dicaeum minullum* 7–9cm FIELD NOTES: Active, agile forager at all levels, attracted to the flowers and fruits of mistletoes. VOICE: A high-pitched trill; calls include twitterings, a sharp *chek*, a ticking *chrik* and a *tik-tik-tik*.
HABITAT: Broadleaved evergreen, semi-evergreen and deciduous forest and secondary growth. DISTRIBUTION: Resident in Sumatra, Java, Bali and Borneo.

5 PYGMY FLOWERPECKER *Dicaeum pygmaeum* 8cm FIELD NOTES: Forages in high understorey or the canopy among flowering mistletoes; encountered singly, in small groups or in mixed-species flocks. *D. p. davao* (5b) occurs in the S Philippines; *D. p. palawanorum* (5c) is found in the W Philippines. VOICE: A loud, sharp, irregularly spaced *tip tip…*, repeated almost continuously; also a high *schenk-schenk…* and a *zip-zip… zip-zip… zip-zip*. HABITAT: Forest, forest edges and secondary growth. DISTRIBUTION: Endemic to the Philippines.

6 CRIMSON-CROWNED FLOWERPECKER *Dicaeum nehrkorni* 8–9cm
FIELD NOTES: Forages mainly in the canopy in fruiting trees, singly or in pairs, and as part of mixed-species feeding flocks. VOICE: A sharp *zit-zit*, a repeated, hard *tit* and a high-pitched, insect-like trill. HABITAT: Hill and montane forest and forest edges. DISTRIBUTION: Endemic to Sulawesi.

7 FLAME-BREASTED FLOWERPECKER *Dicaeum erythrothorax* 9cm
FIELD NOTES: Occurs in small parties or alone, foraging in the canopy in fruiting trees.
VOICE: A repeated *tcheep tcheep tcheep*. HABITAT: Lowland forest and scrub in riverine areas.
DISTRIBUTION: Endemic to Buru in the Moluccas.

8 HALMAHERA FLOWERPECKER *Dicaeum schistaceiceps* 9cm FIELD NOTES: Formerly considered a race of the previous species; habits and actions presumed to be similar.
VOICE: Presumed to be similar to that of the previous species. HABITAT: Primary, degraded, open and secondary forest, riverine forest edges, scrub and cultivation with trees.
DISTRIBUTION: Endemic to the N Moluccas.

9 ASHY FLOWERPECKER *Dicaeum vulneratum* 8–9cm FIELD NOTES: Forages from low down in shrubs to the treetops, singly, in pairs or as a member of mixed-species flocks.
VOICE: A hard, staccato *tst*; song consists of high-pitched, metallic, disyllabic or trisyllabic notes. HABITAT: Hill and coastal forest, forest edges, plantation edges and old gardens.
DISTRIBUTION: Endemic to the S Moluccas.

1

2b ♂
xanthopygium

2c
cinereigulare

2

♀

♂

♀

2d ♂
dorsale

3b ♂
obscurum

4

♀

♀

3

5c ♂
palawanorum

♂

5

5b ♂
davao

♀

♂

6

♀

9

7

♀

♀

8

♂

♂

♂

175 FLOWERPECKERS

1 BLACK-FRONTED FLOWERPECKER *Dicaeum igniferum* 9cm FIELD NOTES: Occurs singly, in pairs, in small groups or as part of mixed-species flocks. Favours flowering trees. VOICE: A rapidly repeated, high-pitched *see-saw*; song comprises a very rapid, descending series of short, thin, dry notes. HABITAT: Semi-deciduous, degraded or secondary forest, coastal monsoon scrub forest, lightly wooded cultivation and clearings. DISTRIBUTION: Endemic to the Lesser Sundas.

2 BLUE-CHEEKED FLOWERPECKER (RED-CHESTED FLOWERPECKER) *Dicaeum maugei* 8–10cm FIELD NOTES: Forages alone or in pairs; often seen around mistletoes and in fruiting trees. VOICE: A high-pitched *tsit* and a high-pitched 2–3-note whistle. HABITAT: Primary, secondary and degraded forest, woodland, plantations, wooded cultivation and bamboo. DISTRIBUTION: Endemic to the islands south of Sulawesi and the Lesser Sundas.

3 FIRE-BREASTED FLOWERPECKER *Dicaeum ignipectus* 7–9cm FIELD NOTES: Restless, agile forager; attracted to mistletoes. *D. i. beccarii* (3b) occurs in Sumatra. VOICE: A high-pitched *titty-titty-titty* or similar; calls include a metallic *chip* and a rattling trill. HABITAT: Montane forest and forest edges. DISTRIBUTION: Resident in Sumatra and the Philippines.

4 BLACK-SIDED FLOWERPECKER *Dicaeum monticolum* 8cm FIELD NOTES: Forages at low levels and sometimes visits the canopy; especially fond of mistletoe fruits. VOICE: A sharp, piercing, metallic *zit*, a repeated *tit*, a rapid ticking and a *tsweet-tsweet*. HABITAT: Hill dipterocarp, montane and heath forest, and scrub. DISTRIBUTION: Endemic to Borneo.

5 GREY-SIDED FLOWERPECKER *Dicaeum celebicum* 8–10cm FIELD NOTES: Favours mistletoe in the canopy; forages alone or in pairs. *D. c. talautense* (5b) occurs in the Talaud Islands; *D. c. sulaense* (5c) is found on the Banggai and Sula islands. VOICE: Calls include a thin, upslurred *seeei*, a repeated *tjjit*, a dry *trri-tri*, a high-pitched *tsip*, and a sharp *chip chip chip…* in flight. HABITAT: Primary and tall secondary forest, forest edges, lightly wooded cultivation and gardens. DISTRIBUTION: Endemic to Sulawesi and the Banggai and Sula islands.

6 BLOOD-BREASTED FLOWERPECKER *Dicaeum sanguinolentum* 8–10cm FIELD NOTES: Favours mistletoe in the canopy; forages alone or in pairs. *D. s. wilhelminae* (6b) occurs on Sumba; *D. s. hanieli* (6c) is found on Timor. VOICE: Song consists of 4–5 jerky, thin, high-pitched, sweet notes; calls include high-pitched clicks and a hard, sharp, buzzing double note. HABITAT: Montane, hill and secondary forest, forest edges, *Casuarina* groves, open and degraded woodland, and lightly wooded cultivation. DISTRIBUTION: Resident in S Sumatra, Java, Bali and the Lesser Sundas.

7 MISTLETOEBIRD *Dicaeum hirundinaceum* 9cm FIELD NOTES: Especially fond of mistletoe; forages from low down up to the canopy. Generally in pairs or alone; occasionally joins mixed-species flocks. VOICE: A dry *tick* note and sibilant calls. HABITAT: Forest, forest edges, mangroves and village trees. DISTRIBUTION: Resident in the E Lesser Sundas and S Moluccas.

8 SCARLET-BACKED FLOWERPECKER *Dicaeum cruentatum* 9cm FIELD NOTES: Forages at all levels, often among clumps of mistletoe. VOICE: A rising and falling *see-sip-see-sip-see-sip* and a ringing *chipi-chipi-chipi dzee-dzee-dzee*; calls include a *chip-chip*, a clicking *tchik-tchik-tchik*, a high-pitched *chizee* and various twitterings. HABITAT: Open forest, forest edges, secondary forest, mangroves, parks and gardens. DISTRIBUTION: Resident in Sumatra and Borneo.

9 SCARLET-HEADED FLOWERPECKER *Dicaeum trochileum* 8–9cm FIELD NOTES: Forages alone or in pairs, especially around mistletoe at upper tree levels. VOICE: Song contains sweet, high-pitched, rising and falling double notes; calls include a short, high-pitched *zit-zit-zit* and a buzzing *seeeeep… seeeeep*. HABITAT: Woodland, mangroves, cultivation, open scrubby areas and gardens. DISTRIBUTION: Resident in Sumatra, Java, Bali, Borneo and Lombok in the Lesser Sundas.

1

3b beccarii ♂

3 ♀

♀

2 ♀

♂

♀

6c ♂ hanieli

4 ♀

6b wilhelminae

♀

♂

5 ♀

6b ♂ talautense

5c ♂ sulaense

♂

6 ♂

7

6 ♀

♂

8 ♂

♀

9

♂

♀

176 IBON; AVADAVAT; ZEBRA FINCH; PARROTFINCHES

1 CINNAMON IBON *Hyprocryptadius cinnamomeus* 15cm FIELD NOTES: Active, gleaning insects from foliage and branches. A regular member of mixed-species foraging flocks. VOICE: A soft, whistled *chuuu, pee chuuu* or *pee chuuu chuuu*, often given by a group of birds together. HABITAT: Submontane and montane mossy forest, and forest edges. DISTRIBUTION: Endemic to Mindanao in the S Philippines.

2 RED AVADAVAT (RED MUNIA or STRAWBERRY FINCH)
Amandava amandava 10cm FIELD NOTES: Forages on the ground or on grass-heads, often in small flocks; winter flocks are bigger and may include other species. VOICE: A weak warble combined with sweet, twittering notes; calls include a thin *teei* or *tsi*, and various chirps and squeaks. HABITAT: Swampy grassland, cultivation, reeds and tall grass near watercourses, secondary growth, scrub and gardens. DISTRIBUTION: Resident in Java, Bali and the Lesser Sundas; introduced to Borneo and the Philippines.

3 ZEBRA FINCH *Taeniopygia guttata* 10cm FIELD NOTES: Gregarious, often in large flocks of up to 100. Feeds on the ground, on grass-heads or in vegetation. VOICE: Song comprises nasal call notes interspersed with chattering trills; calls include a sharp *tya, teea* or *tcheea*. HABITAT: Dry grassland with scattered trees or scrub, lightly wooded cultivation and the edges of scrubby monsoon forest. Often near water. DISTRIBUTION: Resident in the Lesser Sundas.

4 TAWNY-BREASTED PARROTFINCH *Erythrura hyperythra* 10–11cm
FIELD NOTES: Forages on the ground on seeds and small fruits; usually in small parties. VOICE: A series of soft notes followed by four bell-like notes; calls include a high-pitched, hissing *tzit-tzit* contact call, given in flight. HABITAT: Primary forest, bamboo, forest edges and adjacent grassland. DISTRIBUTION: Resident in Java, Borneo, the N Philippines, Sulawesi and the W Lesser Sundas.

5 PIN-TAILED PARROTFINCH *Erythrura prasina* 15cm FIELD NOTES: Forages singly or in pairs; also in small parties, especially when bamboo is in seed. *E. p. coelica* (5b) occurs in Borneo and the W Philippines; yellow morph is uncommon. VOICE: A series of abrupt clinking or chirping notes; calls include a sharp *teger-teter-terge*, a high-pitched *tseet-tseet*, and a shrill *tzit-tzit tzit* in flight. HABITAT: Bamboo thickets, rice fields, forest edges and secondary growth. DISTRIBUTION: Resident in Sumatra, Java, Borneo and the W Philippines.

6 GREEN-FACED PARROTFINCH *Erythrura viridifacies* 12–13cm
FIELD NOTES: Forages in pairs, alone or in small flocks, with over 100 individuals occasionally at rich feeding sources. VOICE: Calls include a *tseet-tseet* or *tisi-tsit*; song comprises a soft *deedeedeedee…*, followed by a chattering *day day day* and ending with a harsh *grey-grey-grey-ray-day-lay-grey*. HABITAT: Montane forest, forest edges, bamboo, grassland and scrub near forest. DISTRIBUTION: Endemic to the Philippines.

7 TRICOLOURED PARROTFINCH *Erythrura tricolor* 10cm FIELD NOTES: Feeds on the ground, in low scrub, bamboo and trees, singly, in pairs, in small flocks or occasionally in larger flocks. VOICE: A shrill, high trill; calls include a soft *ti-ti-ti-ti…ti-ti-ti* and thin, high-pitched, sibilant upslurs. HABITAT: Monsoon forest, forest edges and clearings, woodland, secondary growth, thickets, bamboo and cultivated areas. DISTRIBUTION: Endemic to the Lesser Sundas.

8 BLUE-FACED PARROTFINCH *Erythrura trichroa* 12cm FIELD NOTES: Forages alone, in pairs or in small groups, from the ground to the canopy. Occasionally joins mixed-species feeding parties. VOICE: Calls include a thin, high-pitched *tsit-tsit, ti-tu ti-tu-tu* or *t-t-t-t*. HABITAT: Montane forest, hill forest and rainforest, forest edges, bamboo, scrub and dense secondary growth. DISTRIBUTION: Resident in Sulawesi and the Moluccas.

9 RED-EARED PARROTFINCH *Erythrura coloria* 10–11cm FIELD NOTES: Forages on the ground, in low vegetation and occasionally up to the forest canopy, usually alone or in pairs. VOICE: Calls include a sharp, repeated *tik*, a sharp *prrrt* and a trilled *tik-tik-tik-tik*. HABITAT: Montane forest, forest edges, secondary growth, shrubs, thickets, dense understorey and tall grass. DISTRIBUTION: Endemic to the Philippines.

177 MUNIAS

1 WHITE-RUMPED MUNIA *Lonchura striata* 11–12cm FIELD NOTES: Feeds on small seeds. Gregarious – usually encountered in small parties, with larger flocks post-breeding. VOICE: A series of rising and falling, twittering notes; calls include a plaintive *peep* and a twittering *tr-tr-tr*, *prrrit* or *brrt*. HABITAT: Forest clearings, secondary growth, scrub and grassy areas. DISTRIBUTION: Resident in Sumatra.

2 JAVAN MUNIA *Lonchura leucogastroides* 10–11cm FIELD NOTES: Forages on the ground or low down in vegetation, usually in small flocks. VOICE: Calls include a short *tit*, a *p-tit*, a *peteet* or a *chirrup*. HABITAT: Cultivated areas, mangrove edges, grassland at forest edges, woodland and gardens. DISTRIBUTION: Resident in E Sumatra, Java, Bali and Lombok in the W Lesser Sundas.

3 DUSKY MUNIA *Lonchura fuscans* 11cm FIELD NOTES: Quite shy and retiring, foraging on the ground and low down in vegetation. VOICE: Calls include a shrill *pee pee*, a thin *chirrup*, and a low *teck teck* in flight. HABITAT: Paddyfields, grassland, grassy riverbanks, forest edges, secondary scrub, cultivated areas and gardens. DISTRIBUTION: Endemic to Borneo.

4 BLACK-FACED MUNIA *Lonchura molucca* 10–11cm FIELD NOTES: Feeds on the seeds of grass-heads and seeds on the ground; usually occurs in pairs, alone or in small flocks. VOICE: A short *tri* or *t'sip*, or a buzzy *tissip*; song contains a run of wheezing *peep* and *whee* notes. HABITAT: Bushy and grassy areas, paddyfields and cultivated areas. DISTRIBUTION: Widespread in Wallacea, on Kangean Island off NE Java, and on Lembogan and Nusa Penida islands off S Bali.

5 SCALY-BREASTED MUNIA *Lonchura punctulata* 10–12cm FIELD NOTES: Forages on the ground or on grasses, usually in small groups, with bigger flocks post-breeding. *L. p. particeps* (5b) occurs in Sulawesi. VOICE: A series of quiet notes, followed by a short series of whistles and churrs, and ending with a long, slurred whistle; calls include a *tit-ti* and a *kit-teee kit-teee*. HABITAT: Open country with scrub and trees, bushy hillsides, secondary growth with grass patches, cultivation and gardens. DISTRIBUTION: Resident in Sumatra, Java, Bali, Borneo, the Philippines, Sulawesi and the Lesser Sundas.

6 WHITE-BELLIED MUNIA *Lonchura leucogastra* 11cm FIELD NOTES: Forages in pairs or small groups, feeding on small seeds. *L. l. castanonota* (6b) occurs in S Borneo. VOICE: Calls include a *twyrt*, a *tee-tee-tee*, and a strong *tik* or *tchek* when alarmed; song is transcribed as *di-di-ptchcee-pti-pti-ti-pteep*. HABITAT: Lowland and hill forest, forest edges, paddyfields, grassland, scrub and around rural houses. DISTRIBUTION: Resident in Sumatra, Java, Borneo and the Philippines.

7 CHESTNUT MUNIA (BLACK-HEADED MUNIA) *Lonchura atricapilla* 11–12cm FIELD NOTES: Forages on the ground, usually in pairs or small parties, with bigger flocks post-breeding. *L. a. formosana* (7b) occurs in the N Philippines. VOICE: Calls include a loud *pink pink* and a clear *peet* or *pee* contact note. HABITAT: Grassland, edges of reed-beds, marshes, swamps and cultivation. DISTRIBUTION: Resident in Sumatra, Borneo, the Philippines and Sulawesi; introduced to the N Moluccas.

8 WHITE-CAPPED MUNIA *Lonchura ferruginosa* 11–12cm FIELD NOTES: Feeds on the seeds of grass-heads, especially rice; often seen in large flocks. VOICE: Song comprises a very quiet series of clicks and wheezing notes, followed by a long, drawn-out *wheeee*; calls with a whistled *veet veet*. HABITAT: Grassland, paddyfields, and wetland areas with reeds, grasses and sedges. DISTRIBUTION: Endemic to Java and Bali.

178 MUNIAS; SPARROWS; WEAVERS

1 FIVE-COLOURED MUNIA *Lonchura quinticolor* 11–12cm FIELD NOTES: Forages in pairs and small groups, feeding on the ground or on seedheads. VOICE: Song is transcribed as *te te te te weeee weeee pti-ti-pti-pti*; calls include a loud *triprip* and a single *peet*. HABITAT: Grassland, paddyfields, lightly wooded savannah, mixed scrub and large forest clearings. DISTRIBUTION: Endemic to the Lesser Sundas.

2 WHITE-HEADED MUNIA *Lonchura maja* 11cm FIELD NOTES: Feeds on small seeds on the ground or from seedheads, usually in pairs or small groups. VOICE: Song consists of a series of clicks and then a drawn-out *weeeee heeheeheeheeheehee*; calls include a soft *preet* or *prit*. HABITAT: Open grassland, marshes, reed-beds, paddyfields, cultivation and village gardens. DISTRIBUTION: Resident in Sumatra, Java and Bali.

3 PALE-HEADED MUNIA *Lonchura pallida* 11cm FIELD NOTES: Forages in small or large flocks, feeding on seeding stems and on the ground. VOICE: A high-pitched, chattering *weeeeeeeee*; calls include a *pseet* or *psit*. HABITAT: Open grassland, paddyfields and grassy scrub. DISTRIBUTION: Resident in Sulawesi and the Lesser Sundas.

4 JAVA SPARROW *Lonchura oryzivora* 15cm FIELD NOTES: Feeds on seeding stems or on the ground, in pairs or small groups. Immature generally brownish with a pink-buff face and dark crown. VOICE: Bell-like trilling and clicking notes, ending with a drawn-out whistle; calls with a *tup* or *tack*. HABITAT: Grassland, cultivation and gardens. DISTRIBUTION: Endemic to Java and Bali; introduced to Sumatra, Borneo, the Philippines, Sulawesi and the Lesser Sundas.

5 TIMOR SPARROW *Lonchura fuscata* 12cm FIELD NOTES: Forages in pairs or small groups, mainly on the ground; regularly perches on stumps and posts and in trees. VOICE: A rising *chip chip chip chip chipchipchipchip*; calls include a *tchik*, a *tchuk* and a *wheeee*. HABITAT: Degraded monsoon forest and grassy areas with scattered bushes and trees. DISTRIBUTION: Endemic to the E Lesser Sundas.

6 TREE SPARROW (EURASIAN TREE SPARROW) *Passer montanus* 13–14cm FIELD NOTES: Usually in pairs, with larger flocks post-breeding; forages on the ground and in trees and shrubs. VOICE: Song consists of a series of call notes interspersed with *tsooit*, *tsveet* or *tswee-ip* notes; calls include a high *chip*, a sharp *tet* and a dry *tet-tet-tet* flight call. HABITAT: Around habitation, including towns and cities, and in lightly wooded areas and cultivation. DISTRIBUTION: Widespread resident in the region.

7 STREAKED WEAVER *Ploceus manyar* 14cm FIELD NOTES: Gregarious, foraging and roosting in flocks; breeds in scattered colonies. VOICE: A trill of high-pitched whistles, ending with a wheezy note; calls include a *re tre cherrer cherrer*, often uttered by displaying males, and a *chirt-chirt* in flight. HABITAT: Reed-beds, reed-swamps, tall grass and seasonally flooded areas. DISTRIBUTION: Resident in Java.

8 ASIAN GOLDEN WEAVER *Ploceus hypoxanthus* 15cm FIELD NOTES: Gregarious, breeding in small colonies. VOICE: Chattering notes, ending with a long rattle; calls with harsh *chit* notes. HABITAT: Marshes, paddyfields and flooded grassland. DISTRIBUTION: Resident in Sumatra and W Java.

9 BAYA WEAVER *Ploceus philippinus* 15cm FIELD NOTES: Gregarious; roosts and forages in flocks, often in the company of other weavers, and joins mixed-species flocks. VOICE: A chittering, followed by a wheezy whistle, a buzz and finally some chirps; calls with a harsh *chit*. HABITAT: Generally open areas with nearby water, including grassland, scrub with scattered trees, paddyfields, cultivation and secondary growth. DISTRIBUTION: Resident in Sumatra, Java and Bali; introduced to Borneo.

179 FINCHES; CROSSBILL; BULLFINCH; BUNTINGS

1 BRAMBLING *Fringilla montifringilla* 15cm FIELD NOTES: In flight, shows a white rump. Non-breeding male similar to breeding female, but head is darker. Forages on the ground, usually in flocks. VOICE: Calls include a nasal *tsweek* or *zweee*, and a *chuk-chuk* flight note. HABITAT: Open forests and cultivations. DISTRIBUTION: Vagrant in the Philippines.

2 MOUNTAIN SERIN *Chrysocorythus estherae* 12cm FIELD NOTES: Shy and retiring, spending much time sitting quietly in low bushes or on the ground, usually alone or in small groups. *C. e. mindanensis* (2b) occurs on Mindanao in the S Philippines; *C. e. renatae* (2c) is found in N Sulawesi; orange form is uncommon. VOICE: Calls include a dull, metallic chittering note; in flight, utters a short tinkling. HABITAT: Alpine and subalpine grassland and heather-dominated meadows with scattered bushes or scrub; on Mindanao, occurs in montane rainforest or dwarf ericaceous forest. DISTRIBUTION: Resident in Sumatra, Java, the S Philippines and W Sulawesi.

3 SISKIN (EURASIAN SISKIN) *Spinus spinus* 12cm FIELD NOTES: Acrobatic forager, mainly in trees; usually encountered in small parties. VOICE: Calls include a plaintive *dlu-ee*, a dry *tet* or *tet-tet*, and a *twilit*, *tirrlilli* or *titteree* in flight. HABITAT: Open forest, forest edges and secondary growth. DISTRIBUTION: Vagrant in the Philippines.

4 CROSSBILL (RED CROSSBILL) *Loxia curvirostra* 14cm FIELD NOTES: Sociable, usually in small parties; acrobatic, often hanging upside down to extract seeds from cones. Regularly drinks from small pools. Male plumage variable, with some birds only tinged red. VOICE: A rapid *twit-twit-twit-twit*, and a loud *chirp*, *chi-chirp* or *chip-churp*. HABITAT: Pine forests. DISTRIBUTION: Resident in the N Philippines.

5 WHITE-CHEEKED BULLFINCH *Pyrrhula leucogenis* 15–17cm FIELD NOTES: Noisy and conspicuous; occurs in pairs or small groups, with larger groups found post-breeding. VOICE: Calls include a ringing *pee-yuu*, a loud, musical *chuck-a peeee yuuuu* and a harsh, insect-like *zrrreeep*. HABITAT: Montane forest, especially mossy forest and forest edges. DISTRIBUTION: Endemic to the Philippines.

6 BLACK-HEADED BUNTING *Emberiza melanocephala* 16–18cm FIELD NOTES: Male in non-breeding plumage has head and back colours obscured by pale fringes. Forages mainly on the ground. VOICE: Calls include a *cheep* or *chlip*, a *dzuu*, and a *chuhp* in flight. HABITAT: Grassy places, fields and scrubby areas. DISTRIBUTION: Vagrant in Borneo.

7 LITTLE BUNTING *Emberiza pusilla* 12–14cm FIELD NOTES: Forages on the ground or low down in bushes or trees. VOICE: Calls include a hard *tzik* or *pwick*. HABITAT: Forest edges, scrubby areas, stubble fields and paddyfields. DISTRIBUTION: Vagrant in Borneo and the N Philippines.

8 YELLOW-BREASTED BUNTING *Emberiza aureola* 15cm FIELD NOTES: Non-breeding males have back and face pattern obscured by pale fringes. Forages on the ground, retreating to nearby bushes or trees when disturbed. VOICE: Calls include a sharp *tsik*, and an abrupt *chup* when flushed. HABITAT: Paddyfields, stubble fields, grassland and scrubby areas. DISTRIBUTION: Vagrant in Borneo and the N Philippines.

9 JAPANESE YELLOW BUNTING (YELLOW BUNTING) *Emberiza sulphurata* 13–14cm FIELD NOTES: Forages on the ground, alone or in small groups. VOICE: Various alternating twittering phrases; call is a short, metallic *tsip tsip*. HABITAT: Scrub, pine forest and cultivated areas. DISTRIBUTION: Non-breeding visitor to the N Philippines.

10 BLACK-FACED BUNTING *Emberiza spodocephala* 15cm FIELD NOTES: Forages mainly on the ground. Face pattern of males is obscured by pale fringes when in non-breeding plumage. VOICE: Calls include a sharp *tzit* or *tzii*. HABITAT: Open bushy areas, scrub, forest edges and cultivation. DISTRIBUTION: Vagrant in the Sula Islands.

1

2b *mindanensis*

2

2c *renatae*

♂ orange form

3

4

5

6

7

8

9

10

FURTHER READING

Ali, S. & Ripley, S. D. (1987). *Compact Handbook of the Birds of India and Pakistan*. 2nd edn. Oxford University Press.

Alström, P. & Mild, K. (2003). *Pipits and Wagtails of Europe, Asia and North America*. Helm.

Baker, K. (1997) *Warblers of Europe, Asia and North Africa*. Helm.

Beaman, M. & Madge, S. (1998). *The Handbook of Bird Identification for Europe and the Western Palearctic*. Helm.

Byers, C., Olsson, U. & Curson, J. (1995). *Buntings and Sparrows*. Helm.

Cheke, R. A., Mann, C. F. & Allen, R. (2001). *Sunbirds: A Guide to the Sunbirds, Flowerpeckers, Spiderhunters and Sugarbirds of the World*. Helm.

Clement, P., Harris, A. & Davis, J. (1993). *Finches and Sparrows*. Helm.

Clement, P. & Hathway, R. (2000). *Thrushes*. Helm.

Coates, B. J., Bishop, K. D. & Gardener, D. (1997). *A Guide to the Birds of Wallacea*. Dove.

Cramp, S. (ed.) (1977–94). *The Birds of the Western Palearctic. Vols 1–9*. Oxford University Press.

Feare, C. & Craig, A. (1998). *Starlings and Mynas*. Helm.

Ferguson-Lees, J. & Christie, D. (2005). *Raptors of the World*. Helm.

Fry, C. H., Fry, K. & Harris, A. (1992). *Kingfishers, Bee-eaters and Rollers*. Helm.

Grimmett, R., Inskipp, C. & Inskipp, T. (2011). *Birds of the Indian Subcontinent*. Helm.

Hancock, J. & Elliott, H. (1978). *Herons of the World*. London Editions.

Hancock, J., Kushlan, J. A. & Kahl, M. P. (1992). *Storks, Ibises and Spoonbills of the World*. Academic Press.

Harrison, P. (1983 & updates). *Seabirds: An Identification Guide*. Helm.

Harrop, S. & Quinn, D. (1996). *Tits, Nuthatches and Treecreepers*. Helm.

Hayman, P., Marchant, A. J. & Prater, A. H. (1986). *Shorebirds: An Identification Guide to the Waders of the World*. Helm.

del Hoyo, J., Elliott, A. & Sargatal, J. (eds) (1992–2011). *Handbook of the Birds of the World. Vols 1–16 and Special Volume*. Lynx Edicions.

Kennedy, R. S., Gonzales, P. C., Dickinson, E. C., Miranda Jr, H. C. & Fisher, T. H. (2000). *A Guide to the Birds of the Philippines*. Oxford University Press.

Lefranc, N. & Worfolk, T. (1997). *Shrikes: A Guide to the Shrikes of the World*. Pica Press.

MacKinnon, J. & Phillipps, K. (1993 & 2004). *The Birds of Borneo, Sumatra, Java, and Bali*. Oxford University Press.

MacKinnon, J. & Phillipps, K. (2000). *A Field Guide to the Birds of China*. Oxford University Press.

Madge, S. & Burn, H. (1988). *Wildfowl: An Identification Guide to the Ducks, Geese and Swans of the World*. Helm.

Madge, S. & Burn, H. (1991). *Crows and Jays*. Helm.

Madge, S. & McGowan, P. (2002). *Pheasants, Partridges and Grouse. Including Buttonquails, Sandgrouse and Allies*. Helm.

Mullarney, K., Svensson, L., Zetterström, D. & Grant, P. J. (1999). *Collins Bird Guide*. HarperCollins.

Olney, D. & Scofield, P. (2007). *Albatrosses, Petrels and Shearwaters of the World*. Helm.

Olsen, K. M. & Larsson, H. (1995). *Terns of Europe and North America*. Helm.

Olsen, K. M. & Larsson, H. (1997). *Skuas and Jaegers: A Guide to Skuas and Jaegers of the World*. Pica Press.

Olsen, K. M. & Larsson, H. (2004). *Gulls of Europe, Asia and North America*. Helm.

Phillipps, Q. & Phillipps, K. (2014). *Phillipps' Field Guide to the Birds of Borneo*. 3rd edn. John Beaufoy Publishing.

Porter, R. F., Willis, I., Christensen, S. & Neilsen, B. P. (1981). *Flight Identification of European Raptors*. 3rd edn. Poyser.

Robson, C. (2002). *Birds of South-east Asia*. New Holland.

Taylor, B. & van Perlo, B. (1998). *Rails: A Guide to the Rails, Crakes, Gallinules and Coots of the World*. Pica Press.

Turner, A. & Rose, C. (1989). *Swallows and Martins of the World*. Helm.

Winkler, H., Christie, D. A. & Nurney, D. (1995). *Woodpeckers: A Guide to the Woodpeckers, Piculets and Wrynecks of the World*. Pica Press.

SPECIES DISTRIBUTION MAPS

Vagrants and most introduced species are not included in the distribution maps section. Species that spend most of their time at sea, have a distribution clearly covered in the text, occur only on offshore islands, are very rare or have a very limited distribution are also not included in this section. Distribution of birds in the region is not well documented and in some cases sources are even contradictory.

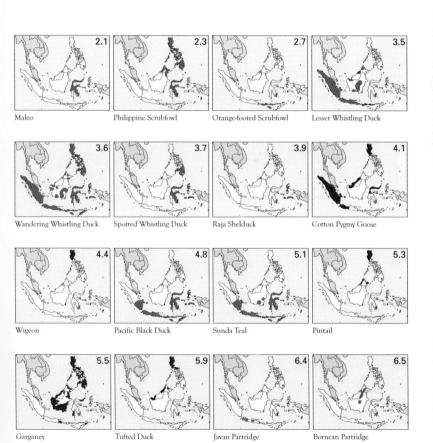

2.1 Maleo	2.3 Philippine Scrubfowl	2.7 Orange-footed Scrubfowl	3.5 Lesser Whistling Duck
3.6 Wandering Whistling Duck	3.7 Spotted Whistling Duck	3.9 Raja Shelduck	4.1 Cotton Pygmy Goose
4.4 Wigeon	4.8 Pacific Black Duck	5.1 Sunda Teal	5.3 Pintail
5.5 Garganey	5.9 Tufted Duck	6.4 Javan Partridge	6.5 Bornean Partridge

373

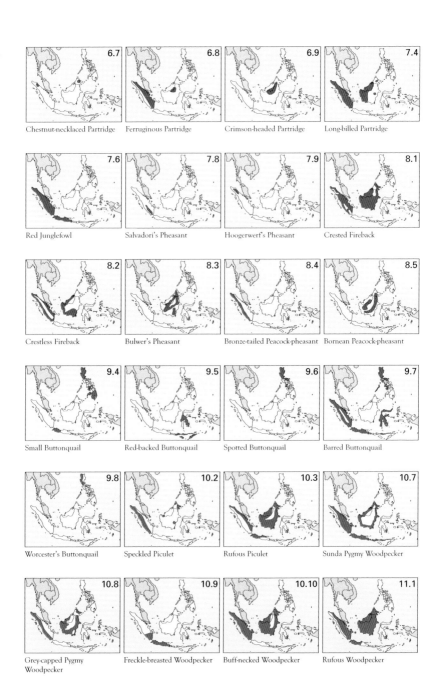

6.7	6.8	6.9	7.4
Chestnut-necklaced Partridge	Ferruginous Partridge	Crimson-headed Partridge	Long-billed Partridge
7.6	7.8	7.9	8.1
Red Junglefowl	Salvadori's Pheasant	Hoogerwerf's Pheasant	Crested Fireback
8.2	8.3	8.4	8.5
Crestless Fireback	Bulwer's Pheasant	Bronze-tailed Peacock-pheasant	Bornean Peacock-pheasant
9.4	9.5	9.6	9.7
Small Buttonquail	Red-backed Buttonquail	Spotted Buttonquail	Barred Buttonquail
9.8	10.2	10.3	10.7
Worcester's Buttonquail	Speckled Piculet	Rufous Piculet	Sunda Pygmy Woodpecker
10.8	10.9	10.10	11.1
Grey-capped Pygmy Woodpecker	Freckle-breasted Woodpecker	Buff-necked Woodpecker	Rufous Woodpecker

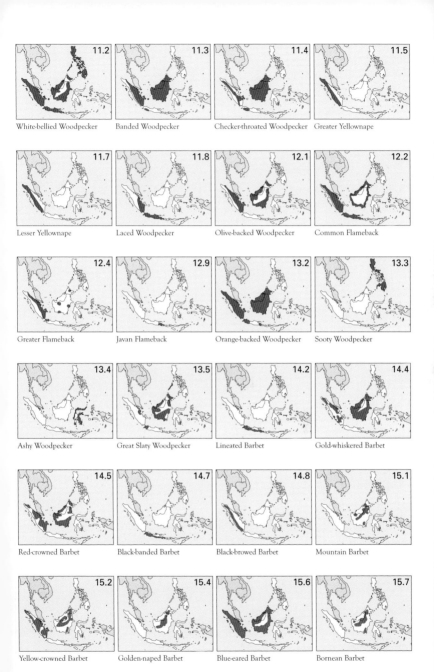

11.2 White-bellied Woodpecker	11.3 Banded Woodpecker	11.4 Checker-throated Woodpecker	11.5 Greater Yellownape
11.7 Lesser Yellownape	11.8 Laced Woodpecker	12.1 Olive-backed Woodpecker	12.2 Common Flameback
12.4 Greater Flameback	12.9 Javan Flameback	13.2 Orange-backed Woodpecker	13.3 Sooty Woodpecker
13.4 Ashy Woodpecker	13.5 Great Slaty Woodpecker	14.2 Lineated Barbet	14.4 Gold-whiskered Barbet
14.5 Red-crowned Barbet	14.7 Black-banded Barbet	14.8 Black-browed Barbet	15.1 Mountain Barbet
15.2 Yellow-crowned Barbet	15.4 Golden-naped Barbet	15.6 Blue-eared Barbet	15.7 Bornean Barbet

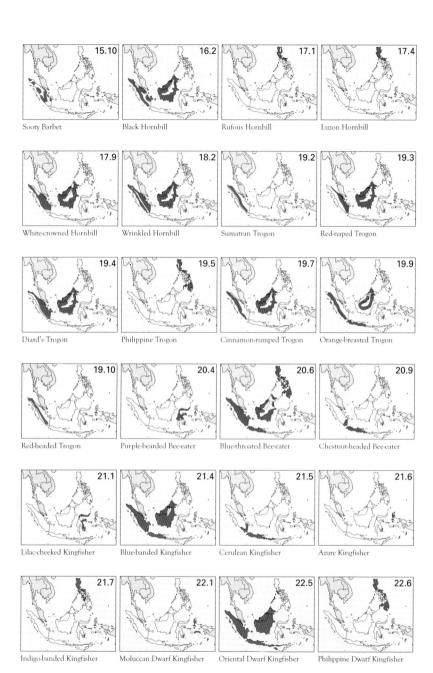

15.10 Sooty Barbet	16.2 Black Hornbill	17.1 Rufous Hornbill	17.4 Luzon Hornbill
17.9 White-crowned Hornbill	18.2 Wrinkled Hornbill	19.2 Sumatran Trogon	19.3 Red-naped Trogon
19.4 Diard's Trogon	19.5 Philippine Trogon	19.7 Cinnamon-rumped Trogon	19.9 Orange-breasted Trogon
19.10 Red-headed Trogon	20.4 Purple-bearded Bee-eater	20.6 Blue-throated Bee-eater	20.9 Chestnut-headed Bee-eater
21.1 Lilac-cheeked Kingfisher	21.4 Blue-banded Kingfisher	21.5 Cerulean Kingfisher	21.6 Azure Kingfisher
21.7 Indigo-banded Kingfisher	22.1 Moluccan Dwarf Kingfisher	22.5 Oriental Dwarf Kingfisher	22.6 Philippine Dwarf Kingfisher

376

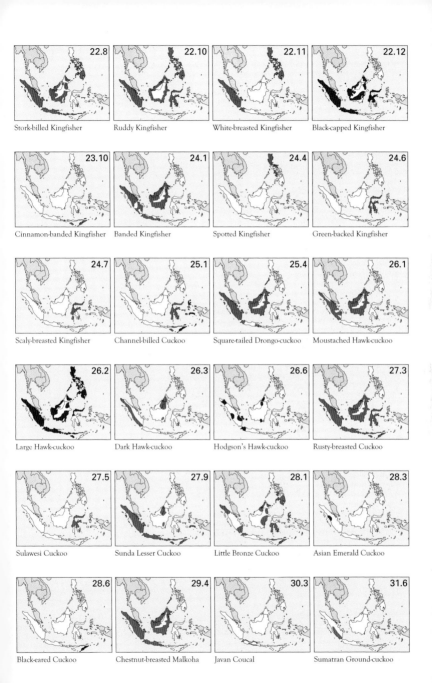

Stork-billed Kingfisher   22.8

Ruddy Kingfisher   22.10

White-breasted Kingfisher   22.11

Black-capped Kingfisher   22.12

Cinnamon-banded Kingfisher   23.10

Banded Kingfisher   24.1

Spotted Kingfisher   24.4

Green-backed Kingfisher   24.6

Scaly-breasted Kingfisher   24.7

Channel-billed Cuckoo   25.1

Square-tailed Drongo-cuckoo   25.4

Moustached Hawk-cuckoo   26.1

Large Hawk-cuckoo   26.2

Dark Hawk-cuckoo   26.3

Hodgson's Hawk-cuckoo   26.6

Rusty-breasted Cuckoo   27.3

Sulawesi Cuckoo   27.5

Sunda Lesser Cuckoo   27.9

Little Bronze Cuckoo   28.1

Asian Emerald Cuckoo   28.3

Black-eared Cuckoo   28.6

Chestnut-breasted Malkoha   29.4

Javan Coucal   30.3

Sumatran Ground-cuckoo   31.6

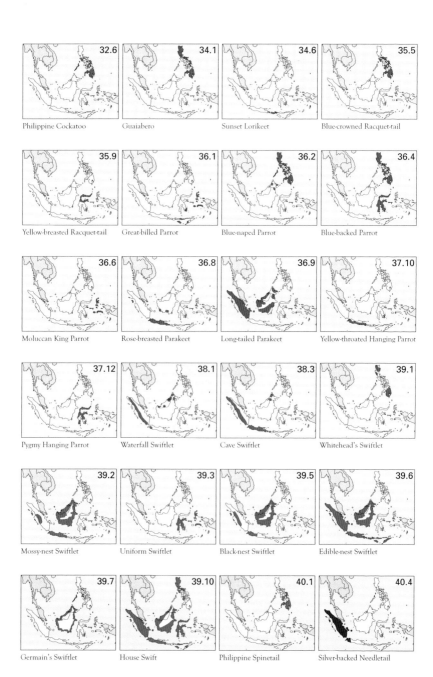

32.6	34.1	34.6	35.5
Philippine Cockatoo	Guaiabero	Sunset Lorikeet	Blue-crowned Racquet-tail
35.9	36.1	36.2	36.4
Yellow-breasted Racquet-tail	Great-billed Parrot	Blue-naped Parrot	Blue-backed Parrot
36.6	36.8	36.9	37.10
Moluccan King Parrot	Rose-breasted Parakeet	Long-tailed Parakeet	Yellow-throated Hanging Parrot
37.12	38.1	38.3	39.1
Pygmy Hanging Parrot	Waterfall Swiftlet	Cave Swiftlet	Whitehead's Swiftlet
39.2	39.3	39.5	39.6
Mossy-nest Swiftlet	Uniform Swiftlet	Black-nest Swiftlet	Edible-nest Swiftlet
39.7	39.10	40.1	40.4
Germain's Swiftlet	House Swift	Philippine Spinetail	Silver-backed Needletail

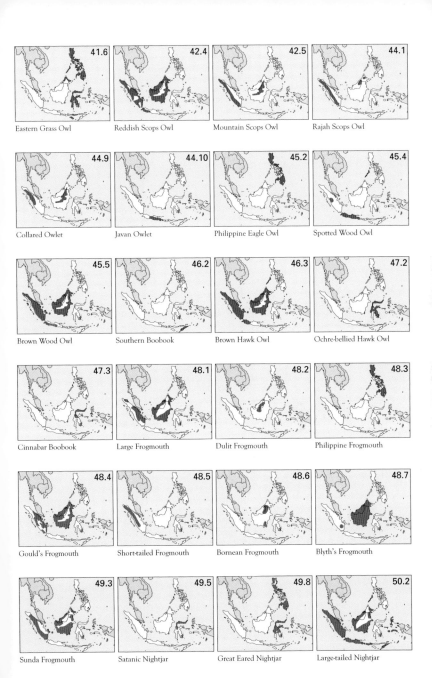

41.6 Eastern Grass Owl	42.4 Reddish Scops Owl	42.5 Mountain Scops Owl	44.1 Rajah Scops Owl
44.9 Collared Owlet	44.10 Javan Owlet	45.2 Philippine Eagle Owl	45.4 Spotted Wood Owl
45.5 Brown Wood Owl	46.2 Southern Boobook	46.3 Brown Hawk Owl	47.2 Ochre-bellied Hawk Owl
47.3 Cinnabar Boobook	48.1 Large Frogmouth	48.2 Dulit Frogmouth	48.3 Philippine Frogmouth
48.4 Gould's Frogmouth	48.5 Short-tailed Frogmouth	48.6 Bornean Frogmouth	48.7 Blyth's Frogmouth
49.3 Sunda Frogmouth	49.5 Satanic Nightjar	49.8 Great Eared Nightjar	50.2 Large-tailed Nightjar

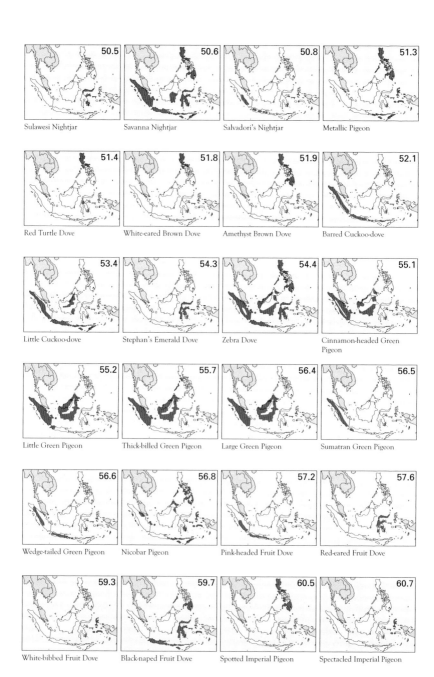

50.5 Sulawesi Nightjar	50.6 Savanna Nightjar	50.8 Salvadori's Nightjar	51.3 Metallic Pigeon
51.4 Red Turtle Dove	51.8 White-eared Brown Dove	51.9 Amethyst Brown Dove	52.1 Barred Cuckoo-dove
53.4 Little Cuckoo-dove	54.3 Stephan's Emerald Dove	54.4 Zebra Dove	55.1 Cinnamon-headed Green Pigeon
55.2 Little Green Pigeon	55.7 Thick-billed Green Pigeon	56.4 Large Green Pigeon	56.5 Sumatran Green Pigeon
56.6 Wedge-tailed Green Pigeon	56.8 Nicobar Pigeon	57.2 Pink-headed Fruit Dove	57.6 Red-eared Fruit Dove
59.3 White-bibbed Fruit Dove	59.7 Black-naped Fruit Dove	60.5 Spotted Imperial Pigeon	60.7 Spectacled Imperial Pigeon

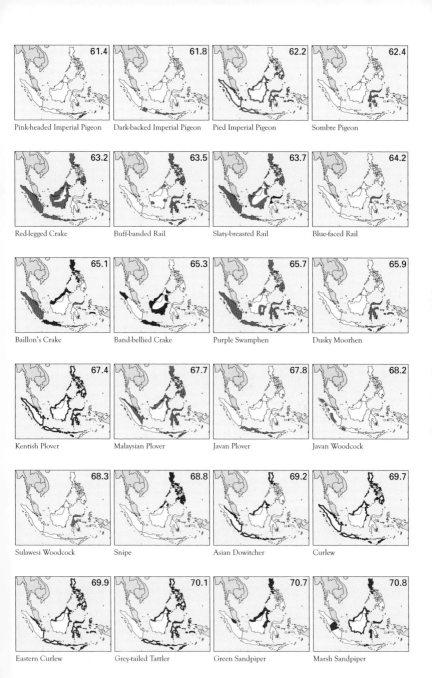

61.4 Pink-headed Imperial Pigeon	61.8 Dark-backed Imperial Pigeon	62.2 Pied Imperial Pigeon	62.4 Sombre Pigeon
63.2 Red-legged Crake	63.5 Buff-banded Rail	63.7 Slaty-breasted Rail	64.2 Blue-faced Rail
65.1 Baillon's Crake	65.3 Band-bellied Crake	65.7 Purple Swamphen	65.9 Dusky Moorhen
67.4 Kentish Plover	67.7 Malaysian Plover	67.8 Javan Plover	68.2 Javan Woodcock
68.3 Sulawesi Woodcock	68.8 Snipe	69.2 Asian Dowitcher	69.7 Curlew
69.9 Eastern Curlew	70.1 Grey-tailed Tattler	70.7 Green Sandpiper	70.8 Marsh Sandpiper

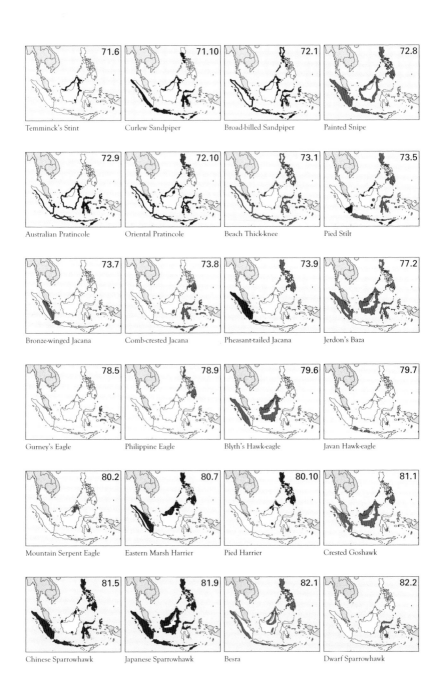

71.6 Temminck's Stint

71.10 Curlew Sandpiper

72.1 Broad-billed Sandpiper

72.8 Painted Snipe

72.9 Australian Pratincole

72.10 Oriental Pratincole

73.1 Beach Thick-knee

73.5 Pied Stilt

73.7 Bronze-winged Jacana

73.8 Comb-crested Jacana

73.9 Pheasant-tailed Jacana

77.2 Jerdon's Baza

78.5 Gurney's Eagle

78.9 Philippine Eagle

79.6 Blyth's Hawk-eagle

79.7 Javan Hawk-eagle

80.2 Mountain Serpent Eagle

80.7 Eastern Marsh Harrier

80.10 Pied Harrier

81.1 Crested Goshawk

81.5 Chinese Sparrowhawk

81.9 Japanese Sparrowhawk

82.1 Besra

82.2 Dwarf Sparrowhawk

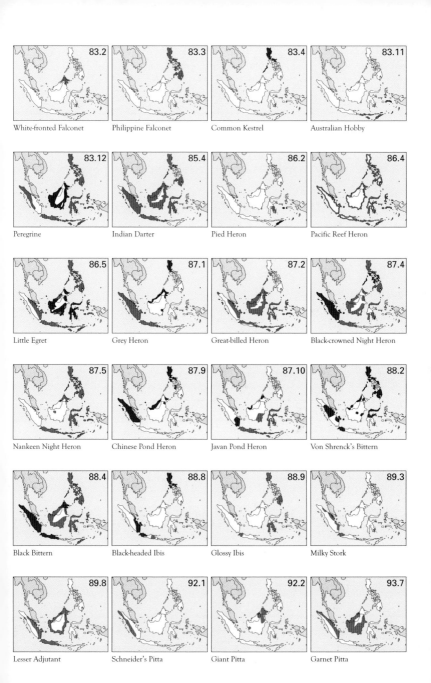

White-fronted Falconet 83.2	Philippine Falconet 83.3	Common Kestrel 83.4	Australian Hobby 83.11
Peregrine 83.12	Indian Darter 85.4	Pied Heron 86.2	Pacific Reef Heron 86.4
Little Egret 86.5	Grey Heron 87.1	Great-billed Heron 87.2	Black-crowned Night Heron 87.4
Nankeen Night Heron 87.5	Chinese Pond Heron 87.9	Javan Pond Heron 87.10	Von Shrenck's Bittern 88.2
Black Bittern 88.4	Black-headed Ibis 88.8	Glossy Ibis 88.9	Milky Stork 89.3
Lesser Adjutant 89.8	Schneider's Pitta 92.1	Giant Pitta 92.2	Garnet Pitta 93.7

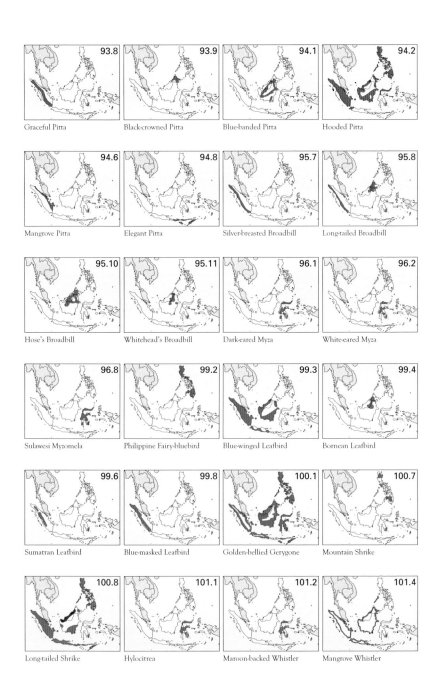

Graceful Pitta   93.8

Black-crowned Pitta   93.9

Blue-banded Pitta   94.1

Hooded Pitta   94.2

Mangrove Pitta   94.6

Elegant Pitta   94.8

Silver-breasted Broadbill   95.7

Long-tailed Broadbill   95.8

Hose's Broadbill   95.10

Whitehead's Broadbill   95.11

Dark-eared Myza   96.1

White-eared Myza   96.2

Sulawesi Myzomela   96.8

Philippine Fairy-bluebird   99.2

Blue-winged Leafbird   99.3

Bornean Leafbird   99.4

Sumatran Leafbird   99.6

Blue-masked Leafbird   99.8

Golden-bellied Gerygone   100.1

Mountain Shrike   100.7

Long-tailed Shrike   100.8

Hylocitrea   101.1

Maroon-backed Whistler   101.2

Mangrove Whistler   101.4

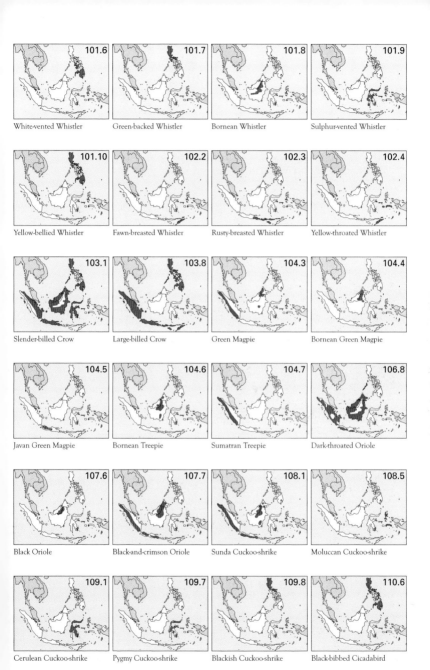

101.6 White-vented Whistler

101.7 Green-backed Whistler

101.8 Bornean Whistler

101.9 Sulphur-vented Whistler

101.10 Yellow-bellied Whistler

102.2 Fawn-breasted Whistler

102.3 Rusty-breasted Whistler

102.4 Yellow-throated Whistler

103.1 Slender-billed Crow

103.8 Large-billed Crow

104.3 Green Magpie

104.4 Bornean Green Magpie

104.5 Javan Green Magpie

104.6 Bornean Treepie

104.7 Sumatran Treepie

106.8 Dark-throated Oriole

107.6 Black Oriole

107.7 Black-and-crimson Oriole

108.1 Sunda Cuckoo-shrike

108.5 Moluccan Cuckoo-shrike

109.1 Cerulean Cuckoo-shrike

109.7 Pygmy Cuckoo-shrike

109.8 Blackish Cuckoo-shrike

110.6 Black-bibbed Cicadabird

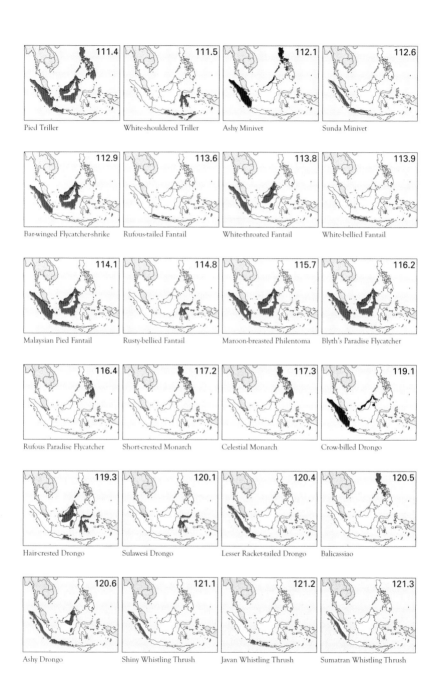

111.4 Pied Triller	111.5 White-shouldered Triller	112.1 Ashy Minivet	112.6 Sunda Minivet
112.9 Bar-winged Flycatcher-shrike	113.6 Rufous-tailed Fantail	113.8 White-throated Fantail	113.9 White-bellied Fantail
114.1 Malaysian Pied Fantail	114.8 Rusty-bellied Fantail	115.7 Maroon-breasted Philentoma	116.2 Blyth's Paradise Flycatcher
116.4 Rufous Paradise Flycatcher	117.2 Short-crested Monarch	117.3 Celestial Monarch	119.1 Crow-billed Drongo
119.3 Hair-crested Drongo	120.1 Sulawesi Drongo	120.4 Lesser Racket-tailed Drongo	120.5 Balicassiao
120.6 Ashy Drongo	121.1 Shiny Whistling Thrush	121.2 Javan Whistling Thrush	121.3 Sumatran Whistling Thrush

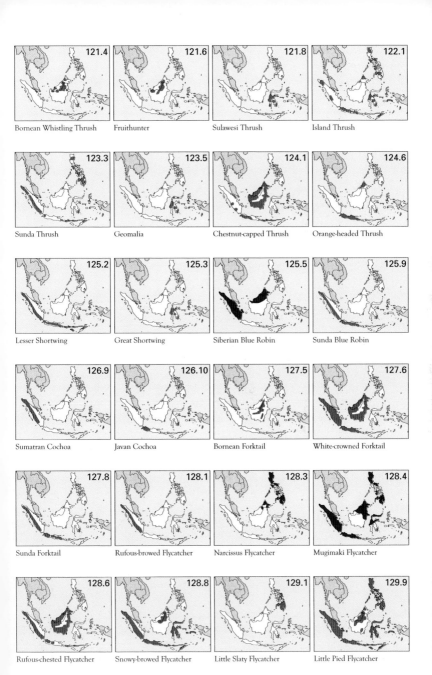

121.4 Bornean Whistling Thrush	121.6 Fruithunter	121.8 Sulawesi Thrush	122.1 Island Thrush
123.3 Sunda Thrush	123.5 Geomalia	124.1 Chestnut-capped Thrush	124.6 Orange-headed Thrush
125.2 Lesser Shortwing	125.3 Great Shortwing	125.5 Siberian Blue Robin	125.9 Sunda Blue Robin
126.9 Sumatran Cochoa	126.10 Javan Cochoa	127.5 Bornean Forktail	127.6 White-crowned Forktail
127.8 Sunda Forktail	128.1 Rufous-browed Flycatcher	128.3 Narcissus Flycatcher	128.4 Mugimaki Flycatcher
128.6 Rufous-chested Flycatcher	128.8 Snowy-browed Flycatcher	129.1 Little Slaty Flycatcher	129.9 Little Pied Flycatcher

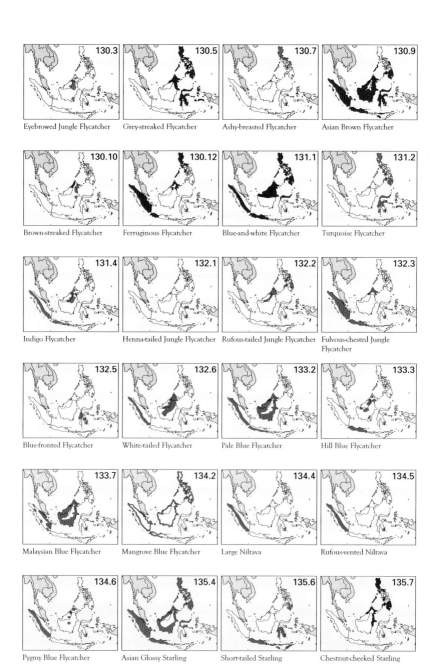

130.3 Eyebrowed Jungle Flycatcher	130.5 Grey-streaked Flycatcher	130.7 Ashy-breasted Flycatcher	130.9 Asian Brown Flycatcher
130.10 Brown-streaked Flycatcher	130.12 Ferruginous Flycatcher	131.1 Blue-and-white Flycatcher	131.2 Turquoise Flycatcher
131.4 Indigo Flycatcher	132.1 Henna-tailed Jungle Flycatcher	132.2 Rufous-tailed Jungle Flycatcher	132.3 Fulvous-chested Jungle Flycatcher
132.5 Blue-fronted Flycatcher	132.6 White-tailed Flycatcher	133.2 Pale Blue Flycatcher	133.3 Hill Blue Flycatcher
133.7 Malaysian Blue Flycatcher	134.2 Mangrove Blue Flycatcher	134.4 Large Niltava	134.5 Rufous-vented Niltava
134.6 Pygmy Blue Flycatcher	135.4 Asian Glossy Starling	135.6 Short-tailed Starling	135.7 Chestnut-cheeked Starling

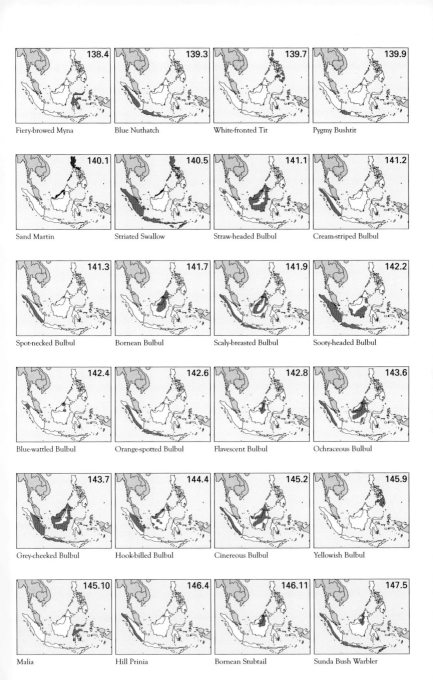

138.4	139.3	139.7	139.9
Fiery-browed Myna	Blue Nuthatch	White-fronted Tit	Pygmy Bushtit
140.1	140.5	141.1	141.2
Sand Martin	Striated Swallow	Straw-headed Bulbul	Cream-striped Bulbul
141.3	141.7	141.9	142.2
Spot-necked Bulbul	Bornean Bulbul	Scaly-breasted Bulbul	Sooty-headed Bulbul
142.4	142.6	142.8	143.6
Blue-wattled Bulbul	Orange-spotted Bulbul	Flavescent Bulbul	Ochraceous Bulbul
143.7	144.4	145.2	145.9
Grey-cheeked Bulbul	Hook-billed Bulbul	Cinereous Bulbul	Yellowish Bulbul
145.10	146.4	146.11	147.5
Malia	Hill Prinia	Bornean Stubtail	Sunda Bush Warbler

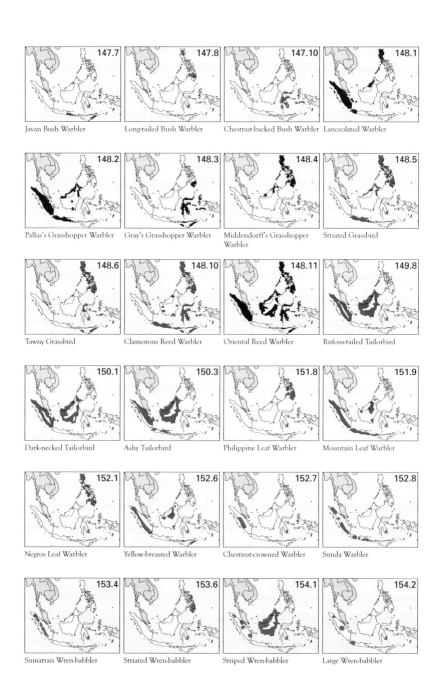

Javan Bush Warbler

Long-tailed Bush Warbler

Chestnut-backed Bush Warbler

Lanceolated Warbler

Pallas's Grasshopper Warbler

Gray's Grasshopper Warbler

Middendorff's Grasshopper Warbler

Striated Grassbird

Tawny Grassbird

Clamorous Reed Warbler

Oriental Reed Warbler

Rufous-tailed Tailorbird

Dark-necked Tailorbird

Ashy Tailorbird

Philippine Leaf Warbler

Mountain Leaf Warbler

Negros Leaf Warbler

Yellow-breasted Warbler

Chestnut-crowned Warbler

Sunda Warbler

Sumatran Wren-babbler

Striated Wren-babbler

Striped Wren-babbler

Large Wren-babbler

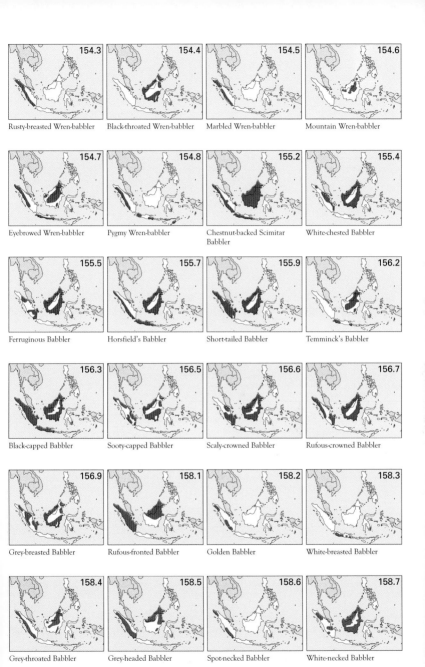

154.3 Rusty-breasted Wren-babbler

154.4 Black-throated Wren-babbler

154.5 Marbled Wren-babbler

154.6 Mountain Wren-babbler

154.7 Eyebrowed Wren-babbler

154.8 Pygmy Wren-babbler

155.2 Chestnut-backed Scimitar Babbler

155.4 White-chested Babbler

155.5 Ferruginous Babbler

155.7 Horsfield's Babbler

155.9 Short-tailed Babbler

156.2 Temminck's Babbler

156.3 Black-capped Babbler

156.5 Sooty-capped Babbler

156.6 Scaly-crowned Babbler

156.7 Rufous-crowned Babbler

156.9 Grey-breasted Babbler

158.1 Rufous-fronted Babbler

158.2 Golden Babbler

158.3 White-breasted Babbler

158.4 Grey-throated Babbler

158.5 Grey-headed Babbler

158.6 Spot-necked Babbler

158.7 White-necked Babbler

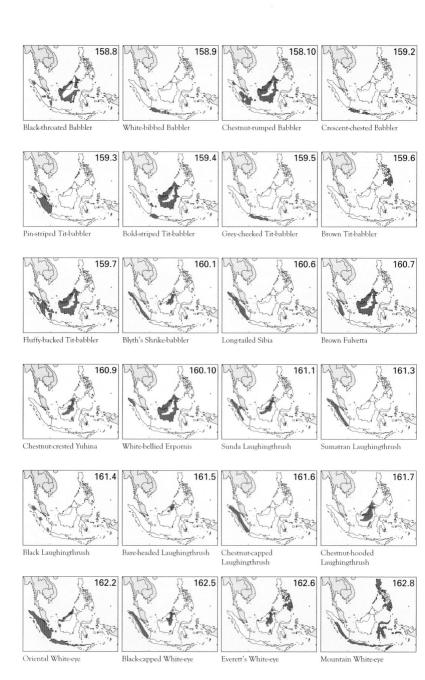

158.8 Black-throated Babbler	158.9 White-bibbed Babbler	158.10 Chestnut-rumped Babbler	159.2 Crescent-chested Babbler
159.3 Pin-striped Tit-babbler	159.4 Bold-striped Tit-babbler	159.5 Grey-cheeked Tit-babbler	159.6 Brown Tit-babbler
159.7 Fluffy-backed Tit-babbler	160.1 Blyth's Shrike-babbler	160.6 Long-tailed Sibia	160.7 Brown Fulvetta
160.9 Chestnut-crested Yuhina	160.10 White-bellied Erpornis	161.1 Sunda Laughingthrush	161.3 Sumatran Laughingthrush
161.4 Black Laughingthrush	161.5 Bare-headed Laughingthrush	161.6 Chestnut-capped Laughingthrush	161.7 Chestnut-hooded Laughingthrush
162.2 Oriental White-eye	162.5 Black-capped White-eye	162.6 Everett's White-eye	162.8 Mountain White-eye

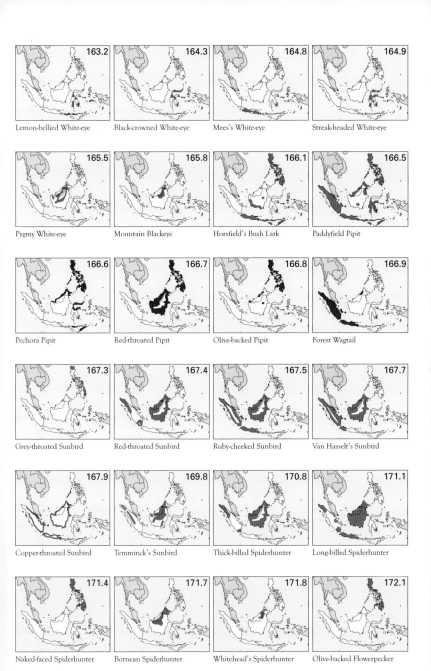

163.2	164.3	164.8	164.9
Lemon-bellied White-eye	Black-crowned White-eye	Mees's White-eye	Streak-headed White-eye
165.5	165.8	166.1	166.5
Pygmy White-eye	Mountain Blackeye	Horsfield's Bush Lark	Paddyfield Pipit
166.6	166.7	166.8	166.9
Pechora Pipit	Red-throated Pipit	Olive-backed Pipit	Forest Wagtail
167.3	167.4	167.5	167.7
Grey-throated Sunbird	Red-throated Sunbird	Ruby-cheeked Sunbird	Van Hasselt's Sunbird
167.9	169.8	170.8	171.1
Copper-throated Sunbird	Temminck's Sunbird	Thick-billed Spiderhunter	Long-billed Spiderhunter
171.4	171.7	171.8	172.1
Naked-faced Spiderhunter	Bornean Spiderhunter	Whitehead's Spiderhunter	Olive-backed Flowerpecker

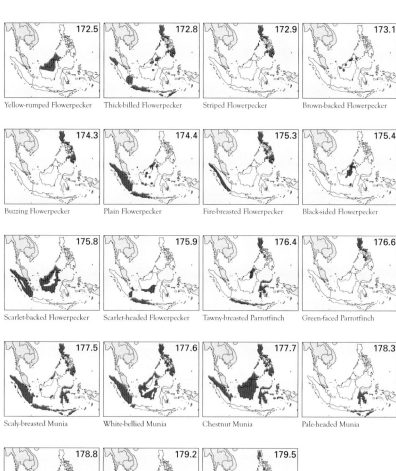

Yellow-rumped Flowerpecker — 172.5

Thick-billed Flowerpecker — 172.8

Striped Flowerpecker — 172.9

Brown-backed Flowerpecker — 173.1

Buzzing Flowerpecker — 174.3

Plain Flowerpecker — 174.4

Fire-breasted Flowerpecker — 175.3

Black-sided Flowerpecker — 175.4

Scarlet-backed Flowerpecker — 175.8

Scarlet-headed Flowerpecker — 175.9

Tawny-breasted Parrotfinch — 176.4

Green-faced Parrotfinch — 176.6

Scaly-breasted Munia — 177.5

White-bellied Munia — 177.6

Chestnut Munia — 177.7

Pale-headed Munia — 178.3

Asian Golden Weaver — 178.8

Mountain Serin — 179.2

White-cheeked Bullfinch — 179.5

INDEX

398

402

405